The Method of the Siddhas

The Divine World-Teacher and True Heart-Master,
Da Avabhasa (The "Bright")
at Sri Love-Anandashram, 1992

The Method
of the
Siddhas

*Talks on the Spiritual Technique
of the Saviors of Mankind*

by
The Divine World-Teacher and True Heart-Master,
Da Avabhasa
(The "Bright")

THE DAWN HORSE PRESS
CLEARLAKE, CALIFORNIA

NOTE TO THE READER

The devotional, Spiritual, functional, practical, relational, cultural, and formal community practices and disciplines discussed in this book, including the meditative practices, the Yogic exercises of "conductivity", the breathing exercises, the life-disciplines of right diet and exercise, the intelligent economization and practice of sexuality, etc., are appropriate and natural practices that are voluntarily and progressively adopted by each student-novice and member of the Free Daist Communion and adapted to his or her personal circumstance. Although anyone may find them useful and beneficial, they are not presented as advice or recommendations to the general reader or to anyone who is not a participant in Da Avabhasa International or a member of the Free Daist Communion. And nothing in this book is intended as a diagnosis, prescription, or recommended treatment or cure for any specific "problem", whether medical, emotional, psychological, social, or Spiritual. One should apply a particular program of treatment, prevention, cure, or general health only in consultation with a licensed physician or other qualified professional.

For a further discussion of individual responsibility in the Way of the Heart, our claim to perpetual copyright to the Wisdom-Teaching of Sri Da Avabhasa, and His renunciate status in the Free Daist Communion, please see "Further Notes to the Reader", pages 386–88 of this book.

New Standard Edition December 1992
Printed in the United States of America

Produced by the Free Daist Communion
in cooperation with the Dawn Horse Press

Library of Congress Cataloging-in-Publication Data

Da Free John, 1939–
        The Method of the Siddhas: Talks on the Spiritual Technique of the Saviors of Mankind/by The Divine World-Teacher and True Heart-Master, Da Avabhasa (The "Bright") – New standard ed.
        p.   cm.
Includes index
ISBN 0-918801-50-8
1. Spiritual life.   2. Siddhas.   I. Title
BP610.B8149   1992b

92-36965
CIP

CONTENTS

by Ray Lynch
Composer, Deep Breakfast, No Blue Thing, *and* The Sky of Mind

Twenty years ago I walked out of a bookstore in Portland, Maine, with a copy of *The Method of the Siddhas* under my arm, wondering about Siddhas, their "method", and what was in it for me. I had no idea how profoundly this book would affect my life, but somehow I was ripe for its truths. At that time, I was many things: ex-Texan, respected lutenist (in New York City), gentleman farmer (in Maine), observer of life (everywhere), seeker of truth (armchair). I was thirty years old and had already achieved noteworthy unhappiness. I had also just received a warning.

One week before, while strolling across my front yard, I was surprised by a sudden and shocking vision: A gigantic pit opened up just in front of me, and, as I peered into its darkness, I knew with uncharacteristic certainty that if I didn't change the direction of my life, I was going to fall into the pit and die. The synchronicity of these events seemed meaningful, and I read *The Method of the Siddhas* with an intensity proportionate to my newly perceived nearness to the precipice. Halfway through the book I realized that I had found my Teacher.

The Method of the Siddhas presented something new to my awareness: a man who understood, who was <u>clearly</u> awake, who had penetrated fear and death, who spoke English (eloquently!), and who was alive and available in California! His words cut across years of enthusiasm, seeking, and suffering while giving the best description of my predicament that I had ever encountered. He spoke the Truth and certainly didn't glamorize or minimize the ordeal required for its Realization. I worried about that part, feeling that I would not be able to do everything that He was going to ask of me, that I was unqualified for the kind of uncompromising relationship being offered. But He was my only true option, and I soon found myself on a plane to Los Angeles, lute in hand, heart in stomach, grateful for something more real than the pit.

How can I summarize the next twenty years? Da Avabhasa's first words to me, whispered in my ear as we embraced several days later, were, "Stick with Me." Later that week He did something equally straightforward but, at the time, quite inexplicable: He threw me a pear. I was sitting on the floor in the far corner of His office when He picked a pear from a bowl of fruit on His desk and, without a word, threw it across the room to me. I caught it, but I didn't understand, so I merely smiled at Him. I had come in haste, unprepared and in great need, and I failed to notice that I had brought no gifts. Giving was something I had to learn (and am still learning). When I caught that first pear, I could have understood and given Him all my suffering then, but I didn't, and so over the years Da Avabhasa (never reserved in His Giving) has thrown more pears my way. His Gifts, I have learned, come in many guises, some delicious and immediately edible, others much more difficult to stomach. The most nourishing and useful ones, oddly, are often the latter.

A year later, Da Avabhasa threw me the most difficult (and most useful) such "pear" in my experience. To appreciate its effect on me, you would have to understand the overwhelming and seductive attractiveness of the Company of such a free Being, passionate in His living, completely open, totally committed to those around Him, and full of humor. I had come to Him because I wanted to be free and happy, as He so obviously was, but after spending only a little time with Him, I found that my priorities had shifted: At the top of my list was the desire to simply be with Him; Enlightenment was second, maybe third. In those early years, being with Him, being "accepted" by Him, being "liked" by Him, was everything.

Now, I had recently married Kathleen (a fellow student) and had begun a relationship that was proving to have, well, a lot of local color. One evening Kathleen and I were at His house when I walked into one of the rooms and saw Kathleen and Da Avabhasa sitting on the floor talking together. Apparently they were talking about me, because as soon as I came through the door, He looked up at me and said, "I don't like him, either." It was like the moment just before impact when wrecking an automobile. I felt the bottom drop out as my worst fears about myself were confirmed. My mind reeled and something in me shut down as I refused to understand what had just happened and, instead, pushed the whole incident below consciousness.

Over the years my relationship with Da Avabhasa continued, but our physical contacts became rarer. (He had since established His residence in Fiji while I was still living in California.) Slowly, and with some difficulty, I began to understand and accept that God (or a God-Realized Adept) was under no obligation to "like" the ego. I saw that my demand to be "liked" and "accepted" was not only immature but actually insulting. How could the ego, self-contracted and deluded, maintain its position in the presence of Consciousness and expect to be congratulated? Given my posture, His comment was not merely beautifully timed but truly kind. It was clearly a Gift, a pear of the first magnitude, and I had managed to suppress it for years.

As the meaning of all this was dawning on me and I began feeling the humor of the incident, my Teacher pulled another pear from His bowl and drove home the real point, rounding out the whole affair. A friend who had just returned from Fiji reported that Da Avabhasa, in the midst of a completely unrelated conversation, had abruptly looked up and asked, "Does Ray know that I love him?"

I was so moved by this gesture on His part that I almost failed to fully consider the question, and to acknowledge that, as the ego, I was more comfortable with being "liked" than with being Loved perfectly. His Love was a challenge, because it was so complete, so unreserved. It had nothing to do with anybody's preferences. It simply couldn't be contained, and it spilled out, unexpectedly, into my life.

It also spilled out into my dreams. The dreams (and there were many during this period) almost always dealt with the great theme of this book, namely the Guru-devotee relationship (or Satsang). One series of dreams, which went on for more than a year, consisted exclusively of telephone conversations. Whenever I called, Da Avabhasa always answered and often spoke with great passion on the nature of our relationship, sometimes pleading and weeping for me to understand. "Satsang is everything!" He shouted over and over, "Nothing else matters!"

Several years ago, after too long an absence, I traveled to Fiji to be with Da Avabhasa once again for a short while. This time I came with my arms as full of gifts as I knew how to make them. Our first meeting occurred in formal Darshan—sitting with Him for the simple purpose of viewing Him and feeling into His Presence. I was sitting in front, eager and somewhat nervous. He came in and sat down, and I was stunned by what I saw. The mechanisms that normally filter my perception were suspended in that raw and most beautiful moment. All the old protective scar tissue covering my heart was ripped apart. As my heart opened, I saw and felt Him fully, as Reality, and I was pervaded and unhinged by the Truth of His Confession: Love is a wound and it will never heal. It was all given in the first ten seconds. I spent the rest of the hour weeping, as did He, as the mutuality of our relationship sank into my being. I was finally understanding the "method" of the Siddhas. Satsang is Love and Love is mutual sacrifice. That is simply the way it works, and there is nothing anyone can do to change it.

Three weeks later, on the day before my departure, Da Avabhasa surprised me with another pear. At the end of my last Darshan, He gave me a framed photograph taken a few weeks earlier. The photograph showed us embracing. Below the photograph, but in the same frame, carefully dried and pressed, was the flower I had laid at His feet when I first arrived. His Gift to me was as unexpected and as powerful as the embrace had been. It summarized perfectly everything I had been shown over twenty years about giving, about relationship, about love.

**The framed photo of Ray Lynch being embraced
by Sri Da Avabhasa**

How can I summarize twenty years with One who Gives so much and Loves so well? I haven't the words, but I can look at that photograph and it's all there. What the photograph shows is fully expressed in *The Method of the Siddhas* and could be grasped instantly. But we seem to need time, and so the Adept, graceful as always, keeps reaching into the bowl to remind us Who He is and, ultimately, Who we are. This book is a reminder and, as you read it, my best advice to you is, heads up! You may not see it coming, but a huge pear is being tossed in your direction.

Sri Da Avabhasa
at Sri Love-Anandashram, 1992

Just This Relationship
Is Sufficient

by devotees of Da Avabhasa (The "Bright")

The book that drew me to my Guru's Heart was none other than the first edition of The Method of the Siddhas. *I can still vividly recall the darkness that enveloped my life before Da Avabhasa Entered it. When I contemplate the Miracle that lifted me out of the mortal sorrow and anguish that was my destiny, and that is the lot of human beings everywhere (whether or not they are ready to say so), I am overwhelmed by a feeling for which the word "gratitude" is but a pale apology. Feeling what Sri Da Avabhasa has Given me, I want to tell everyone about it. I want to shout aloud to the whole world that the Divine Being is here, Present, in the flesh, now; that we are neither damned nor condemned to pass our lives in the frantic pursuit of fleeting pleasures; that the "unreasonable" Happiness we glimpse in moments or in peak experiences here and there is our Real Condition and that it is freely Given in Sri Da Avabhasa's Company.*

These are the words of one who has been touched by the unparalleled Wisdom and Grace that Sri Da Avabhasa offers you through this book. It is but one among countless such accounts—testimonies to the transforming power of what you are about to read.

◆ ◆ ◆

The Siddhas are men and women of perfect Spiritual accomplishment. The method, or the "Spiritual technique", of the Siddhas is an infallible sacred science. Rightly practiced, it cannot fail. Fully embraced, it can only produce the most remarkable transformation in us, for the method of the Siddhas is more powerful than any merely natural science. What the Siddhas have to offer is more

1

fundamental to us than the oxygen in the air we breathe or the pulse of blood in our bodies. It is more intimate to us than anything else we now know or could ever know.

Although little known or appreciated in the West, the method utilized by the many Siddhas, or true Gurus, who have appeared in this world is nevertheless a time-honored process. It is the mechanism whereby Grace meets and overcomes need, pain, limitation, and even death. And Da Avabhasa (The "Bright") is the most fully equipped Master of this "method" who has ever lived.

What, exactly, is this "method" of Grace? And to what is it leading us?

SRI DA AVABHASA: The Guru appears in the midst of the dreams of ordinary waking life like sunlight in the morning. When you are still dreaming, still asleep, the sun comes up. It gets brighter and brighter, and the light comes into the room. At last, the light, the day itself, becomes sufficient to wake you, and then, all of a sudden, you are not dreaming, and everything is all right. The Guru is simply that sunlight process, that intensification, rising on you always, without any other special activity. The Guru's relationship to you, your condition of relationship to the Guru, just that relationship, is sufficient. . . .

And, luckily, all beings are already alive with their intuition of Reality. Therefore, they have this affinity with sunlight, with the true waking state, with the Guru. . . . When your eyes have opened in the morning light, everything will be obvious to you. And you will know that you have never slept, that you have never dreamed, that you have never been limited to any thing that has appeared. You have never been in any condition that you have assumed. There was only Reality, your true Nature, which is Bliss, Consciousness, the unqualified Intensity. (The Method of the Siddhas, *pp. 265, 282–83)*

The Manifestation of Grace:
Da Avabhasa (The "Bright") Appears

In February 1939, as the world was about to be engulfed in the darkness of the second World War, the great Indian Spiritual Master Upasani Baba was visited by the Shankaracharya of Jyotirmath, the Spiritual leader of millions of Hindus. They spoke of many things, but especially of the state of the times, when Spiritual Wisdom seemed in danger of extinction. The Shankaracharya confessed his despair to Upasani Baba. It seemed to him that only an Avatar—or a human Incarnation of the Divine Being—born to show the way to ordinary people by relating to them directly, could restore the world to Truth.

Spontaneously, Upasani Baba burst out with a prophetic declaration. The Divine Being, he said, would shortly take Birth in a European country. (In the East, "European" refers to Caucasians as a race rather than to any geographical place.) This Incarnation would be all-powerful, the Swami continued, bearing down everything before Him, and would reestablish the ancient Wisdom.

The two men spoke from a place of mutual understanding, grounded as they were in one of the world's most sophisticated and long-standing Spiritual traditions. They had, from birth, known the incomparable value of the relationship to a true Teacher, a God-Realizer capable of imparting his or her own Realization to others. The relationship to such a Siddha has always been the very cornerstone of the Hindu tradition—and, if we study history, of all religious traditions.

The response of the Shankaracharya is not recorded, but we may imagine that he was both elated and stunned—elated because the Birth of such an Avatar is a rare and most auspicious occurrence, and stunned because this One would be born in the West. The East (and, to a lesser extent, the Middle East) has borne witness to the Appearance of a steady stream of Great Realizers, but, until now, there has been no such legacy in the West.

Nine months after Upasani Baba's dramatic prophecy, on November 3, 1939, a boy child was born to Frank and Dorothy Jones on Long Island, New York. His parents named him Franklin Albert Jones.

The One thus Born now speaks to us in the pages of this book.

◆ ◆ ◆

How can we come to accept the appearance of the Divine in human Form? One woman tells how her heart opened to this discovery:

To those of us raised in the West and the Westernized world, the appearance of a Siddha is the most confounding, but essentially the most compelling, news we could ever hope to hear.

When I first encountered Da Avabhasa through His description of His Divine Birth in The Knee of Listening, *His Spiritual autobiography, I was*

3

plunged into a maelstrom of emotions. I realized that having been raised a Christian I allowed that the Divine could become Incarnate—but only once, two thousand years ago. I was happy to celebrate each Christmas that Jesus of Nazareth had appeared, and that "God is with us". The possibility that the Divine could Shine before my eyes in my own lifetime—not abstract, not past-tense, but intimately, gloriously, bodily present—was inconceivable. I had never entertained such an idea.

But committed as I was to my own ingrained point of view and presumed experience of the Divine, when I met Da Avabhasa through His books, I was able to let go. I admitted to myself that despite my doctoral studies of Christian liturgy and its music and my passionate appreciation of the lives of Christian saints, I knew very little to absolutely nothing about God. I had to see that my whole life had been built on inherited religious views that left no room for profound, revolutionary surprise, no room for the obvious Truth that God is absolutely Free to Appear.

The deepest passion of my being was stirred by the chance that a living Revelation of God could be here now. Suddenly, inexplicably, there was no more debate—I felt my heart to be already His. In the depth of my being, the relationship to Him had already begun.

◆ ◆ ◆

Da Avabhasa's early Life of struggle to incarnate Divine Help in the human world culminated when He was thirty years old, in a small temple on the grounds of the Vedanta Society in Hollywood, California. He described the "Vedanta Temple Event" as follows:

In an instant, I became profoundly and directly aware of what I am. It was a tacit realization, a direct knowledge in consciousness itself. It was consciousness itself, without the addition of a communication from any other source. I simply sat there and knew what I am. I was being what I am. I am Reality, the Self, the Nature and Support of all things and all beings. I am the One Being, known as God, Brahman, Atman, the One Mind, the Self.

There was no thought involved in this. I am that Consciousness. There was no reaction of either joy or surprise. I am the One I recognized. I am that One. I am not merely experiencing Him. (The Knee of Listening, *p. 241*)

Da Avabhasa wrote *The Knee of Listening* in the voice of one who was formerly unenlightened and then Awakened to the Divine Condition. But Sri Da Avabhasa had no need to be born for the sake of His own Enlightenment. He was already that One, and had Enjoyed Perfect Divine Realization before His birth as Franklin Jones. His descent into flesh was therefore not merely the birth of an exemplary devotee destined to fulfill the God-Realizing Process in this lifetime; it was, rather, the Birth of One Already Free and Awake beyond all limits, driven to Incarnation by no karmic necessity of His own but only by a great compassionate Impulse to Awaken all beings. The Vedanta Temple Event was not the end of Da Avabhasa's Ordeal. It was the beginning of His Work in the world.

Da Avabhasa has said that He was born "in a time of terrible necessity". His early childhood years were the era of World War II. He came to live and do His Divine Work in a world in desperate straits, in the Spiritual desert of modern secular materialism. This book is a sign that when the need is greatest, the greatest Gift may be Given.

We have before us, in the message of this book and in the Realizer who stands behind it, an incomparable opportunity. The more one studies Da Avabhasa's Wisdom-Teaching, the more one views His total Work of Blessing and true redemption, the clearer it becomes that Sri Da Avabhasa is the culmination of the many God-born Siddhas who have appeared throughout history, and that He is the full, potent epitome of the Love and Blessing they have all taken birth to animate and to inject into the human world.

In the ancient East, even ordinary people—the farmers and the housewives, the shopkeepers and the children—understood that there is a great process of God-Realization, made possible by the devotional relationship to the Siddhas, the Incarnations of Grace. In these cultures, ordinary people would generally not come across such an individual, for Adepts usually lived and taught in isolation, away from the commerce of mundane life. But even ordinary people who were fortunate enough to come into the presence of a Siddha knew enough to fall to their knees and bury their faces in the dust, in gratitude for the extraordinary and auspicious Gift of the mere sighting of such a Realized Being. To do more than that—to be accepted as a formal practitioner and to live in the Company of such a Realizer—has traditionally required exceptional Spiritual insight and an intense one-pointed capacity for self-discipline and meditation, qualities for which most of us are not distinguished!

No one knows this better than Da Avabhasa. The greatness of His Realization is shown in the scope of His embrace—for He has Worked, with a diligence that has no equal, to make His Instruction accessible to the most ordinary of us and to make the opportunity to live and practice in the fold of His Blessing available to absolutely everyone who will choose it.

The Yoga of Grace:
Constant Resort to the Guru

Understanding our need for Grace perfectly, and clearly seeing our weakness, Sri Da Avabhasa has made it as easy as possible for us to enter into the process of genuine human and Spiritual transformation. He has used the traditional Hindu story about the love between the God-Man Krishna and his most ardent followers, the "gopis" (the cowmaidens who, seeing Krishna, fall hopelessly in love with him), as an allegory for His own relationship to all who would receive His Spiritual Help. This legend, Da Avabhasa says,

is a play upon the romance between Krishna, or the Divine manifested in human form—the Spiritual Master in God—and these ordinary women, who become madly involved in an absolute attachment to Krishna, and who, as a result of this attachment, become more and more ecstatically absorbed in the God-State.

The whole purpose of the meeting between the Spiritual Master and the devotee is to serve the establishment of this love-relationship. Everyone who approaches Me must enjoy such distraction whether or not we meet in physical company. (December 16, 1975)

In other words, it is Sri Da Avabhasa's Spiritual Attractiveness, acting like a repolarizing magnet, that draws our attention away from our egoic distress to feel His Love and Freedom, His ineffable Divine Happiness. When attention is steadily yielded to Da Avabhasa in this way, the limits of the ego are first brought to light, then seen to be unnecessary, and finally outshined in the feeling of His Limitless Being. Ultimately, by this Means, we receive Da Avabhasa's Blessing to such a degree that we realize He is not only most intimate with us but that His Divine Condition is actually our very own!

SRI DA AVABHASA: It is stated in the traditional writings that, of all the things one can do to realize one's freedom, the best thing one can do, the greatest thing one can do, is spend one's time in the Company of one who is awake. That is Satsang, living in relationship to the Guru and in the company of the Guru's friends. All other activities are secondary. And Satsang is not a strategic method, not an exercise or meditative technique one applies to oneself. It is simply the natural and appropriate Condition. It is Reality. It is itself Truth, or enlightenment. There are no other means given to disciples.

There is nothing that one can do to save oneself, to become enlightened, to become realized. Nothing whatsoever. If there were something, I would tell you, but there is nothing. . . .

All the means of transformation belong to the Truth Itself, to the Guru, to the Heart. Therefore, Satsang is Itself . . . the only true spiritual practice. Living, working, sitting with the Guru is sadhana. It is meditation. It is realization. (The Method of the Siddhas, *p. 164)*

◆ ◆ ◆

Da Avabhasa never ceases to prove the simplicity and the power of the relationship He offers. One woman devotee describes a moment in which Da Avabhasa Granted her this certainty most tangibly:

Upon arriving at Sri Love-Anandashram, His Great Hermitage Ashram in Fiji, for retreat in 1992, I was Graced to receive a hug from Sri Da Avabhasa—an extraordinary Blessing that I will always cherish. When He first motioned to me that I could come forward and receive His embrace, I was nervous. To meet face to face with Sri Da Avabhasa is always a test, because the ego is exposed in the Shine of His Love. I was afraid that "I" would get in the way, that my own tendency to superficiality would prevent me from being vulnerable enough, loving enough, responsive enough to Him—as I so much wanted to be. And I discovered, again, that I could not "do" anything, I could not successfully make any effort to "overcome myself" in order to "be loving" to my Heart-Master. I could only receive the Help that Da Avabhasa was so Graciously Giving me to surrender as best I could to What and Who He Is. I felt His Love pouring into my body, and His great Heart easing me in every way. He held me so close, with such strong arms, that I could feel my self-concern and my superficiality dissolving, layer by layer—so that my gratitude, my attraction to His magnificent Being, and my human love for Him could come forward in the most natural way. He literally drew me out of my self-consciousness, without my doing anything about it, except for the simple act of feeling Him and cooperating with Him.

In this embrace, as in all things in my life, Sri Da Avabhasa showed me again that He is the Guru, the One who accomplishes the entire process. His embrace contained human love, but it also had so much more in it. His Love is boundless, centerless, overwhelming—I felt such joy and freedom in feeling Him. Then He held my face with His hands and kissed me several times. By the time my Beloved Heart-Master released me, all I could do was sit at His Feet and look at Him in love. I felt the deepest peace all over my body and in my heart, and I had no attention left over for anything but the great love I feel for Him. He had Given me the very thing I wanted, the greatest Happiness I have ever tasted—which is the ability to feel and to love free of reserve, and, through the joy of devotion to Him, to radiate back to Him the very Love that He always already Gives to me and to everyone.

◆　◆　◆

After Da Avabhasa had Re-Awakened to the "Bright" Divine Condition of His birth in the Vedanta Temple Event, the Guru-Function, the Maha-Siddhi (or Great Power) whereby He could draw others beyond themselves and grow them Spiritually, Awakened spontaneously in Him—and it has functioned in Him continuously since that time. Before this time, when "Franklin Jones" had closed His eyes in meditation, the internal phenomena of His own body-mind would appear to His consciousness; afterwards, when He sat in meditative repose, the content that arose was no longer His. Instead, thousands of beings would appear to Him in meditation, and He would literally meditate these, His future devotees.

SRI DA AVABHASA: For years, I would sit down in meditation, and all my own forms would appear—my own mind, my desires, my experience, my suffering, my feeling, my energies, my this and my that. But, at some point, it all came to an end. There was no thing, nothing there anymore. None of that distracted or interested me. Meditation was perfect, continuous. Then I began to meet those friends who first became involved in this way. And when I would sit down for meditation, there would be more of these things again—all of these thoughts, these feelings, this suffering, this dis-ease, this disharmony, these upsets, this craziness, this pain, these energies—all of this again. But they weren't mine. They were the internal qualities and life-qualities of my friends. So I would sit down to meditate, and do the meditation of my friends. When I would feel it all release, their meditation was done. And I began to test it, to see if this meditation went on in some more or less apparent manner for these people who were not with me. And I found that this meditation went on with people whom I hadn't even met. People I saw in dreams and visions would show up at the Ashram. So the meditation went on. It was the same meditation I had always done. The same problems were involved, the same subtleties, but the content of the meditation was not mine. (The Method of the Siddhas, *p. 268)*

Gradually and mysteriously, the first handful of these individuals made their way to Sri Da Avabhasa. He provided photocopies of the manuscript of *The Knee of Listening* for them to read, and relayed Instruction to them as they met to study and discuss what they had read. But, in general, He lived privately and did not Instruct these individuals personally, nor had He yet fully presumed the role of Guru in relationship to them. Eventually, the gathering of those who were attracted to Him grew in number so that it became necessary to obtain a place where He could meet with them.

A storefront was secured on Melrose Avenue in Los Angeles. The building was gutted, and Sri Da Avabhasa Himself designed the layout of what was to be the new Ashram. The members of the newly formed group worked together to renovate the building—creating a small book-store in front, then behind it a meditation hall perhaps three times as large.

Up to this point Sri Da Avabhasa had given Spiritual Instruction to His household intimates, but in the manner of an elder brother or a more mature devotee. Thus, for example, it was His custom to sit side by side with them during their daily meditation. But the very architecture of the new Ashram indicated that this was about to change: There was to be a Chair for Him at the head of the room. No longer would He sit with His devotees apparently as an equal. Instead, all sat facing Him as their Divine Guru.

On the evening of April 25, 1972, Sri Da Avabhasa took His Seat at the head of His new Ashram. Thus, the Avataric Incarnation, the Very Divine Consciousness, Present in bodily (human) Form, Assumed His Role as the Divine World-Teacher, and turned the Wheel of His Dharma—the purest Wisdom ever spoken to human ears. In the Talk He gave on that first night, and thereafter, Sri Da Avabhasa no longer spoke with the voice of the exemplary devotee—He Spoke as Sat-Guru, One who lives the Force of Truth to all who turn to Him.

The Talks in this book, which document Da Avabhasa's Instruction to His devotees in roughly the first year of His Work, were given in response to the genuine need of the people who came to Him. For when Da Avabhasa opened the doors of His Ashram, He welcomed neither a group of advanced practitioners who were fully prepared to make use of His Divine Instruction about the advanced and the ultimate stages of life nor a group of true beginners possessed of at least a rudimentary understanding of Who sat before them and how to relate to Him as their Guru. No—this Divine Adept gazed out upon a ragged assortment of confused and alienated people, the jetsam of a society in chaos. Thus, the collection of Talks that comprise this book is a uniquely precious document—it is the record of a God-Born Being speaking to Spiritual beginners and Teaching them from the ground up, offering the greatest of opportunities to the most ordinary of people.

As the community of His devotees has grown and matured, Da Avabhasa has felt increasingly free to require from His devotees the level of responsibility that is traditionally expected of those who approach the God-Realizer. Such responsibility is appropriate, for without right preparation the aspirant is unable to truly receive or make effective use of the Sat-Guru's Blessing. Da Avabhasa's responses to the questions posed to Him by raw beginners throughout *The Method of the Siddhas* therefore belong to the past history of His Work. Today, those who come into Da Avabhasa's Company must have thoroughly studied His Wisdom-Teaching on the Way of the Heart, must understand the nature and necessity of the Guru-devotee relationship, and must have already conformed their lives to Da Avabhasa's detailed Instruction on the Way of the Heart. Nevertheless, the essence of His Instruction remains unchanged from the evening when He first opened His Ashram.

The Revelation of Understanding and the Heart: Da Avabhasa's Teaching Ordeal

D a Avabhasa's task was formidable and unprecedented: No Divinely Realized Adept had ever endeavored to Liberate such unprepared and reluctant devotees. He entered into this Work with a burning Intensity born of His Passionate Commitment to the Liberation of all who come to Him, moved by an unfathomable and unyielding Love. He once said:

SRI DA AVABHASA: *If My devotees are to live with Me, they must know that I love them. They must be absolutely certain of it. If I am to be effective as a Teacher, devotees must know I love them.*

You must not abstract Me from that reality. You should rather observe that I fully incarnate love and that it is a major aspect of My Work with you.

We live together in the Domain of Love, which is the incarnate form of the Spiritual Principle. I live this Principle to you, and you should likewise live it to Me and to one another. (June 29, 1983)

Da Avabhasa has continuously manifested that love among His devotees, in a manner always perfectly consistent with what is required for their Liberation. One man, who came to Da Avabhasa in 1972 on the brink of suicide, despairing of any real happiness despite his successful business career and suburban family life, recounts how Da Avabhasa nurtured the bond of love between Himself and His early devotees, patiently Instructing them in the Spiritual nature of their relationship to Him:

I was once Graced to go on a trip to Mexico with Da Avabhasa for two weeks, just the two of us. On about the third day of our trip, I got very sick. Da Avabhasa decided to send for a doctor because I was really in bad shape. I was lying in bed with a high fever. The doctor told me I had Montezuma's revenge, a dysentery-like disorder. I took the pills he prescribed for me, and I got much worse. I became so ill that I could hardly move.

Da Avabhasa would sit beside me and feed me soup with a spoon. He also tucked me in bed and kept changing the sheets, which were continually getting drenched with my sweat. After about four of five hours of this intense fever and sweating and delirium, He read a passage from a

11

Tibetan text that He had brought with Him. In this text, there is a detailed description of what can occur in the devotee when he or she meets the Spiritual Master. And as Da Avabhasa read these symptoms to me, I realized that this was a perfect, exact diagnosis of my ailment. Each of my symptoms was elaborated, literally word for word, in this ancient text! Da Avabhasa finished reading, closed the book, and said, "So I didn't want you to think it was only Montezuma's revenge!"

I had been Da Avabhasa's devotee for only six months, and I could see that He was Working to prepare me for a truly Spiritual relationship with Him. It was a moment of Grace: The Divine Adept Showed me His Love by feeding me soup with a spoon!

During the months when the Talks in this book were Given, Da Avabhasa lived among His devotees in a manner more traditional to His role as Guru—meeting with His devotees on formal occasions of Silent Blessing and also Discourse, and sometimes spending time with them while they functioned in the Ashram. After a year of such Work, in which the fundamental tenets of His Wisdom-Teaching were elucidated and the principles of the Guru-devotee relationship were made known to His devotees, a change in the manner of His Working took place.

Just as the archetypal artist is a mad ecstatic, an oracle, a man or woman possessed by a vision that must be communicated, so is the God-Realizer in his or her urge to communicate Realization. Da Avabhasa has always been prepared to go to any lengths to Liberate His devotees, unfettered by egoic conventions of speech or behavior. In the Spiritual traditions, such Freedom is called "Crazy". Now, Da Avabhasa saw that a more creative and daring approach would be necessary if His Wisdom-Teaching were really going to take its foothold in this world. Da Avabhasa has spoken Humorously of the years that followed:

SRI DA AVABHASA: My life is a little bit like going into the world of enemies and dragons to liberate somebody who has been captured. You cannot just sit down and tell a dragon the Truth. You must confront a dragon. You must engage in an heroic effort to release the captive from the dragon. This is how I Worked in the theatre of My way of Relating to people, particularly in the earlier years, and in the unusual involvements of My Life and Teaching. You could characterize it as the heroic Way of Teaching, the Way of identifying with devotees in that context and bringing them out of the enemy territory, gradually waking them up. (August 23, 1982)

Life in Da Avabhasa's Company during the years of what He calls His "Teaching Work" was a living experiment, a constant investigation of the many sides of life. Periods of strict ascetic discipline alternated with parties wild with abandon, righteousness and indulgence were encountered equally, rules and forms were introduced and then eschewed—but the extremes of this entire span of years served one purpose: the understanding that Satsang with Da Avabhasa alone is the "method" by which His Way of the Heart unfolds.

Da Avabhasa's Sacrifice, His Work to Help His devotees to surrender the ego in the face of His unconditional Love, has always been Extreme, Heroic, full of Genius, Compassion, and Daring. At times, His identification with His devotees has been demonstrated in ways that have been more than graphic. One evening in 1983, for example, a devotee fell on his left side and broke his ribs. The next day Da Avabhasa noticed that the man was clutching his chest in pain as he laughed. Da Avabhasa inquired of the cause. The man told Him what had happened, and nothing more was said. At the time, Da Avabhasa was Working intensely to help His devotees move beyond the limits of their emotional and sexual addictions. Two weeks passed, and the man's ribs were still painful. Da Avabhasa forcefully yet lovingly discussed with the man a particularly dramatic incident from the man's past. Da Avabhasa's Divine Power relieved the man of the emotional scar—the guilt, anger, sorrow, and shame that had kept him emotionally bound for many years. Through the Siddhi of Da Avabhasa's direct Work with him, the man's emotional trauma was relieved. What is more, mysteriously, his painful broken ribs were healed.

After this confrontation with His devotee, Da Avabhasa lay down to rest on His porch. Soon He began to feel an ache on the left side of His chest and sharp pains as He breathed. A doctor who was called to examine Da Avabhasa found that two of His ribs had fractured spontaneously. They were the exact same ribs and fracture sites that had been broken in Da Avabhasa's devotee.

As extraordinary as this account is, it is not altogether uncommon—for, during the years of His Teaching Work, Da Avabhasa would often take on the physical suffering of His devotees, contracting their illnesses and purifying them in His own body. But whatever physical symptoms He might have been manifesting at any given time (and there were often harrowing physical crises associated with His Teaching Work), Da Avabhasa had fully Submitted to assume the more fundamental suffering

13

of His devotees—which is egoity itself. He Worked face to face with His devotees in a living, theatrical ordeal of Spiritual Instruction, by acting as a Mirror to reflect back to them their contracted thoughts, emotions, and desires. His Life was not His own—His human existence, the struggle He endured, night and day, had become the very Means by which His devotees would understand the profound suffering of their egoic choices and accept His Graceful Help instead.

For years Da Avabhasa expended Himself in a Herculean effort to liberate His devotees by these means. Finally, in 1986, that manner of Working had utterly exhausted itself and a new phase of Da Avabhasa's Revelation of Grace began—one that would profoundly expand the potency of the sacred relationship that Da Avabhasa offers and that He describes in the pages of this book.

Da Avabhasa's "Bright" Emergence: the Ultimate Means

Sri Da Avabhasa has always worn His Love on His Face and on His Body, living as a vulnerability and a passion that no ordinary human heart can touch, much less tolerate. He has said of His Birth:

SRI DA AVABHASA: The Great God is willing to Love you and all beings, and that Divine Will, or Purpose, must be fulfilled. It is My unique Impulse. Whoever you say I might have been in times past, I am not anyone but you. And here I Am, Incarnate, to do this Work. A thousand years may pass before anyone understands anything about My Appearance here. So much suffering accompanies it. So much was required of Me to Submit to your company.

DEVOTEE: How is such a decision made?

SRI DA AVABHASA: By Love. By Divine Self-Realization, which is Love. To encompass the totality of conditional existence in Love—that is the Sign of Divine Self-Realization, Which embraces all to the point of death. Therefore, submit to love, to be compassionate, to serve. Such submission never destroyed Me. It cannot destroy Me, for the One Who I Am can never be destroyed. But Love, the Impulse to Kiss you, just to Kiss you, to not deny you, made Me a Body to Live with you. Can't you see it in My Face? (September 15, 1987)

14

On January 11, 1986, Da Avabhasa spontaneously relinquished His previous manner of Working with His devotees. But this turnabout was not simply a matter of changing His mind about how He would relate to His devotees. Da Avabhasa literally gave up the "persona", the bodily vehicle, through which He had played out a great drama of taking on the qualities of His devotees in order to reflect them to themselves. This crisis of change was a profound kind of death, and it manifested as a Yogic Swoon so dramatic that it appeared, for a brief time, that He had physically died as well.

It was some weeks before Da Avabhasa attempted to communicate the meaning of this profound Event to His devotees:

SRI DA AVABHASA: You have heard descriptions, by Yogis and other Spiritual figures, that before Realization one tries to go beyond the world to Realize God, and then after Realization one comes down into the body just so far, down to the brain, down to the throat maybe, down to the heart maybe, but typically not any lower than the throat.

I have until now invested My Self more profoundly than just down to the throat or the heart, but not down to the bottoms of My feet. I remained a kind of shroud around this Body, deeply associated with it, with all the ordinary human things, playing as a human being often in very ordinary ways, but, in My Freedom, somehow lifted off the floor, somehow not committed to this sorrow and this mortality.

Then I left this Body. And I suddenly found My Self reintegrated with it, but in a totally different Disposition, and I achieved your likeness exactly, thoroughly, to the bottoms of My feet, achieved un-Enlightenment, achieved human existence, achieved mortality, achieved sorrow.

To Me this is a Grand Victory! I do not know how to communicate the significance of it. For Me, it was a grander moment than the Event at the Vedanta Temple or any of the other Signs in My Life that are obviously Spiritually auspicious. To Me, it seems that through this will-less, effortless integration with suffering, something about My Work is more profoundly accomplished, something about it has become more auspicious than it ever was. I have not dissociated from My Realization, or My Ultimate State. Rather, I have accomplished your state completely, even more profoundly than you are sensitive to it.

I have become this Body utterly. I have become the Body, and it is Full of Divine Presence. (January 27, 1986)

By a process of Grace great beyond all explaining, Da Avabhasa had, in His Divine Emergence, found a way to fulfill the Great Impulse that had caused His birth.

SRI DA AVABHASA: I have used the metaphor of kissing to describe My Impulse to serve everyone, all the billions (of humankind), directly. It is an obvious impossibility as a physical matter. But in My Divine Emergence, it was accomplished. I have, by totally taking on this Body, by bringing this Realization fully into the context of this Body, established a Vehicle that serves everyone if they will give their attention to Me. This is the method of the Kiss, then, this Incarnation, My Divine Emergence, the establishment of this Means. (December 11, 1988)

Sri Da Avabhasa's Impulse to "kiss" all beings expresses His Intention to rouse every heart with the Love and Bliss-Force of His own Divine Being—like "the kiss of the Prince and Sleeping Beauty", multiplied as many times as there are living beings.

But Da Avabhasa's Intention to touch every heart with His Love and Blessing is not allegorical. Through the most profound ordeal, He has brought into the human world a Mechanism so potent with Blessing that It conveys the kiss of His heart-awakening Grace to everyone who will turn to Him. His Own Divinized Body, His full Emergence into a human Form is that Mechanism of Grace. Da Avabhasa's Divine Emergence is the Means by which the relationship with Him, the time-honored method of the Siddhas, has achieved unprecedented effect.

◆ ◆ ◆

Da Avabhasa's Divine Emergence is an ongoing process through which His Blessing-"Brightness" continually magnifies Itself. While on retreat at Sri Love-Anandashram in 1990, one woman was Graced to understand something of the Miracle that His Divine Emergence is, and the Power that is now communicated through Contemplation of His Divinized Form:

The heart of my retreat, and of all retreats in Da Avabhasa's Company, was the opportunity to receive His Darshan (a traditional term for the sighting of a God-Realizer). On the formal occasions in which He Granted His Darshan, Da Avabhasa would typically walk a hundred yards from His House along a path lined with flowers to one of the halls of the Ashram where retreatants waited for Him. When we were alerted to His imminent arrival, we would turn around as one to see Him moving toward us with the majestic ease and power of a lion. Usually, during this period, He would be wearing a traditional Indian style of dress, a length of cotton cloth in His characteristic colors of indigo and white wrapped around His waist, and sometimes a shawl of similar color.

The effect of His entrance can hardly be described. For a devotee, these moments are the most precious in life, prepared for and looked forward to through one's whole life of practice. Here in Person is the Beloved of one's heart, today perhaps fiery-eyed, perhaps Blissfully tender, Radiating the Supreme Mystery and Beauty of Divinity.

Da Avabhasa would take His seat and begin to scan the room, meeting the eyes of each devotee. Then after a time, He might close His eyes and simply sit in Silence, Magnifying His Love-Bliss for maybe an hour or more. The "language" of His Silence is heart-feeling, expanded to Infinity as limitless Happiness.

As I would Contemplate Him and feel His Feeling, many emotions, thoughts, and bodily or visual experiences would arise—some difficult, because being in His physical Company often releases suppressed thoughts and emotions, and some blissful. Like others present, I would sometimes have kriyas—involuntary movements such as bodily shaking and rapid breathing—and spontaneous vocalizations of prayers and praise.

While many moments of heart-breaking joy, self-revelation, and self-release were Granted me by my Guru through His Sublime Darshan, it was when I was leaving the Island that the Blessing He had Given me during those weeks became fully evident.

As the boat sped away from Sri Love-Anandashram, I felt the characteristic feeling of Da Avabhasa more and more strongly. I felt Him especially pressing upon me at the heart, but that same feeling also radiated in the faces of the other travellers, in the whole boat, in the air, in the sunlight, in the sea. He was simply Present, and His Transmission of Love was soon pouring through my whole body. He was answering my prayer to be undone by His Love. Through my tears and the salt spray, I watched the Island recede—this incredibly Blessed Spot of earth where the Divine has set Foot and made His Abode. The whole day was one of feeling His "Invisible Touch" and being carried in His "Secret Embrace", of discovering the tangible reality of my relationship to Him at a depth I had never felt before. I knew that it was prior to this life and could never be broken.

I realized I had been relieved of the most basic of human fears, fear of being apparently adrift in this puny body, of spinning out a little life surrounded and soon to be engulfed by the great Ocean of the unknown. I did not realize how primal and real that fear was in me until I felt Him take it away. Now it was not my vision anymore. The Mystery in which I was floating was only Da Avabhasa. I knew by some Graceful intuition that He is the unfathomable Ocean of Divine Consciousness, the Radiant Being, the Divine Love-Bliss, and that my relationship to Him as That is eternal. Nothing can limit it or bring it to an end.

At the end of that day, in a hotel room near Nadi International Airport, I read from His Wisdom-Teaching:

> *If You Will Only Consent To Be Attracted and Distracted By Me, You Will Feel Me, For My Given and Mere and Blessing Company Always Moves The Heart.*
>
> *If You Feel Me, You Are With Me.*
>
> *And If You Are With Me, Your Heart Cannot Fail To Realize Me, Who Is The Heart Itself.* (The Dawn Horse Testament, p. 688)

◆ ◆ ◆

Ultimately, it is Sri Da Avabhasa's ever-increasing Emergence as the Person of the Living "Bright" Divine that makes this book significant. For *The Method of the Siddhas* conveys His Offering of the most fully Empowered form of the Guru-devotee relationship that has ever existed—the relationship to Him, the consummate Siddha.

The opportunity to practice in His Company, to use His Instruction and to be attracted by His Divinely Emerged Form, to give attention to Him—these are the bases for a life that is sane, whole, focused in self-understanding, grounded in true feeling, capable of discrimination, integrity, and strength of purpose, alive with the invigorating demand to keep growing, equipped with the means to cut through the vagaries and the desperation of the ego, made round and human with gratitude and the excess of love that spills over from the relationship with Him into every relationship, every circumstance, a life that is even swollen with joy, with the constant celebration that the Divine Person is not only Standing before us, but He is Standing as our own hearts in this very moment.

The bond of Love that exists between Da Avabhasa and all who turn to Him—rather than any technique or exercise—is the "method" whereby

He relieves us of our suffering and draws us into Divine Love-Bliss. As you read this new edition of *The Method of the Siddhas*, we urge you to carefully consider and embrace the great relationship that Sri Da Avabhasa offers to you, and that He so eloquently describes in these sublime Talks.

The Mountain Of Attention, 1992

Notes to the text appear on pages 351–60.

Sri Da Avabhasa
at Sri Love-Anandashram, 1992

PART ONE

The Method of the Siddhas

Sri Da Avabhasa in Los Angeles
April 25, 1972

1.

Understanding

O n April 25, 1972, the date of this Talk, Da Avabhasa formally invited people to approach Him for the first time at His Ashram in Los Angeles. Thus, it was on this date that His Work as Divine World-Teacher truly began. Before this time, previous to the establishment of His Ashram, He had Taught only a few individuals who had begun to respond to Him as Teacher. In addition to marking the inception of His open Spiritual availability to all who are moved to respond to His Wisdom, His Grace, and His Person, the occasion of this Talk also marked the moment when Da Avabhasa's devotees formally began to acknowledge and to relate to Him as Sat-Guru.

In this first Talk, Da Avabhasa described the process of understanding that had been one of the fundamental discoveries of His own life, and that is the necessary foundation upon which Satsang, or the relationship to Him as Sat-Guru, must be built. In the thousands of hours of Discourse and the many volumes of Written Instruction that have ensued since this Talk was given, Da Avabhasa has only underscored and reiterated the Call to understanding that He elucidates here.

Since April 25, 1972, Da Avabhasa has been involved in a progressive and open Communication and Demonstration of the Way of Truth, the Way of the Siddhas, or "Completed Ones", who come in the forms and activities of God. Both His Communication and His Demonstration of the Way of the Siddhas have been unparalleled in their vigor, their comprehensiveness, and their purity. The Discourse He Gave on this night is thus the cornerstone of a consummate Revelation of Spiritual Instruction and Blessing.

As was His custom at that time, Da Avabhasa first sat with His devotees in silence for perhaps an hour, Transmitting the sublimity of His own Heart-Realization to them. Such was the mood and appearance of His Spiritual activity during the earliest days of His Work. Then He Spoke.

SRI DA AVABHASA: Are there any questions?

No one replied, so Sri Da Avabhasa spoke again.

SRI DA AVABHASA: Everyone has understood?

QUESTION: I haven't understood. Explain it to me.[1]

SRI DA AVABHASA: Very good. What haven't you understood?

QUESTION: Well, you said, "Did everybody understand?" and everyone seemed to understand but me. Would you explain it to me?

SRI DA AVABHASA: Explain what?

QUESTION: Well, you could start with the word "understanding".

SRI DA AVABHASA: Yes. There is a disturbance, a feeling of dissatisfaction, some sensation that motivates a person to go to a teacher, read a book about philosophy, believe something, or do some conventional form of Yoga. What people ordinarily think of as spirituality or religion is a search to get free of that sensation, that suffering that is motivating them. So all the usual paths—Yogic methods, beliefs, religion, and so on—are forms of seeking, grown out of this sensation, this subtle suffering. Ultimately, all the usual paths are attempting to get free of that sensation. That is the traditional goal. Indeed, all human beings are seeking, whether or not they are very sophisticated about it, or using very specific methods of Yoga, philosophy, religion, whatever.

When that whole process of seeking begins to break down, one no longer quite has the edge of one's search left. One begins to suspect oneself. One begins to doubt the whole process of one's search. Then one is no longer fascinated with one's search, one's method, one's Yoga, one's religion, one's ordinary teacher. One's attention begins to turn to this sensation that motivates one's entire search.

When one begins to re-cognize,[2] consciously to know again, that subtle motivation, this is what I call "understanding". When one begins to see again the subtle forms of one's own action, which are one's suffering, that re-cognition is "understanding". When this becomes absolute, perfect, when there is utterly, absolutely, no dilemma, no form in the living consciousness to interpret existence, when there is no contraction, no fundamental suffering, no thing prior to Consciousness Itself, this is what I call "'radical'[3] understanding". It is only enjoyment.

The traditions call this enjoyment the "Self", the "Heart",[4] "God-Union", "Satori", "Nirvana", "Heaven". But it is simply Consciousness Itself. There is no thing prior to Consciousness Itself. You are not some piece of Divinity seated inside the body, which somehow must get released from the body and go <u>back</u> to its spiritual Home and Source. There is no such entity. The Home and Source is also the very Nature of the "entity". There is Consciousness Itself, and the apparent entity is within Consciousness Itself. When Consciousness Itself enjoys Its own State, or Real Nature, even in the midst of conditions, even where there is life, that is perfect "understanding". When, no matter what event appears, there is only the enjoyment of Consciousness Itself, not transformed or modified by events, when no implication arises on the basis of events to seem to change the Nature of Consciousness Itself, that is perfect "meditation". When there is the perfect enjoyment of Consciousness Itself, that is called "liberation". All of that is "understanding".

There is a subtle contraction in the process called "Man", and it seems to change the quality of Consciousness Itself. The contraction itself "creates" (or seems to imply) the identification of Consciousness Itself with the contracted sense—<u>that</u> form, <u>that</u> body, <u>that</u> mentality. And in that act of identification, that form, that body, that mentality, differentiates itself from <u>other</u> forms, <u>other</u> bodies, <u>other</u> minds—<u>other</u> beings (or selves). Then the rest of life is spent, through exploitation of the movement of desire, to overcome that "creation". Through the movement that is desire, people seek constantly to "create" a connection, a flow of force, between the contracted identity and everything from which it has differentiated itself. The usual Yoga, religion, spirituality, philosophy, all your strategies, even your simple psychological strategies, your lifestyles, have this same form. They are all attempts to release energy between this contracted, separated one and all from which it is differentiated. Thus, all ordinary activity is founded in this dilemma, this self-"created" contraction.

Traditional spiritual life is a search in this same form. There is dilemma, and there is the spiritual method, which is an attempt to overcome this dilemma. When the individual begins to see again the dilemma that motivates his or her strategic method, that seeing is understanding. As long as he or she is simply seeking, and has all kinds of motivation, fascination with the search, this is not understanding—this is dilemma itself.

25

But where this dilemma is understood, there is the re-cognition of a structure in the living consciousness, a separation. And when that separation is observed more and more directly, one begins to see that what one is suffering is not something happening to one but it is one's own action. It is as if you are pinching yourself, without being aware of it. You are "creating" a subtle pain, and, worse than the pain, a continuous modification, which is "mind", which the living consciousness identifies as itself. The more one observes this, the more one's search is abandoned, spontaneously, intelligently. One simply sees one's motivation, one's actual suffering. One can only live that suffering. It does not move, until conscious life becomes a crisis. Then one sees that the entire motivation of life is based on a subtle activity in the living consciousness. That activity is avoidance, separation, a contraction at the root, the origin, the "place", of Consciousness Itself.

In the beginning of this crisis, one only observes the contraction as a sensation, as a sense of dilemma, as a search. But the more directly one observes it, the more clearly one recognizes the action itself. At first, one sees the avoidance, the strategy, the life-technique. Then one begins to observe this activity in terms of what it is excluding, what it prevents, what is always being eliminated from the living consciousness and the lifetime of consciousness. That which is always excluded is the condition of relationship.

Ordinarily, one is unaware of relationship, as relationship. One only lives the drama of separation. But when one becomes directly aware of this contraction, this separation, this subtle form, one observes or enjoys relationship as that condition which is always already the case. Relationship is always already the condition of the living consciousness. When this contraction is observed perfectly, "radically", there is only relationship, and no obstruction. Then, spontaneously, it is also perfect awareness. That perfect awareness is called the "Heart", the "Real", what always already is the case.

The Heart is always active, always accomplishing the thing that desire always seeks but never finally realizes. The Heart is always unqualified relationship, always Force, conscious Force without obstruction. But the life of desire is always already based on separation. Separation has already occurred in the usual human being, so desire tries to heal the sense that arises as a consequence of that separation. But there is no ultimate success by the means of desire, even "spiritual" forms of desire. There may be temporary releases, fascinations, but desire never "radically" escapes

26

its own dilemma. This is because it does not deal with the dilemma. The search is concerned only with desire and the objects of desire. But beneath that is this subtle contraction.

Therefore, the Heart is always already the absolute continuum, the flow of Power, without obstructions. It is always already like desire fully satisfied, because the flow is always already accomplished. Always already accomplished, not the result of any motivated action.

The Great Siddhas,[5] the realizers whose understanding is perfect, are those who live consciously as the Heart. They function as the Heart for living beings. And that function is simply unqualified relationship, unobstructed flow. The pressure of the Presence of such a one awakens and constantly intensifies the flow of Force in living beings. All obstructions tend to fall away in the presence of this Force. Where it moves, there is either surrender or flight in its course. The Great Siddhas communicate the living Force of Reality. They live It to living beings. They simply live the natural state of enjoyment with other beings. And those who stay to live in friendship with one who understands tend also to understand.

QUESTION: I have to go, but I have one more question. You said the Great Siddhas live as the heart. What about the mind? Do they live as the mind also?

SRI DA AVABHASA: What is it?

QUESTION: Do they live as the mind as well? It is connected with the heart.

SRI DA AVABHASA: What mind?

QUESTION: What mind? The mind that they exist in. There is only one mind.

SRI DA AVABHASA: There is? Which?

QUESTION: Of course their brains are functioning too. Right?

SRI DA AVABHASA: And?

QUESTION: And?

SRI DA AVABHASA: What is the point you are trying to make?

QUESTION: Well, I asked you the question about the mind.

SRI DA AVABHASA: Yes. What mind?

QUESTION: What mind?

SRI DA AVABHASA: The brain?

QUESTION: Yes, the brain.

SRI DA AVABHASA: Ah, well that is something very specific. You are talking about the brain, or the "One Mind"?

QUESTION: Well, there is only one mind, of course.

SRI DA AVABHASA: You are talking about the mind now, and not about the brain?

QUESTION: Well, I was asking you what is the relationship between the mind, the brain, and the heart.

SRI DA AVABHASA: You are talking about the physical heart?

QUESTION: Not necessarily.

SRI DA AVABHASA: Well, which?

QUESTION: You can answer however you like.

SRI DA AVABHASA: I do not have need for the answer. What specifically are you asking?

QUESTION: Well, actually you answered me, because I wanted to see what you wanted to say.

SRI DA AVABHASA: No, that is not what you wanted to see. Don't play games. I am not here to entertain. All these little dramas you are playing have no place. I have no interest in them, and neither have you. I am not here to "lay something on" to you. I am not concerned with that. If you want to discuss something with me for a real purpose, that is something else. But if you want to play at polemics, and idle cleverness . . .

28

QUESTION: That's not what I want.

SRI DA AVABHASA: No, no. That is what you want.

QUESTION: Do you think that is what I am trying to do?

SRI DA AVABHASA: Yes.

QUESTION: Why do you think that?

SRI DA AVABHASA: What is all of that? [pointing to the man's expression]

QUESTION: What is what?

SRI DA AVABHASA: What has all of that [pointing to his expression] got to do with anything, hm? You are very upset. What are you upset about?

QUESTION: I'm not upset at all.

SRI DA AVABHASA: Yes you are, my friend. [to another] Does he look upset to you?

ANOTHER: Yes. I recognize that. [to the questioner] You know what that is? It is fear—stone-cold fear.

SRI DA AVABHASA: Something here is upsetting you. I would like to talk about that. That would be worth talking about.

QUESTION: I don't feel upset.

SRI DA AVABHASA: You don't feel the least upset?

QUESTION: No.

SRI DA AVABHASA: Very good.

QUESTION: If what you say of me were true, why would I have come here tonight?

SRI DA AVABHASA: I think you have good reasons for being here, but I don't think that is what we are dealing with at the moment. Before we can deal with your good reasons for being here, you must overcome the social dilemma it represents to you. Yes? The whole spiritual life, or the thinking associated with spiritual life, which you bring here is perhaps somewhat threatened. Well, that is fine. But you all have to get beyond simply being threatened by one another. And before you can get beyond that, it must be acknowledged. The obviousness of it must be acknowledged. The obviousness of your strategy, your cleverness, your inability to be direct, to love. You must acknowledge this "creation" of artifices. All of that must be understood. If you have not understood that, what is there to defend? I could sit here and have a discussion with you about the mind, the brain, the heart. But what does all of that have to do with anything? Hm? We could talk about the shape of clouds. But what _is_ going on? What is this sensation, this feeling that you have, that everyone has?

QUESTION: What sensation do you speak of? I am not sure what you mean.

SRI DA AVABHASA: Exactly. What is that sensation that you have at this moment? Your awareness?

QUESTION: I am sorry, I don't understand what you are talking about. You are saying awareness is a sensation, right now?

SRI DA AVABHASA: What exactly is the Nature of your awareness at this moment?

QUESTION: I don't know how to answer that. But I know it exists. I am aware of it.

SRI DA AVABHASA: Of what?

QUESTION: My awareness.

SRI DA AVABHASA: You're aware of your awareness?

QUESTION: Yes.

SRI DA AVABHASA: And is it always truth, sublimity, and beauty?

QUESTION: It just is, brother, it just is!

SRI DA AVABHASA: Good.

QUESTION: Yes!

SRI DA AVABHASA: Then why are you so uncomfortable?

QUESTION: You keep seeing that, so there must be something.

SRI DA AVABHASA: What is this attitude that you are using at this moment? I am not "concerned" with it, you see. I don't want to put you down for it. But I want to get to it, because it is the primary quality in all your comments to me. Hm? You are aware of it. How you use your body, your eyebrows, the tone of voice, your manner of expressing yourself.

QUESTION: What is wrong with that?

SRI DA AVABHASA: I am not saying there is anything wrong with it.

QUESTION: Well, then, why are you making any mention of it?

SRI DA AVABHASA: Because you are using it to communicate to me. It is your communication.

QUESTION: Well, so what?

SRI DA AVABHASA: What is this attitude? What is that? That is an attitude, isn't it?

QUESTION: Well, obviously it's me.

SRI DA AVABHASA: What is the purpose of it? What are you doing with it? What is its nature? You have communicated differently at other times. Sometimes you laugh, sometimes you cry.

QUESTION: Yes.

SRI DA AVABHASA: All right. You are not laughing or crying now. You are doing this! What is it you are doing?

QUESTION: I am in the process of communicating with you.

SRI DA AVABHASA: Why in this particular form?

QUESTION: Because that is the form I choose to use.

SRI DA AVABHASA: Yes. And it does not have any resistance in it at all?

QUESTION: Well, it has a resistance. Yes, it has. I feel that there is a lack of communication going on.

SRI DA AVABHASA: OK. That is what I am talking about.

QUESTION: When I'm communicating with somebody or somebody is trying to communicate with me, if I feel there is a lack, sure I feel a resistance.

SRI DA AVABHASA: Exactly. That is what I am feeling.

QUESTION: You feel it too, huh?

SRI DA AVABHASA: Yes. And if there were simple, direct communication between us, it would be unnecessary for you to have that sensation and to communicate it to me as you now feel you must. But what is actually coming through is that fear, that resistance, that upset about the nature of this communication. And that is exactly what I have been talking about tonight. It is exactly that contraction, that resistance, that formation of awareness, that _is_ suffering. Behind that are all the thoughts, illusions, memories, experiences, searches. But that contraction, or resistance, is always first. That is always the subtle structure everyone is living. Wherever you go, wherever you are, it is that subtle sense, that subtle resistance, that subtle discomfort, that subtle unpleasantness, that failure of love, of energy, of presence. And _that_ is exactly the thing I am talking about. And this present sensation of which you have become aware is the quality by which it is <u>always</u> experienced. It may also be very elaborate. It can take on all kinds of forms, but this present sensation is the "contraction" I am talking about. It is not unique to you. I just happen to feel it functioning like this at this moment in you. But you are no different from anyone else. Everyone is suffering the same tendency and activity. And its results are always the same. Everyone is suffering exactly the same thing. There

32

are only different life-methods, styles, complex experiences, whatever. But the essential structure is common to everyone.

There is first the periodic awareness of that sensation, then the awareness of it as a continuous experience, then the observation of its actual structure, the knowing of it all as one's own activity, a deliberate, present activity that is your suffering, that is your illusion. The final penetration of that present, deliberate activity is what I have called "understanding". It is simply the penetration of that process which structures all conscious events, all of your experience. And the primary, even the most obvious, effect of this subtle activity of suffering is the destruction of the consciousness of relationship.

That is exactly how it was functioning between us in the last few minutes. There was the sense of an obstruction in this relationship. But when it is not there, when the contraction does not take place, when it is not meditated upon, when it is no longer a matter of concern, when there is simply this unobstructed relationship, there is no dilemma. Then there is no one superior to the other, no problem, no jealousy, no distinction. There is only enjoyment. And where life is constant as that enjoyment, there is the Infinity of Liberation, the Perfect Consciousness of Truth, the Siddhi[6] of the Real. But it is always simply that basic enjoyment, that unobstructed, spontaneous, moment to moment existence as relationship. It is what is called "love". It is simply the Force of the Heart, the Real, which is unobstructed, unqualified existence. When there is no resistance, no contraction, no separation, there is just this ease of pleasure in one another. And where there is that ease of pleasure, there is no problem. Give it a name, if you like. It is simply your natural state.

What I call the "Heart" is Consciousness. It is called "Atman", the very Self, or Nature, of the apparent individual. It is not a separate organ or a separate faculty. It is identical to what is called "Brahman", the Formless, Absolute, Omnipresent Divine Reality. It is Very Consciousness, Absolute Bliss, Unqualified Existence. It is intuition of unspeakable God. Anything secondary that we could call "mind", "body", or "brain", any function at all, is contained within the Heart, like an event in a universe. Within that universe is the appearance of living beings. Naturally, if you speak of the physical body, or the psycho-physical entity, there is the physical heart, there is the physical brain, and there are many other functions, physical ones and subtle ones. But all of these are contained in that perfect Consciousness, that unobstructed Nature, the Heart. From this "point of view", there is no dilemma in the appearance of things, no misunderstanding of it, no threat. All of this is a form of enjoyment.

It is common for those who constantly live in the obstructed state to possess an elaborate, dramatic conceptualization of things. But that conceptualization of things is not equivalent to things themselves. It is simply a display of modifications of energy, of subtle internal energy, appearing as functioning mind. It is only a structure, a figure, an imposition, a distraction, and its root is this contraction of which I speak. It is utterly beside the point whether my conceptualization of things is bigger than yours, or mine has all seven parts in it while yours has only four. It is only that we have a different traditional structure, different theatre. It doesn't make any difference what these minds contain. It is not merely the saint who can understand. Every fool can understand. It doesn't make any difference what is inside. It all has to go. Because it is this contraction, this obstruction, this self-containment, that every human being is suffering.

When the obstruction is no longer the force that is patterning one's state, then it becomes possible for one to enjoy the very state of things, the real structure of things, directly, prior to conceptualization and the ordinary drama of one's life. From that "point of view", which is already free and true, perhaps something meaningful can be said about the structure of things, but, from this very "point of view", nothing is either gained or lost by the existence of the manifested structure of worlds or the description of it. If the principle of suffering is released, something can be said, but the speech is not necessary.

A person came to Bodhidharma[7] and said something about his "mind" that is similar to your remarks. He sat in the presence of Bodhidharma, trying to attract his attention. He did this for a long time, without success, so that, finally, he was moved to hack off his arm, which he presented to Bodhidharma. You must have heard the story. He held this arm up to Bodhidharma, who, at last, turned to him. He was willing to have a brief discussion. But he wasn't upset, excited, or particularly interested in the bleeding and mortal condition of this seeker. The person wanted to know something about his mind. He wanted to be liberated from his perpetual disturbance of mind. Bodhidharma said, "Show me your mind." Show me this mind that is upset, that you want to understand, that you claim to possess. According to tradition, that was sufficient to enlighten the man. He saw that what he was upset with, what he thought he was suffering or owning, had no tangible existence. There was not in fact any "thing" that he was suffering or owning. He was simply obsessed. His suffering and his "mind" were present self-"creations". All Bodhidharma did, or served to do, was to bring about this spontaneous re-cognition of the nature of that which the man was presenting all the time as himself, as his state. So, there was this sudden turnabout.

The traditions are filled with such meetings between questioners, or seekers, and their teachers. It is always the same story. The individual has some very elaborate search going on in himself or herself, some very elaborate structure of mind that he or she always presents and that he or she wants to defend or overcome. But, whatever his or her number or game, the usual man or woman always communicates one thing to others. It is his or her own mind-form, his or her own state. It is always this that people present to one another and to life. By the performance of one's own state, one destines oneself to certain reactions of life, certain experiences. One's state also becomes one's action and one's destiny. True "spiritual life" is always that process whereby the present and chronic modification of Consciousness Itself—this compulsive state, this action that becomes dilemma, seeking, and suffering—is undermined in understanding. True "religion" is the crisis of the living consciousness. True "religion" is the crisis in which unconsciousness is undermined. It is the crisis of one's ordinary, common state, where it is utterly turned about, undermined. That is the essential event to which all traditions try to bring seekers, regardless of the lore and technique peculiar to the time and place. It is always a crisis. It is not some "self-possessed"[8] artifice. It is not a defense of the person's limited condition. It is where all of this is utterly destroyed. The Christian tradition talks about "spiritual death" as the basic event. It is a sacrifice, a cross. In the East it is the crisis of satori, or of the difficult, long term of sadhana,[9] or of self-purifying action. But it is always the crisis, the turnabout, the obliteration of that form in which the person is helplessly alive. And if that has not taken place, there is no spirituality, but there is simply the same thing that always was, the same obsession with forms, the same suffering, this disability, dilemma, disappointment, or whatever emotional quality is manifested in the individual case.

When there is no defense left, when the bottom falls out, when there is nothing to stand on, that is "liberation". As long as there is something left to defend, something with which to resist, as long as there is something still left to die, the same state persists, the same suffering, the same search. When it is all "dead", when the greatly feared event has already occurred, then there is no longer the thread of seeking or the defense of its hidden dilemma.

The kind of resistance we discussed in relation to the questioner who opened this discussion is exactly the thing that everyone brings to the teacher. The drama between the disciple and the teacher is always the hour-to-hour confrontation with that condition. It is not special in anyone's case. It is the very thing that "creates" the spiritual drama. It is the very thing that is dealt with throughout spiritual life, in always more subtle forms. There is no particular enjoyment in it. There is no special honor in it or any special dues that come across because you deal with this suffering and resistance. The teacher must always deal with the state that people bring to him or to her. And that state is never "radically" free. The new disciple is never a form of enjoyment. He or she is not blissful. He or she is not Truth. The teacher must function with the communicated obstructions, and he or she must do so consciously and deliberately. The teacher must not forget the suffering and dilemma of the disciple. Therefore, the teacher must not simply console and fascinate the disciple with promises, words, and smiling notions. The teacher must constantly deal with the obstruction in the disciple, until the disciple is no longer suffering that. But in order for the disciple to no longer be suffering that, there must be a crisis, a difficult confrontation. And it is always absolutely difficult. Even between the teacher and the calmest, most apparently loving devotee there is that obstruction. It is only on the surface, in the personal strategy, that the new disciple appears to be calm and loving. But he or she is also bound up with his or her suffering. Some appear to be very loving and capable of service. Others appear very resistive and angry. There is no real distinction. It is just a difference of qualities, but essentially the same event is going on. The same thing is brought to the teacher in every case. The same thing has to be lived by the teacher in every case. Therefore, from the human point of view, there is no great privilege or pleasure in performing the teaching function for people. It is simply that the Heart functions in that manner. Always, spontaneously, it moves into relationship. It moves through the structures of the living consciousness. It flows through. It breaks down the obstructions. The Heart is always already enjoyment.

The person in whom this whole strategy has broken down looks like a pane of glass. There is no "peculiarity" about such a one, no resistance. That whole structure of force in which he or she lives is open. But when you meet the usual man or woman, you immediately experience the limitation on life that he or she will accept or demand in your relationship to him or to her. And this tends to stimulate, by reaction, your own limitation. So everybody complains that ordinary experience with people is unsatisfying. But when that contraction opens even a little, the force of delight and of love begins to flow, and the obstructions begin to break down, until, finally, the "person" is shattered. At last, the whole ordinary form of his or her existence is absolutely destroyed. He or she no longer lives from the point of view of this contraction and all of the assumptions about life that it requires. Consciousness has fallen out of the usual form, and the "point of view" is that of the Divine Self, the Heart, the "radical" intuition of Reality, or God. Such a one no longer contains the least trace of a separate self sense. It doesn't even tend to arise. And yet, the apparent functions of life remain.

Those who live in genuine spiritual community have value for others who come into contact with them. They will only allow people to live as the Heart, to function in relationship with the Force of the Heart. They will not indulge a person's strategy. They will provoke the crisis of his or her suffering.

[At this point the young man who had been questioning Sri Da Avabhasa got up to leave. He had obviously felt quite antagonistic toward Sri Da Avabhasa. It was not clear why he felt it was necessary to assume a superior manner, but his contempt as well as his insecurity had been made plain to all. After he left, many of those present expressed their relief with laughter and criticism, but Sri Da Avabhasa continued to remind them that the drama they had just witnessed was a kind of exaggerated version of the process that is enacted between the teacher and every one of his or her disciples.]

SRI DA AVABHASA: It is always the same. Every one is like that. He wasn't extraordinary. He just played the obvious drama that he played. He was good. I appreciated his questions. It was good that something that dramatic or emotional could take place. You should read the documents which record the history and teaching in the Ashrams of various teachers, such as Ramana Maharshi or Ramakrishna.[10] It is always the same thing. This Ashram is not going to be any different.

QUESTION: Would you please speak about this contraction, and how the form of enquiry you describe in *The Knee of Listening*[11] passes beyond all the forms of separation?

SRI DA AVABHASA: A lot of words could be used. The traditions describe different "knots" that are opened, and the goal of spiritual life is often said to be the opening of these various knots. There is a knot in the navel, a knot in the heart, and a knot in the head. There are many knots, but these are perhaps the primary regions discussed in the traditions. What they are really talking about are functional forms of contraction in the organic and subtle processes of life. The chakras, or subtle centers through which the life-force moves, are like the shutter of a camera. When they are contracted and closed, no force flows. If there is a force trying to make them open, the resistance of the contraction "creates" pain, heat, and all the various Yogic manifestations, many of which are described in *The Knee of Listening*. As a living center of consciousness opens a little bit more, then the mind begins to get a little "flowery". So there are little visionary things, and perceptions and insights. When it is completely open, there is just the blissful, Divine Force of Consciousness Itself. Then the life-force moves on, until it hits the next obstruction. The life-force is ultimately the Force of the very Heart, the God-life, the Power of Reality, moving through the various centers of life, which are chronically obstructed, or contracted. And the various experiences associated with the release of these centers characterize the process of Yoga, or the traditional paths of spiritual life. But what is ultimately the case is not all of these experiences. They just take place because there are obstructions. If there are no obstructions, there is only Absolute Consciousness, no dilemma, nothing to be accomplished. There is no body in which to accomplish anything. Therefore, one in whom understanding and enquiry are perfected passes from limited and even extraordinary forms of knowledge and experience into the intuitive and spontaneous life of Reality, or God.

QUESTION: Is the activity of the mind and thought an obstruction?

SRI DA AVABHASA: What is your experience?

QUESTION: My experience is that in spite of what I will or wish, I have lots of strange thoughts.

SRI DA AVABHASA: If you close the eyes meditatively, you turn yourself mainly to concentration on mind-forms. But if your eyes are open, there are people, functional demands, and the whole cosmic event. And while you are sitting there with your eyes open, you will become aware that all of this thought is also going on. You will begin to feel, almost see, how thought slides between you and all contact with the moving world.

Thought is an actual, solid obstruction. It is a form of matter, a modification of energy. What you call the mind is wavelengths of force, functioning, taking on forms, through the subtle processes of electrical interchange. So when you have a thought, you have modified the energy flowing through the brain regions. In other words, you have <u>contracted</u> it, and you are always concentrating on that contraction. If you pinch your arm, attention centers at the point of pain. If you have a thought, attention centers at the point of thought. Whenever there is distraction by a particular entity, form, function, or whatever, there is loss of direct awareness, of relationship. When there is concentration, everything else is excluded. The "ego" is just another form of concentration, of distraction. In the case of the ego, the distraction is not a particular thought but the separate self sense that all contraction generates. The ego is an activity, not an entity. The ego is the activity of avoidance, the avoidance of relationship.

Therefore, any thought, any function, anything that "creates" form, that appears as form, that seems to be form, is produced by concentration—or contraction. Thus, apart from understanding, all processes, even life itself, tend to become an obstruction. The root of it all is called the "ego", but it is actually contraction, in countless forms, endured unconsciously. The unconsciousness is the key, not the acts of concentration themselves (which are only more or less functional). Apart from responsible consciousness, or present, conscious understanding, functional contraction tends to become the assumed condition of life. Unconscious contraction "creates" separation, which manifests as identification, or the sense of separate self.

The root of true spirituality is not some activity like desire that seeks to get you to the super-Object. Genuine spirituality is understanding of the whole process of motivation. It is to re-cognize the root of it—this contraction, this separation. When you no longer have any more options, when you have worn yourself out doing your number, and you have tried all the trips and methods, paths and lifestyles, strategies and places to go, all the forms of concentration, whatever they are, then all of that begins to break down. You discover that you just don't have the "jazz" left to really carry it on anymore. You find yourself more depressed, just a little bit too much depressed to meditate or to hunt for sex. You just don't have the jazz, the necessary fire of motivation. Then upsetness begins to overwhelm you. The crisis begins to come on. You don't really have a path (or a strategy) anymore. You may talk a lot about it, feel a lot about it. It remains a part of your mind, but you don't really <u>have</u> a path (or a

39

strategy) any longer. That is really the most hopeful sign. The ego is beginning to rot! When fruit begins to rot, then it falls with seed into the
earth. But as long as one is very righteous, as long as one has got one's
"trip", one is not ripe. It is only when the trip begins to kick you in the
face that you begin to soften up, bruise a little bit, feel your fear, your
suffering, your dilemma, this constant upset of all your mortality.

We are all going to die. We are all going to lose this present awareness, this present enjoyment. I can't endure that dilemma from day to
day. From the moment I was born, that upset me. I wasn't the least interested in tolerating moment to moment existence as that kind of suffering.
Life wasn't worth the involvement if its summation had to be death, zero.
What difference does it make how turned on I can get if I must fall out
the bottom, arbitrarily. Everything is wonderful today. But you wake up
tomorrow and the world of lovely friends is delivered to you dead, the insane parcels of everything disappearing. So all righteousness, all ordinary
spirituality, all the search for consolation, is nonsense. It is a refusal. It is
unreal.

The usual perception is that of the agonizing fact of identification, the
act that is ego, this refusal of one another, this lovelessness, and this living craziness. And all of your ordinary processes are bound up with that
craziness, until you begin to get sick of it. Then you are no longer talking
about your trip, your Yoga, how groovy it is and how you're going to get
there, "everything is so soul-beautiful", and all this crap. You will become
obsessed with your darkness, your heaviness. You will try to feel good,
but you know you feel lousy. You really feel upset. It is really bad. It is
really an annoyance. You are only upset, so what difference does the
search make? If you go through that long enough, you begin really to get
upset, and your meditation becomes concentration on your upset.
Whereas before you were always doing your number to avoid that upset,
now you can't do anything but be upset. And while you are meditating
on your upsetness, you happen to get involved here, in this Ashram, and
you get even more and more upset all the time. You come to me, and I
make you more upset. You think you are supposed to be having a very
groovy spiritual experience here, becoming more and more turned on.
But when you come around, people yell at you. They call your attention
to your crazy number. You are trying to do your best, but everybody is
hitting you over the head. All such experience is very aggravating, but it
begins to reinforce the real meditation that has now started to go on in
you. It is this crisis, this falling apart, this rot. And it will persist, until you

begin to observe, somehow, this activity of yours.

When you begin to see what you are doing, when you begin to re-cognize it, you will see it first of all in very direct, human terms. You will see it in the simple, human, practical things that you do. Later, you will begin to see it in subtler terms. You will observe the whole quality of your mind, your ordinary activity, your game, the drama, the event that is always going on, until you begin to see it most precisely and very subtly. When you see it absolutely, that is "radical" understanding. When you see the thing itself, the simple thing, that is the end of it. You fall apart. You scream, or you can't say anything, but it just ends. All of a sudden, the whole process is not going on anymore. And this apparent event, unlike all other apparent forms of action in the manifested worlds, is not followed by a re-action.

In *The Knee of Listening*, I have described my Great Re-Awakening. When there was this simple, "radical" turnabout, there was nothing about it that would have appeared remarkable to anyone who might have observed me. I didn't smile. I didn't feel "high". There was no reaction, because there wasn't anything left over of the thing that now was thrown away. There was no thing to which I could react. There was no one to react, to feel good about it, happy about it. There was no peculiar emotion. The Heart was all. Its quality became more and more apparent. There was a preliminary period of that fundamental enjoyment which lasted for perhaps several months. During that time there was no longer this whole complex life in dilemma, but I didn't really function in any manner different than before. I didn't experience any comparative impression about what had occurred. I didn't really interpret it clearly and fully for a good period of time, even though I consciously enjoyed a state that was untouched, unqualified, by any event or circumstance. That state of enjoyment would seem remarkable in itself. But I hadn't begun to function as it in relation to manifested life. Only when I did so, and then only gradually, was I able to estimate and know what had occurred. It was as if I had walked through myself. Such a state is perfectly spontaneous. It has no means to watch itself. It has no means to internalize or structure itself. It is Divine madness. The very Self, the Heart, is perfect madness. There is not a jot of form within It. There is no thing. No thing has happened. There is not a single movement in Consciousness. And that is Its blissfulness. It was not the fact that certain functions of internal life had been stimulated. It was peculiarly free of vision, movement, and all the blissful phenomena characteristic of the activities of Yoga-Shakti.[12] And when such phenomena did happen to arise, they were of another kind, or they were known from a new point of view. Their qualities had become cosmic and universal rather than Yogic or personal in nature. Until there is only God, the living One.

The mind acts as an obstruction. When the process of understanding begins in you, you may enquire of yourself as I have described in *The Knee of Listening*. In that case, you will enquire of the mind, you will enquire in this moment of thinking, and you will understand it. When the living consciousness moves into relationship, the mind falls away. The mind is replaced by a form of intensity. The more that simple intensity is enjoyed as existence, the less obtrusive the mind becomes. Even though it continues to arise, it becomes less and less obtrusive. You notice it less. Now you think you are the mind. You are thinking, thinking. But the mind is actually something that is arising in Consciousness Itself. It is only a modification of your own Nature. One who understands simply does not notice the mind in the usual manner. It is not that one has quieted one's mind. One is not the mind. There is no separate one there to be the mind. The "mind" is simply one of the functions that spontaneously arise. But if you identify with it, then you have already separated yourself. Only when that whole structure of the separate self is undermined by "radical" perception of its root does thought resume its natural, or prior, state.

Ramana Maharshi advised seekers to find out Who it is that asks the question, thinks the thought, whatever. The "Who" is not an entity. When Ramana Maharshi spoke, he used the symbology and language of Advaita Vedanta, the classic monistic, or "Only-One-Reality", school of Hindu philosophy. The imagery of this traditional way of describing the process of Truth deals in statics, things in space. So there is the ego—the objectified, solidified self. But I speak more in terms of process, or movement. I speak in terms of concepts of experience with which the modern mind is more familiar, and which are more appropriate in this time and place. I do not speak of "the ego" as an object within a conceptual universe of objects, because people today think more in terms of process, of energy. Therefore, presently, the concept of the static ego is not very useful. It doesn't very well communicate people's actual experience. To say "Seek the 'I'—find out 'Who' the 'I' is" is not very meaningful, because today people don't tend to approach the Conscious Nature via the mental structure assumed by that question. But everyone is dealing with activity, with process, movement. Therefore, what is called the "ego" in the traditions is today more appropriately and conclusively re-cognized to be an activity.

And understanding is that re-cognition, that direct seeing of the fundamental and always present activity that is suffering, ignorance, distraction, motivation, and dilemma. When this activity is thus known again, there is spontaneous and unqualified enjoyment of what it excludes—that which is always already the case, always already there.

The process I describe as "understanding" is ultimately the same that Ramana Maharshi was describing. The same state or enjoyment is being communicated and served by me. It is the same Force of Truth. It is all absolutely the same. However, since you are all presently existing, you cannot simply and naively embrace the fixtures that you have inherited. There must be conscious re-cognition of your present condition. Therefore, the old concepts and methods are not necessarily useful, even though they may be pleasant and consoling. There must be an absolute penetration of the form of life. Thus, it must be approached within the living, present structure in which it is suffered and entertained.

QUESTION: On this basis, how does formal meditation stand? You don't seem to think that formal meditation has much great benefit.

SRI DA AVABHASA: If you understand what you call your "formal meditation", that understanding is meditation. The understanding of your activity is meditation. If you have an inclination to do some particular kind of sitting, concentrating, Yogic method, whatever, all of that is an activity that you are already <u>tending</u> to do. The point is not whether to do that or not. The point is the understanding of that whole ordinary motivation, the process in this moment that is producing this particular tendency that is "formal meditation". Intelligence is the fundamental meditation. The living consciousness is itself meditation. The usual individual is always already seeking, so it is not a matter of doing or not doing some particular kind of motivated search. One is always already seeking, whether at this moment one is doing it in the form of a conventional Yogic technique, or in the next moment one is doing it in the form of a sly glance at somebody as one passes him or her on the street. You <u>are</u> always already doing it, so the point is not whether you <u>should</u> do a particular form of it or not. There is simply and always the process of your own action. When there is the engagement of action by real, unmotivated intelligence, understanding begins to develop as a spontaneous, real process in consciousness. As this process of intelligence matures, it tends to appear to become more formal, so that one actually sits down and actively meditates for a half hour, an hour, or even longer periods. Thus, one may appear to everyone else as if one is doing what they recognize to be <u>motivated</u> (or remedial) meditation. But that is not in fact what one is doing. One is living the conscious intelligence. It is just that, from a practical point of view, if the body is relaxed, sitting in a natural pose in which its fluids and energies can move freely, such is an appropriate manner in which to enjoy the critical activity of real intelligence. Even so, the same intelligence can be active under any conditions, whether formal or random and circumstantial. There is simply the endless return to this re-cognition of your own activity. The gathering of our Ashram, our conversation together, our sitting together, the reading or study you do, your life with one another, everything you are doing, constantly reawakens this re-cognition in some form or other, through crises, endurance of the resistance of your suffering, whatever. As you pass through ordinary life in this manner, and you see this same quality, always this same disturbance—that seeing, that understanding, which is to exist no longer trapped in the unconscious process of action, <u>is</u> meditation. And such meditation is the necessary foundation of all true spiritual activity, the life of Truth.

The form that arises in the living consciousness at any moment is the avoidance of relationship. It is the obstruction. The whole quality that arises in the living consciousness, which appears as forms of body sense, awareness of life, thought, the whole spontaneous event of waking, dreaming, and deep sleep, is, in itself, in the case of the usual man or woman, the avoidance of relationship. Whatever arises is a manifestation of this same process. Once you begin to re-cognize it, once you catch the little pieces of it that are prominent, then you begin to see yourself fully. Understanding begins in that manner, in very practical observation, in the real observation of something that is obviously and practically a hindrance, an avoidance of the condition of relationship. When real observation of that kind has begun in you, this intelligence that is understanding has a practical basis. To that degree, you are able to respond with the intelligence of understanding to the events that arise for you. The more there is of this re-cognition, of this practical re-cognition, the more understanding has become your intelligence. At the point when you really begin to see the all-embracing technique and strategy of life, when you really begin to see the structure of your suffering, at that point the form of enquiry I have described in *The Knee of Listening* becomes, for those so inclined, a natural extension of consciousness. And it will be used in even a very formal manner, but its use is rooted in understanding itself.

Genuine enquiry in the form "Avoiding relationship?" is utterly dependent on prior understanding. Without understanding, enquiry is just like anything else. It is just a question in the head. It is just another preference. And understanding itself depends on Satsang,[13] the Company and conditions generated by the Siddha-Guru,[14] the one who lives Truth in the world.

People do in fact tend to use the enquiry ("Avoiding relationship?") as a "method". They may read about it, or they may even have begun to engage themselves in the preliminary stages of life in the Ashram, and they begin to "meditate" by using this form of enquiry or some other form of looking at themselves. But in such cases, enquiry is always used in the spirit of method and seeking. Everything tends to become the search, until understanding, or real intelligence, is alive. But even though such people are going on with all of that, if they are involved in the conditions of practice in my Company, everything will eventually break down, if only a person has the endurance for it, or the need for it, the looseness for it, or only the inability to go out and play the ego-game again, whatever it is. Some such inner quality must keep a man or woman in place, so this work can take hold in him or her. And the supreme, or most potent, inner quality is faith in the Guru, devotion to the Guru, and surrender to the Guru.

Sri Da Avabhasa
at Sri Love-Anandashram, 1992

2.

The Avon Lady

SRI DA AVABHASA: [Laughing] What is there?

DEVOTEE: Is there free will?

SRI DA AVABHASA: What would that be?

DEVOTEE: I don't think we have free will. I think only God has free will.

SRI DA AVABHASA: And who are we?

DEVOTEE: Part of God.

SRI DA AVABHASA: Does God have free will?

DEVOTEE: Then what about evolution? If there is such a thing as evolution, we will all get to God eventually.

SRI DA AVABHASA: You are assuming that you are not there for the moment.

DEVOTEE: Well, I am not aware that I am there.

SRI DA AVABHASA: That "awareness" that you are not there is what our work in the Ashram is all about. What kind of free will are you concerned with? To do what?

DEVOTEE: Well, if we have free will and there is evolution, why do we have to work at it? Why not let evolution take over and eventually we will all be evolved into illuminated Masters.

SRI DA AVABHASA: Are you trying to become a Master?

DEVOTEE: I didn't think you could leave this plane of existence until you were a Master.

SRI DA AVABHASA: What is wrong with this plane of existence?

DEVOTEE: There are other planes to work on. Eventually all attain the state that Jesus attained, without physical bodies.

SRI DA AVABHASA: Where did you hear all of this?

DEVOTEE: I don't know.

SRI DA AVABHASA: You are making a lot of assumptions to begin with. God, Masters, evolution, free will or not, getting there, other planes. What has all of that got to do with you?

DEVOTEE: I am somewhere, but I don't know where.

SRI DA AVABHASA: Well, that would seem to be the first order of business. That is just it, isn't it? You are very confused, and there is suffering, apparently. You read all these books, and you do all this thinking, all this hoping about Jesus and whomever else, about getting there, and doing this and that to get there. That is suffering. And it is true, why go through all this effort to get there? I wouldn't use the excuse that you are going to get there anyway because of evolution, but there is something very meaningful in this doubt about the whole attempt to "get there". You have discovered this feeling that the trying to get there is very closely related to suffering. There is suffering, and there is the trying to get there. Those two things, I would imagine, are very real to you: the conscious suffering involved in life, and this whole attempt to get free of it.

This whole attempt to get free of it is a very elaborate, very involved notion. You have to do so many things before you "get there". There is all of this "stuff", which doesn't do one thing to your suffering. The concept of Jesus doesn't do anything for your suffering. The idea of becoming like Jesus doesn't do anything for your suffering. The effort to become like Jesus doesn't do anything for your fundamental suffering. Your constant evolution to become like Jesus doesn't do anything for your continuous suffering. Suffering persists as the basic content of your consciousness. On top of that, there is all of this seeking, wondering, thinking about how to get there, how to get free of suffering. If you were already free of suffering, it wouldn't make any difference to you whether this room appeared, or a ballroom in Vienna, or a seventh plane party! The fact that suffering is gone would be the thing that makes you happy. When suffering no longer distracts you, you see that you are already happy, that you are happiness. From the purely practical and real point of view, the thing that concerns you is not other planes, God, Jesus, or "getting there". Suffering is your concern, because it is already your real experience.

DEVOTEE: It seems to me that if you look at any realized man or woman, you see how far you have to go.

SRI DA AVABHASA: How do you know how far you have to go? How do you know where such a person is?

DEVOTEE: Well, I'm still suffering, so I still have far to go. If I am not in a perfect state of living, if I am not here now, then I am separate.

SRI DA AVABHASA: What is this suffering?

DEVOTEE: Well, there are different forms of suffering. Not being realized is suffering.

SRI DA AVABHASA: What is it right now? As a perception right now, what is this suffering?

DEVOTEE: Being trapped in the human body.

SRI DA AVABHASA: What is there about that that is suffering?

DEVOTEE: I don't want to be in it.

SRI DA AVABHASA: Are you in it?

DEVOTEE: Now I am, yes.

SRI DA AVABHASA: What makes you think you are a something that could be inside the body?

DEVOTEE: Well, that is how I feel now. Since I assume it now, it's real now.

SRI DA AVABHASA: Your assumption makes it real?

DEVOTEE: Yes.

SRI DA AVABHASA: Is your assumption the thing you are suffering?

DEVOTEE: Well, you could say that, yes.

SRI DA AVABHASA: That which is called "realization", "liberation", "God-union", or whatever, gets represented to people in various symbolic forms, as something with lots of planes and worlds, colors, lights and visions, figures and forms, methods, universes, "inside" and "outside", going here, going there, distance, direction, shape. These are all concep-tual communications, symbols, pictures for the mind. Fundamentally, they exploit your suffering, by motivating you to acquire whatever it is they represent or hide. True spiritual life is not a motivation to these symbols, a belief in them, nor even the acquisition of what they represent. True spiritual life is the process in consciousness in which there is understand-ing, or re-cognition, of suffering, the present experience.

Where there is no suffering, that which stands out or becomes the ob-vious is called "heaven", "nirvana", "liberation", the "Self", "Brahman", "God", "God-union", "Truth", "Reality". When there is no dilemma, when Consciousness Itself ceases to take on form or become identical to form, this is what is called "liberation". The process that is involved is not one of search based on suffering. Ordinarily, if you suffer, you immediately seek to get free, and you attach yourself to all kinds of hopeful signs. But true life, or spiritual life, is the reverse of that. Ordinarily, you are seeking, pursuing forgetfulness from your suffering, your dilemma, your contrac-tion, this separation, this unconsciousness. You pursue the absence of that in delight, enjoyment, distraction, search for perfection, search for all kinds of acquisitions, food, sex, money, good weather, lunch, until this whole process begins to become uninteresting. You try every resort, either by contemplation or by actual adventure. You look at every "movie" on the subject. You seek, until that whole movement in yourself, that whole reaction to your suffering, which is this search for the absence of suffer-ing, begins to wind down. Now you begin to realize its hopelessness. The search begins to lose its ability to occupy you. It becomes less exotic, less fascinating, less hopeful. Some quality in consciousness begins to turn away from this whole process of seeking, this whole reaction to your suffering, and rests in the suffering itself. Even a vague disinterest in life's pleasures may come over you. You begin to realize that you are actually suffering, whereas before you were completely occupied with your seeking, and suffering wasn't really the object of your contemplation. It was just some vague "whatever". The search was what involved you. But now you begin to fall out of your search. You begin to live this suffering. Suffering becomes your experience, your obsession. It completely absorbs you. It becomes the object of your meditation. Your actual state becomes absorbing—this rather than all the things to which you attached yourself to forget this, to get rid of this. Then you begin to see your suffering, to re-cognize your suffering. You begin to see, in fact, what your suffering is. That subtle sensation that is motivating your whole search becomes the thing that occupies you. You can no longer do anything about it. You see what suffering itself is, at this moment. You begin to see it precisely. It is a present activity. You begin to re-cognize it, to know it again in consciousness. You see this contraction of your own state, moment to moment, this separation, this avoidance of relationship. You begin to see this more and more exactly, specifically. It becomes an overwhelming re-cognition, until that portion of yourself, that quality of yourself that enjoys the re-cognition, that is the intelligence of this re-cognition of suffering, becomes your intelligence, becomes the very quality of consciousness that you live, with which you approach all experience moment to moment. Then, instead of simply suffering, you may enquire of the nature of this experiencing, moment to moment. You see beyond this contraction that is your suffering. And you begin to enjoy that which your chronic activity and state always prevent.

Your suffering is your own activity. It is something that you are doing moment to moment. It is a completely voluntary activity. You cognize it in the form of symptoms, which are the sense of separate existence, the mind of endless qualities, of differentiation, and the whole form of motion, of desire. You are always already living in these things, but their root, the source of it all, the thing whose form they are all reflecting, is this contraction, this separative act, this avoidance of relationship, which constantly "creates" the form in your living consciousness that you cognize as suffering. Where it is re-cognized, known again, this activity and its symptoms cease to be the form of the living consciousness. Then what is always prevented by the usual state becomes the form of the living consciousness. Where there is unqualified relationship, where there is no contraction, where there is no separation, no avoidance, there is no differentiation, no necessary mind, no necessary desire, no identification with separate movement. Then the living consciousness falls into its own form, without effort.

Symbolically, this is called "knowing", or "cognizing", the One Divine Self. But in fact it is not possible to fix attention on the Divine Self. Your own Divine Nature, or Reality Itself, cannot become an object of attention. The actual process involves attention and re-cognition of this suffering, this contraction. Where suffering is thus "known", what it prevents is suddenly, spontaneously enjoyed—not as the "object" of enjoyment, but as the enjoyment itself. Then, prior to effort, motivation, or attention, there is only the Divine Self, Reality, the Heart. Where there is this re-cognition of suffering, the whole structure of experiences, concepts, searches, strategies, that is your ordinary life, your search, ceases to be obsessive or even particularly interesting. It loses its significance, its ability to qualify what always already is. This undistracted state, this natural enjoyment prior to the activity that is your suffering, is called "realization", "jnana",[1] "understanding". It is the enjoyment of Reality, that is Reality, what is otherwise symbolized as God, the Masters, whatever. From the "point of view" of the Divine Self, the storybook "Masters" are of no more significance than a hamburger at McDonald's. The "Masters" are only more imagery that tends to fascinate and occupy the seeker, the one who is already suffering. But the search and the seeker are themselves of no real concern. They are already secondary, because the "seeker" is only a reaction to his or her own suffering. The prior action, the thing that is really occupying and motivating every human being, is suffering itself.

Therefore, suffering is the appropriate and spontaneous subject of meditation, rather than the artifices to which seekers attach themselves. The seeker's illusions are not the appropriate subject. They are no solution. They are more of the same. This room is of no concern to somebody who has never even been to the United States. If a person lives in Germany, but reads a lot of books about this Ashram, his or her reading does not "create" an actual involvement with this place. It is not the equivalent of being here. It may be playful, humorous, enjoyable, but it is not itself equivalent to being here. Reading about Jesus and wanting to be like Jesus is not the equivalent of being Jesus. It never will be the equivalent of being Jesus. Your talk about "Jesus" is like your statement that you are in your body. You are suggesting Jesus to yourself, but in fact Jesus is not here.

DEVOTEE: Isn't the experience here?

SRI DA AVABHASA: What is that?

DEVOTEE: It is the love.

SRI DA AVABHASA: If there is love here, why does it have to be Jesus? What is added to this moment by thinking that the love that is here is Jesus' love? Why does it have to be Jesus? Maybe it is Sam Smith, whom nobody ever heard of! Why does it have to be Jesus? It is only because the mind is associated with that symbol, and it consoles itself with that symbol. Rather than penetrate your own suffering, rather than penetrate the unloveliness, the unloving quality of your own lives, you console yourselves with the images of things you do not contain. When you understand that, when you see what you are doing, it really becomes impossible for you to turn yourself on with symbols. You can read about Jesus and think that love is his love, but sooner or later there is going to be a real need for love, a real dissatisfaction with no-love, a penetration of this whole plaster mind that doesn't really do the job. Then you will see that all of these consolations are forms of your own mind. They are entertainments, distractions, for a purpose that is always hidden. Then you will begin to observe this motivation, this need to be consoled. And that is a very difficult affair, because in this process of re-cognition there are no consoling images. There is nothing by which to be consoled.

There is a "death" declared in all the traditions. There is a "spiritual death", a dark night, the death of the ego and all the imagery it uses to support itself, to console itself, to occupy itself. But consolation is the ego. The thing Jesus recommended was re-birth, or realization through spiritual death, the cross. "Pick it up and follow me, suffer the world." He didn't recommend that you think about his aquiline profile every day and feel good until he comes again.

All the traditions, even those that Westerners tend to associate with, are talking about a crisis in consciousness, spiritual death, as the event of salvation and liberation. In that death there certainly is death. There is no thing. There is the holding on to everything, and the falling away of everything. When it takes place, there is no longer any resistance, there is no longer any one to die. When this death has occurred, what is enjoyed from that "point of view" has been named "love", "salvation", "liberation", "realization", "God-union". But there must be this death, a crisis in consciousness, a crisis in that ordinary process of surviving and seeking which is itself responsible for the "creation" and maintenance of these images that console you. All such images are forms of seeking. You are responsible for their "creation". They are phantoms that you hold on to for reasons. The observation and re-cognition of those reasons—even their very motivation, that sense which supports the whole process of consolation—is spiritual life. And that is also what Jesus recommended. He didn't say that he was love, but that God is love. Where Jesus is not, only love is. Truth is love. Reality is love. This is love. This love has nothing to do with images of some cosmic super-guy. Truth is love. We are love. This is love.

DEVOTEE: What about born-again Christians and other people who go through a sudden change and become very light and happy?

SRI DA AVABHASA: We would, of course, have to be talking about somebody in particular to make much sense out of it. There are all kinds of testimonials, all kinds of salvations, and all kinds of claims made by people. There are thousands of religious and philosophical methods that have been tried by human beings, and all of them have a certain amount of "success". There are always a few individuals who make great claims for some particular remedial path. Christianity is one for which there are many such testimonials, because it has been going on for a long time, and many, many people have tried some form of it. There have been a number of great men and women among the Christians. There have also been a lot of mediocre people. Some of those mediocre people have also enjoyed a revolutionary change in their state, for reasons that others find hard to understand. Many other people have claimed to have gone through the enlightenment experience with various Zen Masters, or whatever. The Christian experience is typically "holy", but the Zen experience is typically "ordinary". The Zen insight may be precipitated by a punch in the mouth, a smack on the head with an oar, or some such crazy thing, and the next moment the "smackee" claims to be entirely transformed, living from an entirely new point of view! So this spontaneous turning around can take place under all kinds of apparent circumstances. Enthusiastic claims are not exclusive to Christianity. They are found in all religious and spiritual traditions. The phenomenon of change is itself the essential or common factor in all of them. And, in general, they are hard to understand on the face of it.

If you took a survey of all religious and spiritual claims and tried to make sense of them, you wouldn't be able to isolate something that occurred, internally or externally, that could justify the claims. And that is precisely the point. In this turnabout, which can appear dramatic or not, nothing is added. Its reasons are not identifiable, because it is not a matter of attaching something to the person's life, externally or internally. It is a matter of a turnabout of the living consciousness itself. One of the things the great traditional Teachers have tried to communicate is the value of that turnabout, and also something about how it actually takes place. If you took a survey of all the apparent examples of this turnabout, you couldn't make sense out of it, so the historical Masters, Gurus, or Teachers have always tried to communicate that process itself, by whatever particular means they had available to them.

For the most part though, except in relatively few cases, the experience to which a religious person may testify represents an emotional and temporary distraction, a kind of mood. It is an <u>experience</u>. It can be described. It can be held on to, and it can be lost. It can even be proclaimed. But what is called "enlightenment", "liberation", or "God-union" in its true sense is profoundly unlike experience. Truth is not an experience. It is not a particular state, and it cannot be identified with a particular style of life, a particular appearance. Seekers of all kinds talk about dramatic events in their lives as if those events were this enlightenment, or Truth. But most of those events are forms of temporary distraction. They are only intense experiences. And people want to hold on to such things. They want to preserve or repeat them throughout life, and look forward to the repetition of them in heaven or the afterlife. But Truth rests on no experience whatsoever. It is not in Itself an experience, It cannot be held on to, It cannot be repeated, It cannot be looked forward to, It cannot be lost, It cannot even be recommended. It is an absolute obliteration of what is commonly called "life".

What is ordinarily called "salvation" is a form of satisfaction imagined by a separate, fearful person. When one is "saved", one's separate life is consoled, distracted, and involved with a remedial path, an image, an experience. But when there is nothing to be satisfied, when there is no one to be satisfied, when there is no one to give a testimony, when there is no one to meet Jesus, that is liberation. When the ego, the separate self sense that is one's suffering, is undermined, and there is a sudden or prolonged penetration of the structure of the living consciousness, of mind, of motion, of self-sense—when all of that is undermined, penetrated, understood, re-cognized, and the very thing that it prevents is enjoyed, there is no longer any one to survive one's death. Then there is no separate one living, there is no "one" to be in a body, there is no one to be out of the body. Nothing has happened. There is no separate one.

DEVOTEE: If we are all already conscious, then we are not in this Ashram to become conscious, right?

SRI DA AVABHASA: What you think is Consciousness is not Consciousness Itself. It is a form in Consciousness.

DEVOTEE: So we are separating ourselves. We are identifying with the form instead of with Consciousness.

SRI DA AVABHASA: But there is no method to be recommended to go and find that Consciousness. Ramana Maharshi spoke about a method, but his way is really quite paradoxical, humorous, and not, as it seems, straightforward. If you remember, he was always saying: Find out "Who" it is that has experiences, that wants to seek, that thinks it is in the body. Find out Who that is. But, of course, there is no method for finding that out. There is no "one" to find that out. It is a spontaneous event, a paradoxical event, the most absolute of all events. It is a gift! It is itself God, Truth, Reality!

The greatest responsibility of human beings is Satsang, to live in the Condition of relationship, the Condition of the Heart, the Company of the Self, the Guru. The essential responsibility of the Guru is Satsang, to live the Heart to his or her friends. The greatest responsibility of those who live this Satsang is to make It available to others. So this Ashram involves Satsang, living Company, a continuous relationship as the Condition of life. It is the one thing done. Nothing else is exchanged—no special techniques, no thing. None of this seeking is exploited. The essential work of those who are responsible for the Ashram is to make Satsang available to others. Everything else is secondary. Everything that serves the availability of Satsang is the responsibility of this Ashram.

There is a danger in all human associations. Because people appear within this human condition, this "dream" world, they tend to live from the point of view of this condition. There is an ancient ritual people unconsciously desire to re-enact. Wherever you see an association of people gathered for the purpose of spiritual life, the same thing is tending to be "created". There is an ancient game called "scapegoat". There is an ancient ritual called the "round dance". People tend to encircle the center—a book, a person, a symbol, a Guru. They tend to encircle such a one, and acquire all things for this circle. The group becomes inward directed. It becomes "occult". Anciently, the culminating product of this cult is the sacrifice of the one in the middle. Traditional societies, throughout the ancient world, did this yearly. The person in the middle was killed, or ritually deposed, and a new person was installed in the center. The execution of Jesus is an example of this same ritual. The addition of this ancient ritual process makes the death of Jesus into the "sacrifice of Christ".

In the *New Testament,* you read how the soldiers tortured Jesus. They played this game called "scapegoat". It is a game of "man in the middle". The tendency of those who become involved in spiritual work is to "create" a cult, a circle that ever increases its dimensions and its content, beginning from this center, surrounding it, ultimately destroying it. The form that the "cult", or spiritual association of human beings, tends to take is the same form that they are living individually. It is self, or ego, in the middle. It is this contraction, this avoidance of relationship, which "creates" the sense of mind, the endless habits of desire. It is what is called "life". One begins to sense this separate existence to be one's very nature, and spends one's life "creating" a circle of content or acquisition all around it. One encloses all other beings one can acquire, all the things one can acquire, all the states and thoughts one can acquire, all the emblems, the symbols, the experiences, the sensations. When one begins to involve oneself in some spiritual association, or, for that matter, any association outside one's own subjectivity, one tends again to "create" that same circle about a center.

The cult is a dramatization of egoity, of separativeness, of betrayal. But true Satsang is an anti-cultic or non-cultic process. It is not inward directed. It doesn't tend to become a cult in the sense I have described. It is inclusive, and the separate and separative self-center is not Its motive. In Satsang the center is always already undermined as a center, as a separate and separative entity. The "center" of Satsang is Consciousness Itself. It is the Light, the very Force, of Unqualified Consciousness. It is communicated directly to one's life, in relationship, so that one no longer needs to turn inward, to "create" survival for the center. Instead, one turns toward function, freely, the Light already assumed. So Satsang, the Company of

Truth, tends to serve life, to move into life, to contact life in relationship, not to acquire life.

My intention with people is not to absorb them into a society or spiritual gang with which they are to become symbolically and ritually preoccupied. I bring them the Force of Consciousness Itself, whereby they can become capable of life. I demand the functional capability of people. I do not require it to be eliminated, resisted, or escaped through some phony meditative impulse. I require that people live a functional life. I do not require the separation from vital life, from vital enjoyment, from existence in the form of life. I require these functions to be known, to be understood, to be lived from the "point of view" of Truth.

Such is the genuine effect of Satsang, the accompanying "mood" of Satsang. It is one of capability for relationship, of no-search, no-dilemma. It is not the tendency to some "other" state. It is the obviation of the dilemma within the present state, the undermining of it. One who understands and whose life is lived as the Condition of Satsang is not necessarily, in his or her appearance, different from any other human being. Such a one hasn't necessarily acquired some psychic abilities, visionary abilities, whatever. Understanding is not itself the acquisition of some particular experience. Such a one might, by reason of his or her tendencies, experience the arising of extraordinary abilities, but not necessarily. Such a one becomes, like the Guru, one who is simply awake within the dream.

Satsang is a natural process in which the contraction that is one's suffering is operated upon by the Guru. The disciple is preoccupied with the search, but all the while the Guru is acting upon the disciple's fundamental, motivating dilemma and strategy. And there are two tendencies by which the Guru is always being confronted by the disciple. One is the tendency to seek rather than to enjoy the Condition of Satsang. And the other is the tendency to "create" this contracting circle, this cult, this ritual of fascination and unconsciousness. The Guru has only one resort in either case. It is Satsang, the Guru's simple relationship to his or her friends.

DEVOTEE: Are all awakened people Gurus?

SRI DA AVABHASA: No. Guru is not a kind of status. It is a specific function. There are some who awaken, but who simply live, without becoming active as the function of Guru. There are others who awaken and do in fact perform that function. Truth, not the "role" of Guru, is the enjoyment of <u>all</u> who are awake.

DEVOTEE: It's hard to figure out what I have read. One "realized" man wiped out his father. Another killed off his whole family. How can such phenomena be explained?

SRI DA AVABHASA: There is a point where one's search becomes inappropriate. This is that point. All of the Scriptures a person reads, all of the remarks and experiences and traditions, come to an end when the import of those Scriptures ceases to be academic. In the presence of the Heart, seeking is inappropriate.

It makes no difference what those sentences mean. That's not the point. The universe devours billions upon billions of entities every second. If we were to judge by actions those to whom enlightenment should go, the universe itself would be the last. Only the righteous fools within it would be enlightened, but the universe would have to wait until the very end on account of its crimes. It is not any kind of significance, any appearance, any suggestion, any implication of what you see that is the Truth. The traditions say that you can't find the Guru in the Guru's actions. In other words, it is not by watching how various people act and speak that you find the Guru. The Guru is always a paradox. The Guru's action is a paradox, like the universe itself.

The old texts that talk about realized beings killing others are allegories for spiritual transformations within a human being. One of the classic statements of Vedanta is that once a person has realized the Self he or she could slay a brahmin[2] and it would not be a sin for such a one. It wouldn't affect such a one. All of these statements are simply suggesting, or somehow trying to imply, the freedom of the Jnani,[3] the Self-realized man or woman. So it is that very Self, that Reality, to which these Scriptures are trying to turn you. If you miss the point, and the Self doesn't become your direction after reading such Scriptures, you are stuck with something you can't understand. You are stuck with something that seems to say what can't be true. So all of these old Scriptures are loaded. There are always two sides. But they only have one purpose, which is to "create" interest in the Truth, in realization. After the interest has been "created", the Scriptures have served their purpose. They just serve to move you along and entertain you for a period of time until this whole possibility becomes significant enough that a crisis, a breakdown in your ordinary functioning, begins to take place. And, hopefully, when this crisis begins, you will also find yourself in the Company of a truly Self-realized man or woman, one who lives as the very Self. When that contact is made, all of these suggestive sentences become obsolete. They lose their function at the point where that meeting takes place. The more you have accumulated before that moment, the more there is that becomes obsolete. And so also the more resistance there is.

Truly, the Divine Self is mad. The Divine Self is unlearned. The appropriate foundation of human life is not an entity, a separate self sense, an ego, even a "soul". Such is not the appropriate foundation for human life. The appropriate foundation for human life is the Heart, the very Self. It is utterly mindless, utterly free, uncontained, unqualified. But, paradoxically, when the Heart is lived, the human being becomes functional, usable, alive, moved. Such a one makes no complicated use of the things an ordinary man or woman uses to survive. Like a child, such a one moves by delight. Such a one is a person of pleasure, of enjoyment. Like a mad person, such a one learns nothing from life. Such a one doesn't believe what he or she sees, doesn't take it to have any limiting significance. Such a one throws away all the things that seem to everyone so profound, so serious. Such a one attributes nothing to them. Indeed, the realized man or woman is like a mad person and a child. But apart from actual realization, or "radical" understanding, what I have just said is a form of entertainment. It doesn't affect your impending death. And your death is what interests the Guru.

DEVOTEE: What about Lord Yama?[4]

SRI DA AVABHASA: Lord Yama, the storybook Lord of Death? He barely enters into it! He is only a symbol in the life-consciousness—as if death were some entity, some being or other. But your death is your concern. It is not the concern of any "other". That "other" is your very Self. So it is only the true Guru who is very interested in your death—your death, not all the things you call your "life". And the Guru is very interested in bringing it about very quickly. The Guru doesn't want a long engagement! The Guru wants a sudden "death" for everyone.

DEVOTEE: What if a person's heart, breath, and mind were suspended for twenty minutes. Wouldn't he or she be free then?

SRI DA AVABHASA: It depends on what has occurred during those twenty minutes. Many people have been in a coma for months, or even years, but they didn't wake up any more immune to death, or any more intelligent.

The "death" I am talking about is not the death of which you suspect yourself. It is not simply that physical event, that vital event. The death I am talking about is the turnabout, the dissolution of the principle by which you live, the fundamental activity that you are animating, dramatizing, considering to be yourself, living to others—your state. It is that death which is significant.

DEVOTEE: Would you like to compare that with, say, the physical act of suicide?

SRI DA AVABHASA: The physical act of suicide is an impairment. It is an obstruction. It takes away from you the functions you have available for intelligence. So the mere act of suicide is not it, any more than extreme fasting, deprivation of the senses, or exclusive internal concentration. None of these psycho-physical events is the crisis of Truth. They are all experiences. They are symbolic at best. They don't achieve the thing that is needed.

We have talked about traditional Yogic methods of seeking Self-realization, or God-union. They are something like sitting in a room, breathing heavily, and looking at erotic pictures. You can generate something that is like passion, but you are never going to make love! It never becomes that. Just so, you can sit and breathe methodically, turning inward, contemplating Divine images or God-ideas, but it is never going to become God-union. God has never entered into it. It is a very hopeful practice at best. There is no God-union until God is there to be unioned with. As a lover depends on his or her loved-one, the God-seeker depends on the living Presence of God before there can be any God-union. And when God appears, you are not going to have to do your spiritual breathing! What there is to do will all be very obvious. You won't have to think about what is necessary to be done to become one with God. It is only the absence of God, the suffering, the ignorant condition, that gets you involved in all of this seeking. It is only where God is already not that all of these practices begin.

DEVOTEE: Well, should we just wait it out until God comes, then?

SRI DA AVABHASA: This deliberate waiting is also another form of that same seeking. Fortunately, or unfortunately, the search goes on in spite of you until this connection is made. Everything you do is that search until God, the Self, the Heart, enters into the picture, as a reality, in relationship.

DEVOTEE: If consciousness is divided between waking, dreaming, and deep sleep, then how do we get behind these three to find the true Self?

SRI DA AVABHASA: That has been the mysterious approach of Advaita Vedanta, of Jnana Yoga,[5] and of other traditions of spiritual practice. They build up this conceptual dilemma, and then they try to solve it. So the Divine Self is pictured as an alternative to waking, dreaming, and sleeping. The Divine Self is pictured or proposed as a something else, another state that is hidden beneath the usual three. It is hardly in the waking state, barely in the dreaming state, only implied in the sleeping state. Thus, in order to get underneath all of this, it appears that you must go through a subtle process of internalization, which is traditional meditation. For a while, you try to go inward. Then you open your eyes again, and, at the same time you are looking at this, the appearing world, you are trying to concentrate on an internal one that is not really in this one. So there is all this "interior" and "out here" at the same time. You go crazy after a while.

The Hindu formula is not complete as spoken. The central formula of the ancients as stated by the Hindus is: The jivatman (the individual "soul") and the Paramatman (the Great "Soul", the Universal Self) are one. Therefore, seekers in that tradition are led into a process of interiorization and union. The formula of Buddhism—its classical tradition—might well be added to this. It is stated in the form: Nirvana and samsara[6] are the same. In other words, the Great Self, the unqualified Reality, is not different from this, the conditional appearance, the world. When taken together, these two reflect, in a symbolic manner, something of the Nature of Reality. This, the entire Force and Form, the Intensity, arising as this moment, is the Divine Self. It is not that there is some hidden Being underneath the three states that is the Divine Self and all of this is just sort of hanging around on it. There is no distinction whatsoever in Consciousness. There is always already no dilemma. There is no inwardness that is equal to the Truth. There is no special subjectivity that is the Truth Itself. There is no special objectivity that is the Truth Itself. But the subjective and the objective are already the very thing, the very Truth.

Even so, there is a dilemma meanwhile. There is suffering, non-comprehension as that simplicity. And since there is suffering, human beings are motivated to recover the sublimity they have been suggesting to themselves and which some have claimed to have enjoyed. But it is only when the whole process of interior and exterior, all these movements, all these searches, all these experiences—when all of that has failed, then suffering itself becomes the point, becomes the experience, rather than all of the seeking that is only a reaction to it. Then one falls into one's suffering, dies from one's suffering, becomes conscious as one's suffering, understands one's suffering, and sees what is already the case. So all the seeking is just a prolongation of the suffering.

DEVOTEE: When the realized man or woman has turned the switch off, how does he or she get to functioning back in this world?

SRI DA AVABHASA: The Divine Self is not behind all of this. The Divine Self is this without a doubt. There is no separation whatsoever. Therefore, Divine Self-realization is perfectly compatible with human existence. One who is truly Self-realized is no longer suffering, no longer inward, no longer outward. The dilemma is gone. Such a one sees the obvious, such a one enjoys the obvious, and all the human functions become functions in fact, usable, realizable, and enjoyable. You are dealing with images. These images imply things about your present state that are not quite true. They are metaphors: the idea of the "switch", the idea of the fourth state beyond the three states. Truth has been represented in the form of images to interest you in realization, to suggest to you what is not realization. But realization is of another kind than this interest, this fascination, developed by means of the texts. All of the traditions agree that the best thing one can do is spend one's time in Satsang, in the Company of the realized man or woman, the Guru. That is meditation. That is the real Condition. That is realization. That is perfect enjoyment.

DEVOTEE: How can that affect you—just sitting with such a person?

SRI DA AVABHASA: One tends to take on the qualities of the things one spends one's time with. If you watch a television program or a movie, you go through a distracting drama. Then, all of a sudden, a commercial! It breaks that whole trance. So you feel disturbed. If you spend your evening in a "topless-bottomless" bar, another game attracts you. If you take drugs, there is that number. If you get amused tonight, smoking cigarettes until dawn, there is that whole form of mind and life. Perhaps you go on a picnic, fishing, or to church on Sunday. There are all these dramas being played. Now, it happens that in the ordinary drama, in all of its millions of forms and in all the millions of people living it, there is a contraction. Every drama is a play of separation, of suffering, of seeking. The contraction is its subtlest element, its foundation, so that when you become involved with all ordinary things, regardless of what they appear to be at this moment, they carry with them the subtle implication of your suffering. Now there is this pleasure, now this, now this entertainment, and now this one. The appearance varies, but it is always the same—the same implication, the same thing by association is being reinforced in consciousness. The Guru doesn't appear to be any different, essentially any different. There is no standout-on-the-lapel thing obviousness about it. But the Guru lives as the very Self. Thus, of all your associations, it is this Company that does not support the contraction. It does not support it. That is what is unique about It. You continue to attempt to live this contraction in various forms, you continue to be entertained, you continue to seek. You even continue to expect what it looks like you should expect from that association. But the Guru does not support the contraction, the very suffering.

The Guru is like an elevator. The Guru is in the hotel lobby with a nice marble casement and a needle above pointing to the numbers of floors. It looks perfectly stable. You know it has been there for a while. You dare to walk up to it. You see buttons on the wall. The doors open. You look inside. It is nicely decorated. A couple of people nicely dressed come out to go to the cocktail lounge. So you step in. You expect to rise, as all the traditions say. But you fall right through the bottom of the floor! The Guru doesn't support it, but the Guru appears ordinary. The Guru's activity is non-support in endless subtle forms.

The effect of this non-support is that the quality of contraction in you begins to become self-conscious. The search winds down, the suffering becomes self-conscious, and, intuitively, you become alive within it. This quality of contraction simply begins to get flabby and fall apart. You begin to re-cognize it, to know it again. Therefore, in that living association, or relationship, with the Guru, the Divine Self is lived to you, whereas in all other conditions it is this contraction, the avoidance of relationship, that is lived to you.

DEVOTEE: Would you describe some of the levels on which the Guru operates?

SRI DA AVABHASA: There is no particular point in describing them. The most it would do is make you self-conscious and wary. On every level that awareness is possible the Heart is active. The important thing is that even though people are suffering they intuitively recognize the living Self. What they will do about that is another matter. But the recognition is there in some intuitive form. Rather than any other kind of information, it is upon that recognition that disciples and devotees[7] must depend, both for the knowing whether a person is Guru and for the knowing whether or not they want to be involved in that kind of relationship. Many have had enough, so that once they see the Guru, they stay to live with the Guru. Through that process they begin to see how the Guru, the living Heart, operates. Others come, and they resist immediately. They defend their state, and so they leave.

The concern of the disciple is the relationship to his or her Guru, which is Satsang. Sitting with the Guru is the disciple's meditation. It summarizes all of the elements of meditation: consciously sitting in relationship with the very Divine Self, or God-Nature. What else could meditation be? So it is simply sitting or living, aware of that. And it becomes more profound, more subtle. It becomes intelligence. It may become self-enquiry for those so inclined. It perhaps becomes something formal-looking to some degree, appearing as what people ordinarily think to be meditation. But that sitting, that relationship to the Guru, Satsang, living It from day to day, living the conditions this relationship "creates" for you—that is true spiritual life. It is meditation, it is spiritual effort, sadhana. And, on top of that, there is entertainment, because life is an entertainment. There is as much entertainment in that relationship as any other. There is a humor to it, but the entertainment is utterly enjoyable. That relationship is humor, it is obvious, because the most fundamental enjoyment is always taking place.

Until one recognizes the Heart alive and lives that relationship, everything one does is a form of the search. Every action reinforces one's suffering. It is not it. There must be a "radically" new life, a "radically" new presence, a "radically" new communication. The Heart Itself must appear. Otherwise, the seeker is like the guy with the girlie magazine in his room. The seeker is not going to make it. And all of the "spiritual" books have no more ultimate significance than pornography for such a one. All of the seeker's "spiritual reading" is perhaps a little subtler than erotica, but the same motivation is behind it. The same suffering is there. It is a form of entertainment. On different days there are different kinds of entertainment. Some days you prefer porno magazines, other days you prefer the *Bhagavad Gita*. But it is the same person, the same search, the same dilemma. This is why certain Zen Masters burned the traditional sculptured images of the Buddha. The same thing must be done for the Scriptures. It is not necessary to go out and burn them in the street, but there must be this understanding of their significance in relation to the Heart, the true spiritual life. The intelligence of the Heart is a genius, a fire, not a little pipe-smoking philosopher. The same Power that wields this universe and devours the billions of beings is the Heart. One who lives as the Heart can read these Scriptures and use them, consume them, destroy them, play with them, do whatever he or she likes with them. Such a confrontation with the Scriptures is alive, but the seeker's confrontation with the Scriptures is mediocre. It doesn't amount to God-union. Only one who is already realized reads such things and comprehends them.

For the one who does not understand, the books are simply a means of gaining one's interest, moving one toward a moment when one will seriously begin. And even then, there are many pitfalls. The person puts down the porno magazine, gets dressed, and goes out to a pornographic movie house! This instead of going out to find himself or herself in human company, in relationship! So it takes more than just putting down the books. There are lots of "gurus" around, lots of movie houses where you go in for a zapping. They entertain you, they take a couple of bucks, they do a number for you. It's in sound and color, two full hours! And what does it come down to? They tell you to go home and do it yourself! You were home trying to do it yourself all night! But now they give you a "do-it-yourself" kit. You take it on home, and you clean up the corner of your bedroom! You throw away all the porno magazines, or at least you keep them in the bathroom under the hamper. You clean up a corner of the room, and you open up the blinds so that the sun comes in on it real nice. Then you get up at dawn, and you do "it" to yourself!

Such a one is in the same condition that he or she was in the night before, even less intelligent. He or she has taken on some strategic path or other, professionalized the search. The night before, that one was just an ordinary person, just a slob. But now that person is a "YOGI"! He or she puts on the outfit, wears the beads, starts collecting money for a trip to India next year. He or she does this number for however long it takes to get sick of all that. And after that the person says, "The hell with it," and messes up the room again, throws away the robe and beads, and takes the porno magazines back in the bedroom. But he or she really hasn't got it anymore. Besides, the person is probably fifty years old by now. So such a person is really not about to go back out to the strip show. The porno magazines aren't really going to give it either. Then all of a sudden the doorbell rings. It's the Avon Lady! Better known as the Guru!

In the building in which our Ashram is presently housed,[8] we have the "movie house" (our bookstore) out in the front, with all of the best traditional literature, the very best "pornography". In other words, we don't carry any junk! People who have become interested, who have left their homes, who are wandering around trying to find something a little jazzier, who have done a little reading, these people see the bookstore. All of the traditional motivations gather them up, and they come in to look at the books. While they browse, they see a couple of signs about our spiritual center. And after a while they begin to feel a little itching in the back of their heads. It is a very unusual movie house. It appears like any other one. It appears ordinary. It is ordinary. The ordinary, from the "point of view" of Consciousness Itself, is the only extraordinary. All the extraordinaries to which people aspire are very ordinary. They have been done thousands upon thousands of times. All of the kriyas,[9] all of the subtle movements, all of the purifications, all of the visions—they have all been done! Thousands upon thousands of times. Everything has been done. All of these realizations have occurred. The internal mechanism of the human being has been exploited and explored for eons. It is not a new medium at all. Therefore, all the ordinary aspirations based on suffering and seeking lead to the ordinary, the mediocre, the usual, more of the same. The one having an "ecstatic" vision is in the same condition as the one watching a TV commercial. Only when all of that has worn down does one begin to see that the principle of one's seeking, one's discovery, one's realization is suffering! That's the truth. Then one begins to become sensitive to one's actual condition instead of trying to do something about it. One sees exactly what it is. That is when the extraordinary living thing occurs. When it begins, there is an unseriousness about all the things that one took seriously before. All the accumulations, all the imagery, all the books, all the symbols, cease to be one's occupation. One becomes occupied with the living Truth. And It precedes all of this mentality.

Sri Da Avabhasa
at Sri Love-Anandashram, 1992

Money, Food, and Sex

SRI DA AVABHASA: There are patterns in one's individual life that are responsible for the quality of "tamas",[1] or inertia, immobility, sluggishness, the backlog of everything. The earliest period of sadhana, or life in relationship to the Guru, deals especially with this "tamasic" condition, the inertia of the disciple, the disciple's tendency to remain in or return to the very state of suffering and ignorance in which he or she began. Therefore, the disciple must find the means, the practical means, to fulfill the Guru's demands for a responsible realization of life. When you are capable of functioning, that is when true spiritual life begins. Until then, it doesn't make any difference how many times you come to see me, or how many lectures you hear. Now is the time to begin to live, and to live is to be responsible for your life, not to continue old patterns. I cannot release you from responsibility. How can I release you from the responsibility of your breath?

When people become involved in any kind of religious or spiritual activity, particularly a group activity of some sort, there are a few subtle notions that tend automatically to be awakened in them. There is the subtle suggestion that spiritual life has something to do with separation from vital and physical life. Indeed, in many of the ancient traditions that is exactly what spiritual life was—an exclusive and terminal inward turning, getting away from all of the life-force, the life-form, the life-mind, the life-appearance, the life-sensation, into some inward, subtle non-life perception, or vision, or heaven, or whatever. Because this traditional association of ideas tends to be blanketed over everything that looks like religion, spirituality, Yoga, and the like, every demand, every quality suggested within religious and spiritual life that involves the physical and vital being, meets immediate resistance.

Money (and, in general, the commitment of life-force in the forms of effort and love), food, and sex are the essential activities of life. Those are the vital processes, the forms of vital appearance and function. And money, food, and sex are the first things that people begin to resist or manipulate when they get involved in anything that is even remotely like religion or spirituality. Religious people, for the most part, are extremely confused and guilty about money, food, and sex. People involved in spirituality, Yoga, and religion are endlessly involved with experiments about money, food, and sex. What are such people always doing? "Should I or shouldn't I?" "What is the right diet?" "Fasting? Macrobiotics? No food?" "Renunciation? Poverty?" They are on and off food all the time, on and off sex. They may be celibate for years in order to get enlightened, but then, just as dramatically, they are seeking the "Tantric bliss"[2] or the restoration of "mental health" in a perpetual orgasmic exercise. Then there are all of the other games of self-denial, no work, no income. All of these things arise whenever anything like spirituality or religion comes into a person's life.

Because of the automatic resistances built into religious and spiritual endeavor, the practical need for money and for the means of survival is a very complicated and frustrating affair for even the most sophisticated religious and spiritual groups. But all of this should be a very obvious matter. We are not in heaven. This is the earth. Everything here costs life, effort, and money. It costs a great deal of life, effort, and money to maintain a religious or spiritual community. The purposes may be spiritual, but a living community must fulfill the same functional laws as any household and any business corporation. Even so, whenever practical demands are made for effort, commitment, love, or money, people tend to lapse into the "tamasic mood". Such reluctance retards life. And the ability of an individual or a group to transcend this tendency is the measure of freedom and survival.

There is the suspicion that if you are "spiritual" you are not supposed to need money, you are not supposed to require anything, and you are supposed to abandon the functions of life. Obviously, though, money is needed in most circumstances, and work, force, love, and energy are necessary for functional survival. Why isn't it obvious, then, why isn't it patently the responsibility of individuals, that they bring life and commitment to their own religious or spiritual community, that they take on its "creative" work, and contribute a responsible amount of money for its continuation? Why isn't that obvious? Why is there always so much wheeling and dealing involved with any religious or spiritual organization? It is because of the traditional illusion of spiritual attainment, which is pictured as a kind of evaporation process, wherein you become more and more "elusive", and finally disappear inside your "something", or dissolve into your "someplace else".

Now, there are people who teach that such goals are Truth. If that is the game you want to play, you must go to such people. There are few and always fewer responsibilities at the level of life involved in such teachings. A certain amount of food must be taken, but some teachers have even suggested that if you begin a fast and never eat again, at death you will merge into the enlightened state. So they have handled that side of it, too. Such "enlightenment" is a cave without money, food, or sex. If that seems to represent the Truth to you, then go to the forest and fast until death!

I think this traditional orientation is utter nonsense. I do not teach it, and I do not support it. The Truth that already is the case is the Truth from this one's "point of view". I live very naturally in the human world, and its responsibilities do not make me "unspiritual". Its responsibilities are a "creative" manifestation, requiring intelligence. All life-conditions are forms of relationship. All of life is ordinary. One who is incapable of ordinariness hasn't even begun to become involved in spiritual life as subtlety.

The first level of sadhana, or spiritual discipline, that I had to endure with a human teacher wasn't any sort of other-worldly Yoga, nor did it involve love and acknowledgement from the Guru, or even kind words. I spent about two minutes with Rudi[3] when I first met him. He told me to get a job and come back in one year! But I was perfectly willing to do that. As it happened, within a month or two later, my spiritual work with him did begin. It wasn't in fact necessary for me to be away a year, but I was perfectly willing for it to be so. I was ecstatically happy to have made this contact, to have a beginning, to have become capable of spiritual life. It was a profound joy to me to have found someone who was obviously capable of drawing me into a condition at least more profound than the one I was living. From that moment, it was one demand on top of the other. It was work. Work was the sadhana, work was the spiritual life. There was no "Come to me and sit and chat." It was "Take out the garbage. Sweep out this place." If I came to sit and talk with Rudi, I was most often told, "Scrub the floor," or, "There is a new shipment in the warehouse, so go and unload my truck." I worked constantly, day and night, for four years. On top of the heavy physical labor, Rudi had me

71

going to seminaries, where I studied Christian theology, masses of historical literature, ancient languages, all kinds of things in which I had no fundamental interest. I had to live in Protestant and Orthodox seminaries, but I was not a Christian. My sadhana was continuous work and self-transcendence. There was no ending of it. Even in sleep and dreams, there was no ending of it.

My time with Rudi did not see the fulfillment of my spiritual life. I moved on to other relationships, and the order of my sadhana and my understanding changed. But his requirements for sadhana in the functions of life and body, in terms of money, food, and sex, were more than useful to me. The sadhana performed in those years became the very foundation of my spiritual life. During that time I was strengthened and stabilized in mind, body, and life. When I came to Rudi, I wasn't prepared for an elusive Yogi. Such a one could have been of no use to me in the beginning. Truth is resurrected from the ground up. The conscious force can never leave the ground if you begin your sadhana in the air. If sadhana is begun as an effort to become "spiritual", then what is merely alive remains a mass of confusion and craziness. So I must insist that all who come to me take on functional responsibility for the powers of life, which are money, food, and sex. My manner of working with people is to take hold of them and establish a relationship with them, so that this relationship becomes their conscious, overwhelming, and continuous Condition. When they become conscious of it on any level, then I give them responsibilities at that level. From that moment, I require and expect them to function at that level. I never pat them on that part of the head again. I expect them to live that function responsibly in the Ashram and everywhere in life from that point on. I expect all of you who are already with me to do sadhana at the levels of money, food, and sex. And to do sadhana on those levels is, at times, going to be just as difficult for you as it was for me. If you are ready for spiritual life, you will be very happy to have something in your hand at last, to function at last, to have begun. All other responses to this sadhana are your unreadiness, your unwillingness, your resistance. They are Narcissus.[4] Narcissus has no support from the Heart, from the Guru, from the Truth, or even from the universe. Narcissus is already dead. Death is his karma, his destiny, his realization. And everyone will only die who lives as Narcissus. Narcissus will die in his own pocket. His head will fall from a sleeve. He will not die a sublime death. He will die alone, unconscious for a long time. He is the destiny of unconsciousness, of foolishness. But all waking comes suddenly.

People have become involved with all kinds of patterns of life that are their suffering. Your sadhana involves that level of complication, or suffering, that you are already living. It doesn't necessarily involve visions. Even if visions appear, they have no ultimate consequence. Suffering is the place of sadhana. Sadhana meets this complication, this resistance, this fear, this stupidity, this lethargy, this craziness, this violence, this separateness, this heaviness, this endless distraction by the current of experience from hour to hour. All of that is terrifying, if you could consciously see it. Sadhana is involved with that. Sadhana requires a great deal of a person. It requires one, ultimately, to be a genius, a hero. It requires one to manifest the great qualities, the greatest human qualities. Everyone who does sadhana must manifest those qualities in his or her own life. Of course, it is not all required or even possible in one afternoon, but functional intelligence must manifest at a certain level even at the beginning.

True spiritual life is not a form of consolation. Its foundation is not a fascinating promise. It is not generated in the form of "Get along, do the best you can, and after death you will go to heaven," or "I will come again and make everything all right, no matter what you do, because everything is really okay, you rascal!" There is a profound sense in which everything is really all right, even now, regardless of the conditions, but that profundity requires the most "radical" kind of humor, intelligence, and discipline to be understood.

So one must become responsive at the simplest level, the level in which one is living, in which one exists. There is nothing very profound about it. And this requires one to conduct, or make lawful use of, the life-force, not to abandon it, not to become separate from it. One must become capable of relationship at the level of the vital, on all the levels of the physical being, ultimately including the whole range of psycho-physical life. When there is no obstruction to relationship, there is no praise, no blame. There is no praise, no blame, in the responsible, appropriate enjoyment of sex-relationship. There is no praise, no blame, in vitality itself, nor in the appropriate management and enjoyment of food. There is no praise, no blame, in the earning and use of money nor in the "creative" exercise of power and "creativity", in the use of functional ability and force. But one who is living in the pattern of separation is enormously complicated in the functions of money, food, and sex. Most of the problems he or she perceives in his or her own case have to do with money, food, and sex. The mishandling of those three things manifests as poverty and lawsuits, hoarding and financial complications, ill health, and compulsions at the level of food and sex. Those are the daily experience of the usual man or woman. The daily round is a complication of money, food, and sex. Ramakrishna used to say "women and gold" were the chief distractions and sources of bondage. He was perhaps a member of the school of "getting away from the vital", but he was right about "women and gold", the functions of money and sex. And we must include food in the list. These are the areas in which suffering is most apparent. Therefore, a person's life becomes very complicated to the degree that he or she has not understood the vital processes, to the degree he or she is living the life of Narcissus in relation to money, food, and sex.

Simply because you have come to this Ashram and have expressed a certain willingness to begin this "radical" life does not mean that you have ceased to live in the usual manner. Since you came here, you have begun to observe the resistances that are in you, the reluctance to function in at least human terms, all of the craziness, and the forms of crisis that make it all so very apparent at times. So it hasn't disappeared simply because you are here. But the process that undermines all of that has begun. Satsang does not support the forms of your reluctance, your "tamasic" tendencies. These things remain to occupy you, until a different intelligence replaces them. And that is precisely what this work is all about. In the meantime, while you are all still a little nutty, you must survive in time and space. Indeed, the Ashram itself must survive. Therefore, rather than have the Ashram accommodate itself to resistance, your responsibilities must be made plain. What is appropriate must be made known in a simple manner, and all who come here must be required to function at that level immediately.

People think they are supposed to be allowed a little time to get through all of their functional problems. People think they are supposed to analyze it for a few years, under very supportive conditions, and get it a little bit straight about two, three, maybe four years from now. But that has nothing whatever to do with the Truth. It is only another sign of reluctance, inertia, "tamas". Spiritual life is not the support of your malfunctioning, with a few little bits of wisdom thrown in until you come out of it. Spiritual life is sadhana, the always present demand of function. How do you think the spiritual crisis was brought about in traditional monasteries and spiritual centers? Certainly not by coddling and consoling mediocre disciples. That is why very few people went to those centers. The moment you stepped in the door, someone was waiting with a stick who took all of your clothes, all of your money, all of your belongings, put you in a little cell, gave you brief instructions about the four or five things you were going to be allowed to do for the rest of your life, and then demanded you do all five before dinner! You found out how you were failing to function by trying to function, by living under the conditions where nothing but functioning was allowed.

True spiritual life is a demand, not a form of therapy. It is a demand under the conditions of Satsang, the relationship to the Guru. It is the practice of life in a world where the living Heart, not your own dilemma and search, is the Condition. The demand itself does not make real sadhana possible. It is Satsang, the prior Condition of Truth, that makes it necessary. Satsang contains and communicates Itself as a demand. And this demand acts as an obstacle for those who are not certain about their interest in this "radical" life. They have read a little about it, heard a little about it, and now it tests them in the fire of living.

Such is how it has always been. The monasteries, the Ashrams, the schools of teachers in the past, were conceived like fortresses in the hills. They were difficult to get to, and very few people ever returned from them. People didn't gaze nostalgically at the place up on the hill, or hear about it on the evening news, and say, "Wow, I wish I could just go up there, you know, turn on to where it's really at, go up there and everything is groovy forever, and really get it on." Traditional spiritual life was never confused with any sort of playful getting high. All of that is only a mediocre interpretation fabricated by people who have no real capability for sadhana or the true and "radical" bliss of conscious existence. True spiritual life is not getting high. From the human point of view, the resistive, narcissistic, ordinary human point of view, spiritual life is the most completely oppressive prospect. And it stimulates massive resistance in such people as soon as they get a taste of it. Traditionally, incredible obstacles were put out front, so that people would not bother even to come to the door. It was purposely intended that people would never even ask about it unless they had already overcome tremendous resistance in themselves. The great oriental temples, for instance, were built with incredible images of demons, guardians, and ferocious beasts surrounding the entrances, so that people would not approach such places in their usual state of self-obsession. Their heads were required to be bowed. The devotee was expected to be crushed within, in a humble state, reflecting awareness of his or her habit of living. The devotee was expected to arrive on his or her knees, and never without a gift. Such people would never come irreverently. They would never display an inappropriate attitude.

75

The traditional forms of approach are perhaps too ritualistic and too pure-ly symbolic. They can be superficially learned and imitated, and so they do not necessarily reflect the inner attitude. However, all must realize and demonstrate the appropriate and genuine manner of approach and life in our Ashram.

Every poor person is welcome to come here, regardless of his or her present state of life. I am not about to throw poverty-stricken people into the street because they can't pay the "dues". But Narcissus is not allowed to play here. He is not supported. He is abused, he is called names, he is cursed. I put on masks in front of him. I say and do idiotic things in his company. We haven't established an artificial environment here in which everyone is supposed to be "Simon-pure". Those who come here have nothing to defend. You can all know one another very well. That is one of the freedoms of such a place as this. So people here are generally very out front with one another about their nonsense. And that is perfectly all right, perfectly allowable, because it is a righteous demand for relation-ship. It is a purifying demand. True spiritual life is such a demand. It hurts at times, it puts you into confusion, it stimulates conflict, it makes you feel ugly, it makes you recognize crazy things about yourself, it forces you to function in spite of your refusal to function, it offends all of the self-imagery that you have built all of your life. But, after all, that is what we are here to deal with. Everything you bring to the Heart to de-fend is destroyed. Everything you defend is undermined. Your game is not supported. It is aggravated. And people often become aggravated in Satsang.

DEVOTEE: What is the nature of the demand you make upon your disciples?

SRI DA AVABHASA: The conditions for understanding are Satsang. Satsang Itself, when It is most consciously lived, is understanding. It is meditation. Satsang is the real Condition. That is why It goes on apart from the search, prior to your dilemma and suffering. One should not approach one's Guru in order to carry on the search. One should approach one's Guru with devotion, as one who has found, and put one's search down at the Guru's feet. The true disciple is one who simply lives with his or her Guru. That is the true spiritual practice, or sadhana, of Satsang. Every bit of seeking, dilemma, and self-obsession that you lay down is your true gift to the Guru. All gifts symbolize that true and inner gift, and make it visible. One may bring a flower to one's Guru. The flower is very fresh and fragrant. When one smiles and puts it on the ground or in a vase, it may all seem like a pleasantry. But what is represented by that flower could be the most difficult crisis of one's life. The truth of that flower, of that gift, is the crisis itself.

When one begins to live one's life functionally, as relationship, when one accepts the simplest level of responsibility and lives it consciously, in spite of conflict, in spite of difficulty, then life itself becomes sadhana, real spiritual practice, an expression of Satsang. Such functional and responsible living is the first gift of a disciple to his or her Guru. Therefore, it is also the first demand of the Guru. I truly expect those who live with me to master life, to establish my Ashram, to live the process of Satsang in my Company, to give it their life-force, to live it with intensity and love, and to make Satsang available to every human being who has the sensitivity to this one. I do not expect, nor do I support, anything less than that. I expect you to function. Confrontation with the functional demand of life is your test from day to day. It is a sign to you of your state from hour to hour. It is on this functional level that people begin to enjoy realization, understanding, and Truth.

I am not interested in dealing with the superficial and smiling level in you. I am always aware of your visible suffering. I always want to deal with that suffering, seeking, dilemma, contraction, and resistance. Satsang deals with that. It undermines your lack of functioning. It is your craziness that must be dealt with here. We can already be friendly, but we can't already enjoy the Heart together. Since that is the case, we must deal with it. We must deal with the obstruction as it is. And Satsang is the appropriate means to deal with it. I do not mean some sort of confrontation, where we have it out with one another, or where you get to yell at me, make demands, get very upset, or go through a whole emotional act. Things happen like this occasionally, but, essentially, that is not Satsang. Satsang in Itself doesn't necessarily have any obvious drama associated with It, and yet these fundamental obstructions are continually dealt with.

I have lived this Satsang with people for a long time, and I have seen the drama that gets played with the symbol of the Guru. I have seen people approach me as if they were either my parent or my child, for months or even years, always being conscientiously pleasant with me, praising me, seeming to be a devoted disciple, but in time I have seen these same people try to work "black magic" on me, obsessed with threats, undermining the sadhana and harmony of other people by secretive means, until they finally separated from me, and remained preoccupied with all kinds of negative judgments about me from then on. Such people never suspect that the drama they are living from day to day is their own. They always suspect that it is in life somewhere, that it is something that comes on them, like bacteria. Everything they deal with on a relational, functional level is interpreted in that symbolic manner. They never suspect themselves. But as a true disciple, one must become very suspicious of oneself. One must have played one's game long enough, so that one knows what one is up to. It is fine that one knows what one is up to. And I know what my true disciple is up to. I find my disciple's drama, his or her seeking, completely acceptable. I find it completely livable, endurable, understandable, and transformable from the "point of view" of the Heart. I am not the least interested in preventing it. I am entirely willing to allow that to be my disciple's present state, and to live Satsang from that moment in those terms. But when we begin to live It in those terms with one another, a "creative" event has replaced the ordinary round of life. There is no longer any suffering or seeking to justify, to defend, to support, to make survive through time. For the moment, particularly tonight, we are looking at this fact: At the level of life there is essentially the failure to function. That is the fact about this gathering. That is the fact, not the Truth.

My disciples have agreed to do sadhana in the functions of life. They are willing to see this contraction, but to function in any case. The first stages in Patanjali's Yoga system are yama and niyama, things not to do, and things that must be done.[5] The first steps in Yoga are the fulfillment of functional prescriptions. The first thing that one must do is get straight. One may not feel like being straight. After all, one is not yet enlightened! But one is just plain going to be straight in a very fundamental sense. This is the demand of all traditions and of all the Great Siddhas. It is agreed, it is acknowledged, it is accepted from the beginning, that one is upset, that one is suffering, that one is not functioning well at all, and that life is filled with pleasures, but also with burdens and fears and obstacles. When one arrives at the door, this is already understood. Nothing needs to be said about it. So the keeper of the door says, "Okay, now that we have heard that, I've got these twelve rules for you to do." And the would-be disciple looks at the list with amazement. One is supposed to do all the things that one wasn't able to do and that motivated one to come here in the first place! These things are not what one is supposed to do when one gets enlightened. They are what one is supposed to do starting this afternoon. And all one gets at the beginning is a handshake and a broom!

One gets up before the congregation, and they say, "This is Jack Umpty-ump, and he has just joined the church." Everybody looks, "Very good", they read a brief prayer over him, and from that moment he is supposed to be straight. He may rise up from there into some magnificent, "creative" spiritual life, perhaps. But his straightness has got to be right out there. It is the first demand. He is not given anything miraculous to make him capable of that. And to fulfill that demand, he perhaps has to go through all kinds of difficulty, all kinds of conflict, all kinds of crises, but, even so, he is expected to fulfill that demand. And he is expected not to burden his fellows with his suffering while trying to fulfill that demand. He can be passing through the most incredible turmoil, and yet he is supposed to be well-groomed, clean, smiling, able to do what is required, loose, straight.

But the therapeutic point of view, the point of view of the search, is of a different kind. A person comes to "the healer". The person is obviously completely incapable of functioning, and he or she is offered somebody who will listen to him or her express that failure day after day, week after week, without adding anything to that misery except more things to console and occupy the person, and by which he or she can further express the same dilemma. The person gets a remedy, an ego-method by which to further express his or her craziness. A consoling religion, an idol of "God", a belief. He or she gets a few brief psychiatric analyses by which to express that craziness. He or she gets medicine and magic to vanish symptoms. But these are all just added to his or her craziness. They give the person a more elaborate expression for that craziness. The remedy tends to indulge one's suffering, because it indulges the search. One's search depends on one's dilemma, and one's dilemma is one's suffering. From the "point of view" of Truth, a therapeutic confrontation is not useful. Only the most "radical" approach to one's suffering is useful.

The Guru does not respond to, support, or act upon the premise of the functional failure and suffering of the disciple. The Guru demands that the disciple function on that level at which some consciousness already exists. The disciple is not given the absolute demand out of the Heart of the universe in one shot, but he or she is expected to function on the level at which he or she is living confusion. That demand of functioning stimulates in the disciple a disturbance, a crisis, a form of conscious conflict. That is the core of sadhana. Of course it is difficult! It can stimulate great physical and mental disturbance at times, particularly in those who have not yet surrendered and found the Truth already present as their Guru. That is why those who begin this way are generally those who have tried the alternatives.

They have tried the forms of indulging their search, and found this strategy does not affect the core of suffering. But when they become sensitive to the Presence of the Heart in the Guru, they become capable of Satsang as enjoyment. Only the true devotee has the force of consciousness that will permit him or her to endure this crisis of conscious life. But one who still pays a great deal of life to his or her suffering and resistance is burdened with alternatives. Such a one continues to suffer, and to be involved in tremendous conflicts that have nothing whatever to do with spiritual life. They are simply the expressions of one's failure to live Satsang as one's Condition. They are the expressions of one's suffering.

All suffering is Narcissus, an obsessive distraction by one's own mind-forms. That is all that suffering is. The modifications of the force of one's own life are one's suffering. Therefore, the quality of dilemma, which is suffering, is present even in the forms of life that are apparently delightful from a social point of view, even apparently successful, apparently making for survival. Whatever one holds in consciousness and defends in the face of all relationships, all conditions, is one's suffering. The endless stream of modifications or formulations of the force of your own living consciousness is the face of Narcissus in the water. Modifications obstruct the living consciousness. They tend to replace relationship with forms within the living consciousness, with contractions of the field of awareness. Therefore, the qualities of experience may change from moment to moment, but always the force of the living consciousness is, by its own modifications, providing the individual with a current of distraction. It is this current of distraction, or psycho-physical modification, that prevents relationship. It is this that implies the center, the ego, the separate one, the dead perceiver. People are really just dummied up with their own machine. They express their suffering through various forms, but it always has the same structure.

Narcissus is a good symbol for suffering. He has separated himself from all relationships, especially the primary relationships of mother, father, loved-one, and environment. He confronts only his own image, which he does not re-cognize as such. Obviously, Narcissus doesn't know that the face in the water is his own image. He does not re-cognize his own image, or quality, as such. And suffering is in the failure of one to re-cognize, to know again, one's own distraction, which is one's own state, one's own quality, one's own modification. When one re-cognizes it, one ceases to be enamored, fascinated, and distracted. One's drama is undone by simple and yet "radical" knowledge. If Narcissus understands his fundamental activity, his insane condition will come to an end. Indeed, all that one is suffering is fascination with the force of one's own activity and experience, which represents the separate self sense (identification, or "ego"), the field of differentiation (the conceptualized world), and the endless adventure of seeking (mysterious motivation, or desire). The things flashing and moving before one, the "objects" of consciousness, imply the separate perceiver over against the field of perception. And where this implication becomes the point of view, the true and prior Nature of the world ceases to be obvious. This structure goes on and on, magnified through all forms, all the types of experience, all the worlds of experience, all the conditions—gross, subtle, and causal[6]—that arise. Every thing that arises is fitted within this structure. So it makes no difference where Narcissus moves, what experience occurs, what technique or search he applies to this dilemma. No matter what occurs, Narcissus fails to know it directly. Even the Divine Vision fails to be conclusive, because he knows it in terms of this structure of fascination and separation. One is always being Narcissus until there is the re-cognition of this primary activity, assumption, and root of cognition. But when this re-cognition occurs, one is like a person discovering that he or she has been pinching himself or herself. The pain was always his or her own event, the theatre of his or her own action. When one finally sees this, it is a simple matter. One no longer needs to go through any sort of complicated affair to get free of pain. All one has to do is take one's hand away. Re-cognition is of that kind.

And the Guru is the water itself, upon which this image of Narcissus is reflected. By causing a disturbance in the water, or the prior Nature of the disciple, the Guru makes himself or herself known. The Guru intensifies the true Nature of Narcissus, so that this re-cognition can take place. However, the Guru does not do it simply by stimulating modifications of your experience, binding you to mind-forms, appearances, visions, distractions. All of that is only a secondary process in the life, not the very communication of Truth. All of that is only more of the face in the water for one who does not understand. But the Guru communicates the water itself to Narcissus. The Guru only intensifies the true Nature of Narcissus.

Therefore, it is not by the elimination of conditions or by the destruction of your responsibilities that you are served. You are served by the communication of your responsibilities in the ordinary manner. It is not by distracting you while you remain irresponsible and in trouble that you

81

are served. It is by the forceful demand for responsibility that you are served.

DEVOTEE: What are the responsibilities of those who live in Satsang with you?

SRI DA AVABHASA: Those who enjoy Satsang with me are responsible for appropriate action in life and in the Ashram. They must remain in regular contact with the Ashram, and assume responsibilities there. They must be employed, or else be responsible for children. They must be responsible for an orderly household. As a general rule, they should avoid recreational drugs, alcohol, tobacco, coffee, tea, and the like. They should eat moderately, and essentially use only foods that are usable and supportive of bodily life and vitality. In most cases the diet should consist of natural vegetables, grains, fruit, and seeds and nuts.[7] The key to diet is to discover what is supportive and to use it wisely and exclusively. Food does not "create" spirituality. The disciple must spiritualize the taking of food, whatever it is, by appropriate sadhana. The problems of excess, laziness, instability, chronic weakness, and irresponsibility are the patterns of Narcissus. The patterns of avoidance are the very material, or fuel, of sadhana. Bring all of that to the Guru. But even while the dilemma of life is being considered and confronted in Satsang, all are expected to function appropriately. Remember that Satsang is Itself a functional relationship to the Guru, to others in the Ashram, and to the world. A responsible, relational, intelligent way of life is the condition for Satsang.

Human beings have gained a great deal by liberating themselves from the earth. The natural cycle of the earth is a difficult condition in which to survive, and if survival is the preoccupation of human activity, the subtler faculties of the human being do not develop. Therefore, people have "created" great cultures and centers of culture, in order to enjoy common freedom from bondage to the point of view of survival against odds, and to develop the subtler, or hidden, faculties of human destiny. But we are living in a period of reaction to the artifices of culture and technology. Many have decided that the ideal is to become a righteous farmer, or a wandering singer of love-full protest songs, and live Mother-Goose-beautiful out in the woods. But it has only been a relatively short time since the great cities have existed. The human experiment has barely begun. The reasons that people have tried to establish great cities are reactions to the ancient bondage to the cycle of the earth. People are trying to transcend the limitations of the natural cycle, so that they may be free to realize a higher order of common life. Therefore, people have, in their relationships with one another, found the means to transcend the limitations of the natural cycle of earth and water.

Countries like India anciently belonged to the earth. The Indian population is barely breaking away into a genuinely human order of life. In India, if one wants to <u>seek</u> for God—which is inappropriate to begin with—one can freely abandon one's life-responsibilities, one's work, one's relationships to family, one's attempts to support oneself, and one can become a wanderer. This is a tradition of the earth and water cultures of India and certain other areas of the world. There are massive areas of land in India that are unowned or untenanted, where one can be irresponsible in relation to the earth and one's own earth life. One can find a cave and sit in it. But when people have begun to live with one another, when they have broken the cycle of attachment to earth and water, they must accept responsibility for their own survival. Therefore, it is inappropriate under the conditions in which "fire", or the cultural and technological means of material and human transformation, is developed for one to be without work or responsibility for one's own action. Either one must work for one's own support—and in most cases that is necessary, because most people don't have the money to live without work—or one must do so simply because it is appropriate to work. Work is a peculiarly human activity. It is the means for transcending the limitations of "lower", elemental conditions. Thus, it is not appropriate for people who come to live in Satsang to remain irresponsible for their own survival, or irresponsible for "creative", supportive action in the human manner. Another thing people bring to the Guru, because of the nature of this time and place, is attachment to drugs. Whatever its function at the time it began, positive or negative, it has no purpose whatsoever in real spiritual life. It is an aggravation. It toxifies the body, and stimulates one illusion on top of the next. The person involved with drugs and its illusory "spiritual" culture is back and forth every day. He or she is not ready for Satsang. Drugs are a heavy alternative until one understands the limitations of that bondage. The other forms of stimulation people use, like tobacco, alcohol, coffee, and such, should be, as a general practice, abandoned as well. They don't have the immediate kinds of effects that are witnessed with hallucinogenic or even so-called "healing" drugs, but they are remnants of a social culture of "gentility", forms of self-indulgence and distraction that reinforce dullness and only kill at last.

People very often ask about diet. For some reason or other, food has become like drugs. People are using it to become realized or spiritual. Neither drugs nor a special diet will make you realize the Truth. People tend to use diet as a form of search. There is no "search" that is appropriate. Therefore, there is no form of diet that is appropriate for the sake of realizing Truth. You will not become Self-realized or understand because you eat only fruit, because you fast one out of every two days, or because you are a macrobiotic gourmet. However, there is an appropriate form of eating and fasting. The appropriate diet is one that sustains and supports the body and the vital force. For the most part, natural, whole, and fresh vegetables, fruits, grains, and seeds and nuts are the basic diet.

How much one eats is just as important as what one eats. People eat too much. Overeating disturbs the bodily functions and makes food unusable. Unused food, as well as unnatural and inappropriate food, toxifies the body and causes disease. Many of the things people think are their spiritual problems are just the results of toxicity. Therefore, you must simplify and moderate your diet. Make it natural and pure. Eat only what is usable by the body.

Satsang and spiritual life do not go on while you indulge yourself and remain irresponsible. Even though you do not understand, even though perhaps you live in dilemma, you must be responsible for an appropriate life. To engage life under appropriate conditions makes you aware of your limitations, your struggle, your search, your dilemma, your resistance. The form of life is sacrifice. Nothing needs to be added to life—no attitude, no special sort of yielding—to make life sacrifice. Life is already sacrifice, and all appropriate action is in the form of sacrifice. The symbols of religion tend to indicate that you should add something, some sort of payment, to life, in order to make it sacrifice. But sacrifice is the form of every function. It is the universal law. It is even the rule of pleasure.

The self-indulgent and irresponsible person is not aware that all action, all manifestation, is itself sacrifice. Speech is sacrifice. Sexual activity, even emotional-sexual relationship itself, is sacrifice. All action tends to break the life-current, the sphere of descending and ascending force. Where action is performed, the internal circle of life, or energy, tends to be broken and released temporarily. Do that enough, do it in ignorance and absolutely, and there is only death as a result. Do it intelligently, and it gives life, it generates life through relationship, for relationship is a universal duplication of the internal circle of energy. To sacrifice oneself, or open oneself, into relationship is to realize the greater Form, the true and perfect Circle, the Completion that transcends limited, or separative, individuality. Therefore, true and conscious sacrifice is a form of completion, not of interruption or separation. Thus, for the intelligent one who understands, death is only transformation, because one is consciously intimate with the real process of life. But the unintelligent person is already broken. In death, he or she is the sacrificial meal for one he or she does not know. Even so, life doesn't become intelligent by doing something to it, by preventing all kinds of things, by never talking, never enjoying emotional-sexual relationship, never laughing, never doing anything. Life is action. There must be action, or conscious sacrifice.

In Satsang, action becomes natural. The natural order of life is awakened by the Force of Truth. One who simply indulges his or her possibilities continually breaks the circuit of descending force. That one never allows the ascending, internal return of force. That one is always breaking the circuit. That one exhausts himself or herself.

In Satsang, there is a natural tendency to return to the normal, the ordinary, the pleasurable, the intelligent. However, one who is simply indulging himself or herself while in Satsang, even though his or her body is in the Ashram, continually prevents return to the normal. Therefore, there are conditions for Satsang. But they are not exaggerated conditions. I ask for a natural ordinariness, an ordinary, pleasurable life. If you bring a relatively normal, pleasurable existence into Satsang, it will tend to become more harmonious, more intelligent, more alive, more enjoyable, subtler, in a very natural manner. The Force that is in Satsang is the Force of Reality. The quicker it becomes in you, the more intelligent, the more "like" Reality, you become.

There is no Satsang without sadhana. Satsang is not just sitting around and "turning on" to spiritual Force. Satsang is a functional, relational life. One of Its forms is this sitting in meditation, along with all the other phenomena that tend to arise within It. There is meditation, and perhaps enquiry, and all the spiritual sensations. But Satsang has many forms throughout the day. It is relational life itself. In fact, what is difficult for a person is not the extraordinary, the thing that requires the great, the dramatic, the heroic. It seems very amicable to go and sit in a cave, or wander as a seeker-tourist in India. Abandoning everything and going to India is an idea that commonly fascinates people who have heard a little about spiritual things. People can imagine doing that. It is very dramatic. But to be an ordinary man or woman, to function alive in the human world, is a notion that people resist. The usual images of spiritual life, of spiritual attainment, implicitly contain the refusal of ordinariness. The common "spiritual" motivation is a form of resistance, this contraction of which I often speak. Some people devote themselves to this illusion of the fantastic which they call "Truth". Whatever it may involve, including every kind of vision and miracle of the occult, it is simply resistance to ordinariness, to the sadhana of sacrificial existence.

Becoming ordinary, functioning in the stream of manifested life, is what people resist. Indeed, suffering is a disorder in human functional life. It is not that Truth is absent. Truth is always already the case. Truth is simply not obvious to people. Truth is not absent. People are suffering. There is this contraction, this disorder, this refusal of functional life, of ordinariness. This suffering obscures conscious Truth. The search for the extraordinary is nonsense. It is adventure without intelligence or real beauty. People indulge in extraordinary seeking in order to compensate for self-caused but unconscious suffering. The adventure itself never deals with its own motivation.

Thus, the plane of sadhana, of true spiritual action, of action appropriate to Satsang, is the ordinary. Not the extraordinary, not the search, not methods, but simple, ordinary, functional life. Such sadhana is the most difficult to attain. But it becomes possible in one who understands. And it becomes simple for one who lives Satsang with the true Guru. And such ordinariness is essential for a natural, pleasurable life. Sadhana is not the extraordinary. Sadhana is not sitting in the cave, preoccupied with the ego-self. Sadhana is simplicity. It is, at its foundation, relational life. It is your conscious humanity. You must live it. You must become a human being. You don't have any choice. Either you become a human being, and function truly as a human being, or your humanity becomes obsolete by non-use. Much of the traditional spiritual search is an attempt to make ordinary life obsolete by inattention and non-use. The popular Indian version of the search, for instance, is detachment and abandonment of all the "lower" desires, the "lower" forms of experience. The concern is only to ascend beyond life. By inattention to life, life becomes obsolete. Life certainly can be murdered by design. But the result is not enlightenment. If non-life were enlightenment, all you would have to do is kill yourself. So it is not making things obsolete by inattention that is the way of Truth. It is re-cognizing what you do under the conditions of the ordinary that is the way of Truth. In that re-cognition, Truth stands out. Truth is always already in life. Truth is not someplace else. Truth is not Itself identical to any experience or any place. There is no inner world, no chakra,[8] no sound, no light, no form, no loka,[9] no experience, no attainment, that in itself is Truth. There certainly are such experiences, such manifestations, but they are not in themselves Truth. Truth is always already the case. Truth is the present Condition, the real Condition of every moment, whatever arises. It is not necessary to do even one thing to make Truth arise in the present. There is only Truth, Reality, or God. It couldn't be more obvious. There is no dilemma. Only perceive your own action, your subtle strategy, moment to moment. Re-cognize it, and see what is always prevented by your own action. That which is always being prevented is Perfect. Where there is this re-cognition, all things, conditions, and states become obvious. Dreams become obvious, sleep becomes obvious, death becomes obvious, birth and life become obvious. All manifestation becomes obvious as Truth, as the very Force, the very Intensity, that is that One Reality, called "God", "Brahman", "Nirvana". But Truth becomes obvious only to one who lives the ordinary, whose thirst for the extraordinary has begun to die, has begun to show itself as seeking only, as a reaction to fundamental disturbance, or dilemma.

Therefore, you must become ordinary in order to live Satsang. By "ordinary" I don't mean that you become sort of empty and nondescript. I mean that you begin to function humanly. And when you function as a human being, you can be a marvelous, intensely "creative" person. But your activity will not be itself a way to Truth. It will simply be an expression of life already in the Truth, which is Satsang. Your activity will simply be appropriate. Your life will be controlled by your human functions.

Just so, Satsang, the conscious relationship between Guru and disciple, is, at Its base, a form of ordinariness. It is a human function. It is the primary human function. It is simply a relationship. It is ordinary. It has many subtle aspects, which may also become conscious, but It is ordinary from the beginning. It is functional. It is a relationship. It is obvious. Satsang is the enjoyment of relationship, being in relationship, becoming intelligent under those conditions, perceiving it in subtler terms, even perfect terms, until fundamental intelligence and enjoyment are entirely awake and alive. Everything that one would call "extraordinary" is an alternative to Satsang. And everything that is ordinary is a form of Satsang. That very thing that you resist—whatever seems oppressive in ordinariness and in the functional condition of being alive—that very sensation, is the cognition of present dilemma, the motivation to seek, the guarantor of suffering and dilemma. That condition, in all its forms, must be endured and lived until it is re-cognized, or known again. Therefore, only ordinariness, the functional endurance of your actual condition moment to moment, is the appropriate condition. Thus, Satsang also provokes a person, because It manifests one's resistance to one's ordinary or actual condition.

Much of that disturbed condition that people bring to the Guru is not a matter of anything subtle or spiritual. For the most part, it is simply a functional disharmony. In many cases, the simple moderation and purification of diet is the most dramatic form of sadhana. The simple moderation and intelligent selection of diet purifies the body. The judicious use of occasional fasting also aids this normalization of psycho-physical life. All "ordinary" sadhana purifies the body, and returns it to a normal condition of vitality. Extreme forms of desire, of functional attachment to non-functional patterns of money, food, and sex, extreme forms of emotion—all the things that people think they should bring to an end through "spiritual" methods—become quiet in a very natural manner in the regimen of ordinariness to which they apply themselves in Satsang.

The use, or transformation, of food is the fundamental process at the level of organic life. Therefore, the simple intelligence of diet is very useful, very appropriate. The thing that is your suffering, this contraction, is not necessarily a matter of exaggerated desires and needs, and every kind of craziness. You need not be half psychotic before real spiritual life becomes useful to you. The way of understanding and Truth is a subtle, intelligent matter for ordinary people to consider. You will simply see that by the intelligent use and moderation of diet the level of organic life, and even the whole of psycho-physical life, tends to become functional, usable, harmonious, free of disturbance, or dis-ease. But appropriate diet is not a means to Truth. It is simply appropriate.

It is not appropriate to cut off a finger each day. To stop cutting your fingers off, however, will not make you realize the Truth. It is simply appropriate to put fingers to proper use. Just so, there is appropriate use of food and life. Obstructing the natural process by excess and wrong use is like cutting off a finger every day. It causes suffering, disability. On the other hand, if you correct your diet, moderate it, you don't realize the Truth for doing that. It is simply appropriate to do that. Seekers propose diet as if it were the way. They talk about lunch as if it were the Absolute, or the very method of Truth. The various food cultists talk about their dietary practice as if it were the means for absolute realization: raw only, yin-yang, grain is basic, only fruit, high protein, seven basics, non-mucus, total fast! All purely idealistic and exclusive views are the refusal of ordinariness. Diet is a simple matter of "lunch". It is a practical matter of experimental self-observation. Extreme assumptions about it, overuse of food, extreme attachment to food-thinking and arbitrary dietary demands, use of foods that toxify the body, fasting for inappropriately long periods—all such things are extensions of the search, the refusal of ordinariness. There is an appropriate diet. There is an appropriate time to fast. But, if it is right, it is, characteristically, simple, moderate, and satisfying.

The appropriate use of food tends to manifest natural control of mind, breath, and sex. You will perhaps discover that the force of sex-desire is secondary to food. If your diet is conscious, the sex-force tends to be harmonized. What you are always contending with as sex-desire, at times trying to suppress it, then to control it, but always finally giving up—that whole drama of sex cannot be separated from "lunch". There is no necessary problem about sex. But it is disturbed by all the jazzy, self-indulgent, unintelligent use of food, drink, and stimulants. You will find that on a natural diet, an intelligently moderated diet, the whole force of sex gradually becomes intelligent. There will be nothing compulsive about it anymore, or it will at least have become available to your understanding and the Force of Satsang. It will become a natural, usable force, a relational capability. Sex, after all, is a functional form of relationship. But people try to deal with it as an intense, internal, and isolated personal demand. They don't bring it into relationship. They don't confine it to the conditions of relationship. So sex becomes obsessive, as any desire that is not made to function in full relationship. But that whole extraordinary disharmony and problematic demand of sex is essentially a matter of improper diet and the inappropriate use of the sources and functions of bodily energy. Thus, in one who understands in Satsang, the whole search for "orgasm", or convulsive release and stasis, through the sex-function as well as every other function of life, is replaced by prior and continuous conductivity of the force of life.

The orgasm is an instrument of procreation, an instinctual, subconscious, and unconscious demand that guarantees the physical survival of the human species. It is not, as some seem to think, a necessary instrument of physical and mental health. It is not the necessary or even desirable accompaniment to emotional-sexual intimacy. It is not appropriate for it to be repetitively or frequently attained within emotional-sexual intimacy. Emotional-sexual intimacy itself is the union. The relationship is the union. Therefore, intimacy, not orgasm, is the fulfillment of the sex-function. Orgasm is only one of its functional, or sacrificial, capabilities.

Intimacy is itself continuous communion. It need not include orgasm, or even the sex act itself, as long as the internal conductivity of vital force is unobstructed in each partner. Indeed, when the search for orgasm becomes the principle of sex-relationship, even intimacy becomes disturbed, its harmonious communion becomes impossible, and the separative qualities of mind and action develop. But in an emotional-sexual intimacy that exists under the conditions of understanding in Satsang with the Guru, the generative thrill of orgasm gradually becomes a controlled, occasional, and perhaps even obsolete activity. It is controlled and even replaced by the prior, regenerative bliss of the higher faculties. In one who understands, there is spontaneous, constant conductivity of internal force, down from above, through the vital and sexual organs, and up through the spinal plexuses to the "creative" mental and supramental functions. Such is the circle of bliss that is natural to human beings. The symbol of emotional-sexual intimacy is a ring, a circle of purity. It symbolizes the unbroken circle of life-force that is continuous within each individual, and which is also the principle of the true sex-relationship, which is intimacy itself. This principle transcends and, ultimately, controls the separative principle to which individuals become attached in ignorance. Therefore, it also transcends and controls the principle of orgasm to which seekers attach themselves in the dilemma of vital obstruction. Thus, true and conscious intimacy, rather than orgasm, is the truly human and spiritual form of the sex-relationship. The exploitation of sexuality outside of the condition of emotional-sexual intimacy in Satsang is always separative, founded in dilemma, motivated to the search, manifested as narcissistic attachment to orgasm and to all the social forms of violent release.

In the continuous communion of love that is emotional-sexual intimacy, the internal forces of the partners are conducted in a circle to the higher centers and not thrown out in arbitrary, frequent, and obsessive orgasm. Thus, the sex-function, in Satsang, is self-transcending, always yielding to a subtler, or prior, fulfillment. And such fulfillment is realized without either the search for orgasm (which search manifests as excess, promiscuity, obsessive sexual aberrations, and obsessive and chronic masturbation) or the search for celibacy (which search manifests as the brittle solitude of devitalized self-consciousness). Loving communion is the human fulfillment of the sex-function. Therefore, in most cases, emotional-sexual intimacy is a most appropriate condition for those who live in Satsang with the Guru.[10] It is appropriate. It does not make you "spiritual". It is itself an expression of your prior and real Condition.

Essentially, human beings are lazy and passionate. They are too lazy to do many things that are necessary, and they are very turned on to a number of other things that are unnecessary and destructive. Ordinary life is spent, from hour to hour, in being turned off and being turned on. That is all the usual life is doing. The opposite must begin. Where a person is lazy, he or she must begin to work, not because it "does something", but simply because it is appropriate. A person must begin to function. Where one is simply crazy, passionate, all over the place with one's desires, one must become practical, intelligent.

The moderation of diet is a key factor in that whole process. To a large degree, that to which one is responding with one's strategy of laziness and passion is one's own enervation and toxicity. Intelligence about diet is one's vital responsibility. And this includes all the substances taken into the body. Recreational drugs are craziness. They are mediocre, like all addictions, all methods. They only intensify or reinforce the fundamental stupidity and insanity. At the very least they toxify the bloodstream and contract the nervous system, producing estrangement from the environment and from the subtle sources of energy. Even one marijuana cigarette contracts the nervous system for a long time. None of that has anything to do with real spiritual life. It is just drugs! It is only self-indulgence and the search. It is a form of suffering.

Arbitrary attachment to an orthodox or idealistic system of diet is another form of addiction. Diet does not lead to the Truth. Diet is not itself Truth. There is no universal spiritual dogma about diet, because diet is not the way. There is simply an <u>appropriate</u> diet, and the individual must discover it if he or she is to remain vital. There are appropriate patterns of life that allow life to live, to be intense, to be sensitive, to be intelligent, to "create". Life is not contained in some dogma about how to live, how to correct yourself. Life is simply the realization of "ordinariness". Appropriate patterns of vitality are a primary instrument for Satsang. They foster those conditions of simplicity and the necessary subtlety, physical and mental, that allows this process to begin. The disciple is responsible for the appropriate maintenance of these patterns of vitality, at the level of his or her physical and relational conditions. Diet is very fundamental, and then on its basis comes the practical observation of your laziness and your passion. You must energize and activate your life where it is dead, and you must harmonize it where it is freaking out. This is why I require you to work and to have regular responsibilities in life, and also to function responsibly in the life of the Ashram.

A human being's perfect food is Truth. This is literally so. Truth is not just a concept. Truth is the living Force of Reality. It is Intensity. It is life, and life-usable. There have been cases of people who did not take ordinary food at all. They lived on the universal prana,[11] or life-force, which is the fundamental substance communicated in food and air. But such revolutionary abstinence is not the appropriate goal of one who eats. It is simply necessary to restore your natural and human relationship to things, which is to fulfill the demands of Satsang. And the process of Satsang Itself is essentially feeding, conversion, and waste. There is no process in the manifested universe that is without these three qualities, or functions. Psychic waste, the subtle by-product of conscious life, is a form of pollution. Where Satsang is not consciously lived, people suffer one another. People are suffering mutual enervation and toxification. They do not have the conscious means to conduct and transform the communicated energy of life. Thus, they become disabled, poisoned, without love or freedom. They have lost sight of the source. Food and life have become mysterious to them. Men and women are obsessed with their toxicity, their dis-ease. Going to the Guru, to Satsang, is restoration of food, life, and the conscious powers of freedom and refreshment. The self-sustaining powers of conversion, of "digestion", go on spontaneously in those who live the conditions of Truth. Then this psychic waste is returned to the natural course wherein it can be converted. In such cases, individuals no longer toxify the subtle life of the human world. For this reason it is said that, of all the things a person can do, Satsang is the best.

It is important to remain vital. People think spiritual life has something to do with becoming weak. Some people get addicted to fasting because of the airy and artificially exalted weakness that comes upon them when they fast. Excessive, unintelligent use of fasting combined with inappropriate diet weakens the vital. The vital loses its ability to inform consciousness when fasting and diet are managed by the ignorance of seekers. People feel this "weakness" is a very spiritual tendency. But it is just vital weakness.

A truly spiritual individual is very strong. Traditionally, in Japan and certain other places, the vital center is valued and protected. Wherever you want to pinpoint its center, in the navel, or just below, the vital area is that entire region of the body extending from the solar plexus, or even the heart and lungs, down to the anus. It should be strong, not weak. There should be force there. You should conduct this force. Sneezing, coughing, vomiting, and generally exploiting vital tendencies are all the same activity. Even laughter and speech are forms of this same psycho-physical ritual. The life-force is thrown upward and outward through the front of the body. The movement is counterclockwise. It is the reversal of force, the rejection of energy. But the force of life should always be conducted fully, spontaneously, clockwise through the body. If your tendency is to be weak in life, in relationships, to be sort of fawning, fey, ambiguous, elusive, empty, not forceful, or even exaggeratedly forceful, then you also will tend to take on vital problems of various kinds. Once you are sick, there are a number of things wrong in the vital circuit.

There are a number of things that you must be responsible for. There is diet, exercise and the taking of good, strong breaths, function, or work, the spontaneous attitude of strength, the whole intensity of understanding in Satsang. There is a conductivity necessary to life, a conductivity of force. People ordinarily are only rejecting, becoming empty all the time by various positive and negative strategies. But there is this natural conductivity, downward, through the frontal functions of the psycho-physical life, and up the spine. This full circle is the law of manifested life. That should be spontaneous, simple. That is health. It is also sanity. That is the human cycle, the psycho-physical circuit. Force, strength, intensity, has got to be brought to the functions of life. You had better stop indulging your games and strategies of seeking. Otherwise you will constantly go through cycles of disease, disturbance, sickness, annoyance, negativity. All of that is a direct result of your activity, your relationship to things. Everything you suffer is a direct result of your own activity, your own involvement with the force and the pattern of manifested and unmanifested existence. I am not suggesting you should begin to become very self-conscious about your physical state and feel guilty if you happen to get a little sickness of some sort. It is simply that you should know in general just what the life-process is, and begin to observe the results of your own action. See the results of your action. See your action prior to results. See your motivation prior to action. See the roots of motivation, or motion, in yourself. This is fundamental intelligence at the level of life. Usually people don't become sensitive to their own action until they see its results. They always only see life fall apart or become difficult, to the point of death.

Episodes of sickness are purifying events. Sometimes these things occur when the living Shakti[12] is activated in various forms. Latent illnesses sometimes appear by such means. But those in Satsang are continuously responsible for the appropriate and ordinary order of psycho-physical life.

DEVOTEE: What about exercise?

SRI DA AVABHASA: Just as you must discover the appropriate diet in your own case, you must discover the kind and level of activity necessary to keep the body supple and strong. All of it is a matter of intelligence at the level of your specific constitution. You must discover what foods and vitamins are necessary to keep your chemistry at a constant level. You must discover what types of activity and uses of life you can enjoy without breakdowns of various kinds. In every person's case, there must be an individual and intelligent self-observation and learning.

There is really no basic human being. Everyone is manifesting a very different karma, or range of tendencies and conditions. Some people need and tolerate much more exercise than others. But, in general, every one, because he or she has a vital, physical body, needs a certain amount of regular, conscious physical activity. I am providing the Ashram with detailed instruction in matters of diet, exercise, and every functional aspect of vital and spiritual life. Those who are my disciples must become masters of the ordinary.

DEVOTEE: What about sleep? Does it also depend on the individual? How much do we require?

SRI DA AVABHASA: You should always feel refreshed, rested, and full of energy when you get up. If you can get that in half an hour, then sleep for half an hour every day. If you get it in five or six hours, then sleep that long. If you need seven or eight hours, then arrange for that. Every one is different. But what every one must observe is how he or she feels upon waking. There is such a thing as overindulgence in sleep. Too much sleep actually weakens you, devitalizes you. If you sleep long into the period of dreaming, particularly very superficial dreaming, that morning twilight dreaming, where you are almost awake, you are sleeping too much. You will feel tired and probably moody on that day. All kinds of subliminal mind-forms establish themselves by such oversleeping, and these subtle tendencies contract the vital during the whole day. You should find that period in your sleep when you can awaken and feel refreshed, without the subliminal twilight of dreams.

The diet is very important in terms of the vital. Exercise is important. Sleep is important. The breath is very important. Therefore, speech and thought are also important. If you feel anything like a cold or any sort of vital difficulty, it is very good to walk, and breathe intentionally as you walk. Deep-breathe while you walk. Walk as an exercise. Don't just sort of flop down the street. Walk very deliberately, forcefully, with spine straight and muscles loose, and breathe deeply, rhythmically. Inhale profoundly, with the entire body, and exhale completely while walking. This helps remove impurities, opens up the breath-system, and feeds you through the transformation of energy in the chemistry of air. It is not that the goal of absolute health has a great deal of reasonableness about it. Whole spiritual systems have been based on the ideal of becoming absolutely healthy, even immortal. This whole event of life is much more complex than that. But every individual should at least be responsible for the basic quantities in his or her life, and this will manifest as optimum health, free of attachment to psycho-physical conditions, good or bad.

Everyone seems to be subject to a mysterious cycle in the vital. There are attacks in the vital. I have called these attacks and their source "vital shock".[13] There are periodic attacks, cycles of compulsive contraction, in the vital. You don't necessarily feel a physical cramp, but very often there is some sort of somatic sensation. These attacks are evidence of various conditions, various associated phenomena, external and internal. The peculiar crises that occur in this real spiritual work, or sadhana, correspond in general to these periods of vital shock. Therefore, you must begin to become as intelligent as you can about the basic vital process. You must not deliberately allow the vital to become weak. Keep the essential vital quantities constant. Learn the secret of moderation, which is continual alternation, or rhythm, of appropriate use and intelligent abstinence.

Under the heading of food, which is very basic to this whole affair, are all the things on which the vital thrives. These not only include the basic quantities in the diet but also the breath, or conductivity of the life-force, or prana, itself. Sexuality and the communication of force as money, effort, and love are also very fundamental functions of life. All forms of exploitation and of willful, exaggerated non-use tend to weaken the vital, break the conductivity of the life-force, and make the functions of life obsolete in the negative, or destructive, sense.

All social activity, all relational life, is communication of vitality, of force, of energy. In various of the world's Scriptures, people are told to love one another. What is being recommended through such language is use of the internal mechanisms of the life-force. These mechanisms harmonize the vital at the level of intercommunication. If you haven't become intelligent at the level of life, if you haven't seen the results of your action and the nature of your action, you can never become subtle enough to enjoy the very Force that is Consciousness, that is Reality. In that case, you will be continually distracted, continually returned, as a compulsive form of attention, to the adventures of dilemma and seeking.

All people enjoy little glimpses of the gracefulness of Reality. At times they may feel a "Presence" influencing them in some manner. But until they begin to go through the crisis of intelligence at the level of life, nothing constant, nothing truly subtle and alive, occurs in their own case. That is why, as a condition of Satsang, I require people to deal with some very practical things. I require them to work, to manage their personal environment, their diet, and their sexual life intelligently. Work and all the things surrounding one's responsibilities in the environment are indispensable means of bringing one into responsible, repetitive contact with the conditions of human existence and human energy. Self-indulgent, irresponsible living is not the proper or workable foundation for Satsang. As long as the self-indulgent, irresponsible pattern is lived compulsively, there is only the endless cycle of vital shocks. And these shocks continually interrupt the process of Satsang. What I require from you is practical intelligence and responsibility at the level of the vital.

DEVOTEE: Would you please discuss the advantages of the sex-relationship for real spiritual life?

SRI DA AVABHASA: It is a relationship. That makes it, in principle, compatible with Satsang. It is no more or less "spiritual" than any other form of relationship, but it is very fundamental to life. You aren't advanced to Truth if you engage it, or if you don't. It is neither one nor the other from the "point of view" of Truth. But there are human and subhuman uses of sex. Only the human use of sex is acceptable in one who would live in Satsang with the Guru. And the human, conscious, responsible, love-use of sex is, in general, an extension of the process of conductivity and regeneration rather than of the exclusive orgasmic violence of generative sexuality. When the truly human functions are optimally realized in human beings, orgasmic, or generative, sexuality becomes a sacrificial and intelligent activity, limited not by an act of will but by the functional realization, or enjoyment, of prior fulfillment, the circle of regeneration, the natural state of human beings. In one who lives the way of understanding in Satsang with me, all functions tend to return to their human, conscious, responsible forms, including the sex-relationship, which takes on more and more of the regenerative character, even to the point of transcendence of the sex act itself.

We have been speaking about how life-dilemma is perceived by human beings in three essential areas of function. These are money (or, in general, the commitment of effort, love, energy, or life), food, and sex. These are the most fundamental human functions. Therefore, they are also the most obvious places where one discovers that one is suffering. Most individuals are chronically obsessed with the functions of money, food, and sex. Most individuals are dramatizing their fundamental dilemma by seeking in relation to the functions of money, food, and sex. Some pretend to be very "subtle", very spiritual, but they, like most others, are simply reacting to money, food, and sex, which appear to them not as simple functions but in the form of problems. Most people are either exploiting these functional possibilities or resisting them, trying to overcome them. But the only reason to exploit any function or to overcome it is the fact that you are already in dilemma, that you conceive of the function as a problem rather than simply a function.

When one understands one's search, one's dilemma, then all of one's functions return to their natural state. Then the functions of money, food, and sex become possible in a very natural manner. Every individual emphasizes each of these functions to different degrees. Since relationship is fundamental, and the sex-relationship is among the most fundamental, and perhaps the most obvious from the point of view of life, the sex-relationship is a very obvious place for Satsang, for sadhana, for understanding.

Until one understands, neither money nor food nor sex is lived as a form of relationship. Instead of living these functions as forms of relationship, one lives them as forms of identification, differentiation, and desire. If anyone is having sex, <u>that</u> <u>separate</u> <u>one</u> is having sex. It is one's own pleasure, one's own satisfaction. If anyone is having food, <u>that</u> <u>separate</u> <u>one</u> is acquiring it. If one has money, energy, or power, they are one's own. Money, food, and sex are conceived as one's possessions, rather than as functional, relational possibilities. Such a one is a seeker, and these things reinforce his or her dilemma, his or her separateness. But when one's life takes on the form of Satsang and the intelligence of relationship, then these things become forms of relationship, and, as forms of relationship, there is no praise, no blame, in the appropriate use and functional enjoyment of them. They are simply the enjoyable and "creative" faculties of the earth.

From the traditional spiritual or religious point of view, sex, for example, is always very ambiguous, very threatening. Traditionally, people are periodically wondering whether they should give it up forever. They try to become celibate for a period of time, then they try willfully to draw the sex-force up their spines, then they try to sublimate it into painting, office work, poetry, and prayer, without otherwise understanding the motive of their lives. There is no true motivation to abandon sexuality, and, in Truth, there is also no true motivation to acquire it. When one understands, all of one's functions suddenly, spontaneously, are alive. One's intelligence is also spontaneous and alive. Then all relationship is a living, spontaneous enjoyment in which there is no loss, no separation. But for the seeker there is only loss and separation. The traditional Yogi, out of fear of loss and separation, prevents the sex-relationship and retains the sex-force in order to possess the intensity whereby he or she can enact his or her adventure, the search. But when a person understands, the sex-force becomes a natural process in relationship, without loss, and without gain. Therefore, in answer to your question, there is no advantage to the sex-relationship whatsoever. It can be very enjoyable, and a profound condition for the sadhana, or real practice, of Satsang. But if one doesn't understand, it makes no difference whether one does or one doesn't function sexually.

Just as in certain forms of Yoga there is attention to an internal mechanism, a subtle process of energy, something like the positive and negative of electricity, just so, in life there is a pattern of communicated force. Men and women live this pattern in the sex-relationship. Many other forms of relationship in the natural environment are also mutual forms of this pattern of energy. The enjoyment of relationship at the level of the vital life includes not only sex but the whole process of vital force, and the whole ordinary activity of energy and exchange, which also includes the communication of money and the taking of food. At the level of life, something is being done that is quite similar to what is done internally, subtly. Whenever a temporary balance is achieved through mutual conductivity of opposing forces, positive and negative, this is felt as pleasure, or fulfillment, on the level of the physical and vital life. Whether there is sex or any other relational function, when there is this balanced conductivity of force, there is pleasure.

Human beings are continually involved in a mutual activity in which something like positive and negative is harmonized. The "electrical" impulse at the level of human nature is the quality of desire in its natural and functional form, as a simple impulse. Because functional desire is there, the survival of the human species is realized through sex. Just so, the survival of the individual is realized through the process of food transformation, and the survival of community is realized through the exchange of force, energy, work, money, "creativity", love, and commitment of life. At the level of life, this necessary and functional mutuality is continually being enacted, satisfied, and also frustrated.

This relational impulse, this very ordinary impulse, is natural to all human beings. In some, relational force is more intense than in others. From the point of view of life, relationship is the natural, or functional, form. But people are also suffering, living in dilemma, avoiding relationship. Therefore, the sex-relationship has become one of the most corrupt forms of experience possible for human life. It is one of the most disharmonious and aggravated forms of opposition that human beings can encounter. It is one of the chief sources of the exploitation and degradation of human existence, one of the chief sources of fascination, preoccupation, dysfunction of intelligence, frustration, fear, guilt, and dis-ease of life. Therefore, like all forms of relationship, it requires a great deal of both man and woman. The essential thing about it is that, in Truth, it is a form of relationship, not of acquisition or of sensation. When sexual union is lived as relationship, the circle of energy, the conductivity of life, is complete, and there is no loss. But when the sex-function is lived purely as a form of obsession, for the sake of release, there is only separation. Therefore, the sex-relationship and the functions of money and food are forms of spiritual theatre. In Truth, they are a "creative" enactment of the form of the living consciousness. They are forms of realization. They are all these things from the point of view of life, and yet, from the "point of view" of Truth, they have no significance whatsoever.

Most people use sex as experience rather than relationship. They have lots of sexual experiences, which are all modifications of their own mind and life. Therefore, they tend continually to reinforce the sense of separation. But where sex is always enjoyed as relationship, it has no effect, positive or negative, on the primary Force of Consciousness. From the "point of view" of Truth, there is no need for self-conscious or willful suppression of the sex-force, but, also from the "point of view" of Truth, there is no motivation to exploit or exhaust the sex-force. In one who understands, conductivity, or self-conservation and regenerative, "creative" use of what otherwise appears as the sex-force, is an inherent capability, freely enacted.

This truly regenerative activity cannot be "taught" or realized apart from the whole life of understanding in Satsang. The relationship between man and woman can no more adequately be described than the Heart. That relationship is simply the expressed intensity of the Heart, of the Self, of Real God. In fact all there is is this one Intensity. This is why it is said in the Hindu tradition that the husband is Siva[14] to his wife. The very Force of prior and unmoved Consciousness is represented in the male. And a man's wife is considered to be Shakti to her husband. She is the very "creative" Power and motion of the cosmos. From the "point of view" of Truth, there is <u>no</u> activity, no moment in time, that is not Siva-Shakti. It is always this union. Union is already the nature of all relationship. Union, or relationship, is always already the case.

DEVOTEE: What form does it take during sleep?

SRI DA AVABHASA: It depends on what is going on during sleep. It depends on the nature of the sleeper, on his or her state of consciousness. To those who are awake in the world, all sleepers only sleep. But those who are asleep may also dream, or pass through many forms of cognition and experience. There is a process at the level of the causal being, the unmoved realm of deep sleep, that also corresponds to the vast complications of the subtle and gross worlds. It is very simple, subtle beyond subtlety. But it could also be called "Siva-Shakti". The perfect union of Siva-Shakti is fundamental and unqualified Intensity, the very Self. There is no ultimate difference. There is no Siva <u>and</u> Shakti. Even here, in the waking world, there is no Siva <u>and</u> Shakti. But it is easier for most people to think in those concrete and symbolic terms. Therefore, one can say that all relationships, all forms of exchange, are ritual enactments of the One Intensity that is Siva-Shakti. And the sex-relationship is one of them.

The very cells of the body are Siva-Shakti. The atom is Siva-Shakti. Simply because the world exists doesn't mean that Shakti is separated from Siva and must return, or that the Yogi is somehow separated from Siva, and must return to Siva in the form, or vehicle, of Shakti. All that arises is already the union of Siva and Shakti. It is not necessary to raise the Kundalini[15] one inch. It is already raised. It is continually rising. And it is continually descending. It is a circle of conductivity about the Sun, the Heart. When manifested existence is lived from the "point of view" of the Heart, all ascent and descent is already and continually accomplished. But when one lives purely from the point of view of ascent, one has a great deal to accomplish, and when one lives entirely from the point of view of descended nature, one also has a great deal to accomplish. Thus, in terms of the sex-relationship, as in any other kind of relationship, the quality of one's awareness, the quality of the ritual, or the drama, that one is playing, varies from day to day. Sometimes it is very serious, sometimes it is very confused, sometimes very complicated, sometimes very frustrated, sometimes very satisfied, sometimes very humorous. And if one doesn't understand, all of this is an obstacle and a dilemma, which provokes one's seeking. But if one understands, all of that becomes enjoyable. Therefore, in terms of sex or anything else there is no exclusive recommendation. Only understand.

DEVOTEE: What is the most common form of avoiding relationship?

SRI DA AVABHASA: It has only one principal form. It is that very act which I have described as the "avoidance of relationship", which one who understands has begun to identify as his or her primary activity. At times, one may find it dramatized at the level of one's ordinary life in some particular form. One may discover particular and strategic forms of it that are characteristic of one, either during a special phase or as a pattern throughout one's life. But there is ultimately only one form that is that, and everything else is an extension of it. At last, for one who understands, there are not many forms of suffering and ignorance, and there cannot be one that stands out among common actions as the primary form of that action of which I speak, for that action is perceptible only to understanding. It is only that in the case of an individual, each individual, it has its chronic appearance.

Those areas of a person's life in which this activity is most obvious are generally functions of the vital process, the vital force, or energy, that becomes effort, work, exchange, love, money, food, and sex. Those are the areas in which life communicates itself most obviously, most fundamentally. The force of life is communicated as sex-force, as food-transformation, and as relational energy. In other words, the activity that is one's suffering does not appear apart from the life-process itself, in its gross, subtle, and causal forms. From the "point of view" of Truth, the life-process itself cannot be called the obstacle. If so, to become realized would only be a matter of killing yourself, or something similar, some sort of revolutionary detachment or even separation from life. But, in fact, life itself is that area wherein one senses one's conflict, feels it dramatized.

The suffering of human beings is essentially a life-dilemma. It becomes a subtle dilemma only after it has arisen in life. People who desire some sort of remarkable subtle experience to transform them are really responding to a very primitive life-conflict. All of their striving to subtlety is really a reaction to life suffered as dilemma. Therefore, it is not a matter of getting rid of one aspect of life, a hang-up somewhere within life. It is a matter of understanding under the conditions of life. And when the force of life is no longer communicated as dilemma, then this avoidance of relationship becomes obvious.

There is no higher world that is the special and exclusive communication of Truth. All worlds communicate Truth in exactly the same manner, so there is no special advantage in any world beyond here. Truth is always already the case. It is the Condition of all forms of existence. If you do not grasp It, then you will pursue subtlety, or a new state. But when your present condition is no longer lived as dilemma, then you are like one who is awakened from a dream. The quality of such awakening is not to have some "other" kind of experience—it is not some vision, some thought, some experience, some form of self-analysis. Waking itself is the freedom. When a person is awake, this contraction, the avoidance of relationship, becomes obvious.

Ours is not a solid universe in which we are inserted like little capsules of force, separated from other capsules of force, trapped within bodies. This is a realm of Divine Consciousness. Consciousness Itself is the primary "event", the primary "fact", the primary "movement", the primary "drama". It is not that Consciousness must Itself evolve. Consciousness must Itself be lived. And It is lived in one who understands.

DEVOTEE: What causes this contraction, or avoidance?

SRI DA AVABHASA: It is not an activity outside you.

DEVOTEE: How does it arise?

SRI DA AVABHASA: It is arising. When it is seen directly, it has no cause. It did not begin in the past. It is presently arising. It is a spontaneous activity whose mystery is understandable only in the instant of re-cognition. Before re-cognition, nothing can be said about it that makes any difference—because it has not begun in the past. It is always arising presently. At the subtlest level, it is a completely voluntary activity. That is why it is a simplicity. That is why understanding is a simplicity. That is why understanding is possible. It is like someone who is pinching himself or herself, unknowingly. You will try all kinds of extraordinary healing methods, psychic methods, Yogic methods, anything to get rid of this subtle sense of pain and agony that you have all the time. You will continue to pursue every kind of means until you realize that all you are doing is pinching yourself. When you realize that, you just take your hand away. There is nothing complicated at all about it. But previous to that, it is an immensely complicated problem, and the sense of life itself tends to be identified with that problem. The cognition of problem, or dilemma, motivates a person to every kind of distraction, and the understanding of it cannot occur before the most "radical" recognition of his or her essential and always present activity. To seek its origin, to seek a cause for it, is like trying to find the beginning of breath.

DEVOTEE: How does it arise in the present moment?

SRI DA AVABHASA: If it is arising in the present moment, how can you think of it in terms of a cause? All causes are past. But this entire process is a present activity.

DEVOTEE: What brings it on or stimulates it?

SRI DA AVABHASA: It is not caused. The only proper investigation of it, the only "answer" to the question one can formulate about it, is Satsang (the Condition of relationship to one's Guru), understanding, and, perhaps, enquiry. There is no satisfactory answer apart from the present re-cognition of it.

DEVOTEE: What do you mean exactly by the word "re-cognition"?

SRI DA AVABHASA: Knowing again. Most of our activities are forms of cognition, or simple knowing. We are experiencing that, that, that, that, that. The search, the forms of motivated Yoga, the remedial techniques people acquire, are also forms of cognition. "Look at this 'chakra', look at this 'light', look at this 'sound', look at this God, look at this deliciousness, look at this, look at this!" "Oh, yes, I am looking at this!" Narcissus is always looking at his picture. "I" is always looking at this. Such is the ordinary adventure, until one re-cognizes, rather than cognizes. Then you not only know what you are doing but you know what it is that you are doing! When you know it again, it has no fundamental importance. Then all of this chattering, "Oh, look, look, I'm seeing this, oh, look, look at this," just comes to an end. This contraction and unconscious formulation of Consciousness Itself no longer occurs. Narcissus realizes, "Ah!" All of a sudden, "Ah!" And the person just gets up and walks back into town. Recognition is, in itself, the utter, "radical" reversal of all dilemma. It is sudden, spontaneous, perfect, and it cannot in any manner be indicated before its accomplishment.

DEVOTEE: You have said this action takes the form of identification, differentiation, and desire. In a concrete situation, what happens?

SRI DA AVABHASA: The ordinary sense that one has, sitting, walking, is of separate existence. One doesn't ordinarily say to oneself, "I am this body, I am this mind, I am this, I am that." No mental process goes on that is itself the communication of this sense to one. One already has this sense. One wakes up alive, one moves in bodily terms, it just seems very obvious. And there is the sense of some sort of subtle limit, size, shape, or difference. That is identification. It is called the "ego". Differentiation is all the forms, all the qualities of cognition, or mind, in which everything becomes an extension of this same thing that one has assumed. Everything becomes a "this". "Look at this, look at this." Suddenly, there are endless planes of significance. The very structure of one's thought is "this, this, this". Spontaneously, everything is already multiplied, distinct. Having already, spontaneously, acquired this sense of separate existence, and while already perceiving, thinking, a range of multiplicity, of separate natures, forms, and forces, one moves. And that motion is desire. This separate one moves. One conceives a realm of multiplicity in which to move, because one is separate. There is something, even a world, that one is up against, so one moves. And that movement is desire. An endless adventure is possible when these three assumptions are made. And that adventure is what people are doing. All ordinary beings who are karmically manifested in the material worlds are living this adventure. Each one lives it with different qualities, different circumstances, different ranges of subjectivity, but all essentially are living it on the armature of this same structure, this same form, this same complex of assumptions. Therefore, the best practical or "concrete" example of it is just this present state, "me", separate, with everything around "me" moving. What you ordinarily perceive to be your condition at any moment is the best example of it.

Now all adventures, all human adventures, are possible from that point of view, and all are built on that point of view. And that point of view is the dilemma. All accomplishments take place within the framework of that dilemma. Therefore, all pursuits, all searches, all activities, all accomplishments, spiritual and mundane, are possible adventures within that same framework. It is not that the spiritual ones are better than the mundane ones. They are all the same adventure. And, of course, the dilemma and its search are manifested between human beings as all kinds of conflicts and preferences. They are reflected at every level of awareness.

The waking life, what one cognizes to be the ordinary waking state, is a continual drama of these three activities of identification, differentiation, and desire. The causal being, which is also the seat of deep sleep, manifests as the activity of identification, or separate self sense, through contraction of the causal center on the right side of the chest.[16] The subtle body, which is also the seat, or condition, of dreams, is the internal or subtle organ, and it manifests essentially as the elaboration, or differentiation, of thought, feeling, energy, and sensation. This is done by contraction of the subtle mechanism, which has many centers, or functions, in the spine and brain. Then the waking state adds this movement of desire, or manifested vitality, the descending and frontal life. The traditional searches are an attempt to return to the simpler origin. When they turn inward in the waking state, away from desire, this is religion. When they turn inward from the subtle life of dreams to forms of subtlety, or light, beyond mind, this is spirituality, or Yoga. The intuitive methods of the would-be jnani or buddha turn beyond life and subtlety into the causal ground. But in fact all of these are simply means of going from one state into another, moving from one condition to another, that is relatively more subtle, or relatively more free of conditions. None of these functional movements is the Truth Itself. But when one comprehends one's own adventure, and one's search occupies one less and less, when one's suffering becomes the only real possibility, when suffering, or dilemma, becomes one's essential condition, regardless of one's state—waking, dreaming, or sleeping—then there is the possibility of real intelligence, of spontaneous re-cognition, of understanding, of Truth.

The "natural" state is neither waking nor dreaming nor sleeping. It cannot be identified with the three characteristic functional conditions. It has been called "turiya", the "fourth" state, beyond the three common states. When it is enjoyed most perfectly, this has been called "turiyatita", "beyond the fourth".[17] Therefore, one who understands is awake while only waking, awake while dreaming, awake while sleeping. Such a one always enjoys this simple intensity that is Reality prior to the contraction of functional life. He or she has become humorous. Mortal seriousness has fallen from such a person. I don't mean that he or she is always giggling, but the subtle aggravation, contraction, that mystery of his or her own suffering, is absent. He or she falls through it, always.

DEVOTEE: Are you saying that desire has to stop?

SRI DA AVABHASA: One of the typical methods within the great search is the attempt to obstruct or stop desire, because it is a very fundamental area in which the dilemma is conceived. The dilemma is most obvious at the level of desire, at the level of life. The seeker either exploits desire or resists it, but neither one of these strategies is appropriate. Both of them depend upon the dilemma itself. Desire itself, the movement of life itself, is not the dilemma.

DEVOTEE: Desire arising out of identification, and differentiation—isn't that the problem?

SRI DA AVABHASA: That quality as oneself is the dilemma, but that same quality lived from the "point of view" of the very Self, or Truth, is without dilemma. Thus, in one who understands, there still is the apparently individuated being, there still is the capability for subtle life, mind and all its forms, there still is the capability for movement, which is desire. One's appearance is not changed. One remains ordinary, but one lives from the "point of view" of the very Self, as the very Self. But where Consciousness Itself becomes identification, differentiation, and desire, this is the dilemma, because it is not true. Consciousness is not that. The sense of that is the dilemma. And it is nothing more than that.

So the attempt to remove desire is a secondary reaction to this dilemma. The dilemma has already occurred, so anything done to the function of desire is secondary. You can do anything you like to your desire, but nothing you can do to your desire becomes realization, understanding, or Truth. All this doing to desire is itself desire, a reaction to desire as dilemma. When dilemma is understood, there is no motivation to do anything about desire itself. Why should you want to do anything about desire? What is wrong with desire?

106

It will seem to you at times that you need to block desire. It will seem at other times that you need to enjoy it. It will change from hour to hour, but your occupation must turn from desire to the dilemma itself. And that is the focus of Satsang. The preoccupation with your methods of dealing with your search is fruitless. The more you try, the clearer this becomes. Each method is just another strategy, another form of experiencing that tends at last to reinforce the dilemma. Each method has its satisfactions. The libertine has his or her satisfactions, and his or her liabilities. The one who pursues sainthood has his or her satisfactions, and his or her liabilities. Both only reinforce this dilemma. When at last they fall out of their search into their suffering, from within their suffering they will begin to intuit Truth.

Sri Da Avabhasa
at Sri Love-Anandashram, 1992

4.

Vital Shock

DEVOTEE: I wonder if you could expand on a discussion you had with some of us the other day regarding the "vital". You were telling us how people become obsessed with anger, fear, jealousy, and the like, as a result of a contraction in the vital, or life-function.

SRI DA AVABHASA: Yes. I've talked about how the Force of Consciousness operates in life through a structure, or pattern, of conductivity, a circle of descending and ascending force. The special point of view of "life", or vitality, is an epitome, or center, in the midst of the body, in the general area of the navel, this lower-body area. This center, or this aspect of the larger circle of force, is in the frontal and descending pattern of life. It is most intimate to human beings. And it is in the area of life, of vitality, that people experience most obviously, most directly, the nature of suffering. It is at the level of vitality that people cognize existence, for the most part. The whole ascending life, the subtle life, is more obscure than this vital life. In fact, generally, when people pursue spirituality, it is not because they are responding to something "spiritual". What makes them seek is not a spiritual motivation, not a subtle motivation. What motivates them is suffering, and essentially suffering in the vital, in the life.

The usual man or woman lives in what I have called "vital shock". This shock ultimately includes more than the vital. It operates even on a very subtle level. But its most obvious and motivating form is the sense of shock in the vital being. Ordinarily, the vital, at its chief center in the midst of the body, is contracted, and one continually feels it, even physically. One may feel a kind of cramp, this tension in the midst of the body. And everyone tries to relieve it continually through various experiences, pleasures.

This vital center is like the shutter in a camera. Like the shutter in a camera, it curls in on itself in order to close, or else it unfurls in order to open. It is like your hand. If you clench your fist and hold it together as tightly as you can, it begins to become painful. Just so, this vital center is alive, sentient, and when it contracts, like your hand, it causes a sensation. It causes not only a physical sensation, but also many other reflections in life and consciousness. Therefore, when this contraction occurs in the vital, you not only get a cramp in the stomach, but you have a whole life of suffering.

Every aspect of vital existence is controlled by this image, this state, this vital shock. The patterns to which people become addicted are simply extensions of this contraction. For instance, here in Satsang with me, you may go through a period of obsessiveness when it's very difficult for you, when you are continually obsessed with various kinds of desires, feelings. At the beginning of that period, something occurred. Something in life, somewhere, suppressed or appeared to suppress the vital. And all of the patterns, the rituals, the strategies, that began to come on to you were reactions to that suppression of the vital. The sensation, or cognition, of that suppression, or "blow", is the form of vital shock that currently obsesses you. But even before you began the present episode, the vital shock was already your condition. There is a continuous vital contraction.

In fact, what people are suffering is not their peculiar life-patterns, or strategies, in themselves, but this original shock, in the form of a primary reaction, this <u>contraction</u> of which I speak. People seek through all kinds of means to become free of their various symptoms, their various strategies, including the cramped sensation in the midst of the body. But if a person understands, or re-cognizes, this contraction itself, this activity, this drama, at the present, he or she doesn't have to deal with all the endless extensions of it. True spiritual life, "radical" life, is to deal with this fundamental, present activity, this contraction, not with the search that is an expression of it. It is not to deal with the symptoms, not with the strategies that it manifests, but with <u>this</u> activity itself, presently. This primary activity, this contraction, is the root and the support and the form of all the ordinary manifestations of suffering, all of the patterns of life that people acknowledge to be their suffering. This contraction, this "avoidance of relationship", is, fundamentally, a person's continuous, present activity.

A person can be set into a whole period of dramatizing his or her suffering by some simple event in life, a frustration of some kind, a threat, a loss, whatever—a vital shock. But release is not a matter of looking into

110

your memory and discovering the various sources or incidents of these shocks in the past—you know, the day your father hit you, the day your dog died, and all the rest. Those are only past instances of this same process. The process itself is always instant, present, spontaneous. It is a reaction to life itself. Life is its own shock. The awakening of Consciousness Itself into apparent identification with the form of life is that shock. Birth is that shock, not merely the original physical event that may be remembered, but every moment's cognition of being alive. All the events within life are just extensions of that life-shock.

In *The Knee of Listening* I mentioned an experience I had at one point, where I remembered, even relived, my prenatal state, my awakening into the body. There was a kind of gloriousness about it, a fantastic form of energy, shaped, as I described it then, "like a seahorse". That was the original awakening of the Kundalini, if you will. But in the same instant there was intense sorrow. The shock was life itself, the shock of embodiment. The "seahorse" is already contraction. The spinal form is already this curve. The ordinary life is already this tendency, this compulsive qualification of Consciousness Itself, this compulsive unconsciousness. Everyone, "after birth", develops a peculiar drama of this shock. Peculiar experiences occur during every life, and each individual develops a peculiar pattern of reaction to that. So everyone is living the drama and strategy of suffering in a peculiarly unique manner, a peculiarly complex, individual manner. But in every case there is one fundamental activity. One thing is the suffering. It is an activity, this activity, this contraction, this avoidance of relationship, this differentiation, this separation. Wherever it occurs, that is suffering.

All ordinary suffering is only a cramp. It is this contraction. Wherever there is this contraction, there is obstruction to the flow of the life-force. There is also the tendency in the living consciousness for there to be the sense of separate existence. If you cramp the hand together in a fist, there is a sensation in the hand, as the hand, that is different from the space around it. When the vital itself is contracted in this manner, the center of the "hand" is the ego, the "me", the separate self sense. The mind of this "me", like its form, is separate, separative, compulsively differentiating. So the whole drama of seeking that is a reaction to this contraction, or reaction to life, always begins with this "me". "Me" is the core of this experience. It is the center of the "fist". Every person seeks by every means to be relieved of his or her suffering, but the suffering cannot be relieved, this contraction cannot be uncoiled, without the "me", which is its center, dissolving. The whole affair, at the level of life, of vitality, involves the dissolution, not only of the physical manifestation of this contraction, not only of the life-drama, but of all its qualities, all of its peculiar psychology, all of its mentality, all of its assumptions. Real spiritual life involves the undermining of the whole point of view of vital shock.

When the contraction unwinds, conductivity replaces obstruction. Then there is conductivity of the descending force of life. As long as this compulsive contraction, or shock, exists, there is no conductivity. There is only obstruction, or limitation and constriction, of the flow of life. This may be experienced as intense stimulation of energy, of force, in the vital, felt as all of the various forms of desire. The fundamental forms of this intense cramp of energy, felt as the fire of desires in the vital, are the dramas of money, food, and sex. And if the cramp of obstruction is too severe, there is loss of vitality, desire, and function in these same areas of life. No vitality, no survival.

One who exploits the apparent condition of desire no longer conducts the force of life. There is only the misuse of it, the exploitation of it, the revulsion of force, the emptying of force. One does this because the contraction is painful. One discovers that if the force itself is diminished, the pain goes away. If the hand falls asleep, there is no pain. If you empty the vital of its force, the cramp is not felt, even though the contraction remains. So one who is self-indulgent empties the vital constantly, and that one feels relief, feels open, feels satisfied. But as soon as one's strength returns, one feels the pain again, unless one has exhausted and contracted the vital to the point of impotence. Such a one tries by every means to satisfy himself or herself, to be free of pain. But all of his or her means are from the point of view of this contraction, this avoidance. One will continue one's efforts until the entire process of the search fails, and one feels its failure. At that point, Satsang becomes possible, the life of understanding becomes possible.

One who is dramatizing, or living, this state of vital shock is not truly alive, not enjoying life. He or she is always self-enclosed, always suffering, always unconscious, always obsessed, always seeking. Among human beings, there is always the same complaint: "Everybody is asleep, everybody is unconscious, everybody is self-obsessed, everybody wants to be satisfied." Everyone who comes to the Guru wants to be satisfied. "When will I become enlightened? When will I have this experience? What is happening to me? I am suffering." Everyone wants to begin spiritual life as a search. People want to carry on spiritual life as an extension of the same thing they've always been doing. They want to be satisfied, they want to be emptied, they want to be free of this cramp. They want to be free of it. Me. But "me" is the center, the core of this contraction.

If you go to the usual and traditional religious or spiritual sources, you are given forms of satisfaction, the means to satisfy your inclination to be free of this cramp. You are given palliatives, seeming remedies, strategies of belief, and even every kind of ego-consoling method designed to satisfy this search at various levels. All of these things are responses to the demand in the vital. But those who come to our Ashram in the impulse of that point of view are not satisfied. They are frustrated here. The search is not the "point of view" of Truth. This contraction and its consolations are not the point of view of Satsang. Satsang, "radical" spiritual life, is the undermining of this contraction, at every level, the undermining of the point of view of this contraction, the undermining of suffering, of seeking, and its separative existence. So it is only those who have become sensitive to the failure of their search who are able to tolerate the quality of Satsang.

Satsang is a paradox. For one thing, this contraction in life is the avoidance of relationship, the avoidance of that essential condition that is the primary law, or form, of the cosmos: relationship. Nothing arises on its own, or only as its "self". People come to the Guru who are separate, and separating themselves from all conditions. But Satsang is relationship. Therefore, Satsang is an offense to Narcissus, an offense to this contraction, not a satisfaction of it. Only one who has become sensitive to his or her own failure can tolerate that offense.

Living in the condition of relationship stimulates tremendous resistance by reaction in people. And the life of Satsang, the sadhana, or truly religious and spiritual practice, of this Satsang, is to live relationship over time. It is the same thing that Yogis and religious practitioners traditionally try to do by putting themselves into a cave and various other ascetic circumstances. The most "ascetic" circumstance is relationship. The condition of relationship stimulates all of the reaction, all of the "sinfulness", all of the impurity that is in a person. All of it is awakened in the Condition and relationship that is Satsang. Satsang is an offense to this contraction, and It stimulates its content.

Satsang is a relationship, a connection, a form of conductivity. The Force of Truth is communicated through that connection. At the same time that all of the subconscious of buried reactions, the whole search, is being stimulated by the Condition of relationship in Satsang, the Force of

Satsang is also added to stimulate and quicken the whole process. This provokes the crisis that is true spiritual life. When this activity has loosened the vital significantly, when functional ease is restored to vital life, then the subtle life, the true subtle life, may begin to manifest itself. But, in the beginning, it is at the level of vitality that this work begins, not at the level of visions and other phenomena. Such phenomena are not what is significant at any rate, although a person may tend to have some experiences. Essentially, at the beginning, there is this apparent work in the vital, dealing with this vital shock. The person who is just entering the life of Satsang is like a patient coming to a hospital in shock. The Force and Condition of Satsang must unloose the condition of vital shock. When the unconscious, compulsive point of view and the strategies stimulated by the peculiar state of vital shock have been critically loosed in the individual by the practical living of the conditions of Satsang, the real conscious aspect of spiritual life, which is understanding, awakens.

Sitting, functioning, living in the Presence of the Guru and the community that surrounds the Guru are the means to release vital shock. But the means are entirely an activity of the Guru, for the disciple cannot do what that Presence, Force, and Condition does. The disciple only lives in that Presence and Force under the conditions communicated to him or her in Satsang. Such is the true grace of spiritual life, for it undermines the vital shock with very Reality, or Truth, and real spiritual Force.

DEVOTEE: It seems that a person who is only seeking is never dealing fundamentally with this contraction, but is merely reacting to the shock of life.

SRI DA AVABHASA: Yes. To its manifestations, its symptoms. The secret of suffering is not in the past. It is not in the universe, "out there". Your suffering is entirely your own. It is your own activity. And it is a "radically" present activity, not caused by something else. So the real activity of spiritual life is not generated from the point of view of this search, this re-action, this suffering. It is not a matter of discovering these devils, or whatever they are—these key memories, these mortal and cosmic events. It is a matter of re-cognizing, knowing again, your own activity, your present activity.

There is a present activity, an absolutely present activity, an only activity, that everyone is performing all of the time. There are conditions and reactions to conditions that build up patterns, but the root of all of this is what is significant. The support of all that, the paradigm of that. You can go on and recall the incidents, the conditions, that conditioned you, endlessly, but you will have done nothing except the practice of your own obsession. Why are you conditionable? Why are you <u>suffering</u> these conditions? Your suffering is your own action. When this contraction does not occur, no conditioning occurs, no thought binds. There is only bliss.

The approach of Truth to life is a "radical" one, not a revolutionary one. It is not a matter of the search from any point of view within the condition of suffering, but it is a matter of the absolute re-cognition of this present activity. You are operating <u>as</u> it.

DEVOTEE: Can you clarify what you mean by "radical"?

SRI DA AVABHASA: "Radical" insight is an irreducible insight. Nothing can go behind it, beyond it. The "radical" point of view is not one of seeking, step by step, through experiences, but of penetrating, prior to any movement at all, the present condition. You could take the point of view of the suffering, the symptom, the whole life-game that you are playing individually, and make that the point of view of spiritual life. That is essentially what people have traditionally and always done. They begin from the point of view of their suffering. Instead of resorting to the Truth, they search for It. They go on this vast circle. But every point on this circle is the same point of view with which they began. Each point is simply a different condition or experience from that point of view. Every individual begins to know that, however far on this infinitely wide circle he or she may go before he or she discovers it. When one begins to suspect or <u>see</u>, re-cognize, the nature of this adventure that one is living, one is "at the center". One is already at the center the moment one knows what this whole adventure is. So revolution is the nature of the search, but Truth is always "radical", always already at the core, the center.

DEVOTEE: What is the nature of Paradise?

SRI DA AVABHASA: Paradise! What is Paradise? What is that?

DEVOTEE: Paradise is where there is bliss.

SRI DA AVABHASA: <u>Where</u> there is bliss! Bliss <u>is</u> Paradise. All of this is already bliss. Bliss is the Nature of this. "Paradise" is an hallucination about what it must be like where lots of blissful people are! But bliss is the Nature of Consciousness. Bliss is the Nature of this event. There are lots of someplace elses, but they will be no more blissful for you than this place if you are not already blissful. The lokas, or spiritual realms, of the Siddhas, the great spiritual beings, are just as dismal as the earth for a stupid person. But the Siddhas are very smart. They find ways to keep the stupids out! If some commonly distracted being gets anywhere near, they say, "Psst. Have you been down to uh—earth?" And they really hard-sell it, so everybody comes down here! But this Bliss, this Unqualified Enjoyment, this Happiness, is the Nature of Truth. The Nature of Consciousness, your very Nature, and the Nature of all of this—the Nature of the cells of the body, the Nature of Light itself—is this unqualified openness, no condition.

DEVOTEE: Does that mean there is no separation between any of us?

SRI DA AVABHASA: Do you <u>see</u> any? Do you <u>feel</u> there is? In Truth there is no separation at all. But from the point of view of the seeker, one who suffers, there is <u>only</u> separation, at every level. When one wakes, when one re-cognizes one's own adventure, one's own state, in every form that it takes, one can't find separations anymore, one can't discover them, and one goes mad. But that madness is intelligence.

DEVOTEE: Higher than that one can't go?

SRI DA AVABHASA: Higher than that? It wouldn't occur to you! It is the seeker who is always going someplace. The one who is already in trouble is always going someplace else, because he or she is suffering, because this contraction has occurred. All of the chakras, all of the so-called "centers" in the subtle body, the ascending conductivity, the subtle life, are in the same form as this vital chakra, this vital center, this life. And they are contracted, closed, not conducting this Force of the descending and ascending Light. When the vital begins to open a little, when Satsang is lived, when this conductivity begins to occur again, movement also tends to begin in the subtle life as well. Then these chakras begin to open, and various phenomena arise. Spontaneous physical movements, all kinds of things that we have talked about, that you have read about, may occur.

But, as you see, they are not in themselves the Truth. Whenever there is an opening of some sort, or a relaxation in any level or center of conscious life, there tend to be experiences that are associated with that level. These experiences can be movements, rushes of energy, a blissfulness, various sensations, various kinds of psychic phenomena, visions, lights, sounds, but all of these are simply things that were stuck around inside this "fist". As the contraction opens up, they sort of klink off. But the seeker, the one who endures that process from the point of view of suffering, thinks that all of these things are it. One's hand opens up, and one sees the rings on one's fingers, the lines on one's hand. Everything becomes very fascinating, and one thinks of that as spiritual life. One thinks that these visions are Truth.

Seekers, for instance, think that the internal Kundalini Force actually ascends. If the Kundalini ever for one moment came down and didn't retain its connection with the sahasrar,[1] the upper region of the brain and its subtle counterparts, you would be dead, from that moment. That circuit always exists, just as the descending circuit exists. It is just contracted in peculiar forms. As it begins to awaken, to come alive again, to be free again, various experiences occur at the different levels, and people think that the energy itself is rising. But it is just that the characteristic centers are opening, in a kind of progress that looks sort of "upward". And certainly there are sensations that are like rising force. But in fact this circuit is always there, always continuous, except it is obstructed by this tendency to contract, to be separate, to avoid relationship at the level of life.

Thought itself, simple thought, mind-forms, are forms of suffering in the seeker. The simplest mind-form, any mind-form, even a blissful thought of Donald Duck, is a condition of suffering, of contraction. If you examine it while distracted, while happy with that image, that thought, if you examine yourself in that moment with any kind of sensitivity, you will realize that you are suffering, distracted only, but suffering. When all of this contraction, all of this life of avoidance, subsides, when all of this identification with thinking subsides, there is only the absolute conductivity of the Form of Reality. And It lives only as Its own Nature.

The momentary or temporary experience of such a relaxation of the vital and subtle contraction is samadhi,[2] Yogic or psycho-physical exaltation, meditative enjoyment. There are many kinds of samadhi. Most of them, the traditional kinds of samadhi, are the samadhis of the life-force, vital and subtle. Therefore, they are temporary, they are symptomatic, they are experiences that occur when there's a peculiar activity in relation to this living circuitry. When certain forms of concentration are coupled with certain movements within, people have these samadhis of the life-force. But the greatest and only true samadhi is Truth Itself, the very Self, or Reality. There are the temporary samadhis of the life-force, and there is the eternal samadhi of Truth, Sahaj Samadhi,[3] not dissociated from any of the states of consciousness, ordinary or extraordinary. One who enjoys that, permanently, is always full, and such a one does not have to go into the trance states for his or her realization of Truth. Perhaps such a one may do so for enjoyment, but not for his or her realization. Such a one may go into trance states, or Yogic samadhis, for fun, but not in order to realize the Truth. True samadhi is to live the present condition consciously, without bondage to vital shock, without contraction, without the avoidance of relationship, without identification with its subtle forms, which are all forms of thought, modifications of Consciousness Itself. When all of these modifications come to an end, not necessarily in fact or terminally, but as a compulsive activity, then there is already "paradise", only bliss, only the Divine Self, only Real Consciousness, only Light, only Truth, only Reality. In such a one, all the forms of wisdom are communicated spontaneously.

This gets us back to the beginning of our discussion, the notion of "vital shock". Every individual "creates" his or her own life-drama. Everything that has happened to you in the past, the things that you feel uncomfortable about, that you feel upset about, when you think about them now, are things that you strategically commanded from beginning to end. Even the most arbitrary experiences are peculiarly appropriate for the individuals who enjoy or suffer them. And the manner of an individual's relationship to events is not only appropriate but also fundamentally intentional. All of these dramas essentially take place in relationships of various kinds, because the avoidance of relationship, the contraction in relation to the life-force, is that activity to which human beings are bound compulsively. Where there is relationship at the level of life, there is the tendency to separate from it, and if the ordinary man or woman cannot righteously separate from it, he or she "creates" reasons to separate from it. Every individual continually "creates" the failure of relationship. And people become compulsively bound to their special methods for complicating and destroying relationship. These strategies are the life-patterns that people are suffering. And their searches are methods of trying to get free of the limitations they are compulsively generating.

If you are going through a period like that now, while involved in

Satsang with me, the symptoms, the feelings, the moods, the thoughts, the whole period of days or weeks, or whatever, of negativity and unhappiness, of obsession, do not have to be "bought". They do not have to be lived. All of that is a secondary affair. The disease has already occurred. These are just the symptoms of the healing. If you will look back at the beginning of any of these periods, there is usually some frustrating event to which all of this is the strategic reaction. Not that you should always be looking for these events in your past. All I mean to have you discover by pointing this out to you is what you do in relationship to the frustration of life, to the suppression of life, to the shock that is life. What are you doing about that? What does your life-drama consist of? It is always this contraction, this avoidance of relationship.

Relationship is always already the case. If you are sitting in the house, weeping, screaming, feeling upset and negative about somebody you live with, then this is your suffering. This activity is your suffering. Remember that person. Remember the relationship. Live the relationship. Let the force of life move again, and there is no suffering at all. You've obviated that whole "tour", including the making up and everything else. None of it has to take place. All of those things are merely the "subtleties" of your suffering. But suffering itself is always the avoidance of relationship. Wherever you re-cognize your activity, that activity was the avoidance of relationship. Where there is relationship lived, this contraction does not take place, and the force of life is conducted as life. And that conductivity is felt as pleasure, as free consciousness, without distraction by thought. It is loving, open, light, forceful. So the key to true spiritual life is not the life-force itself, not any activity, not Kundalini, not any of these secondary manifestations that occur in Satsang. Such things are not the key to true spiritual life, but only some of its possible phenomena. The key to true spiritual life is this re-cognition of your own activity.

In Satsang, the simple relationship to the Guru tends to stimulate all of this. There is also the communicated Force of Truth, or Real Consciousness. All of this tends to intensify and to build a person up at the beginning. One is also given conditions at the level of life, simple conditions, practical ones, functional things for which one is appropriately responsible. Gradually, the stronger one gets, the simpler one gets, the more experienced one becomes in Satsang, the more one begins to listen with free attention, so that one begins to observe oneself, to move toward this insight, this re-cognition of which I speak. And that is the real event of Satsang. Without this re-cognition, one can have all the spiritual phenomena one likes, but they will be only more experience, more suffering. However, if one lives from the point of view of Satsang, these other phenomena can arise and be of interest, and they will provide conditions in which understanding must take place.

When perfect understanding occurs, it will not be your enlightenment, because when it occurs there is no one left. I don't mean that you will be dead, that you will be unconscious, that you will be in oblivion, but the entire principle which is the center of this contracted life will have disappeared. When you open your hand, what happens to your fist? When you release the contraction, the "me" is gone, the search is gone, the whole principle of suffering is undermined. In Satsang you are moving toward the time when this "radical" insight will become significant, real activity. Until they enter into Satsang, people are looking for release from their symptoms. They want to seek, they want relief. They are not prepared for Truth.

Every moment there is this curvature being "created". Why do you think there are thoughts all of the time? Why one thought after the next? Why doesn't it come to an end? The Light is curving compulsively. Why is there suffering all of the time? This activity is compulsive. It is not true life. That's not "how it is". There is compulsive activity, automatic activity, unnecessary activity. There is compulsive curvature, shaping, contraction of the "radical" Force of existence.

DEVOTEE: Why does it happen?

SRI DA AVABHASA: Once you already have this shape, this human body, why is there such a strong tendency to walk around and talk and be a human being? It has already occurred! That is the shape of it. It's not that it is wrong. It is not that you should make a judgment about it. It is very easy, from a superficial standpoint, to get out of sympathy with your own craziness, and then start to resist it again. But all of that is more of the same. When there is this absolute turnabout, this perfect re-cognition of your own activity, then it no longer exists. But the judgment about it, the feeling that you are sort of screwed up, is another form of the whole process. It is more of that vital shock. The whole affair of Satsang is a movement of conscious intensity, looking forward to the moment when you begin to see it, to know it.

When present activity is truly known, the dilemma no longer exists. That doesn't mean that from that moment no more thinking goes on, no more life goes on. This activity that is one's suffering is not life itself, nor has it "created" life. It is only the obstruction to life, an illusory pattern within life. But it is utter, fundamental, inclusive. You can't even pick your nose without doing this. You can't see without being involved in this activity, this avoidance of relationship. You can't think, feel, move, breathe, you do not live one moment, without performing this activity and experiencing its manifestations. So, from the point of view of the dilemma, everything is a form of this activity. The cosmos seems to be made out of suffering to someone who is wedded to dilemma. That is why people become atheistic, insane, chronically depressed. The whole universe seems to justify despair to them, because everything has become a form of it, an extension of their own activity. Their own activity has become the means and form of their perception. Therefore, re-cognition takes place also at every level, absolutely, at every single level, down to the cells, and as high as it can go. On every level where this contraction occurs, this re-cognition also can take place. When it has occurred, when this activity, this contraction, this avoidance of relationship is thoroughly undone, undermined, and only the Truth is lived, then something about the nature of the phenomenon of universal and cosmic life begins to become clear. From the "point of view" of Truth, life is allowable and good. Perhaps one might choose other forms of life, but in itself the present form becomes clear.

In its simplest form, its most intimate form, its most obvious form, the activity I'm talking about is the avoidance of relationship. And it is to be seen in a very simple, practical observing of life, of you alive in relationship. There is really no subtlety whatsoever to this seeing. It is the crudest kind of self-knowledge. But it is also the most unavailable from the ordinary point of view, because what is to be known is the ordinary point of view.

DEVOTEE: Is it possible, as some have said, for a person to die and then be re-born as an animal?

SRI DA AVABHASA: This whole question of reincarnation and the knowledge of processes like that can be approached from a couple of points of view. For most people it is a matter of experimental living and experiencing. By the use of various internal and psychic means they recollect past lives, see images of other people's lives, see their destinies, whatever. These are the usual means, particularly among Westerners, whereby people

121

have approached such phenomena, to discover if they are true or real. But there is another approach, which is the way of the Great Siddhas, the "completed" ones. That is the way of Divine Self-realization, the realization of Truth. When there is this perfect re-cognition of which I speak, when there is perfect understanding, such a one lives only as Truth. Then one also knows what birth is, what mind is, what life is. One sees it is all the result of tendencies subtly manifested in the Light of Consciousness, which take form in and as the manifested world. One knows this with absolute certainty. One sees this clearly. Truth, therefore, is the basis of one's knowledge of all phenomena, including reincarnation. But one may enjoy this realization without the least suggestion or recollection of reincarnation in one's own case, without remembering, even vaguely in a dream, a single moment of any past life. This is because Self-realization, or perfect knowledge, is not compatible with "birth". One who lives as the very Self has no sense whatsoever of being born as this body, no sense whatsoever of containment, of existing now, of being limited now to one's own mind, one's own life. If one has this kind of relationship to the apparent phenomena of one's present existence, how could one possibly get involved with knowing anything at all about the past of one's dying personality? What could possibly interest one about it? How could such a one possibly discover anything about it? Every time that one zeros in on his or her own mind, he or she sees billions of worlds and other beings. How is that one going to pick himself or herself out? Where is that one? How does that one find a destiny for himself or herself in the midst of the universes, when he or she cannot even discover his or her own life as a substantial and separate event? So this Fullness of Truth has also made it impossible for such a one to get serious and experimental knowledge about his or her own past or future as an individual. But that one's root-awareness of the structure itself, which comes out of the Heart, shows him or her clearly the nature of all patterns, without otherwise giving him or her experience on the plane of recollection, on the plane of mind, on the secondary planes of life.

If you examine the nature and fundamental structure of life itself, it is clear that something like regression, or rebirth, apparent rebirth, in animal form after once having lived in human form, is possible, just as it can occur in dreams. In dreams you can take on various forms in various worlds. The same condition applies to birth in these waking realms of life. But if you begin to become sensitive to your present condition, you may become terrified even of moving into this human condition again!

An affinity for plants and animals is another thing altogether. The vital, descending life in human beings is made up of mechanisms that are found elsewhere in nature. It is made of the same forces, the same kind of functional life. In one of my talks I made an analogy between the human mechanism and a man walking a dog.[4] We are like a mind walking a dog. The vital mechanism is an animal and vegetal mind, a mind like that which governs the organisms and compounds of nature below the human being in the scheme of processes. Therefore, in the vital level of consciousness, human beings have a strong affinity and identification with animals, plants, natural phenomena, nature. Because they partake of that same functional life, that same level of energy, they recognize it in the environment, and enjoy association with it. Someone once asked Ramana Maharshi about the practice of retiring to the forest. As it is described in certain of the old texts, such as the *Bhagavad Gita,* one should set up a seat in the wilderness, in a forest area, under nice circumstances, with streams nearby, etc. This person asked Ramana Maharshi's permission to do this. But Ramana Maharshi pointed out that when people go out and do this sort of thing, to get away from humanity and all of the complications of ordinary life, they begin to become fascinated with animals instead, and animal life, vital life. They sympathize with it, enjoy it, and gradually become like it. As a consequence, they wind up in a worse condition than before. The relationship that one tends to take up with living beings, animals, plants, nature, is a direct indication of one's relationship to the vital, and that is all. If you become very sympathetic with the vital movements in yourself, the forms of vital desire, you will also tend to be very "sympathetic" with animals. If you tend to exploit your own vital life, you will tend also to fail to manage animals, plant life, and the like. If you resist utterly, and are vitally contracting to the point of interference with your own vital life, even with life itself, you will tend to have the same effect on other life-forms. No one, for instance, can tolerate being disliked by their friend's animals! If you go to visit a friend, it is very upsetting if the dog doesn't like you, if the cat doesn't like you. It is very upsetting if you can't grow plants, if flowers die quickly when placed near your bed! But all of this—your relationships to plants, to animals, to life-forms—is a precise dramatization of your relationship to the vital in your own case.

In many people who are unconscious, the vital is smarter than they are. The vital takes over, absorbing their lives from birth to death, and they never exceed it. You must have at least seen photographs of people who are wedded to the earth, who live in isolated farmlands. How unconscious these people seem, from the point of view of one who has been brought up in cities, or in sophisticated social regions. How unconscious these people seem, asleep in the vital without their minds: "They don't speak very much, they are quiet, they are slow, they seem stupid. They seem like cattle, but they are often strangely violent." City people, however, tend to be contracted in relation to the vital. Western people are essentially very resistive to the whole vital life. Americans, for example, are obsessed with sex—not really obsessed with the having of sex but with the failure of sex, and the wanting of it. There is very little actual or successful having of it, because the whole sexual process is so obstructed. The whole participation in the life-force has been undermined by Western society's bondage to its idiot, symbolic religious path—the Jesus-Yahweh number. Not that all of that was necessarily or actually contained in the work of Jesus and the Hebrew men of knowledge, but it is contained certainly in the religious movements that have come down to us. There is a strong suppression in relation to the vital. So everybody is trained in his or her "vital shock" from the beginning, trained to resist his or her entire vital life, his or her lifeline. Money, food, and sex are problematic for everybody, in the sense of a chronic resistance, a chronic doubt about whether or not one is supposed to have anything to do with such things.

Many people come to the Ashram whose emotional-sexual relationships have broken up. There was a case the other day of a relationship that had broken up because the man tended to get into the "celibacy" number. In many other cases, people have come who may not have broken up a relationship over this, but they have just never really been able to sustain a sexual relationship over any length of time, and part of the rationale is that they want to become celibate. They want to become swamis and nuns! For the most part, this "swami" idealism that many Westerners are getting into is an attempted solution to their resistance to vitality, their chronic social reaction to the vital condition, to life.[5] The popular swing toward swamiism, toward artificially induced spiritual celibacy, is a form of emasculation. It is a form of impotence. But there can be no spirituality without the life-force. If you cut off the life-force, you have gone back to zero. The spiritual process makes immediate use of the life-force and its conductivity. Really, the problem of spiritual life, for anyone, West or East, is not whether to be celibate or not. Your choices about sexuality are always a manifestation of your dilemma, not your wisdom, until you understand. The core of it all is the re-cognition of this contraction in the vital.

DEVOTEE: Why is it that so many of the Eastern teachings we read seem to insist on celibacy as necessary for spiritual life?

SRI DA AVABHASA: Examine the cultural life from which the Eastern wisdom comes, especially among the Hindus. It is essentially among the Hindus that celibacy is insisted upon, not really so much, or at least so universally, in other cultures. This is because the traditional Hindu notion of spiritual realization is one in which the vital and subtle life has been abandoned, and the conscious existence has returned to a high or highest state, never to be reborn. Therefore, the processes by which they seek realization necessarily involve the reduction of the whole pattern of life, even the subtle life, to the point of abandonment. Such is the precondition for realization in their terms.

Now, when this pattern of conductivity of which I speak is restored, such a person may, because of his or her subtle tendencies, be celibate. In fact, when this current is felt very intensely at the level of the life-vehicles, very often the sexual impulse just disappears for various periods of time. In some people it disappears permanently. And there is an internal process that replaces their sexuality entirely. But the arbitrary demand of celibacy—in the sense of idealistic avoidance of emotional-sexual intimacy, or avoidance of appropriate realization of sex in the form of such intimacy—as an absolute practice for all, is of relatively recent origin even among the Hindus. The ancient Rishis[6] were almost always sexually active.

The Guru is not some impotent old rascal. The Guru should be able to populate the earth. The Guru is strong. The Guru is alive. The Guru enjoys mastery over the sex-impulse. The Guru may, as a spontaneous practice, be entirely celibate, even in emotional-sexual relationship. But the Guru is not in any case empty or obstructed in relation to the life-force.

In Western culture it is generally not terribly appropriate or necessary to be celibate in the exclusive sense of the avoidance of sexual realization in the form of emotional-sexual intimacy. However, it is absolutely necessary from the spiritual point of view for the whole dilemma in the vital to break down. And it is not just in terms of sexuality that this dilemma is manifested. It is money, or life-exchange, food, and sex. It is the whole vital life. Many people have what appears to them a functional sex-life, one that is enjoyable and seems to work fine for them. But their relationship to the force of life may itself be very mediocre. They may have functional problems in other areas, in other forms of life or psyche, in the environment, in relation to diet.

In the East, particularly among the Hindus, there is a tendency to de-vitalize, to separate from the vital. In the West there is a tendency to ex-ploit the vital. There is that tendency, but on top of the tendency to exploit the vital there is a vast system of taboos against the vital. So, in relation to the vital, the West has a peculiar problem, and the East has another pecu-liar problem. In the East there is an orientation to what is beyond the vital, and in the West the orientation is to the vital. In the East they say you are here for the wrong reasons, because you are suffering from illusion, you have left the Truth, you have left God. In the West they say you are here because God sent you. And in each case there are peculiarly different dramas at the level of ordinary life and vitality. But from the point of view of the real process of conscious life, the vital is a primary seat of spiritual activity.

Suffering is felt, seen, experienced, from day to day essentially in vital terms by human beings. The best "cave" is an ordinary life, a relational life, a functional life. That is where you find your discipline, that is where you become strong, that is where you become truly responsible for your-self. Relationships are the best circumstance of spiritual practice. Intimate relationships, functional conditions, these are the best "Bodhi Tree".[7] These are the true "ascetic" practices. Emotional-sexual commitment is the primary ascetic practice, as everyone who is so committed knows! Anyone can be apparently "religious", anyone can be apparently "spiritu-al", but anyone who lives with the Guru knows how difficult and de-manding true spiritual life really is. It is easy to play imaginary games about religious and spiritual things, but to live spiritual life as the condi-tion of relationship is a very difficult task. To think about sexual experi-ences, to think about men, women, pornography, whatever, to have sexu-al desires and images, is one thing, but to live sexuality as a relationship is very difficult. So with spirituality as a relationship, it is also very diffi-cult. But just as there is no real sexuality without relationship, there is no real spirituality without relationship. There is no fulfillment of spiritual life without the Guru, and without truly living conditions for sadhana.

In all traditional religious cultures you find the professionally ascetic people. They are not necessarily living spiritual life any more than anyone else. In most cases such "asceticism" is a form of self-indulgence. It is an expression of the failure of life. It is an expression of the contraction from life. A vital and subtle shock is the origin of all ordinary spiritual and reli-gious means. But under the real conditions of spiritual life, intelligence begins to arise in relation to sexuality. The individual becomes very sensi-tive to that process and its true nature.

Simple exploitation of sexuality is another method of trying to exhaust this contracted vital. Most people use sexuality as a means of letting off steam, as a form of release. They are attached to the goal of orgasm. They manage to achieve temporary physical stasis by the revulsion, or shedding, of force. But one who lives genuine spiritual life is always conducting the force of life, as vitality and as subtlety. Such a one lives these functions that appear in the circuit of force appropriately, in relationship. Such a one gets smart! When one employs sexual energy out of relationship, or purely for the sake of orgasm, when one simply exploits it, one only empties oneself, and one discovers that one suffers. So the truly spiritual man or woman has simply become intelligent. His or her way of life is not a result of preferences to be lifeless, sexless, or anything else. Such a one becomes intelligent. Such a one becomes capable of relationship. Such a one becomes capable of the real use of the vital functions. Indeed, such a one knows when not to use them, and how not to indulge or exploit them. One allows this force of life to conduct itself fully. One need not, because of the contraction in the vital, simply release this force by vital means. One is not compelled to enjoy it only in the belly or only in the sex organs. One can enjoy it in the top of the head. One can enjoy it in the face. One can enjoy it in the spine. One has got all kinds of places where one can enjoy it. The subtler one becomes, the more one's enjoyments increase. One discovers the source of energy, so that one doesn't weaken oneself, so that one doesn't become involved in a pattern that only empties oneself, that weakens and kills oneself.

There is a process, a spontaneous, internal, Yogic process, that can be felt in the sex organs, in which the force that normally becomes sex-stimulation is felt going in the opposite direction, backward and upward. Instead of seeking release in the sex-function, that energy can be felt pulling, drawing, towards the spine, upwards. When that particular process is very active, intensely active, there is natural celibacy. Then even in the emotional-sexual relationship, the event of orgasm is not sought, but the relational force of love and shared pleasure is intensified.

The Kundalini process is closely associated with what is otherwise felt as sex-energy, although it doesn't simply come from the sex organs, and is not itself literally or exclusively sex-energy. It is the ascending movement of the circle of total energy in which the human being lives. It is a continuation of the conductivity of the descending force. Its lowest terminal in the body is at the base of the sex organs. And that terminal is the turning point, from descent to ascent, but not the origin of the energy itself. The muladhar[8] is this turning point. The intense Kundalini manifestations are generally associated with this reversal of the sex-current. A person who is going through a period of strong kriyas, or some such episode of intense internal activity, will often quite naturally be celibate during that time. Or the person will discover that if he or she exploits himself or herself sexually, through orgasm, while going through this process, certain unpleasant things occur, physiologically and psychically. And so one learns by experience of processes of this kind how to deal with one's sexuality. Therefore, the use or non-use of sexuality is a matter of intelligence, not a matter of preference, not a matter of "how it is supposed to be if you are getting spiritual".

Perfect "celibacy" is death. Then the cycle of life-force turns from descent to ascent, draws up completely into the sahasrar, and never comes down again. That is precisely what the traditional Yogi whose point of view is willful celibacy is trying to do. He or she is trying to die consciously, and literally. Now, the Yogic process of "spiritual death" will take place in any case, whether you have literal separation from life as your peculiar goal or not. True celibacy is Yogic, or spiritual, "death". Yogic death is part of the nature of real meditation, but it doesn't in itself imply the literal end of life or the diminution of life-involvement. Continued living of an ordinary, functional life on every level is perfectly compatible with the realized state, because life itself is an expression of what is Real. It is a manifestation of the Conscious Light. It has tended to take on this peculiar form because of certain tendencies, which are modifications of that Light, but in itself it is not false. Only its complications are false. The life of Truth is absolutely compatible with life itself, with vitality, and with sexuality as regenerative union.

The bellies of the Yogic Siddhas are often full, soft, and round. They are not devitalized beings, even if they happen to be celibate. That swelling of the abdomen is a Yogic manifestation. When the living energy is fully conducted, the abdomen becomes Yogically full of energy. Swami Nityananda of Ganeshpuri[9] was such a Yogi. He spent his days sitting and lying around, letting this current circle about. He rarely allowed it to turn outwards. That is why he hardly ever spoke.

I have told you that speech is a form of sacrifice. It is a sacrifice of the life-force. It is not entertainment. People generally talk in order to empty themselves. That is another form of throwing the force out of this contraction so they don't suffer it anymore. Whenever there is speech, whenever there is communication with the environment, whenever there is relationship, whenever there is use of the life-force, it is sacrifice. Sexuality is a form of sacrifice. It <u>does</u> tend to make you empty, unless you know fully how to make use of that process, how to conduct its generative energy into the cycle of regeneration. If I sat here and talked endlessly, occasionally going to sleep and taking food here, the talking alone would eventually kill me. I would die from speech! Any exploitation of the life-force will kill you, and people are in fact dying from this abuse. People are dying from a complex exploitation of the life-force. They don't conduct it. They only <u>use</u> it. They don't refresh themselves. They don't live this circuit of energy even a little bit. Some of the Yogis <u>only</u> lived it. So they left. Others continued to be communicative at the level of life in various ways, knowing the consequences, knowing what they needed to do to remain fresh. That is why I look forward to the time when I can speak less and write less, or at least have such control over it that I only need to do it when it seems absolutely useful and necessary. Because this current is continuous. When I am sitting, my teeth are clenched, my tongue presses against the roof of my mouth. The circuit is continuous, and as it flows even the cells are transformed.

The death of a Great Siddha is really not separation from anything. The Siddha is simply gone into meditation perfectly. After death the Siddha's body is meditation. And the Siddha's disciples have access to him or her through real meditation, because meditation itself is the Siddha's eternal or perfect Form. The Siddha simply abandons his or her bodily sacrificial function, outward movement, psycho-physical game, and goes permanently into his or her Divine state. The Siddha was already in it before, but he or she abandons the functions that were attached to it, at least those which were the manifestation of his or her present life. This is why people prize the "samadhi site", the burial site, of their Guru. Because the Guru has gone into meditation in its most intense form while associated with that body. Many people find the Force communicated from the Guru seems to get stronger after the Guru's death, because it has become completely without complication by the life-form. The Guru has moved into the most intense manifestation of that Real Consciousness.

It is said that Saint Jnaneshwar[10] consciously took mahasamadhi.[11] He had a tomb built for himself, and he went down inside. He was a young man, only about twenty or twenty-one years old. He went down inside and sat in his chair. They sealed it over, and he just didn't come out anymore. It is also said that about three hundred years later another Indian Saint somehow got into Jnaneshwar's tomb and approached the body. He reported that the body was apparently still alive. It had a certain heat to it, and it wasn't the least decomposed, because the Yogic activity was going on in this body permanently. The site of Jnaneshwar's tomb is a very potent one. Not that he is conscious of trucking with that body anymore. Swami Nityananda's tomb is also like that, very strong.

DEVOTEE: Can a Guru who has died still be Guru for the living?

SRI DA AVABHASA: It is limited only at the level of life. He or she can't function as Guru in any manner that requires a physical presence. So he or she usually tries to leave genuine disciples in the world who can continue certain aspects of the Guru-function. One who has had real experience spiritually can read a book written by someone experienced in spiritual life and see things there that he or she knows are true. It corroborates his or her own experience. Just so, one who is already living the real form of spiritual life can approach the burial site of a deceased saint or go to holy places, and benefit from the pilgrimage in that same sense of corroboration, or recognition. The current of spiritual Force continues to be emanated by such beings after death, but Truth is not lived by them bodily in the world. At times people appear to have experiences on a subtle level with people who are dead. In my own experience, in the case of Swami Nityananda, Ramana Maharshi, Sai Baba of Shirdi,[12] and others, there have been very concrete and complex experiences of their subtle influence. Likewise, because my visits with him have been only occasional, my experiences of Swami (Baba) Muktananda[13] have most often been of a subtle, although perfectly concrete, variety, arising entirely apart from the gross physical medium. Just so, my own work with my disciples is fundamentally subtle.

DEVOTEE: Are there other people in the world who are like you?

SRI DA AVABHASA: I don't know what it is to be like me. Those who are living Truth in the earth plane can't necessarily be discerned by obvious signs. They are ordinary. Perhaps also in some sense extraordinary, but they are real. Of those who are appearing publicly as teachers, very few have anything directly to do with Truth.

DEVOTEE: You have said that all people are suffering. I have the feeling that you and those Teachers that you have had and all the Great Siddhas are the only people who are not suffering.

SRI DA AVABHASA: The only ones who are not suffering are those who are living Truth. And who those are that are living Truth is to be seen. Truth is the most profound Reality, the most "radical" Reality. It is the Nature of all beings and the Nature of all life. It is already all human beings. When I see people in the world, I don't see them as garbage, all screwed up, simply insane, as nothingness that I am supposed for some reason or other to turn into Divinity. I see everybody already as that same Reality. I am no exclusive form of It. But I see people suffering. While they are being Truth only, I see them suffering. The fact that they are suffering doesn't make them any less the Truth, any less the same thing that is all beings, all things. It simply means that they are suffering. If you look at all beings from the "point of view" of Truth, there is only Truth, and the Truth has this little chronic problem!

From the point of view of human beings, it all seems very heavy, because their point of view is the point of view of this limitation. But once they themselves begin to see from the "point of view" of Truth, they see that every thing is already Truth, and every one. To realize that you are already Truth doesn't make you any more than anybody else. It makes you the <u>same</u> as everybody else. It is the sameness of very Truth, that sameness from which all the functional inequalities of relative, conditional existence arise.

There is a certain obnoxiousness that comes into this illusion as well, in the form of righteousness, in the form of false claims, in the form of exploitation. That is also part of this illusion. And, at times, I speak critically about that. I must, because people are suffering from their illusions. If I see a phony making great claims, I am likely to tell you so. Why should I stand for such lies, that exploitation of people, that reinforcement of suffering?

DEVOTEE: I am curious about this notion of responsibility, especially from your point of view. Why should you care at all that a person is suffering from having a false Guru?

SRI DA AVABHASA: It is a natural function of the intensity of Truth, as It moves into life, to purify. When the Force of Satsang approaches an individual, It can't do anything but be the Force of Truth when It gets here. It doesn't start to fade out on the way and become a black widow spider! It is Truth, It arrives as Truth, and It functions as the Truth in that life. It does only that purifying work. It becomes only that intensity of Light, and

It leads only into the process of Truth. Where Truth is lived in the life-plane, It only functions as Truth. Not out of some sort of "concern", some karmic concern to save the world, but as a natural extension of Its own Nature, Its real activity.

DEVOTEE: So in other words it is a spontaneous thing?

SRI DA AVABHASA: When a person starts to gain some sort of position among others by representing Truth to them, he or she is implying something about the great work of the Divine Siddhas. It is not that I am going to start taking out newspaper advertisements about various people, exposing them. I don't have anything to say about it socially. And I am not going to go over to these people or to their disciples and get into arguments with them about the Nature of Truth. But there are many here who know of various teachers. I am here speaking to you. I am not somewhere else, speaking at a paid lecture. So in order to serve the very thing I am attempting to communicate, when there is somebody specific we are discussing, I must clarify what is being represented by him or her. That is simply a responsible extension of the work that I am doing. Apart from that, I don't have any concern for it. As a social event, I have no particular concern for it. I enjoy seeing people become sensitive to the real manifestation of Truth, and begin to see the falseness of charlatans, people who are themselves deluded and who are only exploiting others.

DEVOTEE: It seems that, from the "point of view" of Truth, the process of being born causes an automatic reaction that is death.

SRI DA AVABHASA: For every action there is an equal and opposite reaction. The action of life produces the reaction of the living, even to the point of death.

DEVOTEE: It seems like we are born with three strikes against us.

SRI DA AVABHASA: Yes. That is why you have got to get smart down here! A living being arising in the midst of life is automatically the reaction to the prior action which is life itself. It is quite a natural mechanism. If it becomes the principle of life, reaction "creates" death. And the natural tendency of organic life is to contract, to become more solid and lifeless. It begins to die the moment it makes its appearance. And there are more than three strikes against you. You are already out, already, before the strikes. I have lost my taste for the usual life. Not that I can't enjoy the quality of real life, but I have lost my taste for this whole affair of suffering and compulsive existence. I see perfectly well what it depends on. I wouldn't choose, on the merits of the experience itself, ever to be born in this human condition again. There is no percentage in it. It gains nothing. It is just a period of time in which to understand. Apart from that, it has no ultimate value. It never goes beyond that. Human life is not particularly delightful. It is an endless concern from birth until death. Every minute is suffering of the limited state, or an attempt to break out of it through various kinds of activity, trying to find the answer. From the moment of its awareness, this life _is_ a question. It seems absurd to be actually existing and yet not to know what actually existing is, and to spend the entire period of actually existing trying to discover what actually existing is! This is an insane condition! It is a compulsive tour of unconscious activity for the most part. If Truth begins to manifest in life, as life, It glorifies life to some degree. But the glory that enters life is not that of life itself. It is the glory of the Fullness of Truth, which is manifested as life, whose modifications are life. The more the life of Truth grows, the more the taste for <u>Truth</u> you acquire, not for life apart from or other than Truth. And when Truth is perfectly enjoyed, life becomes secondary, perhaps profound, but unnecessary. Your death in Truth should precede your physical death by at least a few moments! Otherwise the tendency to regain this condition is there automatically.

The Condition that is Truth is far superior to this limitation. And those who live Truth while alive are not glorifying life in itself. They are glorifying Truth. When you enjoy Truth, you are already free. And if you are free, what has all of this compulsive limitation to do with you? Such a one lives Truth until death, and then slips away. And everyone will slip away in Truth sooner or later. The Guru is only looking for company on the way out! The Guru has already discovered who you are. The Guru already is living with you in another sense, as real life, as love, as Truth. The Guru no longer requires your physical existence or his or her own. The Guru looks forward to your perfect enjoyment. But the Guru sees that those who are living in the earth plane are not clear about this, not certain of it, a little confused. So the Guru communicates it in as many forms as he or she can. But all the Guru is trying to do is to take you away, to take your separate life away, to snuff you out of darkness into Light.

Real meditation is not unlike death. The same process goes on in this spontaneous meditation that happens in death. The only difference is that in death the life-force permanently moves out of this vital mechanism, but in real meditation, in Sahaj Samadhi, in the true state, the life-force may continue to conduct itself in this form. One who has lived this whole process and knows it well, knows very well that he or she is not merely alive. Such a one knows absolutely well that being alive is not one's real limitation. It is absolutely clear. Such a one is not believing it, not thinking it. Such a one is already dead, presently dead, presently not alive as the limitation that is the psycho-physical life, the body. If that one were alive as that limitation, he or she would still be afraid. If it were still clear to me that I was alive as the limitation of life, I wouldn't have any time to sit with you in this Ashram. I would be busy hysterically doing all the things that occupied me in the search.

When that "death" is attained and only Truth is enjoyed, there is no more of that search. Then there is only the "creative" enjoyment of living this process in relation to other beings. And that "radical" meditation is continuous, perfect. No embodiment, no identification with the life-force, no identification with the subtle forms of existence, no identification with the levels of mind, with thoughts, with visions, with lights, with phenomena of any kind. They are not lived. That is the paradox of the jnani, the person of real knowledge. Ramana Maharshi said he was like somebody asleep while awake. While awake, while the manifested forms are flying around, while the body hangs out and all the feelings and sensations are there, while the thoughts are running along, the one who understands has no sense at all of any containment, any limitation to that process. Such a one doesn't have to meditate in the traditional way at all in order to feel free of that. Such a one doesn't have to stop the thought-process in order to be free of thoughts. His or her samadhi is perfect, endless. The whole life-phenomenon takes on a kind of indefinite, fluid, homogeneous quality, a paradoxical form, a kind of brilliance, so that it loses its capability to define existence or Consciousness. Everything becomes Consciousness, everything becomes his or her very Consciousness, everything becomes his or her own thought. Such a one has nothing left but humor while alive. And his or her humor is of a "radical" kind. Such a one is not necessarily always laughing. His or her humor is of the nature of no-identification with all of this. The freedom of such a one is extreme, beyond the point of wildness, so that he or she is no longer wild. His or her extremes are manifested as ordinariness. His or her extremes are his or her natural appearance. Walking into a room is a maddening extreme from his or her "point of view". It is odd. It is wildly imaginative! When such a one contemplates his or her own Consciousness, when he or she contemplates being Consciousness Itself, he or she almost, or even actually, falls into trance. So, instead of contemplating Consciousness, such beings look at people, they talk, they do ordinary things—because everything has become insubstantial and unnecessary for them. Their blissfulness has exceeded all of the conditional Yogic states, all of the phenomena of spirituality, because those states again are forms of containment, forms of self-modification. Such enlightened beings have lost the taste, the motive, for mere experiencing. They live only as that unmodified Reality, lightless, soundless, formless, without qualities. And yet, everything is Its modification. Therefore, when living the humor that is their formlessness, their qualityless existence, they, paradoxically, live. For such a one, all life is paradox. And life is no longer a question. For such a one there is not the least trace of dilemma left in the universe. Such a one has no question, and no answer. Such a one is only humorous.

In many cultures, such "humorous" people have taken on the role of a fool. They acted crazy, so that people wouldn't burden them with demands for "wisdom"—because they really didn't have anything to say. They just enjoyed bubbling in the street. And bubbling is really what it is all about. Having to work with everyone at the life-level, the vital level, from day to day tends to become very humorless, because everybody is very serious about his or her life-problems. Every day people come here with their crisis, their revolution this week, their number. All of that is very heavy, very disturbing for them, and rightfully so. But to deal with it, to manufacture seriousness over all of that, has none of the beauty of bubbling. So the more people begin to enjoy Satsang, in Its subtle form, in Its absolute form, the sillier the Guru gets, the more absurd the Guru gets, the more the Guru begins to act in forms that symbolize or express his or her true state. Such humorous people become very "odd", and everything they do is a symbol of their own state. Just so, everything that anyone does symbolizes his or her own state. The humorous person becomes less and less involved in trying to communicate to people the contracted nature of their ordinary state, and he or she begins simply to manifest his or her own free State as a playful activity.

An Ashram must be very straight for such a person to act so freely. So you only find people of that variety acting so freely in very traditional cultures. In Swami Nityananda's Ashram he was free to bubble all the time.

So he became a symbol for the Divine Self, because he took on very few functions at the life-level as Guru. Baba Muktananda always assumed a great many functions, and, as a consequence, he has generally seemed to have less of that kind of quality that Swami Nityananda had. However, over time, even Baba Muktananda is showing more of the "silliness" of the Truth. Ramana Maharshi, like Swami Nityananda, also was a relatively functionless person. The more functions the Siddhas have had, the less of a symbol they seemed to pose in the world, the less they seemed to symbolize or play the Truth while alive. That doesn't mean they were of a lesser nature. It is just that they took on various functions, the functions of this sacrificial activity. Even so, all such people, in spite of their many functions, remain paradoxical, humorous figures.

**Sri Da Avabhasa
at Sri Love-Anandashram, 1992**

5.

Walking the Dog

DEVOTEE: Would you explain what you mean by "relationship"?

SRI DA AVABHASA: What does it mean?

DEVOTEE: I'm not sure. Perhaps simply not to avoid reality.

SRI DA AVABHASA: What is relationship?

DEVOTEE: To be with someone is to be in relationship. Talking to you is being in relationship.

SRI DA AVABHASA: What if there is no one there?

DEVOTEE: Then you are in relationship to your surroundings, and to yourself.

SRI DA AVABHASA: What if there is no thing there?

DEVOTEE: Then you are in relationship to no thing.

SRI DA AVABHASA: Then what is the problem about relationship?

DEVOTEE: I guess I am trying to dig into it and grasp something that is not there.

SRI DA AVABHASA: What is not relationship?

DEVOTEE: It seems to me there is nothing that is not relationship.

SRI DA AVABHASA: Did you appear on your own?

DEVOTEE: No. Not that I know of!

SRI DA AVABHASA: Is there any thing that arises on its own?

DEVOTEE: No.

SRI DA AVABHASA: Is there any thing perfectly, or "radically", separate from any other thing?

DEVOTEE: Intellectually I may think there is. But I don't really think of things as separate.

SRI DA AVABHASA: Do you think of yourself as being separate?

DEVOTEE: I'm afraid that is my state of consciousness. I am thinking of myself as separate.

SRI DA AVABHASA: That is the point! There is only relationship, no separation, only mutuality, interdependence. If anything has arisen, there is only relationship. Yet most of the time you do not observe that fact, you do not observe relationship. Most of your time is spent being obsessed with your separateness. This separateness is not true. But all of the time you are thinking this separateness. All of the time you are acting as if it were so. All of the time you are meditating on it. All of the time you are seeking to become free of it. And yet, among all things that arise, this thought is not true, and it is truly the least valuable of all that arises. Understanding is the re-cognition, or knowing again, of that assumption of your separateness.

If I ask, "What is there?" you might think: "This space. I move around in it. I am this one." When you think about that, it doesn't strike fear in you. You live that, with a grin on your face, as if it were so. But that is not the problem. The problem is that "I" am suffering, that "I" am in dilemma, that "I" need this, that "I" haven't realized this, that "I", that "I", that "I". This sense of separate existence, this contracted form of living consciousness, is suffering. And it is obviously so to everyone, whenever they fail to be distracted and so fall only into the mood and condition of separate, mortal existence.

But Truth is not even the destruction of that. Truth is not the suppression, the quieting, or the explosion of that, nor the union of that with anything. Truth is not <u>anything</u> done to that "I", or with it. Truth is in the spontaneous re-cognition, or knowing again, of the entire process in which this "I", this separate sense, also appears. Therefore, Truth is not a conditional state—it is not a state of inwardness, of attachment to mindlessness, quietness, or formlessness, nor of attachment to vision or lights, to sensations, sensual or supersensual. Truth is in the "radical" re-cognition of all of that. Truth is in the knowing again of your entire adventure, which is a span of possible qualities, from ordinary suffering to the intuitive contemplation of very Self, Reality, Guru, and God. But Truth Itself is a "radical" simplicity. It cannot even be called the "Self" or "ultimate Reality". There is no-thing. Reality cannot be cognized, not even as an <u>ultimate</u> object outside your own apparent consciousness. Truth can only be already enjoyed, already the case.

Understanding is simply to observe this separation, this contraction, of which I often speak. <u>Really</u> observe it. When you really observe this contraction, only relationship stands out. To truly observe it is to <u>see</u> what it is. Not just as a symptom, the "feeling" that "I am separate", or "I am suffering", or any other form of thinking, thinking. But to <u>actually</u> observe it is to comprehend it as the avoidance of relationship. To re-cognize this separate self sense is to turn consciously into relationship.

The natural state of consciousness is not "me". It is not in any sense the feeling of being apart, observing things apart, or feeling the dilemma of being separate. The natural state of consciousness is no-contraction, no-dilemma. Instead of this turning away, it is relationship. It is all of this—connection! All of this relationship. The natural, or true, state is no-obsession with this contraction, no-obsession with "me", no-obsession with all of "that", separate from me—simply, no-contraction. When there is no contraction, what is there? There is only relationship, presently enjoyed as the natural, or effortless, state of consciousness.

Natural consciousness <u>is</u> relationship. Natural consciousness is not separate "me". Natural consciousness is relationship. To enjoy the natural state of consciousness is to be conscious as relationship, or no-contraction, which is effortless existence. And when natural consciousness is enjoyed as it is, <u>as</u> relationship, not <u>in</u> relationship but <u>as</u> relationship, then it is also seen that relationship contains no "other" and no "me".

There is a fundamental quality that you are familiar with all the time in your ordinary occupation: feeling others, feeling in connection, observing relationship in that simple sense. That quality is the natural quality of the living consciousness. It is one's own natural form! Natural consciousness is not "in" relationship, experiencing an "other". Natural consciousness is itself relationship. Therefore, one who perfectly enjoys no-contraction sees there is only Consciousness Itself. Indeed, such a one has never passed a single moment of involvement with anything but Consciousness Itself, his or her own real, or ultimate, State. All of the time one spent "observing" everything outside oneself, thinking all of this was outside oneself, was actually the observation of the endless modifications of one's own real, or ultimate, State. But as long as one was busy separating oneself, contracting, avoiding relationship, the Force of Consciousness Itself appeared as "me". And that is the dilemma.

The usual man or woman "observes", but only intellectually, mentally, whatever, that there is only a vast universe of interconnected events, phenomena, forces. And yet he or she remains continually, chronically, obsessed with the notion of being separate, self-contained, isolated, containing only twenty volts, or whatever it is, always becoming empty, threatened to death, becoming more and more "compact", until he or she disappears. People fail to live the principle of their own observation. They continue to remain obsessed. And the adventures of obsessed human beings are endless. There are endless ways to play it, but none of it makes any sense whatsoever.

I am continually impressed, newly impressed from hour to hour, with the insanity of human beings! Animals, plants, inert things have much more intelligence! They are simpler, more pure. While driving a car or walking down a street, I have often seen people walking their dogs. And the dogs almost invariably appear more intelligent than the people who are walking them. The guy walking his dog seems insane. He is obsessed with his idiotic program of existence. But the dog is just breathing, walking, pissing on the grass. No sign of disturbance at all. The dog sits down at the corner, and I see his clear eyes! But the guy is everywhere else, costumed, crowded into time, bent, driven, mysterious to himself!

The only release from the burden of the insanity of this world is humor. There are two forms of that humor. There is mortal humor and Divine humor. Ordinarily the best people do is mortal humor. Thus, you tend to laugh about this image of the man and the dog. But the only true humor is Truth. The comic humor of your mortal appreciation of things is only laughter. It doesn't change the conditions or even truly understand them. Mortal laughter does not change the condition of human beings, apart from the generation of temporary amusement. But Divine humor, Truth, delights people and also utterly transforms their lives.

Until this Divine humor, this Truth, awakens in people, they are intimidated by "animals", or the vital forces of life. Without a little of Truth, they haven't even got enough of manhood (man or woman) to be the master of a dog. A good dog is too straight for most people. And I have met very few people who could master a cat! Just so, people are intimidated by their own desires, their own moving life, their own vital nature. Animals and other vital beings are just extensions of a human being's own vitality. Every man or woman is endlessly "walking a dog". The animal hangs below your chest, and you walk it night and day. You are intimidated by it, completely obsessed by it, absolutely distracted by it, incapable of being the master of it, unwilling to go through the period of mastery, of training, of responsibility. And so, the "dog" takes over.

When people come to visit you at your house, you all sit around and talk about the dog! Have you noticed that whenever somebody has a pet, people who visit tend continually to talk about the animal, and to the animal? And when conversation drifts away from the animal pets, people talk about the same thing in themselves. They talk about sex, conflict, desire—their obsessions! People are always talking about the dog. Therefore, people are ordinarily humorless. They have no transcendent humor. They only learn how to "create" the ridiculous to entertain one another. The usual entertainments are forms of mortal, or comic, humor. And the means to make others laugh is to take on the form, or "costume", of the dog. Put on a dog costume and go to visit a friend. Your friend won't be able to believe it. Fantastic! Your friend will laugh. Your friend will go out of his or her mind.

There are many forms of the dog, many varieties of the "dog costume". The dog costume is all your adventures, your acquisitions, your knowledge, your every thing, "you". This contraction of which I speak is the dog costume. It is this avoidance of relationship, this falsity, this thinking separation. But true humor is not to appear in the dog costume among your friends. You must restore their humor by showing them the nature of the costume of their mortality, their unhappiness, all the forms of this contraction, this avoidance of relationship.

The ordinary humor is a revulsion, like vomiting. It is heaving the force, the vital force, upwards, throwing it away, casting it out. All the ordinary obsessions, including the entertainments of comic laughter, are forms of revulsion, like vomiting. In that case, the force of life falls down the spine and is thrown out the front. But when a person understands the nature of the whole activity that is his or her obsession, then all of the activities of revulsion tend to subside, and the current of life returns to its natural course, descending and ascending. Thus, the natural conductivity of the life-force is clockwise. But in the usual man or woman it is counterclockwise.

In the ordinary person the "dog" is always hanging out. The ordinary person always appears as the ridiculous imitation of the dog—laughing, grinning, being stupid, insane, confused, self-indulgent—all the things of which animals themselves are actually free. But when a person understands, the "dog" is overcome, is mastered.

Therefore, spiritual life is real humor. It is Divine life, the life of Truth. It is a person's "straightness".

The usual man or woman is always distracted, always concentrating on some invisible point, obsessed with self-awareness, this sense of separation, distracted in endless thoughts, concerns, experiences. People are simply obsessed, distracted, only fascinated. What is amazing, in this manifestation of billions of beings, with billions of human beings, is that one can appear to be born among so many and yet have so little company for a lifetime. Because every one is <u>obsessed</u>! Every one is moving that way, the other way, at light-speed.

Once I worked as a chaplain in a mental hospital. In such places you see the symbol of ordinary men and women. There is <u>no</u> communication in such an asylum. Indeed, the disturbance of communication, or presently engaged relationship, is perhaps what is identified as insanity. Therefore, the Guru appears in the asylum of ordinary people. And what is the function of Guru? It is to distract you again, to stand before you and command attention, to draw you into relationship, to draw you out of your chronic obsession. And that will not happen to you while you are sitting apart in your room, strategically meditating inward! What are you looking at in this turning inward? The same thing that you are <u>always</u> looking at! The same obsession. The usual meditator is just another obsessed person, unaware of relationship as his or her actual condition. So the function of Guru is to continuously draw you into conscious relationship. The Guru works to draw the thread of attention into the form of life. And where the connection is made again, where relationship is consciously lived, the energy of life returns, flows, tends to move, into its natural course again. Therefore, in that relationship, or Satsang, there is the intensification of living energy, until a moment arrives when the disciple is not totally

144

distracted, no longer totally obsessed, not totally inward-turning, but somehow equalized, tacitly aware of relationship. At that stage, insight arises. It is always a very practical insight. The individual sees the avoidance of relationship, if only in one particular form of action. One sees in the particular form of certain kinds of one's chronic action the characteristic activity of one's own avoidance. One observes it very directly, without complication, as one's actual activity. In that instance one sees both one's avoidance and relationship itself. One sees one's natural state, and one sees oneself contracting. Only then has practical wisdom arisen.

This process of intensification and insight continues, in terms of particular actions, particular thoughts, the concrete, actual forms of the disciple's tendencies, movements, "dog costume". At some point, perhaps, the "real meditation" I have described in *The Knee of Listening* may begin. It is the positive approach of intelligence to the particular forms of thought-stress, of action and thought, moment to moment. The "religious" quality of understanding may be manifested at this stage. Its center is the massive vital region above and below the navel. In this case the "dog" has begun to turn to his or her "master". Then at some point, the disciple begins to become "subtle". Suddenly, spontaneously, one finds one's attention is moved out of the vital center, and one finds oneself seated in the "mind", mysteriously within, and even above, where one observes the pattern of one's own thought and life. Now one sees patterns as they arise, not already arisen, not in gross forms and already binding life-conditions. One observes thought-stress, the modified Force of Consciousness, rising out of the heart. One feels it rising. One re-cognizes it to be contraction, separation, modification, obsession. And this moment to moment re-cognition vanishes the force of thought as it rises out of the heart. In yet another moment, this same one may find himself or herself spontaneously to have fallen out of the Light of Consciousness above, even the sahasrar, the epitome of subtle cognition, into the causal being, which feels itself into life from a point in the heart, on the right side of the chest. There the whole force of manifested existence is felt as a single point, the point of unqualified relationship. In the complex life-state, the individual felt relationship in particular forms: "me" and "that". Later, he or she felt relationship as confrontation with the force of thought and subtle forms of cognition. But now he or she senses very existence as a point only. This "point" is the foundation condition of one's living, conscious existence, moment to moment. It is the foundation structure of conditionally manifested existence. Now the disciple has come from the life-center to the subtle center and, finally, to the causal center. And this imageless, form-less, unqualified, spaceless "center" manifests as a point, the point of the heart, tacitly sensed on the right side of the chest. In this state, thought is already vanished when subtle enquiry is transcended. Now the force of this "radical" intelligence, this re-cognition, is active in terms of this single point of consciousness, which is the epitome of all conditional experi-ence. But, suddenly, there is the re-cognition of this point itself. There is seeing that this "point" is also only modification, only a form of con-traction. When this re-cognition arises, the "point" vanishes, or dissolves. And the State Which remains—and Which is called "Nirvana", "Liberation", "Mukti", "Moksha", "Bodhi",[1] and the rest—is, simply, unqualified, or un-conditional, Consciousness Itself. Yet in that same instant of re-cognition, the entire form that has been transcended, or resolved, in this total pro-cess will return. It rises out of the Heart, and it is reflected above as the Light of very Consciousness. That Light in turn is reflected below, in the circle of descent and ascent, the manifested condition of psycho-physical life. The usual form returns, but the separate one does not return with it! In such case, Consciousness is no longer implicated in the process of identification, differentiation, and desire. Very existence no longer ap-pears limited by its own modifications. Then the Force of very existence, rather than the force of thought, rises out of the Heart, and appears above as perfect Light, the Light of Consciousness Itself. It is reflected downward as the energy of life, or all the apparent life-modifications of Consciousness Itself. It descends as Fullness, and it ascends again as Fullness. Such a one appears in the world as before. All forms have re-turned. All the functions remain. There is no peculiarity in such a one, no thing tangible that makes him or her stand out, unique and separate from the ordinary. But there is in such a one this Fullness, this "Brightness",[2] this Force, this very Consciousness. And this may be discovered by others.

The very functions in which people ordinarily perceive their bondage, their suffering, are the means of their deliverance when brought to them in the form of the Guru. In the Guru, these functions in which ordinary men and women perceive their bondage are open, and the Fullness, the Force, the "Brightness", of Truth manifests in and through them. Those who move into relationship with such a one enjoy the process of intensifica-tion that flows between Guru and disciple. And the disciple becomes in-telligent with that intensity, because that very intensity is the Shakti of Truth, the Living Power of Real God. The Shakti of the true Guru is not simply or exclusively the Kundalini Shakti, which is always returning to

Truth, seeking the Truth, seeking the union that is Truth. The Shakti that flows through the true Guru is already the Truth. It is the Force of Truth. It is the One Intensity that is always already Truth.

Where that Intensity is enjoyed in Satsang, the secondary, or functional, forms of the Shakti, such as the Kundalini, all of which are modifications of that One Intensity, may also be experienced. The qualities that are experienced in the individual cases are unique. The forms of modification, or Shakti, in which the individual is characteristically bound, or contracted, are unique from case to case. So the living spiritual process of Satsang manifests itself progressively but uniquely in each individual. But the key to all these spiritual manifestations is the Guru-disciple relationship itself, the Condition of Satsang. All the spiritual qualities rest on Satsang. All of them are Satsang. Satsang is the Great Condition, the Only Condition. It is always already your Condition, but, because of self-contraction, It is not lived. It is denied, forgotten, resisted.

The drama of Narcissus is what obsesses all human beings. Therefore, the Great Condition of Satsang is denied in all the usual events of the world. Thus, the function of Guru arises in the world, to re-establish conscious Satsang, and to make possible the re-cognition of the strategies which prevent It. The true Guru re-establishes Satsang, by virtue of the Siddhi, or great spiritual Power, of Truth. Then, in the case of the true disciple and consummate devotee, Satsang again becomes the Great Condition, the conscious Condition, even of the world.

Therefore, spiritual life begins with Satsang. And sadhana, or true spiritual practice, is to live the Condition of Satsang for a lifetime, even eternally, always recollecting that Condition, living in It, becoming intelligent with It. Truth in life is to live the primary condition of relationship under all conditions while enjoying Satsang with the true Guru at all times. When such sadhana is lived consciously, moment to moment, you have something against which to observe your own contraction, the on-going pattern of Narcissus. Thus, Satsang is the Condition that makes it possible for you to see your own tendencies.

A person's tendencies are always forms of contraction, the avoidance of relationship, which, ultimately, is always turning from Satsang. So every day, hour to hour, there is an endless drama going on in those who live this Satsang. There is the repetitive cycle of coming and going. Every day there is a question of whether my disciples will return. It seems never to end. It is the same every day, in everyone's case. In everyone's case there is the continual wondering in the mind: "Should I go back there, or shouldn't I? I don't want to put up with this anymore, or do I? Don't I really have it already? The Presence always surrounds me already. And my Guru is crazy anyway!" Every day there is a new symbolic form of self-sufficiency, a new "temptation" from Satsang and the discipline of Truth. Therefore, the disciple must become sensitive to what he or she is up to. One must re-cognize one's own game. Previously one was only played by life, and now one seems to play it by ritualizing one's drama in Satsang. Satsang is not here to make you forget that drama of your suffering. The Guru has not come to console you with pleasant and hopeful distractions. The Guru always functions to return you to that state, that activity of avoidance. Satsang does not fulfill your search. Satsang acts, by a subtle frustration of your search, to return you to your dilemma, so that it may be understood. The power of intensification that is alive in Satsang is active in the very seat of dilemma. The Shakti of Satsang operates in the dilemma. The crisis in consciousness is sadhana. The suffering and the intensity is sadhana. Sadhana is not merely the pleasantness. It is not the easy, drifty-blissful, smiling, and stupid meditation of a person sitting cross-legged in a dog costume. Sadhana is living intelligence, conscious in dilemma, but with intensity. The sadhana of Satsang with the true Guru makes a difference!

It is not that the disciple shouldn't go through the dilemma of his or her suffering. One must go through it. It is only that, even though one is going through it, one should continue to maintain oneself in the Condition of Satsang. The greatest mistake people make is to abandon Satsang when they begin to experience Its "tooth". No, even this crisis in relation to Satsang Itself must come. It comes in everyone's case, now or later. And it comes in an incredibly powerful and seductive form, usually very soon after one begins to experience the Guru's discipline. And it always involves the feeling that you should abandon Satsang, abandon this mad Guru. The first form of this crisis is always a personal conflict with this way and this place. And if the disciple gets through that one and stays, the next time it comes in the form of self-doubt rather than Guru-doubt: "It's not working for me. This sadhana is not possible in my case. I'm damned. I'm too crazy. I'm not ready for it." But if the disciple gets beyond these two times, from then on, for the most part, he or she deals with all such phenomena as qualities of his or her hidden strategy, this avoidance of relationship, the drama of Narcissus.

When the disciple becomes capable of enduring this repetitive crisis, when he or she is able to live it as sadhana, as the very spiritual process, then the intelligence of Satsang becomes intensity, and insight becomes possible. But if real understanding is to arise, the Condition of Satsang must not be abandoned. Narcissus endlessly abandons Satsang. That is his business, his role in life. And that is what the ordinary man or woman is up to. He or she is always abandoning the condition of relationship.

Many so-called spiritual seekers are just Narcissus in drag. They don't have enough gut for spiritual life. They are not interested in the demand that is the Guru. They are dogs coming for a bone. Such dogs only come to the master for a bone. A dog whose mind is set on the bone his master possesses will do any ridiculous thing to acquire it. The dog rolls on the ground and whines and barks and jumps through hoops. He does what-ever he must, until his master gives him the bone. And then he runs away with the bone. He wants to see nobody. The dog doesn't want anybody around him when he is chewing his bone. He doesn't want to be touched. He doesn't want to be approached. He makes a vital circle around himself, and he just works on his bone. And if it is a good, big bone, so that he can't do it all in one sitting, he usually hides it some-where, to protect it, after he has finished his chew. And he doesn't go back to his master again until he's out of bone. He does not go to his master in order to be with the master, to delight in the master, to be mas-tered by the master. He only goes for another bone. Such is the ordinary spiritual seeker. "Give me initiation into your Yoga. Give me the secret mantra. Give me the breathing exercise. Teach me the 'Kriya Yoga'.[3] Give me Shaktipat.[4] Give me the Divine Vision." The seeker always asks for the "bone"! And should he or she in fact be granted one of those things (any one of the traditional forms of initiation will do—mantras, energies, be-liefs, whatever), the person goes. Such people leave to play their games with those techniques or consolations. They consume them in solitude. They don't want to be touched. They don't want to be interrupted. They don't want to be reminded of what is outside, in relationship. But the Master waits for the true disciple to come and submit to him or her. Satsang is the relationship between the disciple and the Guru, not be-tween the disciple and his or her "bone".

The relationship to the Guru is Satsang. That is the discovery. That is the process. That is the secret of the Great Siddhas. That relationship is the Yoga. It is the universal process. It is the single means. It is very Truth. Everything else, all "bone" chewing, is only a ritual re-enactment of the process that arises spontaneously and alive in relation to the Guru. At best, "bone" chewing is a ritual re-enactment. Therefore, true spiritual life is not the activity of spiritual <u>seekers</u>. It is the activity of those who discover their spiritual search is false, fruitless, founded in dilemma, a manifestation of the same suffering that all other men and women are suffering. True spiritual life begins when the spiritual search is abandoned and Satsang is begun. And Satsang is a difficult Condition, a spiritual discipline that must be lived from day to day. Anyone can spend an hour at home every day doing a concentration exercise. Anyone can do ritual repetition of a technique from day to day. In that case, nothing is required beyond your own willingness to conform to a certain pattern. But the relationship that is Satsang is a living Condition. It generates conditions that awaken the functions you always prevent. It demands relationship. It demands fulfillment. Therefore, it is difficult, and it does not fulfill a person's search. It continually turns one from the search into relationship.

When a man or woman lives that Condition, that relationship, when he or she actually lives Satsang, It becomes enjoyment. It becomes easy, spontaneous. But as long as one resists that Condition, the Guru's Company and Its implicit demand will make one darker, heavier, more obsessed with self-enclosure and the strategies of Narcissus. It is said in the traditional Scriptures that, for one who is prepared, the Force, the Shakti, that is Reality, or Truth Itself, will turn him or her into the Divine. But for one who is not prepared, that same Force will drive him or her into hell. Those who are not ready to live the Condition of Satsang, but who somehow come into the Company of those who do live It, tend to become obsessed, angry. Their separativeness becomes dramatized. Their narrow mood becomes absolute. Such people always find the means to eliminate themselves from the Company and the conditions of Satsang, because Narcissus is unwilling to meet the conditions. He is unwilling to live relationship as the condition, the very nature, of conscious existence. He resists the form and condition of life. He contracts from it into the reflecting medium of his own functions. If the Force that emanates from Satsang enters his obsessive enclosure, its intensity aggravates him, so that he runs farther into the wilderness. But if he begins to see his own activity, his own obsession, his own contraction, and turns into Satsang, he becomes full of humor, easy. He becomes an effortless human being, full of spiritual experiences, unconcerned about spiritual experiences. The responsibility of those in Satsang is to live Satsang as the Condition of their lives hour to hour, day to day, and to maintain that relationship in very practical terms. They must live an appropriate life, an ordinary pleasurable life.

Coming to the Guru for techniques, methods, and even experiences is a form of self-defense. It is the defense of one's condition, one's search, one's suffering. The seeker who comes to the Guru, however holy or serious he or she may seem to be, comes to defend himself or herself, to be righteously served, to be satisfied. But spiritual life is not the satisfaction of the search. I offer no "bones", no strategic methods, no consolations, no beliefs, no thing! And I will never give the seeker a "bone". Those who have come for "bones" have no business waiting, because it is not going to happen. All of that has nothing whatever to do with Truth. It's all a lot of bullshit! That's all it is, and I don't spend any time tolerating it. Your trouble is an illusion. Your search is a reaction to your suffering. Your actual dilemma has barely been conceived by you, barely experienced. You come to me for another consolation, to prevent awareness of your suffering. You come for distraction, a fascination, a charming vision. You want to be consoled. But why do you want to be consoled? What state are you in that you should want to be consoled by me? You are suffering! Yes? Since you are only suffering, why are you defending all of this nonsense? It is time to be rid of all of that. It is utterly unnecessary. It can be abandoned! All of that is what I want surrendered as gifts around my feet. I want to see all the beards, all the hair, all the clothing, all of the suffering, all of the sorrows, all of the long faces, all of the usual Yoga, all of the kriya shakti, all of the visions, all of the beliefs, all of the philosophies, all of the conventional religion and spirituality, all of your racial and personal history. I want to see your birth and your death. I want all of it! Such are the implications of Truth. But because people arrive here in my Company not simply suffering but to defend their search, they come with conditions. How can I satisfy these "holy demands"? I do not represent the traditional Yoga. I do not represent conventional jnana, or traditional Vedantic Self-knowledge. I do not represent the traditional "enlightenment" of the Buddha. I do not adorn my body with symbols. I have no symbolic significance whatsoever. These are all your own images. Since you are only delighted by images, you will always end up doing sadhana at your own feet!

What is appropriate is not offense with me, but, finally, at long last, to be offended with yourselves. All your lives you have been angry with various people, dissatisfied with various people, criticizing them. You have been critical of society, of life and experience, of birth, of mortality, of politics. You have been capable of anger, of fear, of doubt as reactions to conditions of life. But it is time to turn all energy to your own event.

The Guru does not come to <u>satisfy</u> devotees or disciples. A satisfied disciple is still the one he or she was. The Guru is only interested in the utter, "radical" dissolution of that whole limitation that appears as the disciple. The Guru is not here to satisfy that limitation, to make it feel comfortable. The Guru is here to return people to their own experience, their always present, chronic experience, their dilemma, their unconsciousness. The Guru is here to return people to that, not to prevent them from seeing it, not to keep them obsessively involved with symbols, or strategically achieved Yogic stimulations of light and sound, or some complex, conditional vision of God, or some mere image of Reality, so they will never experience and recognize their own state. The Guru moves by non-support. The Guru <u>undermines</u> the disciple. The Guru skins the disciple! The Guru does not torture the disciple for fun, but the Guru undermines that process which is the disciple's suffering.

The Guru assumes that suffering is what brings people to Satsang. But people in this time and place tend to assume it is their search that has brought them to the Guru. Arriving at the Guru's feet is a form of success for the seeker. But when such a devotee begins to turn from the illusions of the search, and the demands for the satisfaction of its goals, to the sense of his or her actual condition, his or her suffering, his or her dilemma, then Satsang has truly begun. Until then, the pretended devotee sits, waiting for satisfaction. He or she hears what is being said. The suggestion of real spiritual life, or conscious life, is there, but the pretended devotee supposes that somehow the search to which he or she has already attached himself or herself is going to be satisfied.

The game of seekers is ended, as far as I'm concerned. I am no longer entertaining that suffering. I am no longer concerned for ordinary life in the sense of this obstructed stupidity, this fascination, this search. It doesn't interest me. If you have become sensitive to your suffering, your dis-ease, then Satsang is available to you. Only as such is it usable to you. Your sensitivity to your suffering will give you the strength to endure the periods of self-criticism, of negativity, of crisis, because you will be very willing to go through them. Then such episodes will become <u>interesting</u> to you, because you won't <u>care</u> about the things that are threatened or undermined by the crisis of consciousness. But if you are attached to your search, you will be unable to endure the crisis of your own transformation. Transformation will threaten the very thing you came to defend. In fact there is no "sadhana", no spiritual practice in the sense of something you can do to be "saved", to attain the goals of seeking. "Sadhana" in that sense is not appropriate. But what in fact is appropriate is <u>always</u> appropriate.

The subtle and the concrete <u>demands</u> of Satsang should awaken sensitivity to what is appropriate. Just as the functions of our Ashram depend on appropriate action, all of life depends on it. In every place or condition there is a functional appropriateness that must be understood. Everywhere in life, what is appropriate must come alive as action. There are no "reasons" to come to Satsang, and there are no "reasons" to do what is appropriate. There are no "reasons" to visit one's parents. Just so, there are no "reasons" to visit the Guru. There are no "reasons" to do what is appropriate in life. What is appropriate is simply obvious, and it is the necessary form of action. The appropriate movement of a planet is its proper circuit around the sun, not its eccentricity. What is appropriate is functional living. It is not done for the purpose of realization, nor does it produce Truth as a result. It is simply appropriate. It is natural, it is spontaneous, it is intelligent.

The Guru always <u>expects</u> what is appropriate to be manifested by the disciple. Therefore, the Guru doesn't always or even frequently tell the disciple what to do. The Guru lives Truth to the disciple, and looks to the disciple for appropriate action as a sign of the disciple's understanding. The actions of the disciple are a very simple indicator of his or her preparation, the condition of his or her life in Satsang. If you do what is appropriate, your Guru enjoys you. If you do not, you will quickly feel abandoned. You will feel separated from your Guru, not necessarily because of some violent attitude, or even some condition your Guru has put on you, but because of a subtle sensation generated by your own inappropriate action, your nonfunctional life, your eccentricity. It is not the overt punishment of the Guru, or the Guru's demands, or the Guru's formulas for living that bring about the appropriate activity in the disciple. It is the disciple's awareness of his or her real orientation, his or her consciousness of Satsang, his or her relation to the "sun", and then to the other "planets", to all beings, to all of life. When the disciple becomes oriented, functional, when his or her movement is appropriate, the "sun", the Light of the Guru, shines on him or her. If the disciple is eccentric, he or she keeps moving in and out of phase with the Light. The disciple's own discomfort communicates itself to him or her as the Guru's displeasure.

What is always appropriate is understanding and the spontaneous surrender of seeking. What is always inappropriate is the search and its defense. The life of seeking is founded in prior dilemma, and it does not work. The search does not obtain true spiritual realization, and it does not permit appropriate functional life. The seeker is not a functional being. The seeker is eccentric. The seeker is elsewhere. The seeker is involved in all kinds of peculiar artifices, attachments, symbols, both internal and external. The seeker doesn't "work". The seeker has no capability for relationship, for simplicity. There is no love, no functional light. The force of conscious life, of bliss, does not move as him or her. The seeker is always a little screwed up, always somehow unhappy. The seeker is a profound devotee of the Guru today, but tomorrow he or she is someone else's Yogi, or he or she has become "already" realized! The seeker comes and goes. He or she is in and out of opposing moods. He or she is always wondering whether this Satsang is the Truth, whether the Guru is enlightened. But in fact the drama and the limitations are one's own, and when one becomes sensitive to that, one's position in Satsang is secured. Then Satsang is no longer threatened, and one will turn from childish games in relationship to one's Guru to the penetration of one's own suffering, one's dilemma, one's contraction, one's separation, one's arrogance.

DEVOTEE: How can one consciously overcome the resistance if, when one becomes aware of resistance through understanding, the appropriate behavior doesn't come?

SRI DA AVABHASA: Understanding is not itself a method for correcting behavior. You have only seen a little bit. You have seen enough of your game to resist it only. Therefore, you want to resist it, you want some means to intensify your resistance so that it can become perfect and press the bad behavior out of life. But real understanding, true insight, is not just to observe some negative pattern, acknowledge it to be negative, and then resist it. It is truly to comprehend that pattern as the avoidance of relationship. It is not to sit around analyzing and observing your craziness. It is to see your craziness as the avoidance of relationship. It is to turn into relationship. If there is not this comprehension followed by turning from the perceived pattern into the condition of relationship, there is no understanding. Where genuine insight exists, relationship is enjoyed, not concentration on negative behavior or concepts. And where relationship is enjoyed, all forms of contraction become obsolete through non-support. But when you only see a little bit, you only see the contraction itself. Through self-analysis, a little self-observation, whatever, you only see the negative symptom. And you acquire preferences. You "prefer" to be a little more spiritual, to be free of certain kinds of compulsive behavior. This is the usual state of the spiritual seeker. The seeker's attempts to correct himself or herself are simply another form of unintelligence. His or her "preferences" have no intensity. He or she is still mediocre. His or her "spiritual life" is still more of the same.

When you have resorted to me, to this Satsang, and have understood your activity, when you truly comprehend the process of your life as the avoidance of relationship, you are turned into relationship itself. You are no longer concerned with negative behavior and the stream of desires or preferences. You are only in relationship. You are blissful. You are happy. You are already free. You are straight! You are no longer entertaining the problem of your obsessive behavior, because its foundation, its structure, its motivation is not being lived. And so, simply as a secondary affair, you notice the obsessive behavior in your life to be disappearing, becoming weak, less obsessive. Your chronic obsessions, your habitual life-obsessions, on the one hand come upon you less and less frequently, and, on the other hand, when they do come upon you, you re-cognize them. You only enjoy prior relationship because you see these obsessions as the avoidance of relationship.

Relationship is the prior condition. The avoidance of relationship is secondary, a re-action to the prior and always present condition of relationship. Therefore, one who understands simply turns from the activity of avoidance to the condition of relationship. Such a one does not willfully turn from the avoidance of relationship or its manifested patterns of behavior. One comprehends one's usual activity, and in this comprehension the prior condition of relationship stands out as one's true and present condition. One simply and spontaneously falls into it. When insight into one's compulsive pattern reveals what one's ordinary activity always prevents, one falls into that—the condition of relationship, the true, given, and prior form. And when one falls from one's contracted state into relationship, there is the sense of release, of freedom, of purity, of clarity, and of real enjoyment. Then obsessive mental and psycho-physical forces are dissolved.

In the process of understanding, the contraction is undermined, not resisted and overwhelmed. It is obviated from the point of view of intelligence, not resisted, suppressed, or escaped from the point of view of the search. Therefore, in all cases, it is a matter of this Satsang, living the relationship to me, to my Teaching, and to my natural, always appropriate discipline. It is never a matter of analytical concern for behavior, for life-patterns. That is the search. That is the obsession. That is the self-analysis game of "finding yourself out", in which you spend part of the day analyzing your craziness, and you spend the rest of the day dramatizing it.

Most people are not prepared at the moment for what could be called genuine "spiritual" life. But the origins of what is truly spiritual are not as profound as all that. The condition of human dilemma is practical and life-visible. Human beings are possessed by patterns of irresponsibility and self-indulgence. It is not some profound technique or some deep psychic meditation that they need to perfect at this moment. A revolution in the life-pattern is required in simple, practical terms. The beginnings do not involve trampling one's sexual obsessions with some fantastic self-analysis, deep insight into the past, or heroic smacking of the flesh. No, it is only to live in this Satsang, to live the Condition of this Satsang, and simply to do what is appropriate, according to my measured instruction. Enjoy the Condition of this Satsang with open intensity, and you simply won't be obsessed anymore! It is not a matter of doing anything about the obsessions. It is doing something about the basic life-pattern in practical terms. Then the minor notes of obsession are swallowed in the greater form. But this becomes really possible only when this Satsang has truly begun, when this Satsang is truly enjoyed.

When this Satsang has turned a man or woman on, and he or she is alive with It, expectant, pregnant with It, full of that Condition, that relatedness, that openness, that profound enjoyment, then he or she can do what is appropriate in life. That is why I present real, practical conditions to those who want to embrace this Satsang: Get a job, get rid of drugs, get into a natural, moderate pattern of diet. Such conditions seem easy enough, and yet there is something for everybody in the conditions of my Ashram. Something here touches every individual's key obsession in some form. Therefore, the life-conditions seem impossible to those who are not ready for this Satsang at all, but they seem somehow possible to those in whom this Satsang is beginning. My conditions are not some massive thing. I do not ask you to become a saint before you come to me. Mine are simple, natural, ordinary requirements, but they are sufficient to turn away those who are not ready for this Satsang, while they attract those for whom this Satsang can live.

This Satsang is humor, delight. There is only enjoyment. Truly. There isn't this crazy asylum. There is only enjoyment. Everything is a form of bliss. Consciousness is a ride. There is no dilemma. And those who truly live this Satsang are living no-dilemma. They may appear to be going through various kinds of practical life-transformation, but this transformation involves no dilemma. My disciples are not even concerned anymore whether they will "attain" the famous states or not. What difference does it make if you go through some fantastic psychic revolution in which all the time you are looking at a blue image with three curves around the outside? What difference does it make if, no matter where you go, you see this thing, and it is blue, and it has three circular shapes here, and it shows a sort of brilliant knob in the center? "I've attained this after two thousand lifetimes." That is only the dog costume! For those who truly resort to me, this Satsang is sufficient. This Satsang is the discovery. This Satsang is the realization. This Satsang is understanding. It is meditation, It is Truth, It is enjoyment, It is humor. It is the principle of life! It doesn't require your strategy, your ordinary strategy of separation. Neither does It support your dilemma and seeking. This Satsang is only Force, Intensity. It is One! The absolute vision is communicated in this Satsang all the time! This Satsang Itself is the absolute vision. It is above your heads! Just sit up a little straighter!

What more can I tell you? I don't know. I can't make it any plainer. My speech is over. I can't convince you. Send in the next group! We were originally going to open this place as a restaurant. Give the public what it wants. On tonight's menu we have choice Medjool dates!

Sri Da Avabhasa
at Sri Love-Anandashram, 1992

6.

The Gorilla Sermon

D EVOTEE: Can drugs be used to expand the mind?

SRI DA AVABHASA: What is this mind you are talking about?

DEVOTEE: I mean the simple act of life.

SRI DA AVABHASA: How can you get closer to that by expanding?

DEVOTEE: Can the simple act of life "create" death?

SRI DA AVABHASA: What arises falls, what appears disappears, what expands contracts. Every action has an equal and opposite reaction. Neither the expansion nor the contraction, neither the action nor the reaction, is Truth. It is simply expansion, contraction, action, reaction. There is the dream, and there is sleep.

The "expansion of consciousness" is not Truth. It is the stimulation of perception. Why must you seek Truth by this expansion? The reason you must pursue the Truth with it is because you are suffering. You are already suffering, whether you expand your mind or not. Even if you succeed in expanding your mind, you suffer. The one who feels the mind expand is the same one who feels the mind is not expanding or is even contracting. He or she is a contraction, a dilemma, a sense of separate existence. That is the motivation to this search. The sense of contraction is the motivation to expand the mind. Simply to experience is to expand the mind. It increases the objects of the living consciousness. But all of those objects of the living consciousness, high or low, beautiful or not, imply the same status of the living consciousness, which is the separate self sense.

159

If you see one thing, a red balloon, "I" am seeing this red balloon. If you see everything, "I" am seeing it. "I" am seeing the seventh heaven. "I" am seeing dogshit on the street. It is always the same. This contraction is motivating the search. The separate self sense is its form. Understand this. That understanding is called "Truth", "Nirvana", "God-realization".

Truth has nothing whatever to do with expanding the mind or not expanding the mind. Truth is not a form of experience. The pursuit of mind-expansion is a form of the search, dependent on separation, motivated by this contraction. And successful expansion does nothing whatever to the motivating condition itself. This separate one only acquires various objects for itself, thus "creating" a feeling of security, an illusion of survival. But it cannot survive. It has no independent and formal existence.

"I" is felt as a limited capsule of energy, surrounded by mystery. It is like a time bomb. It has a certain amount of time until it terminates. If you experience a lot with it, it burns out quickly. If you throw it off a cliff, it smashes. "I" assumes itself to be this limited little thing under the conditions of life. And people manipulate it from the point of view of whatever strategy they happen to choose. But always this original assumption is your suffering, your limitation.

It is really a simple matter. The usual man or woman thinks: "This body and its psyche are dying. This world is dying. Everyone is suffering, everyone is seeking. There is mortality, there is frustration and limitation." But none of that is Truth. Those interpretations are not Truth. The world itself is not Truth, nor is life, nor psyche and body, nor death, nor experience. No event is itself Truth. All that arises is an appearance to Consciousness, a modification of the conscious Force that is always already the case. All of this is a dream, if you like. It is an appearance in Consciousness. Truth is very Consciousness Itself. Truth is to all of this what the waking state is to the dreaming state. If you awaken, you don't have to do anything about the condition you may have suffered or enjoyed in the dream state. What happened within the dream is suddenly not your present condition. It is of no consequence any longer, once you are awake. If you persist in dreaming, and your point of view remains that of the dreamer and his or her role within the dream, then your possible actions are numberless. But none of them will "work". They will simply occupy you in the dream. They will modify the dream state, but no action in the dream is the equivalent of waking. There are simply forms of fascination, of occupation, of seeking, until you awaken. Nirvana, Reality, the Great Siddhas, the Masters, Truth—all of that is simply waking, no-illusion. It is not a condition within this appearance. It has nothing whatever to do with the "mind", regardless of whether it is expanded or contracted.

Perception is simply what it obviously is. There is no reason for any perception to change in order for Truth to appear as a consequence. The dream doesn't have to be changed in any manner for the waking person to feel that he or she is awake. Nothing has to happen to the dream. Only waking is necessary. To one who is awake, the dream is obvious. There is no illusion, no suffering, no implication, regardless of what appeared in the dream. A blue god, a dirty old drunk, the gorilla of death—it makes no difference. It makes a difference within the circumstances of the dream, to those who are dreaming. But to the one who is awake, it no longer makes any difference. Perception, waking consciousness, is obvious if you are truly awake. If you are asleep, if you do not understand, if consciousness evades you, there is nothing obvious about this at all. Then life is a very serious predicament, very serious. What do you have in such a case? "A few more years and everything is dead." It doesn't make any difference what the drama is, what you manage to "get on" during that time.

There have been some who have been wide awake while they appeared in the "dream". Subtly, by not supporting the dream, they awakened others. The significance of the work of the Guru is not in anything he does <u>within</u> the dream. He simply does not support it. He does not live as it. He does not believe it. He does not take it seriously. Apparently, he can feel and act as he pleases. He persists in the common or ordinary manner. But he does not support the dream. He does not live from its point of view. He does not live its structure to others. He does not live this contraction to others, this avoidance of relationship, this separate self sense. Simply because he lives in this manner, others tend to become awake. But while they are awakening, they persist in dreaming to various degrees. Forms of the dream persist. The search persists. Often, they get a little distance from it, it seems to break up at times, seems to disappear. It becomes vague, it becomes uninteresting, it becomes unserious, it becomes serious again. They play.

You are just beginning to wake up. Satsang is the dream wherein the Guru appears. Now it is as if you are beginning to wake up in your room. You are in bed, and it is morning. There are a few things you begin to notice which indicate that you are in another state. Those who are waking in Truth begin to notice something. They begin to recognize the "signs". They begin to recognize the activity of dreaming. They begin to sense something very odd about the Guru.[1] Before their actual awakening, the Guru appears as all kinds of things to them. The Guru suggests all kinds of fantastic things. All the things they can imagine while they dream, everything unbelievable, is what they think the Guru is. The Guru may appear to be extraordinary, a doer of famous things. The Guru may appear playfully as that. But the Guru is simply awake. Nothing is happening. Nothing has been accomplished. All the Guru has been is awake.

The Guru is like the sunlight in the morning. The Guru intensifies the light of morning until you awaken. Until the light awakens a person, even the true Light of Consciousness, he or she continues to dream, he or she tries to survive within the dream, manipulates himself or herself within the dream, pursues all kinds of goals, searches, none of which awakens him or her. All ordinary means only console a person and distract him or her within the dream. The Guru, the one who would awaken you, is not a person, not an individual within the dream. The Guru is your very Consciousness. The Guru is the Real, the Self, the Light, the true waking state, the Heart, breaking through the force of dreaming. It is not that you are some poor person who needs some other poor person to help you out. It may appear to be so within the dream, but essentially it is your own Nature appearing within the dream to awaken you. The Guru is your awakening, and your always already conscious state.

Even while dreaming, you may experience suggestions of waking. You may become momentarily aware of the body, momentarily aware of lying in bed. For a moment, the images may stop. Just so, the Guru within the world is truly your real Consciousness. The person of the Guru in the world is like an image in a dream. But, in fact, the Guru is more like your own moments of wakening awareness that move you into the waking state. The Guru is not some separateness, some individual. The Guru is very Consciousness, the Real.

No images. Images, blackness, brilliance—all these things are appearances to Consciousness. They are objects. Nothing needs to happen to them for Consciousness Itself to exist. Nothing needs to happen within the dream to verify waking. Waking is its own fullness. While awake, anything can appear. True Awakeness is the foundation of this world-appearance, it is its support, it is its very Nature. Real Consciousness is not antagonistic to this world or to any form within it. It is the Truth of all appearance, disappearance, or non-appearance. Even when it is enjoyed, human life continues. Perhaps it is enjoyed even more. It is used. It becomes functional to an extraordinary degree.

The usual man or woman barely functions at all. A couple of good days a month. The rest of the time he or she is healing or exploiting himself or herself, trying to get straight, trying to work, trying to get with it. Every now and then a little clarity, where he or she just stands up, walks across the room, opens the door, and goes outside. The rest of the month, dreaming and thinking, when just to walk across the room is part of an enormous search, an unkind adventure, an approach to victory against odds. But all he or she is doing is simple things, simple functions.

One who understands, who is awake, functions very well under the conditions that appear. Those conditions may be forms of this waking world, or they can be subtle forms, subtle worlds, any of the possible forms. Under all conditions, understanding is appropriate. There is no experience, no state, that is itself identical to Truth. Just so, the Truth is not different from any experience or state. It is the Truth of all of that.

The Guru is a kind of irritation to his or her friends. You can't sleep with a dog barking in your ear, at least most people can't. There is some sort of noise to which everyone is sensitive, and it will keep them awake. The Guru is a constant wakening sound. The Guru is always annoying people with this demand to stay awake, to wake up. The Guru doesn't seduce them within the dream. The Guru doesn't exploit their seeking. The Guru is always offending their search and their preference for unconsciousness. The Guru shows no interest in all of that. The Guru puts it down. The Guru is always doing something prior to the mind. The Guru always acts to return you from the mind, from fascination.

The Guru is not what the dreamer thinks the Guru is. The dreamer thinks the Guru must have a certain appearance, say and do certain things, have certain magic powers, produce certain magic effects. The dreamer associates all kinds of glorious and magical things with the Guru. But the Guru is always performing the awakening act, putting an end to the dream. Therefore, the Guru doesn't satisfy the seeker. Those that come to be satisfied are offended. They are not satisfied. They feel empty, they don't feel their questions have been answered, they don't feel they have been shown the way. They came for some thing.

Within the dream, the dreamer is always being satisfied by the Guru. The dreamer climbs up on the top of the mountain, and the Guru is sitting in a cave. The Guru hands the dreamer a little silver box. When the dreamer opens the box, there is a blue diamond in it. The dreamer takes it out and swallows it. Then the dreamer's body explodes into a million suns, and the dreamer shoots off into the universe! But the Guru does not function in that manner. The Guru isn't noticed by someone who is seeking for such satisfaction, who is looking for the "signs" of the Guru, who is "hunting" the Guru. The Guru doesn't assume any particular visibility that can be counted on. The Guru is likely to remain unnoticed. People are likely to be offended if they don't feel any force, any energy, in the presence of one who is supposed to be Guru. They tend not to notice or value someone who is simply awake. They are looking for the one who has the blue and yellow light over his or her head. All of this, until they become dissatisfied with the search. When they stop being sensitive to their own search, they begin to feel simply desperate. Then all that is left is this contraction I have so often described. When the search begins to wind down, and you begin to realize you are suffering, then you become sensitive to the Presence of one who is awake. You become attentive to the very Nature of one who is awake.

It is stated in the traditional writings that, of all the things one can do to realize one's freedom, the best thing one can do, the greatest thing one can do, is spend one's time in the Company of one who is awake. That is Satsang, living in relationship to the Guru and in the company of the Guru's friends. All other activities are secondary. And Satsang is not a strategic method, not an exercise or meditative technique one applies to oneself. It is simply the natural and appropriate Condition. It is Reality. It is itself Truth, or enlightenment. There are no other means given to disciples.

There is nothing that one can do to save oneself, to become enlightened, to become realized. Nothing whatsoever. If there were something, I would tell you, but there is nothing. This is because one always approaches the Truth from the point of view of the search. One seeks the Truth. But the search is itself a reaction to the dilemma, an expression of this separation, this avoidance of relationship. So none of this seeking, nothing one can do, becomes or attains the Truth.

All the means of transformation belong to the Truth Itself, to the Guru, to the Heart. Therefore, Satsang is Itself the only sadhana, the only true spiritual practice. Living, working, sitting with the Guru is sadhana. It is meditation. It is realization.

To enjoy Truth is simply to be awake. Someone asked Gautama Buddha, "What is the difference between you and other people?" and he said, "I am awake." I have often used the contrast between the waking and dreaming state to symbolize the difference between "radical" understanding and all the forms of seeking. All attainments, all forms of cognition, all forms of mind, however sublime, belong within the "dream".

When extraordinary and even miraculous conditions are actually enjoyed or experienced, they reveal themselves to be essentially of the same nature as the ordinary experience of suffering that provoked the search to begin with. In my own case, there is no <u>consolation</u> in samadhis, or trance states, no consolation in visions, no consolation in going to other worlds, no consolation in any realization that can be attained. At last, even the subtle force of re-cognition itself dissolves—that whole process which I have described as enquiry in the form "Avoiding relationship?" comes to an end in Truth Itself. Even its spontaneous form, its true form, its utterly useful and intelligent form, dissolves in its own enjoyment. When understanding is perfect, it becomes obvious that all that has occurred, all that has ever occurred, has been a modification of your own Consciousness. This whole thing that has been upsetting you, all this movement, all this seeking, all this attainment, this whole revolutionary path of spiritual life, has been a modification of your own state. Even this attainment, this knowledge, this jnana, is a modification of your own state. There is a conscious instant in which it becomes obvious that this is so. And that is, if one can still apply any name or significance to it whatsoever, "radical" understanding. It is absolutely nothing.

But the ordinary Yogi, whose spiritual principle is the search, is involved in fantastic dramas of experience. Such a one has all kinds of things to do to, with, and around himself or herself, with the body and mind, with all the ego-ornaments, the suffering, the extremes, the whole endless number of searches, strategies, or ego-works. The ordinary Yogi-ascetic has a fantastic, a fantastically distracting, a <u>fascinating</u>, life! It is a great, great adventure. Even the ordinary jnani, the philosophical ascetic, the man or woman of conditionally achieved Self-knowledge, is absorbed in a "fascinating" life of silence, of acquired peace, of strategic formlessness, separated by a waking sleep. He or she is absorbed in his or her own phenomena. But for one who has understood, there is no drama. Such a one has nothing with which to fascinate people. No sign, no act, no word, no costume can represent it. No closing of the eyes, no blissful smiles, no shuddering, no reports of visions—nothing is useful any longer to keep his or her disciples interested from day to day. Nothing is happening anymore. Such a one has become ordinary. The only forceful communication is that which such a one can no longer communicate by any conditional means, neither by purposive silence nor by speech.

Truth does not specially appear under the form of anything extraordinary or fascinating. It is the most subtle communication, the most absolute communication, the most obvious communication, and Its only condition is the obvious. The Condition of Satsang, or relationship to the Guru, stands upon the obvious condition. Relationship itself already exists as your condition. What has to be added for that to take place? Nothing! Your true condition is expressed in every ordinary or present situation. Relationship itself is, in every moment, already the case. Therefore, Satsang Itself, the relationship to the Guru, reveals the Truth by first revealing the most obvious of all conditions.

DEVOTEE: Will you say something more about the state of turning around when we re-cognize our consciousness? I think you once spoke about an intuitive feeling of something prior to our ordinary state.

SRI DA AVABHASA: What is re-cognized is not Reality. What is re-cognized is your activity. Pick up an apple, then put it down. You can see yourself doing that. The seeing doesn't involve anything apparently extraordinary. You can also "catch" yourself thinking certain thoughts. The re-cognition of which I speak is that kind of thing. It is to see yourself, but in the most intelligent manner, the most direct, most all-inclusive, manner.

Of course, people already, intuitively, live in Reality, as the Self, as the Heart, as Real Consciousness. They already do that. That is why all of you can sit here in various limited conditions, but none of you is screaming in fear. The implications of all that is ordinarily being done in the living consciousness are not presently suffered. It takes some profound event to awaken the latent sense of fear. Understanding is very Reality, what is always already the case, clarifying Itself, enforcing Itself. Reality is the present impulse. It is always the present movement, but, temporarily, It appears under the form of the search, then of weariness from the search, then of real insight, of understanding, perhaps of real enquiry, until It appears under no form at all apart from the simple, spontaneous, obvious re-cognition of all that arises. Where the present activity is re-cognized, where the avoidance of relationship is known again, the natural, or ordinary, state is already Reality.

It is not Reality that is being cognized or found. It is separative activity that is being found, re-cognized, known again. When present activity is known again, then what it is always removing from the living consciousness stands out. And in the perfect form of that re-cognition, everything is obvious. There is no dilemma. There is no longer the sense of a separate one in trouble, suffering, needing to survive, needing an attainment for his or her happiness. There is no identification with subjectivity, either as a separate "I", or an ego, or as the whole display of internal life. Then all that you had piddled around with for years, thinking it to be your own consciousness—all of this subjective mind, pattern of brain waves, psycho-physical drama of impulses and shapes—becomes obvious in Reality. Then only the very Force, or conscious Intensity, that is Reality stands out, utterly free of all that arises, and yet not distinguishable over against any thing or state that arises. Then Consciousness is lifted out of that image of barriers "created" by skull and skin. Psycho-physical existence no longer serves to "create" the image of the limited and only apparently necessary form of consciousness. As Ramana Maharshi said, the body-idea is the root of suffering. The I-am-the-body idea is the original limitation. This "idea" disappears in one who understands. Where there is under-standing, the limited identification with the separate body or the separate self dissolves spontaneously, not as a result of one's doing anything to it, but by virtue of the spontaneous, prior enjoyment of That in which it arises.

The seeker is always trying to do something to his or her separate self. First one is just exploiting it, enjoying the strategies of life-games, until one begins to break down a little bit, in despair of one's ordinary destiny. Then one begins to turn towards "spiritual" life, or to some sort of remedy, but even then one is always trying to do something to this separate and personal state, to get rid of one's suffering, to make one's mind quiet, to get "one" with something, to get free, to get out of this THING. That is the point of view of the seeker. He or she is always only modifying that original sensation, trying to get rid of it with deep, relaxing sighs, with all the efforts of pleasure and transcendence, but always he or she comes back to it again. Because the seeker is always working from the original point of view that is his or her suffering. The seeker's dilem-ma is his or her self-image and the separative principle of his or her ac-tion. As the seeker, one only plays with one's original limitations, until the game begins to lose its ability to distract and entertain. Then the energy one formerly had for seeking begins to dissipate, and one falls into one's actual state, which is suffering, this separateness. Hopefully, at this point one also moves into association with a true Guru and begins the life of Satsang, of Truth. In such a case the Truth is lived to the seeker, and he or she lives It as his or her Condition. Gradually, one becomes less and less involved with the suffering and seeking images of oneself. One be-comes less concerned with the usual process of one's life. One is doing less and less about it. One is trying less and less to get free, to get realized, to get to God, liberation, and pleasant sensation. One is not trying to stop doing all of that. It just begins to wear down, while one lives the conditions given by one's Guru. One simply notices it. One ceases to be occupied with it, because the Truth is being lived to one. It is being lived as oneself, by the grace of the Guru. That enjoyment which does not support separation and seeking is the ground of one's true understanding. It replaces the ordinary operating basis of one's life. One simply forgets one's adventure of suffering, that's all. Another intensity, the Power of Satsang, distracts one until one realizes that It is not truly outside of one. Therefore, Truth is not a matter of doing something to this ego, this separate sense, this identification with the body, or anything else. It is a matter of living the Truth, and Truth obviates what is not Truth.

At first, it is essentially the Guru who lives the intensity and generates the conditions of spiritual life in relationship to one who approaches him or her. But, over time, these responsibilities are passed over to anyone who becomes a genuine disciple. The intensity that is Reality comes on the individual first as a sense of Presence, perhaps, or of subjective energies and sensations, various "spiritual" experiences. But then the process begins to assume the more fundamental characteristics of Consciousness Itself, the intuition of Reality. Finally, present existence becomes both Force and Consciousness, a single intensity, which is Reality.

One of the oddities of teaching in this time and place is that people arrive already committed to some form of madness. Because there has been so much of the search, people don't arrive simply suffering, knowing full well they are only suffering, regardless of what kind of a good time they had last weekend. They don't come even in this condition of mortal sensitivity. Nowadays there is very little of the simplicity that you read about in the Bible and other Scriptures. This time and place is unlike the "old days" in Israel or India. Now people come committed to the search. They come to defend it, to make arguments about it, to get angry about it, to feel displeased about the criticism of it, to resist the Guru, to "hunt" the Guru, to offend, fight, and blame the Guru. There has been some element of this always, but it is a peculiar quality of this time and place that people come to defend their search. What must be demanded of them is the understanding of their search. Their search is always offended by the word and life of the Guru.

DEVOTEE: What are we seeking?

SRI DA AVABHASA: Listen. There is a dilemma. Hm? Is there a dilemma? There is no dilemma? When you walk out of the door of the Ashram, and the usual activity resumes, there may seem to be a dilemma, but is there a dilemma? There is no dilemma. There is only the sensation, the appearance, the assumption, of dilemma. If you understand it, you understand in this moment that it has no existence. It does not exist. In that case, the question about how the dilemma comes about is unnecessary and itself untrue, because, as soon as you look for the dilemma, it has no substance. But some continue the assumption of dilemma and suffering. And the <u>assumption</u> is your own activity. At the same moment in which you assume there is suffering, dilemma, that your search is appropriate, the dilemma is not discoverable. In fact, there is only "this", there is only the obvious, only the event itself, prior to dilemma, or "experience".

The dilemma never arises. As soon as you begin to feel it, if you examine it, you realize it has not occurred. It has no substance. If it is something that has no substance, no existence, how can we be in it? If you understand, there is no dilemma. If you do not understand, there appears to be a dilemma. But as soon as you ask yourself about it, as soon as you enquire into it, as soon as you examine it, you realize it does not exist. The seeker goes on reinforcing his or her assumption, but that does not mean the dilemma exists. If it existed, there would be something you could do about it. It would be substantial. It would be different from something else. It would have some kind of cognizable shape, limitation, dimension, consequence. Then ordinary "magic" and "Yoga" would be appropriate, seeking would be appropriate. But as soon as you examine it directly, you cannot find it. You can only assume it, but you cannot find it. Therefore, since it cannot be found, since dilemma does not exist, the search is not appropriate. The search is only what you do when you assume the dilemma to be the case. As soon as you understand the assumption, the search falls away.

DEVOTEE: I've found that the dilemma often manifests in a number of different sensations. The external level that generates them is not real. But the reaction feels real. Would you explain this?

SRI DA AVABHASA: Why do you assume that your internal reaction is more real than the external forces to which you react? What you are saying is that your assumption of dilemma, or suffering, is real in any case, even if external or conditional circumstances do not justify it! This assumption you want to make about your own contraction is the assumption that I have been talking about. It is your assumption, isn't it?

DEVOTEE: Well, yes, the assumption is a mental thing, but the sensation is something else.

SRI DA AVABHASA: On the mental level there is an assumption, but can you distinguish it "radically" from what you call the "sensation"? It is all one process, and that whole process is what I mean by the assumption. If you put your hand in a fire, and then draw it away in reaction to the heat, haven't you assumed it to be hot? Haven't you acted as if it were hot? You may think about it afterwards, and say it was hot, but whether you think about it or not in that instant in the fire, there is this response, this reaction. Thoughts are of the same nature as pain, or any other reaction. All personal events are forms of contraction. They all have the same quality, the same structure.

Withdrawing of your hand because the fire is hot is of the same nature as thinking that the fire is hot before or after you touch it. It is just as much an "assumption", in other words. To assume something is to suppose, act, or react as if it were so. It doesn't require thinking. Thinking is not the only form of assumption, of supposing. You suppose on all kinds of levels. Your affirmations about things are not simply mental. There are mental assumptions, there are physical ones, there are vital ones, there are mechanical ones, subconscious and unconscious. The mental or the conceptual assumption is one form of it, but there are many forms. And the mental doesn't exist in isolation.

DEVOTEE: Would you please clarify what you mean by "dilemma"?

SRI DA AVABHASA: We have been speaking about it in the same sense that it was used in *The Knee of Listening*. All forms of seeking, all pursuit, all searches for the goal, all strategic Yoga, all spiritual processes that pursue an attainment of some sort, are responses to a felt dilemma, however it may be categorized, however it may appear at any moment. The dictionary definition of dilemma is "two assumptions", an impasse, a predicament, a living state, or condition, of contradiction.

The root of the search is something prior to the seeking itself. The seeking does nothing to its own motivation. The seeking simply fulfills its particular desire. Its function is not to modify its own motivation, its source, its root, the dilemma itself. A search can never exceed its own motivation, its fundamental assumption, which is dilemma. Therefore, I have spoken of spiritual life in terms of the re-cognition, or knowing again, of motivating dilemma, or suffering, rather than the pursuit of attainments. I have talked about spiritual life, or real life, conscious life, as the spontaneous re-cognition, the "radical" understanding, of this motivation, this suffering, that is prior to one's seeking. Traditionally, spiritual life has been oriented to the search and to the realization of the goals of seeking.

DEVOTEE: When you speak of "relationship", do you mean relationship to oneself or to another?

SRI DA AVABHASA: All forms of it. Relationship itself, as the essential condition. What I have called "dilemma" here is this sensation, this motivating sense, this assumption, this feeling of contradiction, this experience which implies and reflects something that has already occurred, which is the avoidance of relationship, this contraction, this separation. The avoidance of relationship is that root-activity that has always already taken place, prior to the search. And one feels it as the dilemma, this subtle sensation, a knot in the stomach, the drive, the movement, the motivation, that "creates" and necessitates one's seeking. Where the avoidance of relationship has not occurred, where there is only relationship, there aren't any of these knots, these motivating reactions.

Apart from understanding, it is certainly true, one does experience and react to the knots of contradiction. The "assumed" forms of suffering are experienced, they are appearances, they are conditions in which one must somehow live and survive. If you have some sort of subtle aggravation, fear, anxiety, anger, you feel the knots here and there. And you go about your search on that basis. You seek to be free of the sensation of the knots. But in spite of all the things that you do, nothing is done to the original state to which you are always responding. As a result, you begin to assume more and more that this state you feel you are in is actual, that it is your real condition. You become more and more convinced that your search is appropriate. And so you become less and less intelligent about the present motivation of your life. You become more and more involved in this pattern of always doing something about it. You always and only react to the dilemma as if it were your fundamental condition. The great seekers are those who make the most dramatic attempts to "do something about it", perfectly, absolutely.

Now, all the forms of seeking that take the dilemma seriously, and "assume" it as the essential fact of life, are of the same nature. This prior contradiction is what they assume, this avoidance of relationship. The dilemma, the "knot", is the foundation of the search. It is the actual "Lord" of your Yoga. Dilemma is the Yogi! Simply to do some mentalizing, some philosophizing, some relaxing Yoga, doesn't do anything to all of that. Only understanding obviates the search and its root. Understanding is Consciousness Itself, the very Force of Consciousness Itself, living, awakening, existing, even apparently acting, prior to this assumption of dilemma. The only thing already free of the dilemma in Consciousness is That Which Is Very Consciousness Itself.

The whole reaction to subtle aggravation has shown itself to be fruitless. When it has been followed to its end, when you have taken the whole course and gotten all the lessons, when you have done all the usual meditations and have gone through all the experiences, when you have read all the books, this dilemma is still it. At the very best, the search itself begins to break down. Then, gradually, the dilemma ceases to be reinforced by any secondary activity. Then the force of life's awareness falls into this dilemma, it becomes only this, it is no longer doing anything about this, nothing. It is not even trying to analyze the dilemma, so that it will come to an end. No thing is being done. Consciousness, for the time being, becomes identical to dilemma. When the search falls away in natural frustration, ordinary consciousness <u>becomes</u> this dilemma. In other words, it is doing nothing else, nothing apart from this. This is the profound stage of practice in my Company when, while holding on to my Teaching, and to my person, the crisis of consciousness is endured. Then there is the re-cognition of the dilemma, and only Consciousness Itself, or that very Reality which appears otherwise isolated as separate or limited consciousness, stands out.

The dilemma, like the search, is ultimately re-cognized to be your own activity, your always present, chronic activity. It is the structure and motivation of the usual drama of every life. When there is that re-cognition, there is understanding. Prior to that "radical" crisis, all the things that you may consider to be understanding are only secondary approaches, secondary experiences, in which the dilemma has already been assumed.

DEVOTEE: How does this relate to the different levels of consciousness?

SRI DA AVABHASA: There are no levels. Temporarily, you consider there to be all of these structures within your being. You assume there to be barriers, separations, forms that you are, forms that you are not, activities that are yours, activities that are not yours, separate functions in yourselves like boxes and drawers, functions here, functions here, functions here, different pieces of yourselves. But there is only one, single intensity that is. It is your Nature. It is all things. There is only this intensity. It has no form, no division, no separation, no "me", no this, no that, no inside, no outside. No suggestion of division arises in Real Consciousness, even where all worlds appear. Therefore, understanding is an absolute, "radical" event. It is not some remedial event, some cure. It is not identical to some thought or cognition, some feeling, some symbol, some vision, some suggestion, some belief, some sensation. Those are all forms of experience, and, therefore, they are secondary. They are all forms of the dilemma.

How could a person seriously exist for one moment consciously thinking that he or she has a thought level, and a feeling level, a this level, and a that level, all kinds of separate "bodies", functions, and the rest? How could you exist for one moment really considering that to be your present and ongoing condition? You would go insane! Indeed, such a picture of life is insanity. In such a case, you are already shattered. Then you are imagining yourself to be a whole bunch of little things with no fundamental existence, no functional or prior Self-Nature, no Force. But in fact you do not assume that. You do not fundamentally assume there are these levels, pieces. All of that is only many words, but the mind is one. Every living being intuitively assumes only his or her Real Nature, the Power of Reality. Therefore, one is able to witness the massive complexity of ordinary life, but, ordinarily, one remains relatively calm and capable of functioning. This is not because one is particularly wise, but because one does not really live as if division, multiplicity, and death were already one's condition. Fundamentally, already, this Unity, this Singleness, this Force, this Intensity, this Consciousness, this Reality that is one's Nature, is also one's present enjoyment. This is so at the rudimentary level of primitive intuition, and it must be so if functional life is to continue.

If you did begin seriously to assume separateness, multiplicity, and division in Consciousness Itself, you would go insane. Indeed, that assumption has taken place in rudimentary, functional life in those who are called "insane". They have become relatively incapable of intuiting their own Nature. The ordinary man or woman has just become incapable of conceptualizing it, of experiencing and generating life from that "point of view". But, intuitively, the same one remains always and already in the Force of his or her true Nature. One assumes, most fundamentally, this simplicity, this intensity, this singleness, this non-separation. One who might be called an "enlightened" being, a realized being, is one who not only intuitively assumes the Condition of Reality but who lives it consciously. Such a one lives without any doubt whatsoever regarding this ultimate simplicity, the only "obviousness" that is the ultimate, or Perfectly Real, Condition of moment to moment existence.

Until it is lived consciously, one's ordinary state appears as a subtle dilemma and a motivated search. Intuitively, every being always already lives as the very Self, the Heart, the Force of Reality, but, in the functions of ordinary consciousness, there is the appearance of particularity, of multiplicity, of separation. All of this appears to run counter to one's intuitive assumption. The appearance, the quality of rising experience, tends to inform one's intuition. This "information" tends to become one's assumed condition. And this assumption corrupts and ultimately superimposes itself on the force of intuition. It does so by reinforcing the process of identification, or "ego" (the stream of self-cognition), differentiation, or mind (the stream of thoughts), and desire (the stream of motivations, the endless movement toward contact, connection, union, and temporary loss of the sense of separate existence).

The ordinary person, the "sane" person, passes into the Force of his or her own intuited Nature during sleep. But during the time of waking, and even in dreams, he or she carries on the search, this movement within the assumed dilemma of experience. Such is the pattern of one's life, until there is "radical" re-cognition, or knowing again, of one's essential activity. Whenever that re-cognition takes place, one not only intuits one's own Nature in the subtle depths, but it becomes obvious in every condition of conscious life that there is, in reality, no separation, no actual identification with the states of birth and death. There is not, in that moment, even the slightest impulse to believe the implications of ordinary experience. The Force of the very Self, of the Heart, overwhelms the qualities of experience and consumes them. The Self, or unqualified Reality, is the foundation of all experience. What the ordinary sane person intuits is already his or her Nature. It is already Reality. But in the one who understands, it is obvious, it is apparent, it is conscious. For such a one it is always, only, and already obvious, and he or she need not go through any sophisticated mental operations for it to be so. It depends on nothing. It is just as obvious as ordinary perception is to the usual man or woman.

When you are dreaming, you take the dream very seriously. You assume your role within it, your drama within it. You respond to the condition that seems to be so, whatever the particular circumstances of the dream. If the gorilla is chasing you up the beach, you feel all the threat. All the emotions become involved, all of your strategies of survival, or non-survival, become involved. If it is a sweet, enjoyable, astral² sort of dream, with all kinds of friends and voices and colors and movements, you assume that to be so. You float around in it. You take it seriously. You <u>assume</u> it to be so. You assume it because you have no other point of view from which to enjoy or suffer the dream except that of the dreamer. But when you wake up in the morning, the gorilla that was just about to bite off your head loses all significance. All of the implications of the dream are already undone in one who is awake. It no longer has any real significance, it no longer has any implication for life. It no longer is a genuine threat to life. It no longer is anything except that appearance. And the only difference is that you are awake. Nothing has been done to the dream itself. You have only awakened, and therefore the dream is obviously not your condition.

Understanding is very much this same kind of thing. Understanding is to the waking state what the waking state is to the dream. In the ordinary waking state you assume all conditions to be so: "my" life, "my" symptoms, "my" knot in "my" stomach, "my" headaches, "my" fear, "my" everything else, "my" circumstances, "my" poverty, "my" need to do this and that, "my" death, the news, the war, and all that appears in life—you all take it very seriously. Here you are, in this spiritual place, this Ashram. You are very seriously here to get out of all of this limitation. Everyone has come here very seriously for this very serious spiritual purpose. Now, since you have come here for such a purpose, if I were to tell you to go home, concentrate on yourself, and have visions, what would I be doing? I would be offering you an alternative within the dream itself. I would be asking you to remain within the condition of dreams. I would only be telling you to dream another kind of dream. I would simply be exploiting the dream itself, which in this case is the ordinary waking state. I would be recommending <u>experience</u> to you as the path of Truth. But all of that is more of the same thing. It is only another condition for you to take seriously and assume to be your own.

Understanding is not a form of philosophy. It is not a method. It is not something within the "dream" itself. It is like the waking state as opposed to the dream. The true Guru, the Heart, is "radically" conscious, real, alive, free, by virtue of his or her very Nature, from the implications of the ordinary waking state, and from the implications of even all conditional states. But the ordinary Yogi, the usual teacher, the philosopher, is a role <u>within</u> the "dream" of waking. He or she operates from its point of view. He or she is identified with it, suffering or happy within it. The dilemma is there. His or her realization, however extraordinary it may appear, is an artifice whose roots are in the condition or point of view of the "dream". Such a one is only recommending some distraction to you, some occupation, some solution within the "dream" itself. But the Heart, understanding, is simply awake. Understanding is the true waking state, the very Self, Reality. It has no philosophy, no subtle vision, no peculiar state associated with it. Like one in a dream, one who understands is not presently affected by the waking state. But, unlike one who dreams or appears within a dream, such a one is always, already, consciously free.

The waking state is simply a "radically" different condition from the dream. That is why you feel free of the dream upon waking. The Guru appears in the midst of the dreams of ordinary waking life like sunlight in the morning. When you are still dreaming, still asleep, the sun comes up. It gets brighter and brighter, and the light comes into the room. At last, the light, the day itself, becomes sufficient to wake you, and then, all of a sudden, you are not dreaming, and everything is all right. The Guru is simply that sunlight process, that intensification, rising on you always, without any other special activity. The Guru's relationship to you, your condition of relationship to the Guru, just that relationship, is sufficient. There is only sunlight on the pillow until that intensity is sufficient to wake you up. It is the kiss of the Prince and Sleeping Beauty. Such is understanding.

But the teachings that are generated in the great search are all exploitations of your dream state. They take it seriously. They assume it to be the present condition, even if it is regarded to be only temporary. And that is the fundamental error of all traditional and remedial paths. They are all generated from the point of view of your suffering. They serve your suffering, and they reinforce it in spite of themselves. Therefore, to the seeker, to the one suffering in dreams, the teachings of the ordinary Yogis and philosophers seem very hopeful. They seem to represent something very desirable.

You are running down the beach away from the gorilla. Now, suddenly, there is a guy sitting outside a hut next to a pool of blue water. He has long hair, and he bears all the great signs of an ascetic. He says, "Just sit down here. Very quickly now, because the gorilla is not too far away. Breathe very deeply, and concentrate between the two halves of your brain." He hasn't changed your essential condition, but he has distracted you. The form of experience that he has stimulated in you by the force and influence of his personality certainly appears to be desirable over against being devoured by the gorilla. But, at last, it is simply a distraction within the dream. It is another form of the dream. It is an event within the dream. All of the searches that people are involved with are attempts to forget the gorilla. And that is their maximum possible attainment. Therefore, when you seem to have forgotten the gorilla, all of a sudden you are smiling again. You feel fantastic! There is no gorilla! There is? No, nothing! People assume that the consolations and exchanges or transformations of state generated by seeking are pleasure, "creativity", freedom, realization, Liberation, God-Union, and Nirvana. But do you see how all such attainments relate to suffering itself?

The gorilla is what is going on for people. It is death. Are you interested in that? Hm? It doesn't make any difference what you do for the next thirty years—if you have that long—you are just going to go back to zero. Some of us were looking at a book this morning called *How to Face Death,* or something like that. How absurd, this notion of facing, or confronting, death. The first thing you lose in death is face! That is why the peculiar forms of morality in the Orient are largely based on the "saving of face". Loss of face is loss of life, loss of real existence. Well, that is what happens in the terminal psycho-physical event we call "death". That is what death is all about. How can you face it? Everything you do to face it, everything you do to prevent the gorilla, has no ultimate effect on the gorilla. All seeking is simply your distraction, your makeup, your false face, your fascination, but Zap! the gorilla gets you every time. Everybody dies. Everybody who has ever lived has died. There are billions and billions of human beings who have died. Multiples of billions of other entities and creatures die every moment, even as a by-product of your breathing. All these breathings disintegrate billions of tiny entities in organic fires. There is no righteousness, no non-killing. The death by slaughter, the consumption and literal transformation of apparently separate entities, is going on all the time. There is no escape from death. There is no sanctity in vegetables, nor even freedom for those who reduce cattle to sandwiches. The entire cosmos is a continuous sacrifice, in which all things, all beings, are ritual food. At best, the search can only modify the apparent circumstances of one's death. Ordinary Yogis or religious people may at last manage to forget the gorilla. They may think they are looking at the blue of Krishna or the white of Jesus, until they lose face. Until the sudden zero, they are looking at Krishna or Jesus. They are only consoled, only distracted. Their realization and their death are kneeling in one another.

There is no philosophy whose force is stronger than the force of death. The philosophies by which people counter or react to death are opposite, and at best equal, to the power of death. Therefore, it is possible to be consoled and distracted, but nothing greater is attained by those who react to death, who make adventure in relation to the gorilla. There is no philosophy, no vision, no attainment, no success that will make death a literal delight, that will make it anything less than it appears to be within the dream itself. But if one simply awakens from the dream, then, as the waking state is already free of the "awful" that appears in dreams, one is already free of the implications of the billions upon billions of deaths that can be dreamed. The one who understands is simply one who is awake. Such a one has no other specific and necessary peculiarities. Such a one is not elaborate at all. It is the one within the dream who is very complex, because he or she has so many things to do. But the one who is simply awake is simply awake. Such a one is "straight". Such a one is the waking sunlight, the very Light of Truth, but that one appears within the dream of human beings as an ordinary person. Such a one may seem extraordinary and a paradox to the dreamer, because the dreamer is very serious about all of this, but the one who is only awake is not serious about it anymore. Such a one does not fundamentally assume the condition of the dream as limitation.

The one in the dream is waiting. It is going to happen any day now—either Jesus is coming or the quake is coming, one or the other. Or the war, or the bomb—it is all coming. And you have got to prepare for it, boys and girls! But the one who is just awake slowly sips a cup of sweeted herbs. Everybody else is "phewww!" hitting the panic button, or else inhaling consolations with their minds. But this one is unreasonable. Such a one just doesn't care. There is no sign in that one of any serious-ness about this whole problem. For the seeker, life itself manifests as a problem, a fundamental dilemma. For the one who understands, there is no fundamental dilemma.

Only the condition of genuine waking is truly and "radically" free of the condition in the dream. But that true waking condition is not the thing that is attained by any of the means generated in the dream, the search. And the means designed within the "dream state" are often mag-nificent, extremely elaborate. They are "created" by practical necessity, and so they are very complex, very elaborate. They take many, many factors into account. Traditional religion and spirituality, Yoga, magic, occultism and mysticism, not to mention all the "sciences" in life, the life-strategies and life-remedies, are all highly complex, and often very successful in relieving the symptoms, or experiential dis-ease, of unconscious life. And the methods and artifices of seeking fascinate those who are simply suffering. Everybody is looking for the "head" or "fix" that distracts to the maximum degree. Everybody is willing to pay money for what is not bread. People are not truly looking to be sustained. They do not require Truth. They only desire to forget or escape the gorilla. But the Guru is not such a "one". The Guru lives only Truth to living beings.

I have talked about the relationship between the Guru and his or her friends as being the essence, the fundamental Condition, that is sadhana, or real spiritual practice. But this sadhana is not a form of concentration on the Guru as some totally separate and merely symbolic entity. That is not relationship. That is your own fabrication, your own suffering again. Where there is relationship, there is no need for all of these symbolizations. And the true nature of sadhana is to live the <u>Condition</u> and the <u>conditions</u> of relationship to the Guru in his or her function as Guru. Within the dream, the potential images may be consoling, and even hopeful, but such consolation or hope is not the equivalent of being awake. Consolation and hope <u>depend</u> upon your being asleep. The forms of seeking exploit your capability for identification with the fundamental dilemma of dreaming, which is its unconsciousness. They may satisfy you within the context of your assumptions, but they are not the equivalent of waking up.

What is required to wake up? What can you do within the dream to wake up? Nothing. There is only the waking itself. All actions within the dream are forms of the dream itself. Waking is another process, and it occurs by other means, by already conscious means. The Guru is not a symbol, a condition of the dream itself. Such a one cannot wake you up. The Guru is the Light of Consciousness, the very Self, already awake, functioning alive. The Guru appears in human form within the dream of life, not to console you, but to awaken you through the crisis of real consciousness. The true Guru is a frustration to the unconscious condition of the dream.

There are those who preach various forms of mental preoccupation and subtle preoccupation. They are all the same. They are all doing the same thing. They are all serving the dream. They are not the Self of Reality. They are not what the true Guru is, what the Great Siddha truly is. The man of understanding, functioning as Guru, is an awakener. He is always already awake. He couldn't care less about your urges and demands within the dream. He refuses to satisfy them. I would rather beat you on the head with a stick than give you an experience merely to console you. I have no intention of satisfying anybody here. All the demands for satisfaction that you bring are frustrated here. What is satisfied, what is made to grow, is that fundamental intuition of Reality that is already the foundation of your existence. That is intensified in Satsang with me, the Condition of relationship between me and my friends. And all the rest, the fascinated search, begins to fall away. In this Satsang, the search begins to reveal itself, until it becomes obvious.

And understanding itself won't necessarily have anything peculiarly dramatic about it. How dramatic is it to wake up in the morning? You don't go, "Wowwwwwww!!!" You don't go screaming, "Fantastic! Oh, Revelation!" All you do is open your eyes and live. You just wake up. The moment of the realization that you are not stuck in the dream has a certain pleasure associated with it, but it is not usually a fantastic sort of fireworks. It is a natural, already happy event. In *The Knee of Listening* I described the Great Re-Awakening in my own case. That ultimate event was not dramatic at all. I was sitting on a bench in a little temple. In the moment of Re-Awakening, I simply opened my eyes and walked out into the street. I didn't talk to anybody on the way, and I didn't say anything about it to anybody at home. I didn't describe this profound event to anybody at all for many weeks, even months. And when I began to talk about it, I tried to make it clear that its true import was extremely subtle. It was not "extraordinary". It was without "drama". I was simply being awake. There was nothing to compare it to. It wasn't the attainment of anything.

Within the dream there are all kinds of attainments. The gorilla is chasing you and Smack! the big purple mountain has a crystal cave underneath. You go running into it, and you enter the water that is there. You go deep. And then there are red brilliant lights. Pearls and sacred ornaments hit you on the head. And you go shooting up like a rocket of gleaming silver and gold fire. You flash to the top of the mountain. Your head explodes into billions of serpents. At last you stand immortal and victorious on the mountain top. You scream at all the gorillas from the top of the mountain. You destroy them and smother them and smash them to smithereens! That is the attainment within the dream. That is the usual Yoga. That is the typical vision. But understanding is simple waking up.

Now, this dilemma, this unconsciousness, this "contraction" I have often described to you, is the "dream". It is the crucial assumption. It is not changed or undone by the fact of the ordinary waking state, nor by any ordinary life-activity or seeking. It is without benefit of this intuited Reality in which you truly live. Therefore, you assume and live that condition of suffering, separation, and fundamental dilemma, until you awaken in spontaneous, "radical" insight, or until you become shattered, insane, corrupted, thoroughly unconscious. If the gorilla eats you in the dream, you feel eaten. You are eaten. Those who dream long enough, who try all the alternatives within the dream, who have suffered all the attainments and failures within the dream, who no longer have anywhere to go, who are only dreaming, who are suffering, who no longer take their search "seriously", for whom the search is no longer the thing to which they resort, who have despaired of their own adventure, their ecstasies, their attainments, their strategic paths, their methods, who are only suffering, who are only in dilemma, who in fact are only experiencing this contraction, the compulsive avoidance of relationship, but are doing nothing about it any longer, who know they cannot do anything about it any longer—they become sensitive to the sunlight.

To move into the presence of the Guru is not something the disciple does. The disciple doesn't actually go to the Guru. The disciple can't decide one morning to go to the Guru. The disciple doesn't know where the Guru is. How can he or she go to the sunlight? The disciple is somebody lying asleep in bed. The disciple doesn't go to the Guru. The Guru is the sun, rising, intensifying the light, until the disciple realizes that he or she is in that presence. That realization is Satsang. And understanding is itself true waking, true knowledge, or re-cognition, of the "sunlight". All seeking for the Guru, all going after the Guru, is an activity within the dream. The Guru cannot truly be found within the dream. Only the imagery of the dream can be found within the dream. Perhaps the human person of the Guru can be found, but the Guru's true Nature and function cannot be comprehended by the "dreamer", by the seeker, or by his or her strategic methods.

If you yield to the gorilla at last, if you give up your search, not willfully, but spontaneously, having despaired of your seeking, essentially you have surrendered, or yielded, to that Reality you have always intuited. And that spontaneous surrendering, that conscious dying, that yielding to the gorilla, is a sign of waking. It is the far end of sleep. It is the beginning of that sensitivity to the morning. As soon as you become sensitive to it, you just wake up and go about your business.

The life of a disciple is a very natural, functional life of real enjoyment, of intelligence. It is a waking life. It is not a life in "bed". It is not spent meditating in the crystal cave. It is a simple, normal, ordinary life of bliss. It is to live already awake. Of course, I have been talking in similes. Perhaps I have impressed you with the idea that the "waking state" is the only condition uniquely free of the limitations of the "dream state". But even though all men and women are apparently awake, they know no other state that transcends the ordinary limitations of the waking state. People ordinarily do not pass into a fourth state (other than waking, dreaming, or sleeping) in which even the ordinary waking state loses the force of its implications. That is why the function of Guru is lived in the waking world. The Guru is that "fourth state", alive in the waking world, under the appearance of the waking condition. Just so, real meditation is not a fixation of the eyes on physical sunlight, nor on the energies, ordinary or extraordinary, that appear and move in the waking life. Real meditation is present enjoyment of the Sun itself, the true Sun, which is Reality. That "fourth state" is awake to the waking state. To recognize the Guru, to enjoy the companionship of the Guru, who is always already "awake", is to be awake yourself. When you truly see who the Guru is, you are already awake. Until that moment, you are still woozy. But if you live in the Company of the Guru and fulfill the conditions the Guru requires of you for your sake, you begin to feel a distance from the dream, from its compulsiveness, its repetitiveness. What is happening in such a case is that the very Self, the Heart, the true Sun, the Guru, is being intuited, enjoyed. And when you truly see the Guru, when you truly see the Sun, then you yourself are awake. The morning sun, the appropriate hour, the physics and biology of one's condition, conspire to awaken one to the ordinary world from one's natural sleep. Just so, Satsang with the Guru, the whole Condition and sadhana of real religious and spiritual life, awakens the ordinary man or woman to his or her perfect, always present, and true State. All of the secondary forms of associating with the Guru are indeed secondary. All of your ordinary waking activities, even those in which you communicate with the Guru, are effective only in the ordinary waking state itself, the "dream" of usual life. They may be appropriate, even necessary, but they are not themselves the way. The way is the Condition Itself, the relationship itself. It constantly exists. It is the sadhana. It is the meditation. There is nothing else that needs to be added to it. The Condition Itself, the relationship itself, is the sadhana.

There is no end to the numbers of living beings who can do this sadhana. The sadhana of relationship to the Guru is what the disciple must always realize and live. Since the Guru always already enjoys the Great Condition, It takes up none of the Guru's time. There is no limitation to the Guru's capability to be that fundamental enjoyment for all beings. The limitations are on the disciple's activity within the life-appearance, and on the Guru's apparent activity within that same appearance. But those limitations are only the forms of pleasure and communication, wherein human beings represent their understanding to one another. Even so, the Guru is rising above the house. The Guru is not this limited state. The Guru is your own enjoyment, perfectly known.

Since this true waking is your Reality, your true Condition, the dilemma cannot be found when it is sought. It is purely an illusion that is assumed by the dreamer, by the one who only seems to be awake. As soon as one gets serious enough about one's seeking to examine one's motivation to seek, one cannot find it. One spends one's whole life within the dream, within this vast adventure, to find the princess in the crystal palace and save her from the dragon, or to wait in the crystal palace to be rescued by the prince. One lives an endless, endless adventure, millions and millions of ages, year after year after year, of numberless complications. But at some point along the way, one examines the motivation, the cause, the root, for which this goal is only the symbol. At last one realizes that one cannot find one's symbolic satisfaction. And this falling into one's dilemma, then falling through it, is the unqualified intuition of one's Ultimate Nature and Real Condition.

There is no "fated" time when this will occur. You need not persist to the end of your seeking before it is appropriate to understand. A person can wake up at any time. You do not have to go through the whole dream process until you seem to find the princess sleeping in her castle or the prince finds you. You do not have to dream the whole sequence of the dream. Karmas, or destiny, are not absolute and necessary in this sense. It is appropriate to wake up at any time. It is only one who continues to believe in his or her own search who must acquire and achieve a great deal before realization is appropriate for him or her. Such a one has twenty more years of striving, or twenty more times to be born for death's sake. That one has an obligatory number of things to do. He or she must do certain things "in" the body and earn a certain amount of money. He or she is "born" with various conditions to fulfill. But the ideal of seeking is really absurd. You can't imagine the <u>dreamer</u> defending all of that, but only one who <u>appears</u> within a dream. And even the one in the dream will not defend his or her "destiny" of seeking in the presence of the gorilla. You can only imagine a person saying it when surrounded by delights, or when he or she is full of capabilities. Then such a person is like a child whose mother wants him or her to wake up to go to school. The child doesn't want to get up. The child says, "No, I'll get up later." He or she doesn't want to go to school. The seeker doesn't want to go to "school". The seeker doesn't want to live the sadhana, the discipline, the real conditions of life that are found in the Company of the Guru. The seeker does not want to understand his or her own adventure.

The waking state promises something relatively undesirable to one who is suspended in the twilight state of a pleasant dream. Such a one is reluctant to understand. He or she is too distracted to be interested in understanding. The ordinary reluctance of people is not truly caused by a premonition that the life, or sadhana, of understanding is so difficult. It is only that they do not yet care about it. Somehow, for the moment, everything seems all right. The usual man or woman possesses relatively healthful physical life, certain satisfactions, certain opportunities, things to do, books to read, a future of places, physical pleasures, mental pleasures. With all of that, who wants to awaken? And most people come to the Guru in that condition. Therefore, the Guru doesn't take them "seriously". The Guru knows they are only enjoying themselves, even if to others the new arrivals seem to deserve only mercy and the grin of salvation. When these seekers come to the Guru, they make all kinds of complaints about their fundamental suffering. "Please give me this salvation, this realization, this release!" But they are not really looking for that. They are unwilling to endure the discipline of Truth.

There are certain limitations to the whole adventure and pleasure of ordinary life. You know you are going to die some time, but, essentially, mysteriously, life is full. Thus, Truth is not likely to enter the usual picture without the intervention of some fundamental, transforming event. But if you are smart, if your life is generated with conscious intensity, you don't have to become desperate before you will turn to the Truth. Your circumstances don't have to become empty, corrupted, and diseased. You don't have to wait for the failure of life itself before you will turn to Truth. Someone who is waiting for life to disprove itself is only enjoying himself or herself. There is nothing truly "serious" about the search or the suffering of such a one. But if one is smart, if one's life is an intensity, one is always turning to Truth from birth. The more distracted one is by the pleasures of existence as the condition of one's life, the more mediocre one's realization, on every level, even on the level of life itself. The one who is just plain satisfied with how good his or her body feels barely functions at all. There is no force, no intelligence, in such a one. Such a person does nothing. He or she just smiles and plays with sexual partners all the time. He or she doesn't "create" anything. He or she realizes nothing. He or she doesn't intensify the quality of life. He or she has achieved nothing more than symbolic existence. And he or she may have to suffer drastic conflicts and upheavals before his or her unconsciousness begins to break up, but the suffering is not truly necessary. It is unnecessary to go through the long term of seeking, of suffering, of breaking down, of corruption, before Truth becomes appropriate. The realization of Truth is not a matter of heavy, self-involved, constricted, willful effort. It is as natural as a simple response to sunlight. It is simply the relationship to the Guru, the intelligent life of real sadhana.

Truly, what one brings to the Guru is not one's dilemma. The dilemma has no real existence. One may be preoccupied with it, but the Guru pays no homage to it. The Guru may appear to take it quite seriously, or the Guru may display only the most playful attitude toward it, even allowing the devotee to suffer or enjoy it temporarily, because it is of no ultimate consequence. Truly, what people bring to the Guru is their intuition of Reality. It is only that they are not consciously living it. But it is the very premise of their lives, and so they come to the Guru, who lives it consciously, who is the Sun to their deep-seated intuition, and the Guru draws it into this instant.

Only the seeker takes the dilemma seriously, but the waking state doesn't take your dreams seriously. It is not the least concerned with your dreams. And, luckily, all beings are already alive with their intuition of Reality. Therefore, they have this affinity with sunlight, with the true waking state, with the Guru. The unqualified Reality is what they are already living, and that is what is consciously discovered in relationship to the Guru. Because they are already holding on to the unqualified Reality, it is Reality that makes people return to It. It is intuition of Reality Itself that leads one to the Guru, and to maintain oneself in the Guru's Company. All "reasons" for holding on to the Guru fall away, and also all the reasons for not holding on to the Guru. None of these reasons has any ultimate significance. The affinity of your true Nature, your intuition of your true Nature, the Heart, is entirely responsible for this sadhana. When you become less concerned for your particular search, for your inwardness, for your adventure, you have simply become more sensitive to your Real Condition. You have felt the sunlight falling on your sleeping eyes. When your eyes have opened in the morning light, everything will be obvious to you. And you will know that you have never slept, that you have never dreamed, that you have never been limited to any thing that has appeared. You have never been in any condition that you have assumed. There was always only Reality, your true Nature, which is Bliss, Consciousness, the unqualified Intensity.

Sri Da Avabhasa
at Sri Love-Anandashram, 1992

7

Relationship and Association

S
RI DA AVABHASA: I was talking to someone here the other day about certain associations one has—with people, with environments, whatever. This person was wondering whether some of his old relationships would continue when he became involved in real spiritual life. He wanted to know if these friendships would necessarily come to an end, or if in fact they could continue if he were involved in this way. I pointed out to him that many of one's involvements are not "relationships" at all, and they are not true friendships. They are "associations". They are essentially forms of one's own desire. Such associations with people, with environments, enable one at will to indulge certain qualities of experience.

As such, these are not relationships at all. They function truly as forms of one's desires. Even though there seems to be someone there—a person, a place, a thing—in fact one is not enjoying relationship. One simply has this association that reflects one's desire and gives one the opportunity for the indulgence of it, the satisfaction of it, the suffering of it. Associations come and go, just as desires come and go, but relationship is, in the context of conditional existence, the very function and form of Consciousness Itself. And, truly, it has neither beginning nor end. Where there is genuine relationship with an individual, a place, a thing, an environment, it is not subject to the quality of desire. Desire doesn't "create" it. The end of desire or the change of desire doesn't bring it to an end. Where relationship is discovered and lived, it never does come to an end. Its quality may change, and there may be apparent separations in time and space, but the relationship itself is fundamental, continuous, real. Where there is relationship, there tends to be apparent growth, intensification, change, but it doesn't come to an end.

Associations, however, come and go. Associations belong to periods of one's life, stages in one's own experience. They are functions of time, space, and desire. Therefore, when some particular desire, or desire itself, ceases to be the point of view of conscious life, associations tend to fall apart, disappear, come to an end. But when there is perfect, "radical" understanding, there are no longer any associations at all. There is only relationship. There is no separation. And relationship is enjoyed under all circumstances, all conditions, with all beings, in all environments. Because people are identified with their own desires and live by the habit of association rather than relationship, there is suffering. Because people do not become more for one another than extensions of their own minds, their own desires, there is no relationship. Therefore, the communication of the Force and Condition of Consciousness Itself does not take place.

Until there is perfect understanding, there is the tendency to mere association through desire, even with those with whom one enjoys the quality of relationship. Thus, all one's genuine relationships also involve conflict. They are always threatened by mere desire, mere association. You move in and out of them. You never truly enjoy them, except in brief moments. Where there are simply associations in the form of desire, your connections tend to disappear, and certain relationships tend to become corrupted, destroyed, impossible at times. But all separation is an illusion. It is impossible for there to be any separation. There is no such thing. It has never occurred. There is no separately existing thing anywhere. There is no separately existing <u>being</u> anywhere. There is no separate anything! Separation is only an impression caused by disturbance, by this compulsive contraction I have often described. When it comes to an end, when the avoidance of relationship comes to an end, there is no difference.

All separation is an illusion, and all attainments are an illusion. There is no separation, and there is no attainment of union. The state of the ordinary Yogi is as much an illusion as the state of the dying, suffering person. The one who suffers thinks he or she has become absolutely small, and the expansive Yogi thinks he or she has become absolutely great. But when one thinks one has <u>become</u> great, one truly suspects that one <u>is</u> small. In truth, there is only the penetration of one's search, the re-cognition of it, and then existence becomes enjoyment.

People are busy communicating their own mind-forms, their own contracted cognitions, rather than the Force and Condition of Consciousness Itself. Thus, people are only punishing one another. Everyone causes pain for everyone else. Everyone reinforces the illusion of separate life. Therefore, everyone is seeking. Everyone suspects it is somewhere else, or that it doesn't exist. But where there is the re-cognition of that whole search, there is only the communication of Consciousness Itself, that very Force, that Power, that Condition, that is Reality, in relationship. And, in its ultimate form, that communication is Satsang—the Communication, Condition, or Company of Truth. Where the Force of Reality, or the Condition of Consciousness Itself, is Communicated in relationship, the enjoyers of It are assumed by It, acquired by It. This Communication undermines the ordinary assumptions until one ceases to believe them, and one becomes intelligent with Truth.

All men and women are, apart from true understanding, simply distracted and turned in on themselves. They appear to have been born, but they are still bent. Every man and woman, in fear of the born-condition, lives not straightened from the curve of the womb. And all other men and women, since they are in the same state, only reinforce that fear that makes people bend and curve inward. But one who understands exists and lives as the subtle Communication of That which makes it possible for people to open, uncurl, or turn into relationship. Therefore, restoration in the process of Truth has been called "second birth".

Until one becomes capable of existence in this apparent, or human, form, open in relationship, one tends to reject the force of existence in a continuously repeated ritual activity. It is something like vomiting. The force of life is abandoned constantly. Even laughter is a form of this ritual abandonment. Sexual indulgence is a form of it. Ordinary perception is a form of it. It is the release of, or the failure to conduct, the Power of life. It is unconsciousness, sleep, the refusal to be born. And its symptoms are a life that is not in relationship, that is not whole, that is full of dis-ease, confusion. Such a life cannot function. It only forever seeks its own release, as if the release from life were the goal of life.

In Satsang, in the relationship to the Guru, this rejection of the force of life, of birth, tends to become quieted, and the life-form tends to conduct the Power of life, rather than reject it. The subtle form of one's life is something like a sphere, in which the life-Power of Consciousness continually moves down from above, and then returns upward again, once it has passed through the deepest place below. It is not rejected. It is conducted. The force of life rounds the heart, like the planets around the sun. And the true Heart, or very Self, is the "Sun" of one's living form. The "Fullness" people begin to feel in Satsang, in the Company of the Guru, is this Power, allowed to be conducted downward in the life-form, and allowed to ascend in the natural manner, by the spinal pathway. Not by rejection, this ritual vomiting, but by spontaneous conductivity, the transcendent life-Power is turned and returned in a spherical cycle that is completely at ease, without dilemma.

Some begin to feel this Fullness in Satsang because they are sensitive to the descent of Force and the opening it allows. Some begin to feel ecstatic and moved in various ways because they are sensitive to the ascent of the same Force. Others begin to experience a relaxing and even shattering of the ordinary structure of psycho-physical consciousness. And the true Nature of all things becomes at times, somehow, obvious. When the "Sun", the Heart of Reality, the Force of Consciousness at the root of this, is enjoyed, that is understanding, _real_ization. From Its "point of view", all of this _is_ obvious.

The spiritual and religious traditions transmit various aspects of this phenomenon of "second birth". The religious search, particularly the form of seeking characteristic of Westerners, is a reception of descending Power, the "Power of God" that "comes from on high", that may even incarnate itself and come down so that people may receive it. The traditional Western man or woman, and, in general, the religious type of person, look to receive this Spirit, to receive the Power of the Divine, and to bring the grace of this Power down into life. The traditional Eastern man or woman, and the spiritual person in general, are sensitive to the ascending movement. Traditional Yoga is a ritualization of this process of _ascent_ to the Divine, just as religion is the essentially formal, or ritual, means for becoming at ease, receptive, _full_ of the Divine. But these two, East and West, are simply exclusive and ritual attachments to one or the other of the principal phenomena of this real process, or "second birth". Therefore, the East is traditionally busy with ascent, knowing little of descent, and the West very busy with descent, the descending Power, knowing little of ascent.

The "second birth" truly is a possibility. It is the only _real_ possibility for human beings. And its process is truly enacted only in Satsang, in the living, present relationship to one who lives _as_ the Heart—not one who only suggests It, who has sometime merely experienced It, who merely envisions It, who only thinks about It, or who only teaches about It, but one who _is_ the Heart, without any limiting qualifications. In such Satsang, in the Company and conditions "created" by such a one, the cycle of descent and ascent is restored in a very simple, natural manner, without the disciple's applying himself or herself methodically to the "creation" of that cycle, or to the strategic restoration of that pattern of energy. The disciple who lives such Satsang as the Condition of his or her very existence does not apply himself or herself to the strategic point of view or the remedial methods of spirituality or religion for the sake of Truth. The disciple's entire spiritual practice of sadhana is to live the Condition of this relationship. He or she is not distracted by any search for the descending force or for the ascending power. He or she turns simply to the Guru, and to the very condition of his or her own life, which is relationship. Such a disciple passes through various forms of crisis until there is spontaneous insight into, or re-cognition of, the ordinary pattern of his or her life. I have described that pattern as the avoidance of relationship. The "radical" re-cognition of this pattern is true understanding. The perfect enjoyment of understanding is absolute Truth.

The subtle process alive in Satsang is not a problematic concern with the descending or the ascending Power. It is the spontaneous, intelligent Siddhi, or real spiritual Power, of the "Sun", the true Heart that is Reality. The true disciple is not engaged in a strategic, or ego-bound, process of reception, or of return, or of both. The true disciple abides simply in relationship, and the primary intensity of the Heart's Light, the conscious Power that proceeds in Satsang, is the entire means for the crisis of intelligence, or re-cognition, in the true disciple. In the meantime, there are secondary phenomena, or enjoyments, associated with Satsang, and these are the reflections of the descending and ascending energy. But they are purely secondary. They are enjoyments. They are like becoming healthy. They are not themselves Truth. One who is distracted by these phenomena contracts and separates himself or herself from all forms of relationship.

Only relationship is appropriate. There is no need to be "concerned" with the descending or the ascending Power. There is no need to seek it, to find it, or to grasp it. All such "concerns" are an expression of primary dilemma.

DEVOTEE: How is this Force, or Light, experienced, so that people reject it? Is the experience itself painful? Or is something threatening?

SRI DA AVABHASA: The ultimate reasons are subtle. They have nothing to do with what can be communicated mentally. What <u>causes</u> laughter? What <u>causes</u> vomiting? There are secondary events to which laughter or vomiting may be the reaction, but the selection or interpretation of a

191

"cause" cannot be justified conceptually, because it is not observed. The observation of a cause is not a pre-condition for laughter, vomiting, or life itself. It is not so much that the forms of rejection are an effect of something. They are the action. The rejection, or reaction, is spontaneous. It is this contraction of which I have spoken. But its basis is subtle, prior to life, prior to thought, prior to perception. The perceiver and the perception are already this. They are already bent. They are themselves this rejection. They are already forms of primary dilemma. The true answer is always subtle and not spoken. Even true or real questions are always subtle. The question put in the form of concepts is not the real question. Your real question is the sensation that motivates your thoughts and words. The answer, likewise, is not a concept, not in the form of concepts or an observation. It must be in the form of "radical", direct re-cognition of the subtle condition that is your question, your suffering, your dilemma, the motivation of your search. Nothing else can satisfy. No explanation is equal to it.

There is a sense in which the whole process of rejection, or the avoidance of relationship, is a spontaneous reaction to the action that is existence, manifested existence. Wherever there is an action, there is an equal and opposite reaction. There is the Heart, or One Reality, there is appearance, and there is the contraction that is the reaction to that appearance. People are living as that reaction. When they re-cognize their own activity, which is their suffering, Consciousness again realizes Its Nature as the Heart, which is always already open, which is prior to manifestation, which is not any form of dilemma. The genuine roots of that whole process that is one's suffering, or disturbance, are not truly explainable in any conceptual terms. They can only be undermined, or obviated, in this re-cognition. Therefore, re-cognition is the root-process of sadhana, the spontaneous and intelligent process of Satsang. There is no "second birth" apart from "radical" spiritual practice, or sadhana. There is no "second birth" apart from conscious Satsang, actual moment to moment living of the relationship to the true Guru, who is the manifested Condition of the Heart Itself. The form and function given as grace to human beings for the enjoyment of this Satsang is the living association with the Guru who lives as the Heart, the One Reality. When people realize they are suffering, that they are bent, that there is a subtle dilemma, they begin to seek. The only places there are in which to seek are the psycho-physical realms of the descending and ascending force, which are the structure of manifested life. Therefore, people go about the business of exploitation and discipline until they realize the failure of the search. When this occurs, one has become capable of Satsang.

DEVOTEE: Is it necessary for us to have a true and conscious relationship with you and with everyone we know if we want to live a true spiritual life, or a life of understanding?

SRI DA AVABHASA: It would only be nicer! If it were necessary, then Satsang couldn't take place. If this process depended on everyone here already enjoying relationship consciously, perfectly, it would never begin. It is nicer when it becomes conscious, when a person begins to move into the natural conductivity of Satsang, when he or she begins to enjoy its true quality, its subtle quality, and returns the force of life and of consciousness in a very natural manner. But it is not required. It is not a precondition. There are no conditions for relationship. It is already the case. Some are conscious of it, and some are not. There are some with whom one enjoys relationship as a real condition, whereas one serves only as a form of association and an extension of desire for them. And the opposite may also be true. In such a situation, where there is an apparent conflict, a person must decide whether he or she has the strength or the interest to live that relationship, whether to release it or else to change the quality or the conditions of that relationship as a daily experience.

DEVOTEE: Does a person have a responsibility to make the other person in a relationship more conscious?

SRI DA AVABHASA: That responsibility is inherent in relationship itself. The very fact of living in that direct, relational manner, rather than in the usual contracted manner, is itself to serve the communication of true intelligence. Do you see? So that responsibility is already satisfied by it. It is not necessary to add to that relational force any sort of secondary motivation to change the other person. Where such motivations appear, one's relationships tend to become an extension of one's own search. To that degree, one falls back into "association" again. Yes? But to live relationship with other beings is even to extend and serve the form of Satsang, the relationship to the true Guru.

Sri Da Avabhasa
at Sri Love-Anandashram, 1992

8.

Meditation and Satsang

SRI DA AVABHASA: Spiritual life is Satsang. It is the Company of Truth. It is a relationship to one who lives as Truth. Satsang is also the very Nature of life. It is the form of existence. Relationship— not independence, not separation, but relationship—is the principle of true life.

All attempts to relieve the life of suffering by various strategic means, or ego-based remedies, do not produce Truth. They may heal dis-ease, but only Truth produces Truth. Sadhana, or spiritual practice, is to live Satsang as the Condition of life forever. Sadhana is not something you do temporarily until you get free. It is to live Satsang forever—a <u>lifetime</u> of Truth.

The beginnings of one's spiritual life are the coming into relationship with the Guru—living in the Guru's Company, which is Satsang, living the conditions given in that relationship, getting straight. There is a Force, a Siddhi, or spiritual Power, alive in Satsang. Therefore, among the experiences of spiritual life are the sensations of Force, or Presence, communicated in Satsang. These are enjoyed as various feelings, peace, kriyas (spontaneous purifying movements), bliss, the qualities of energy. But, in truth, spiritual life is not something that happens to you. It is not a process that takes place independent of your conscious existence. If it did, all you would need to do is to wait for it to come to an end in liberation, or some such state. Spiritual life is <u>conscious</u> life. It doesn't really exist until your consciousness comes into play, becomes active. Spiritual life is an intelligent process. It is not a kind of mediumship, wherein you simply enjoy certain experiences and certain energies. The Shakti, or Force aspect, of spiritual life has one purpose. It is to communicate to you the energy alive in the Truth, to purify, harmonize, and intensify your life, so this <u>conscious</u> process can begin. All of the Shakti experiences are simply means to strengthen and intensify your life so that you have the energy, the force, with which to live this conscious life. Sadhana is a process in consciousness. It is intensity. It is force of consciousness. It is intelligent. It is not just energy that you witness. Consciousness does not happen to you.

All of you here tonight have begun to live in Satsang with me. To some degree, you are committed to It. You have begun to live It as the Condition of life. Some of you have these experiences of force, of energy, of movement, of internal awarenesses, of various kinds of purification. In some cases, Satsang appears simply as a very practical influence. But now it is time to begin to <u>use</u> this Teaching which brought most of you here. I want to read you a couple of pieces from *The Knee of Listening*, from the very beginning of that portion called "The Process of 'Real Meditation'". It is a long section. I am only interested in getting into the very beginnings of it here, because the beginnings of it are the practical affair which is the foundation and unending circumstance of real, or spiritual, life.

> "The usual meditation" (traditional meditation, the motivated remedy) "is only a consolation, an effect, and a good feeling. It provides no radical reversal of ordinary consciousness, and, thus, when situations arise out of meditation, the person has no control over the process of identification, differentiation, and desire."[1]

I spent years with all kinds of people who were going through the phenomena of Yoga, of Kundalini Yoga,[2] dealing with presence, force, miraculous spiritual experiences. I have never seen anyone <u>fundamentally</u> changed by these experiences. I was never thus changed by any of these experiences. Their intention is not to change you. They <u>are</u> change. They are phenomena only. They depend on the Force, Guru-Shakti, the Force aspect of Satsang. The phenomena themselves are not the point. They are there only to assist in the intensification of the quality of your life. You are not intended forever to sit in them, to bathe in them and watch them perform. These phenomena, if they need to happen in you at all, will happen in any case. They are a <u>relatively</u> minor aspect of spiritual life. Enjoy them. But see that they are not themselves spiritual life. They will not lead to liberation. They are not Truth. They will not affect the motivating character or source of your peculiar life one iota. Thirty years of shakti experiences will occupy a fool, but they will not awaken him or her. Increase of energy or experience does nothing whatsoever to the fundamental quality of conscious life. At most it intensifies it, providing the functional strength, so that conscious life can begin as a real process.

"Only radical understanding avails." (In other words, no motivated process, no simple influence of energy does.) "Only radical understanding avails. It is the viewpoint of reality itself. It is not attachment to some body, realm, or experience that is seen as the alternative, remedy, cure, and source of victory. It knows that every motive and action is made of avoidance. Thus, it has no recourse except to understand. And understanding and the one who understands are Reality, the Self, the 'bright'.

"The Yogic search only enjoys forms of Shakti, the bliss of energy. Only radical knowledge is real bliss, dependent on nothing."

Satsang with me must begin, the influence of Satsang, the Condition of Satsang, must begin. You must begin to adapt to Satsang, make It your sadhana, meet the conditions of spiritual life in a very simple manner, take on the qualities of an ordinary, pleasurable life, assume responsibility for the relationship that is Satsang with me. And begin to listen.

You will simply begin to listen, and when this process in consciousness has begun, you will begin to observe yourself, see yourself under the conditions of life. This process of self-observation, carried on here in our discussions about this contraction, or avoidance of relationship, and in all your study, reading, and living of this way, at some point becomes communication received, real observation of how, yes! this contraction, this avoidance, is the quality of your life.

"When you see that you are always seeking, understanding is emerging. When you see the pattern of Narcissus as all your motives, all your acts, all your seeking, understanding is emerging. When you see you are always suffering, understanding is emerging. When you see that every moment is a process in dilemma, understanding is emerging. When you see that every moment is a process of identification, differentiation, and desire, understanding is emerging. When you see that every moment, when you are at your best as well as when you are at your worst, you are only avoiding relationship, then you understand. When you see that which already is, apart from the avoidance of relationship, which already absorbs consciousness prior to the whole dilemma, motivation, and activity of avoidance, then you have finally understood.

"When you have understood" (when this insight has become real), "understanding will become the natural response of your

197

intelligence to any experience, the total content of any moment. Then approach every moment with understanding, and perceive the original truth within it. . . .

"Therefore, when you have understood, devote yourself to understanding in the midst of all experience, instead of any kind of remedial action that arises as a means to handle the problem of life at any moment."

That depends on making Satsang into "radical" spiritual practice, true sadhana, your way of life, the very Condition of your life.

From the beginning, embrace and enjoy the Condition of this Satsang with me. In this manner, begin to listen to me, and, thus, become spontaneously available to the intelligence of this Satsang. All of this will spontaneously become self-observation. When this self-observation that is spontaneously awakening in you continues under all conditions of life, you will begin to observe this contraction of which I speak. You will begin to see this avoidance of relationship. It will become clear to you in your living experience. When it has become clear to you, when it takes place as a certainty, as your very knowledge, then that very knowledge can be used positively, directly. It becomes your approach to life. It is your intelligence. Examine this chapter on meditation in *The Knee of Listening*. See what is involved in the beginnings of it.

My work is not the exclusive Kundalini Yoga. It is the all-inclusive, universal, and perfect way of God. Many of you have begun to become sensitive to the spiritual Energy, the Force, the Shakti, revealed to you in and by and as my Company. And no doubt about it, there is a living Force in this Satsang. This work is not simply an intellectual or mental liberation. The Force alive in Satsang is the very Force of the Heart, the living Reality. But It is not unconscious. It is conscious. And the way is conscious. True sadhana is an intense, forceful way of consciousness. So it is not a matter of forever receiving the blessing of Shakti and allowing it to do things to you. Begin to listen. Accept the conditions of this relationship. Remove the ordinary obstacles. Abandon them. If you truly engage and use this relationship from day to day, more obstacles and more demands will be generated for you than you could ever have imagined as a discipline for yourself. The relationship will discipline you. You don't have to be concerned with spiritual techniques, purifying methods, things to do to yourself, apart from the responsibilities for practical maintenance of life which were discussed with you when you entered the Ashram.

Listen! There is this contraction, this avoidance. All human beings are living this avoidance of relationship. Apart from understanding, that is all anyone is doing. Nothing else is happening. Only this contraction of living and subtle forms. It is suffering. It stimulates by implication the notions people have about the very nature of life. This contraction implies a separate self, separate from the world and all other beings. The appearance of many, much, and separate me is an expression of your suffering, but the Force, the intensity, the bliss, of Reality persists and is felt even under the conditions of ignorance. Therefore, it appears as the drama of desire, the search for union between the separate me and the manyness. Everyone's life is the drama necessitated by this fundamental contraction. Everyone's life is the adventure he or she is playing on this contraction. Everyone's life is bullshit! The drama of an ordinary life is without significance, or real intensity. It is deadly ignorance. No Truth, no Satsang.

Satsang must begin. Satsang must be enjoyed as the Condition of life. Then the whole drama of which even traditional spirituality is a manifestation comes to an end, dies. This contraction becomes flabby and opens. The real Force of conscious existence comes into play and becomes the way, the sadhana itself.

Meditation is not something that takes place in the dilemma. Real meditation is not a method to get rid of your suffering. It is not perpetual preoccupation with your own thoughts, the content of your life, in order to get free of them, get aside from them, make them be quiet. The "you" who does all that is itself the dilemma. It knows nothing. It is itself the suffering. It is itself obsession with the endless stream of its own thought. Therefore, the attempts by such a one to do something about the "mind", to make it quiet, to make it see visions, whatever, are within the form of this original motivating dilemma. Such strategies are expressions of one's separate life, attempts to fortify and save one's separate life, which is already an illusion.

Real meditation arises only in Satsang, only under the <u>conditions</u> of Truth, already lived. There is force in such meditation. Real meditation is an intense fire. It is a marvelous intelligence, a brilliance, a genius, a living force. It is not a pious attempt to quiet your little thoughts. It blasts the hell out of these thoughts! From the "point of view" of the very Self, the Heart, the Truth, the Real, there is no concern for all of these thoughts, all of these dilemmas, all of this mediocrity of suffering. It is nothing.

When Satsang lives as the principle of your life, and Truth becomes the form of your meditation, It consumes thought. It is a Presence under which thoughts cannot survive. It is an intelligence that needs only to look at some obstruction for it to dissolve. This is the process that comes awake in Satsang, not some strategic method, some ego-based remedy. The whole point of view of dis-ease is false. Spiritual life is not a cure. Spiritual life is the life of Truth, Satsang. One who is looking for a cure is obsessed with his or her dis-ease.

The first true thing one does when one comes into contact with one's Guru is to relax the obsession with one's dis-ease, one's trouble. Therefore, the original activity one enjoys in relation to one's Guru is not sophisticated meditation. What one does is nothing very sophisticated at all. One comes and relaxes one's search. One begins to find oneself in the Condition of Truth, in Satsang. One begins to enjoy that Condition in a very practical fashion, enjoying the force of It, the intensity of It, the beauty of It, the blissfulness and happiness of It. Only then does one begin to observe and become intelligent, sophisticated. Yes? So the "beginnings" of Satsang may last for a very long time.

The more you persist in the drama of your resistance, the longer you prevent Satsang. If you come into association with one who you suspect might be alive, functioning as Guru, but spend the next forty years wondering about it, you have never entered into Satsang. Satsang is not simply coming into a room and sitting. Satsang is the relationship itself, the relationship to the Heart, the very Self, the paradoxical person of the Guru. The drama of the avoidance of relationship to the Guru is the paradigm, the epitome, the archetype of all the dramas played in all relationships. It is better if, upon meeting one's Guru, one surrenders one's search and enters suddenly into that relationship. But in most cases there is a period of time, of drama, of wondering, of in and out, of yes and no, of wondering again, of thinking, none of which is spiritual life. None of that has anything to do with spiritual life. It is only the drama of suffering, resistance, reluctance. Spiritual life begins for a man or woman when that relationship openly becomes the Condition of his or her life. Then one becomes willing to accept the conditions it demands of a person. One begins to enjoy the Force of that Presence, the Condition that is that Satsang. One becomes alive, intense with that Force and Condition. Then this intelligent activity in the living consciousness begins to awaken.

Observe your connection here. Examine your relationship to this one. See the drama you are playing in terms of this Satsang with me, and live this Satsang instead. I am only interested in this Satsang as a real process. I have no interest whatsoever in gathering an enormous organization of silly, fascinated people. I am concerned that this real process begins in fact, in whomever it is possible for it to begin. If there is no one, I will stay home. If there is only one, I will deal with one. If there are fifty, it will be fifty. If there are fifteen million, that is fine too. But I am not willing to do what is necessary to acquire a following through fascinating promises, strategic, or ego-based, methods, mere consolations, experiential illusions, and one-shot-liberation baloney.

Conditions are continually being given to you here. And these conditions are always appropriate. They are the pure instruments of Self-knowledge. But if you don't live this relationship, this Satsang with me, It will always be an offense to you, It will always "create" an obstacle for you. Then Satsang will only make you angry and uncomfortable. Live this Satsang with me, learn the real conditions of spiritual life, observe your resistance to it, be purified of your seeking, understand and surrender this search. Lead an ordinary, pleasurable life. Remove exaggerated, self-toxifying practices in life, all the absurdities, the forms of self-indulgence. Become more sophisticated with your desire. Come here as often as you can. Simply sit in this relationship, enjoy the force of it, begin to observe yourself. Ask me questions about your sadhana. Not the usual questions: "Where is George Washington today?" or "What is the shape of the next universe?" These are not your real questions. What do you care about all of that? That is not the point. You are suffering only. If you have to fly a rocket between here and Mars, then it becomes a practical necessity to discuss what the conditions are between here and there. When you are elsewhere, it is appropriate to consider what it is like in other worlds. After death it is appropriate to examine what it is like after death. If you are dying this evening, then we can deal with the death process. But you are only suffering. You are resisting Satsang Itself!

Ultimately, all of this avoidance of relationship is only the resistance to Satsang. It is the resistance to making Satsang the Condition of life. It is dramatized in relation to the Guru because, whatever the Guru is in Reality, the Guru symbolizes the possibilities of spiritual life. Therefore, people feel very free to aggravate their relationship to the Guru. But they should be dealing with their own ignorance, their suffering. Come to Satsang with real need, not with anything to defend.

The world is absolutely insane. But your spiritual life does not depend on the world. You are not going to get up from Satsang today and suddenly find that everything and everybody in the world is absolutely beautiful. You are not going to find that all your suffering has been taken away by magic. The world is going to "create" obstacles. The world does not want to function. People do not want to function. They are not yet alive. If you are coming alive in Satsang, you are going to have to be intelligent in your relationships, intelligent in life.

Require Truth. Take yourself to Satsang, the Company of Truth. Don't believe the usual company of life, of resistance, of avoidance. The world will "create" conditions that will awaken your own aggravation, your own ignorance, your own game. It will demand your game of you. It will demand that you suffer it, and that you live it as well. When a person is still weak, still beginning, the world seems a vast alternative to his or her spiritual discipline and to Truth. The patterns of sudden desire seem so much more pleasurable than this sadhana. Therefore, one must make good use of the Company of one's Guru and the Guru's Ashram. When one becomes stronger, one will also make good use of the world.

The same thing you enjoy as Satsang is itself understanding. That blissfulness of relationship is already realization, already Truth. The more profoundly you enjoy It, the subtler Its Nature appears to you. Satsang does not proceed toward a goal of Truth. Satsang is Truth. It is the life of Truth. It is the Force, the Consciousness, that is Truth. Over time Truth Itself produces change, apparent transformation. But Truth is the very Condition of spiritual life, not its end phenomenon. Therefore, from the moment Satsang begins, the demand of Truth is put to you in the form of an obstacle. If sadhana, the practice of Satsang, required no conditions, anyone could come for "initiation", regardless of his or her state of preparation. Then I would give that person a little technique of some sort, and flatter him or her with promises. No, the way is Truth Itself, the Tao[3] is itself the way. Truth is the way. Therefore, the "initiation" of spiritual life involves the communication of this obstacle, this demand that is Truth. The first form of that demand is the person of the Guru. Thus, the first form of a genuinely spiritual encounter is generally the life-drama of one's association with the Guru. Even so, it is not the Guru's function to destroy the resistance of the world by magic. If one responds to the teaching, one must prepare oneself, and make an appropriate approach to Satsang.

The first obstacle, and the primary obstacle, to spiritual life is the relationship to the Guru. However, the relationship to the Guru is also the fundamental Condition, the principal content, and the graceful source of spiritual, or real, life. If it were not for that, everybody could become spiritual by the mere practice of some method or another. They would read books. They would manipulate themselves with arbitrary beliefs. But spiritual life is a relationship, a living demand. It "creates" an obstacle from the very beginning. And that obstacle provokes the crisis and fundamental sacrifice that real life requires.

Nothing is offered by me but Satsang with me. Nothing is given but this relationship, because it is Truth. Those who finally live it as the Condition of life receive everything, because this relationship is also the medium of Truth. Everything rests on one's ability to realize this relationship. I know very well who lives it and who does not. It doesn't even require any psychic powers to know it. If a person lives Satsang with me, I live Satsang with him or her. With those who do not, I must be involved to some degree in the drama of their resistance. Essentially, this involves the application of conditions to their demands, so that the resistance in them is set aside, broken down. Chastisement, or an apparently negative approach to someone, as you may see in some cases here, or in your own case, is not in fact "punishment". It is a form of Satsang, the communication of Truth. It is only that the individual involved in such a case is, for the time being, incapable of assuming the Condition of Satsang, and the responsibilities of Truth.

DEVOTEE: When the enquiry "Avoiding relationship?" is really effective in my daily life, it arises spontaneously. Sometimes it takes the form of an internal mentalization of the question "Avoiding relationship?" At other times it seems to be only a process of intelligence, or spontaneous movement of consciousness itself. In other words, sometimes it arises as intelligence itself, and at other times I find myself using the internal mentalization of the idea, the mental enquiry. Why are there appearances of different qualities of enquiry? I have an idea about this. Perhaps it is that, when I am distracted more, the internal mentalization serves to bring me back to the present, to what I am up to, and serves to dissolve the tendency to distraction of mind.

SRI DA AVABHASA: Real meditation is begun by sitting in Satsang with me—either here in my physical company, or at home alone, or even while active under the ordinary, functional conditions of life. In that conscious Condition that is this Satsang, a kind of quieting arises, and, at the same time, an intensification of your self-awareness. Depending on the peculiar quality of your state at that time, you will become attentive to forms of desire, differentiation, or identification. Impulses are the form of desires. Thought, or separation of things that arise, is the form of differentiation.

203

The various forms of separate and separative self sense are the form of identification. Therefore, when various of these qualities begin to draw your attention, this enquiry may begin. And generally it begins as an internal, or mental, verbalization. The enquiry ("Avoiding relationship?") is evoked randomly—not repetitively, but as a real question—and followed until there is a real answer. And the "answer" is not itself a thought, but a spontaneous re-cognition of thought, of action, of the forms of identification, differentiation, and desire. When enquiry truly arises, founded in prior insight, then the very forms and processes that have attracted attention tend to fall away. They cease to distract you. And you simply and spontaneously fall into the condition of relationship, which is always already the case, prior to the obscuring activity of the avoidance of relationship. In this same sitting, you may proceed through various forms. At first these arise as forms of desire, perception, awareness of life-activity. Then the process may move into subtler forms—forms of thought, forms of impression, memory, images. Then it may move into the various subtle senses of separation, the qualities of self-sense. All the time, for one who chooses it, this verbal enquiry, randomly activated, adapts to the various qualities that are arising. But in the depth of consciousness, there begins to arise a sense of what is always taking place at any and every moment of enquiry. It appears as a kind of "shape" in consciousness. A subtle activity begins to form an impression and then a direct comprehension in consciousness. Then the mental form of enquiry tends to fall away. Instead of mental enquiry, this other activity that has always taken place at every moment of enquiry begins to move into every instant of awareness. It moves in terms of the same processes that were arising before, including forms of desire, thought, and separate self sense, but without mental verbalization. Then, in each moment, these qualities vanish, as they did when enquiry was mentalized.

At first, what is enjoyed in this whole process of enquiry is a kind of intensity in relationship, a sense of relationship itself, with great intensity. But the subtler this process becomes, the more there tends to arise a re-cognition that the only thing that is ever happening in every instant is a modification of the very Reality that exists. Every impulse, every desire, every thought, every sense, every sense of separate self, all of these begin to appear as one activity, a continuous modification, a shaping of what is, of That which is also one's own Nature, or Condition. This is the subtlest form of re-cognition. And no sense of limited, or qualified, relationship exists in this re-cognition at last. The very point in space by which one

204

approaches everything, this separate self sense, is seen, felt, and known to be a modification, an arbitrary shaping of one's own existence. Wherever this "shape", this contraction, this modification, this formation of awareness, is re-cognized, it is obviated, it is disappeared in the instant of re-cognition, until there is absolute, perfect enjoyment of That which underlies all of this activity. At last only It is enjoyed, only It is lived. And that is called "Self-realization", "Liberation", "Nirvana"—all those names.

There are various traditional forms of dhyan, or meditation. But perfect, absolute, "radical" understanding is the most intense, the endless, or eternal, Form of meditation. When that meditation is itself perfect, "radical", absolute, when re-cognition has become total, when every thing has been re-cognized, so that nothing arises that is not at the very same instant already re-cognized, when regardless of the condition that arises, regardless of the activity that is performed, whether one is sitting as if in meditation, or walking, or performing ordinary activity, the Real Form is only obvious, when re-cognition is constant, this is the Fundamental State. This is true Samadhi, Sahaj Samadhi, constant realization of one's True State, prior to all conditions in the worlds. This true Samadhi, or realization, is not itself an experience, a kind of trance or any kind of "Yogic" state. It is only enjoyment of and as that Reality which one has always been, and which all things are. One who simply enjoys and lives this enjoyment is one who understands. In such a one true spiritual life has begun. That one lives in the Heart, at the "foot" of Amrita Nadi,[4] the Form of God. And when such a one moves into association with other beings, he or she begins to speak very strangely about the nature of life.

All human beings are only seeking, all are involved in this peculiar activity, the avoidance of relationship, and all are pursuing an answer in the forms of their present experience. Therefore, human beings want a truth that consoles their humanity. But very Truth has nothing whatever to do with human identity, limited to what presently appears. From the "point of view" of Truth, this birth is an obsession, unnecessary, already non-existent. But people want to hear about birth and reincarnation, experience and afterlife, fulfillment and fascinating "creativity". Truth is the most "radical" penetration of this whole event. And only at that moment is there happiness. Until then, every thought—every thought, regardless of its content—is in the form of dilemma. You can be thinking, "ice cream cone", or, "Run Spot, run", and you may imagine, because of the content of your thoughts, particularly if they are "good" thoughts, that everything is all right. But all thought is in the form of a dilemma for one who does not understand.

Observe the entire content of an instant of thinking. Not just its apparent content, the verbal sentence, or concept, or image you have in mind, but the entire event, including your involvement with the thought, your relationship to the thought, and the tendencies generated by the thought, the tendencies generated by thinking itself. Apart from Truth, all thought is dilemma. The quality of thought is dilemma. The quality of ordinary life is dilemma. Apart from "radical" understanding, or real meditation, life is only suffering, search, endless self-"creation", endless qualification of the Force that is Reality. Every thought is "shape".

DEVOTEE: Suppose you are sitting, looking at a very beautiful lake. You are sitting by a lake, and you are looking at it, and you are thinking it is a very beautiful lake. What would be the dilemma about that?

SRI DA AVABHASA: As I have said, the content of the experience is apparently only delicious. But witness this entire event. No one has ever been utterly relieved in the presence of a lake! If you were to become truly sensitive to the current of your ordinary awareness, you would find yourself getting angry in gardens, terrified on vacation! It is only that you are chronically unaware of the nature of your own event.

What is occurring in this moment by the lake, sitting, looking at the lake? It seems to be very beautiful. But it seems only beautiful because you are thinking of it in contrast to other experiences. You have been very busy, harried, distracted, demanded, frustrated, and so you go and you sit in the country. You "create" an interval, to eliminate the conditions of all these things that ordinarily distract you. You sit in the country, and you relax. You feel a little vital, psychosomatic peace. This sitting in the country by a lake, and all things like it, are actually forms of traditional practice. This seemingly natural repose is actually a sophisticated practice of meditation. There is a long and ancient tradition for it. We could justifiably claim that "a lake in the country" is as fixed and formal an object of meditation as the "Our Father", the "Name of Ram", or "Om Mani Padme Hum".[5] As you spend your several days in the country, that first moment of ease into distraction begins to disappear in the currents of usual awareness. And you begin to become sensitive to all kinds of movements within—thoughts, feelings, sensations, desires, demands, frustrations. When the power to distract is lost, no country lake can remove from you the pain of ordinary existence. It is the same with those who sit with me in Satsang. Nothing apparently is going on. It is a nice room. It is very quiet here, generally attractive. But you can sit here, in Satsang, and go through the most incredible internal drama. And where does all of that come from? It is not caused by the room. Sometimes it is good, sometimes it is not so good—good trip, bad trip. Just so, in the country. In a matter of time you pass from rest and return to the same internal self-revelation. If you were forced to remain in the country and it became your condition rather than your distraction, you would find out that you are disturbed, still disturbed. Then your search goes on in the country, as everywhere else. You discover that the very condition of being someone looking at a lake is a form of suffering. It is a symbol for Narcissus. Compared to running away from a shotgun, perhaps it seems like pleasure. But if you examine the content of experiencing itself, even at ease and pleasure, every instant is this shaping, or limitation, of the fundamental sense of existence. There is the generation in the living consciousness of the separate self sense (this "me" watching the lake), of differentiating thought ("lake" is different from "city", different from "shotgun"), and of desire ("Oh my, this forever"). Consider all the various desires awakened on vacation! What is disturbing people (and all human beings are disturbed, regardless of their relative condition) is not simply their external condition, or their present experience. What is disturbing is their human condition, their birth. You are disturbed by the fact that you are sitting here, that you are alive in some separate sense, in a world of conditions. This is the disturbance. And as long as that condition exists in the living consciousness, there is suffering. That is the suffering. You can change the images, you can change the apparent conditions, you can "change" the world. You can go from here to another world, another condition. You can go into another state while alive, a drug state, a Yogic state, a different house, a different country, a place in the country. You can modify all the conditions, external and internal, but you will never change the essential condition that is your suffering. Only the one who understands is always already free.

What are people like on vacation? What are people like who are sitting in the country? Most of the time they are obnoxious—all these people on vacation, who are all of a sudden so terribly "fulfilled"! How do they treat one another? What kind of tolerance do you have for frustration on a vacation? Practically none. There is no peculiar intelligence required to sit by a lake and feel quiet. Any ding-dong can do that. There is no sighted person who can't feel pleasure looking at a sunset. What is so extraordinary about that? People talk about country, earth, and vacation as if they were a real alternative to the demands of Truth. Anybody can go down to the ocean and feel comforted. But what has that got to do with your death? What has that got to do with your genuine state? All it has done is distract you from your chronic state. Temporarily, distractions make you insensitive to your common state. Vacations are for that purpose, only to desensitize and rest you for a brief period of time. They are sleep and refreshment in life. They are not a way of life. And sitting by a lake, or any ordinary or extraordinary distraction and pleasure, is not a way of life. Even traditional, strategic, or ego-based, spiritual activity is only a temporary distraction. Truth is not a matter of any of these distractions. It is a matter of intelligence, the activity of real intelligence. If there isn't this activity of real intelligence, you are only distracted, and you are only suffering. Eventually, every individual begins to realize that he or she is only suffering. Eventually, people realize they are fundamentally disturbed. The more sensitive you are, the more obvious it is to you. The less sensitive you are, the more experience you require before it becomes obvious. The more force there is in intelligence, the more obvious things are, and the more intense is your conscious life. The less sensitive, the more distracted, you are, the more in terms of time or experience you require. But the ultimate event is the same in every case. This intelligence, this sensitivity, this real observation of ordinary activity, arises. And <u>that</u> is Yoga, true Yoga. That is meditation. That is spiritual life. That is religion. That is the way of Truth. Truly, there is no satisfaction in mere birth. Life is not a form of satisfaction. Life is a form of modification and motivation. It is ego-self-"creating". It is also very-Self-realizing. It is for the purpose of experiencing, or dramatizing and elaborating, latent tendencies, and, by a process of "radical" understanding, of transcending and transforming the given drama by the grace of Truth.

People who get a little religious, or whatever, like to make all kinds of pious statements about what this all is. But this is simply a realm of dramatized desire. Of course, all things arise within the Truth, or within the Real, but as soon as the Truth Itself becomes obvious, "you" disappear. So this world is not itself the Truth. Truth is that real activity, that real intelligence, that is the transcendent <u>core</u> of all manifestation. When Truth becomes active and alive, when this real process takes place, the whole form of motion that <u>demands</u> this limited and compulsive experience, this birth, is dissolved. Thereafter, if anything arises, humor is not lost. Therefore, one who understands continues to live, but with humor, and such a one dies with humor.

The peculiar quality of all such people is unique. Ramana Maharshi, from the moment of his "realization", wanted to get out of here. From that moment, he wanted nothing to do with life. There came a certain stage in his continued existence when people surrounded him, asked him questions, and wanted to serve him. He consented to live the function of Guru among them, but he never wanted it to last particularly long. He was really very anxious for his death. Not anxious in the sense of a neurotic need to die. But he was more than happy for life to come to an end. And his death was very ordinary. It was a lot of festering and pain and moaning and groaning. Because he understood very well what this ordinary life and death was all about, his death was a demonstration of the nature of this common pain, illusion, suffering. There have also been other "saintly" people whose life appeared as a kind of flowery, miraculous pleasure. Even so, you must remember that these people also have all died! The quality all such beings have in common is this "humor", this freedom in the midst of conditions. And all such people demonstrated this "humor" by their lives, in different forms, in different times, and for different people.

There is no moment of this usual birth that is not in the form of desire, of thought, and of separate self sense. Nothing is going on but these, which are the usual qualities of human beings. And none of these truly arises separately. They are a complex event, a single event. And that event is the usual condition and limit of human beings. If you begin to become aware of your activity, your state, your condition from moment to moment, you see there is nothing but this. Nothing but desire, thought, and separate self sense. The ones who are regarded by the various traditions to have been enlightened Sages, or else Saints, or even true Yogis, were those who had become extremely sensitive to this fact. At some point, usually relatively early in life, they became incapable of distraction and fell into their ordinary state, which is fear. When there is no distraction, there is only fear. The great ones are those who have utterly passed through their fear. They re-cognized it, knew it again. Other people are of the same nature as these great ones. They are perhaps momentarily insensitive. They are capable of binding distraction. And the differences between all beings and all disciples are the differences in their capability for binding distraction. The kinds and degrees of distraction to which they are subject, and the intensity of their distraction—these are the differences. These qualities "create" the differences. And the experience of individuals in this great process of Satsang is one in which their capability to be bound by distraction is undermined, frustrated, turned about.

Therefore, periodically, every individual passes through a time of crisis, of great resistance and fear. Ultimately, every disciple and every devotee must go through the same process the Guru has already gone through. Perhaps not precisely in the same apparent form, but, within the pattern of his or her own conditions, that same process must occur.

Thus, spiritual life is this undermining and frustration of the capability for binding distraction. That is why spiritual life has often been described in harrowing terms. That is why one who is a disciple must be very responsible for the basic quantities in life, for the relationship to the Guru, and for the dramatization that he or she is tending to "create" as a result of this spiritual process in the world. Spiritual life is a crisis. Therefore, spiritual life does involve discomfort at times. When discomforts of the crisis occur, this does not mean that spiritual life is failing, or that you are not good enough for it. Crisis and discomfort must occur. The crisis, or turnabout, is what it is all about. It is supposed to occur. You are supposed to suffer the purifying events. You are supposed to encounter resistance in yourself. You are supposed to discover all kinds of garbage in yourself. So why should there be any special resistance to it when it occurs? There may be discomfort, and you may wish you didn't have to go through it. But apart from that, there is no reason why you should be overwhelmed or completely disenchanted by the fact that you are witnessing a period of intense conflict, crisis, suffering, and disturbance. The more time you waste identifying with all of that, the less sensitive you become to the event. Therefore, Satsang, devotion to Guru, and a loving and intelligent approach to all of life should naturally increase or intensify in the periods of apparent discomfort.

All of these apparently disturbed or crisis episodes in this real process of spiritual life are themselves very intelligent, very meaningful. They have a great deal to show you. The more capability you have for passing through these times, the more useful they become. The man or woman who is really using this process can be passing through this crisis almost continually, with great frequency and intensity, and yet, like a soldier on the march, such a person never misses a step, never reveals it in any peculiar, outward manner. He or she continues to function, and apparently only enjoys life. He or she doesn't get involved in a whole drama of upset. But in the beginning, when a man or woman is just beginning to pass through this kind of crisis in consciousness, there tend to be reactions and breakdowns whenever this crisis process begins. In the beginning there is very often an emotional collapse, even a physical collapse.

There are these episodes that have an almost psychotic quality to them. And it is during those times that the person is wondering whether to come here or not and all of that. But as one passes through these purifying episodes, one begins to realize how one must function in terms of the real spiritual process.

When this event begins to arise in the mature disciple, there is always already something familiar about it. One knows the signs, one knows what is about to occur, and one knows the kinds of reactions that will build up. One knows that, instead of clenching one's teeth and resisting it, one should find some more work to do during that time. Instead of planning a vacation or a binge when one sees a crisis coming, one cancels all forms of entertainment or ordinary distraction, every thing that one would normally use to distract oneself from one's usual state. One plans a lot of work for the coming days. One plans on an ordinary, functional life. One makes good use, really good use, of these episodes. The more intelligent one is, the better the use one makes of them. The less intelligent one is, the more capable one is of binding distraction at that time, the more one will look for means to dramatize one's state, and to distract oneself from the lesson that turns purification into transformation.

You must know that everything I am doing is a means to bring about this crisis. I desire this crisis in you. I don't want it <u>not</u> to happen. I don't want to console you. I don't want you to be happy in your unconsciousness. I want you to become sensitive to your actual state. I want you to know very well what you are always up to. I want you to become capable of seeing yourself under all kinds of conditions. I want you to see the machine of your ordinary activity. And I want it all to collapse. I want it to come to an end. I want the death of all of that. If that death does not occur, there will be no release, no real enjoyment for any of you. There will just be the continual round, the self-"creation" of this unconscious event of life and death, that is already distracting you. I look to "create" the various means necessary to serve this crisis, because to serve this crisis is to serve understanding, to serve the joy and true bliss of liberated realization, of "radical" understanding. Every instant in Satsang is working to bring this about.

DEVOTEE: Could you say something about faith in relationship to Satsang?

SRI DA AVABHASA: The truth is not that you must believe or have faith in order to find God or to get to heaven. The truth is that your present activity of contraction is destroying your present enjoyment of God. Where there is understanding, where this whole activity of the avoidance of relationship is obviated consciously, you discover that there is no longer any doubt or withdrawal from relationship, because doubt and withdrawal are merely contractions of your own state. Disbelief, lack of faith, and separation from God are your own activities. You do not need to "create" some feeling of faith over against those activities in order to find God again.

When you understand your own activities, you stand already faithful, already continuous with Reality. You don't "believe in God". That is just a formula for controlling the mind. When you understand your own contraction relative to Reality, the contraction becomes unnecessary, just a shirt that you wear. Then you'll find that nothing like doubt or faithlessness is present in you. But a kind of fullness persists, an enjoyment in which you no longer make these negative assumptions. You will act on the basis of this sense of continuousness, of non-obstruction. The more you live in that manner, the more you will see the Nature of that Condition in which you already exist.

Without understanding, without presently recognizing your own life of avoidance, all your attempts to have faith in God are forms of bad faith, or seeking. Their motivation is dilemma. In such cases you believe in God in order to get rid of your dilemma, whereas faith arises in one who has understood his or her assumed position, no longer claims it, and rests in the natural, or prior, position.

The usual man or woman is always recommending some prescription that you can apply to your state of suffering in order to get better. But even the traditional teaching doesn't originally come in that form. The traditions of the West, in which language like "sin" appears, do not just say, "Believe in God." They say, "Repent," acknowledge your sinfulness, and in that acknowledging turn to God. Understanding, then, is the principle that precedes faith. A critical undermining of the concept and activity of sin precedes faith even from the traditional point of view. Just so, in the East, where words like "karma" and "maya"[6] prevail, spiritual life is not just a matter of believing in Nirvana or Brahman[7] with all your might until you become That. It is a matter of undermining the principle and condition of illusion. Even in the traditional terms, something like understanding precedes the release into Reality.

Therefore, understanding cannot be eliminated from the whole affair of spiritual life. You cannot be told merely to believe and have that be the way of Truth and life. Such instructions are just more stuff. But if you have perceived and undermined the self-contraction, which is exploited

212

by the search, then you are already not turned away. You already see what Really Is. You already see Reality and practice It. All absence of faith, or all the doubt and conflict that you find in yourself, is not caused by anything outside you. It is your own reaction to everything that occurs apparently outside you. It is your own activity.

Divine realization is not going to occur until you become responsible for that activity. All of your hoping to be faithful and have everything turn out all right is not going to affect the sum of your life in any sense. No amount of experiencing will affect it, because, fundamentally, you are in this crunch, living separatively, and seeing the world as mystery, illusion, something independent, multiplied endlessly, and mortal. All those perceptions are fabrications made by your own activity. When you take a drug, you tend to have certain kinds of experiences. Likewise, if you live this life of contraction, you tend to have certain types of experiences. But when the contraction is undone, these typical qualities of life, such as faithlessness, doubt, and fear, cease to "create" your vision, and they cease to qualify your fundamental Nature. Then, instead of living in these qualities and trying to get out of them, or suffering them, you live in your fundamental Condition and use It. You function in and as It, and It reveals Its Fullness to you.

How long must you sit and look at the stuff in yourself? Understanding is not a matter of watching this stuff as if it were on a television screen and saying, "Oh, yes, what a dummy I am, one crisis after the next. Avoiding relationship? Son of a gun." That is the lazy approach to it. If you are just luxuriating in life, if you merely have enough vitality to get it on with your basic consolation from day to day, then you don't bring much intensity to the observation of yourself. Somehow it must become important to you that you understand.

The cultic "guru" merely fascinates and pleases you and lulls you to sleep. The cultic "guru" just keeps you asleep in front of the TV set. The cultic "guru" doesn't really serve you. The cultic "guru" exploits you, perhaps because he or she has so much doubt about the world and about the Divine. And the cultic "guru" suffers a false vision of disciples. The cultic "guru" doesn't dare to master the disciple, doesn't dare generate another difficult moment for the "poor" disciple.

The true Guru does not have such an option. The true Guru has to get up and arm-wrestle that idiotic disciple. The true Guru must curse at the disciple again and again, and be difficult with the disciple, and also continue to maintain himself or herself with humor. Disciples and devotees

213

are as much a test for the true Guru as his or her own sadhana ever was. If there is anything that can make you lose your humor, it is a disciple! But the true Guru cannot get into the habit of believing the disciple, whatever his or her number, whether he or she plays stupid, or "poor me", or is getting angry, or is having a difficult time, or whatever he or she seems to be doing. None of it is true.

Disciples must not be consoled and fascinated and made unconscious. They must be quickened. As egos, they do not want the crisis of this real intelligence to occur. They want to be served with all the things that will allow them to continue in the drama they are already "creating", in order to justify irresponsibility, self-indulgence, and the cycle of concerns that is their peculiar suffering. So the true Guru, knowing the disciple only wants to sleep, must continue to shake and offend him or her. And the true Guru must be offensive with humor, so as not to wind up causing a negative effect on the disciple, and must actually serve the disciple's transformation, the disciple's understanding.

DEVOTEE: In *The Knee of Listening,* you describe the loss of the "Bright" as the loss of faith, and you equate faith with Satsang.

SRI DA AVABHASA: Genuine faith is the principle of spiritual life. It is Satsang, and it is commitment to living the Condition of Satsang.

DEVOTEE: But isn't Satsang more than faith? Isn't there more substance to it than simple faith?

SRI DA AVABHASA: Real faith is not just the simple-minded belief that everything is going to be all right. No—faith is the "radical" assumption of the Condition of Satsang. Therefore, faith is not independent of understanding. Only understanding permits the principle of faith to be alive in you. The conventionally religious person lives faith as a sort of forceful believing, independent of understanding. The faith I am talking about, however, is founded in insight, in "radical" understanding of your true Nature and Condition. True faith is the "radical" assumption of the Perfect Condition, which cannot be assumed without understanding, and which is spontaneously assumed when you understand.

Just so, Satsang, or the spiritual relationship to the Guru, is not independent of understanding. You cannot live Satsang without living understanding as well. Satsang is not merely belief in the Guru and aesthetically emotional feelings toward the Guru as an individual. Such belief is conventional religion. Satsang depends absolutely on understanding. Satsang is the Condition, and understanding is the Process. In one who understands, the quality of understanding is faith. Such a one uses his or her true Condition, uses the Divine life, uses God, uses the Guru.

One who truly lives in Satsang with the Guru knows no limitation to spiritual life, which is always full, always being fulfilled—perhaps not always in the form he or she expects it, but self-fulfillment is not the principle of this process anyway. People do not live as Consciousness. They do not use God, and they do not live in the Divine Condition. They do not use the Guru, and they do not live in Satsang. They lack faith, or the assumption of the Condition of Satsang.

When you assume Satsang—not through an act of will, but through prior understanding—when you truly live in the Condition of Satsang, then you are making use of the Guru. Then you are making room for the Guru, you have become available to the Guru, you have become available to God, you have become available to the Divine Reality with which you are identical, so that the perfect spiritual process can begin in you.

However, if you live without faith, obstructed, self-involved, committed to the egoic life and to the principles of identification, differentiation, and desire, then the Great Principle, which is God, Guru, and your very Nature, cannot operate. In that case your life is a struggle. It is limited to the range of experiences that are karmically determined, and, whether they are good or bad, you will only experience them as mediocrity, all because you lack faith and do not assume your real Condition.

People do not live as if they are identical to the Divine Self. They live as if the most supreme spiritual principles do not exist. Even those who begin to adapt to the conditions of spiritual life assume these principles only in mediocre ways, depending on how they feel on any given day. They do not assume spiritual practice as a discipline. They may experience extraordinary phenomena and changes, but the perfect transformation, the perfect enjoyment, does not arise for them. Every day such individuals wonder, "Should I or shouldn't I?" "Is there or isn't there?" They find all kinds of reasons, depending on their apparent condition that day, to doubt the Guru, their own motivations, and the Divine Nature of things, and they remain in doubt. Doubt, rather than faith, is their fundamental condition.

Doubt, which is felt in the vital, is simply another description for the vital contraction. It is the assumption of separate life and the principle of identification, differentiation, and desire. Where there is faith, there is no

215

vital contraction. You no longer assume the cramped-up capsule that you emphasize by your internal habit and assumption. Rather, you are open, round, and completely available to what perfectly transcends the limited state. The Divine Self, or God, perfectly transcends it, and the true Guru perfectly transcends it. The mediocre person, regardless of how intimate he or she may be with the Guru, the Guru's Teaching, and all the instruments of Satsang the Guru has empowered, never sees the great affair, the great event, the great process. The mediocre person only gets little hints of it every now and then, and they are not sufficient to change him or her. The mediocre person has remarkable experiences here and there perhaps, but they are not sufficient to transform the principle of such a person's usual life. One who truly lives the principle of Truth, however, lives Satsang perfectly and lives by faith, lives the assumption of the Divine Self, the Guru, and God. These become his or her continuous, intense, and "radical" assumption, and he or she truly lives Satsang absolutely. Then such a one begins to see the process of Satsang at work in his or her life, because only such a person has truly made room for these great functions. The power of the community of such devotees who live Satsang, who live by faith, is very great.

In the Buddhist tradition it is said there are three things to which the aspirant must resort. In their language, these three are called the "Buddha", the "Dharma", and the "Sangha": the Siddha-Guru (or descended spiritual Master), the Teaching (including the living spiritual Power and the discipline), and the company, or community, of those who are living the Truth. The first event that occurred in our work together was the meeting in which you and I established a relationship. The next quality that began to be developed was the understanding of what spiritual life is, what this relationship is, what this process is, and what it demands. So the Guru, the Teaching, the discipline, and the communication of the spiritual Power of Truth have been the things that have held your attention in the early stages of my establishing this Ashram. In the last few months you have seen me begin more and more to emphasize the Ashram as a living process, an activity, a responsible activity of communion, or community. I have been "creating" various functions, first by bringing them to life in myself, and then passing them on as responsibilities in others. So we have been working in the last few months to "create" the Sangha, the company, the community, of this way.

The ordinary person is avoiding relationship in complex ways. Therefore, it is necessary, in the midst of this work, wherein you re-cognize this avoidance, for relationship to be the condition. There must be living, working, functional relationship. So there must be the opportunity for those who are living Truth to live It in relation to one another, to examine together the Teaching, and to turn as a living community to the Guru. Community is the natural condition of all true spiritual activity.

People who are moved to approach spiritual things are generally motivated by their illusions. They use what they gather through reading and the usual meditation to isolate themselves further, to console themselves, to generate forms of self-imagery, good feelings, immunity, various narcissistic qualities. But I intend for this Teaching always to be displayed in relationship, because it is only in relationship that it begins to make any sense, that it begins to show itself. So there must be this functional confrontation with the Teaching by those who are using it. That confrontation is the use of it.

Many of you have at one time or another expressed to me your feelings about organized spirituality, organized religion, whatever. People commonly have negative and resistive feelings toward all forms of community and human relationships. And the reason, the ultimate root of these feelings, is the tendency towards separation itself. In a certain sense you can see that it is completely justified. There is a great deal about organized spiritual and common life worthy to be resisted! On the other hand, Truth is manifested only in this relational condition, and It is perceived in relationship. It is a crisis that occurs in relationship. Therefore, the community of Truth, the community that lives this Teaching, is absolutely necessary. But what makes it a thing to resist is your lack of involvement in it, your separation from it, your dramatized resistance to relational and community life. The spiritual community must be alive. Every one must be alive within it. Every one must be active in relationship and must function within it. So if you do become active, responsible, alive, and intimate with others who are living this way, the whole sensation of resistance to so-called "organized" spiritual life will disappear, because you will be dealing with the problem of community only as that which it truly is: an expression of your own avoidance of relationship. But if you do not live this way, if you do not move into functional relationship to this way, you will only see it externally. Everywhere you will only see your reasons for separating from the Guru, the Teaching, and the community, because you will have made it into something without life, something worth resisting. Therefore, it is the responsibility of those in this Ashram to live this way, to become active in it, to use it, and to become responsible for it.

Sri Da Avabhasa
at Sri Love-Anandashram, 1992

9.

One-Pointedness

DEVOTEE: When in Satsang with you, I've started to have this experience of being drawn into some kind of trance, almost like a sleep. I've been trying to deal with it, but I don't know whether I should hold back, hold onto it, or let go.

SRI DA AVABHASA: It makes no difference. Why does this experience seem to cause a question in you?

DEVOTEE: I wonder if a decision, or will, is required, or is it all you?

SRI DA AVABHASA: There are two things here. You have this experience that comes on you in Satsang, and you have your search. The experience is not what you are really asking about. What are you observing about yourself?

DEVOTEE: Well, I'm trying to get the answer. I'm trying to find out what to do. I'm still searching.

SRI DA AVABHASA: And what is this searching, this getting? What does this trying to find the answer involve? What is it you are doing when you are asking these questions and manipulating yourself? What are you up to all the time? What are you doing? You are disturbed!

DEVOTEE: Yes!

SRI DA AVABHASA: That is the truth. Always disturbed. You come here disturbed, and you go through some changes. Then you feel very restful. Then you start wanting to wake up, but you also want to go back to sleep: "Should I do this, should I do that?" You are disturbed! You are asking questions. You have this dilemma. That is true. That is the whole point.

The point is not the answer to this question, not whether you should allow yourself to go into this trance state or not. Such answers are only a response to this question. But this question is what you are all about! It is this chronic disturbance, this dis-ease, this contraction, this avoidance of relationship, this whole process in all its forms.

And all of this is going on while you are just sitting here! But "just sitting here" is a potent means of making you gradually aware of your ordinary activity. That is the point, not these experiences in themselves. The entire process is to make you aware of your ordinary state, your ordinary activity, to see it directly, to know it, to re-cognize it, to know it again. Understanding is the point of all this. Since understanding is the point, the experiences themselves are not what it is all about, nor your reactions to the experiences, nor your questions about them, nor their content, nor their interpretation. What you do about this particular experience is no more significant than the interpretation of dreams. The having of dreams is significant. The fact that they occur is already their meaning. That is their significance. Their very activity, the fact that they occur—that is the process. Apart from the process itself, it makes no difference what a dream "means". It is a process in consciousness, having its own value. So also with the process of your experiences in Satsang. But while this process is going on, you are disturbed. And this disturbance manifests as endless changes in your state. You are wandering, and wondering about it. So it begins to seem that even this simple experience, just sitting here, has become a question! It is as if the sky were a question! But in itself it is not a question. There is no question. "You" are the question! Your state is the quality of dilemma, of dis-ease. Your state is your question.

The Force of Satsang produces phenomena at various levels. It represents itself in many forms. But the value of it all, the ultimate purpose of it all, is for you to see your own activity. If you were not always becoming a question, always contracting, there would be nothing to ask about these phenomena.

And what is this process of becoming a question, a fundamental dilemma?

You must have had the experience of listening to music through a pair of stereo headphones. The sound appears to arise from some point in the middle of your head. If you become very attentive to that process itself, the point of hearing seems to be generated in the very midst of your head. If you become even more attentive, this point of "hearing" will become the thing in which you are interested, and you won't hear the details or even the sounds of the music anymore. The psycho-physical organism as a whole operates in very much the same manner. The functional mechanisms of perception, such as the ears, seem to "target" phenomena. When one is weak, when one has suffered through not living these phenomena from the "point of view" of Truth, one becomes obsessed with this point of awareness, the target itself. One begins to identify with it. Perception, or experience, "creates" the separate self, the ego, and one begins chronically to live in terms of this target as if it were the source and center of life.

No matter what phenomena arise, you habitually manipulate them in such a fashion that this target becomes the focus and apparent source, or origin, of your attention. This target becomes the chronic implication of all experience. Just so, this trance experience arose in your case. As usual, there was the attempt to return to the point of view of this target, to give it all "significance", until the experience itself was lost in the dilemma. The target became the obsession. In this manner, the intensity, or potency, of all experience is used to reinforce Narcissus, the sense of separate, independent self.

That target is "me", ego, but it is also a question. It is always in the form of a dilemma. Because it is a form of contraction, a point, it is always separate, even from the phenomena that cause it! When this target becomes the obsession in consciousness, the living phenomena of one's spontaneous existence are no longer clear. If you are focused compulsively upon the target of the sound, you can't differentiate the patterns of music any longer, you can't enjoy the sound, you can't turn to the source of sound, you contract from it continually. So the sense of existence as this contracted point is the dilemma. When you speak from the point of view of separate self, it is always as dilemma. And when you begin to perceive, to turn back to, the spontaneous world from this point of view, everything seems mysterious, threatening. Then everything assumes the form or quality of a question. And there is a continual return, folding back in on that target, or point, again and again, until this activity is re-cognized, known again.

When re-cognition takes place, this "point" is seen to have no fundamental and fixed or necessary reality. It is simply a functional means of organizing phenomena. The apparent implication, the separate self, the ego, that "point", is unreal, a temporary and dependent event. It is a secondary "creation". It is purely a functional phenomenon, a psycho-physical habit. But this habit persists, until there is a turnabout—from compulsive orientation upon this point, this target, to what is <u>prior</u> to that.

What is the nature of sound and of hearing prior to that target? Before there is the avoidance of relationship, before there is this contraction, with its sensation of separate self, what is the Nature of Consciousness? The whole psycho-physical mechanism is a mass of these targeting agencies. From top to bottom, inside and out, the whole life-process amounts to this sense of a point, a target, and people identify compulsively with that, so that they begin to live from its point of view, forgetting entirely the origin of this point.

Now, Satsang is like the origination of sound. It is received by people in the ordinary manner, through this targeting mechanism, and they compulsively try to orient themselves in relation to the experiences of Satsang, so that they can continually regain the sense of this point, this target, this ego. As if <u>that</u> were the significance of these experiences! But when they remember they are in Satsang, when they turn to the origin of this phenomenon of Satsang rather than upon this target of experience, something happens quite naturally in consciousness. It is not at once illumination, or perfect knowledge. It is a spontaneous and momentary release of the separate point of view. It allows the Force that is being communicated to fill this mechanism, to harmonize it without the compulsive contraction, the compulsive generation of this point of view. Over time, this fullness begins to become a kind of intelligence, an effortless receptivity, a new event in consciousness that begins to see this activity perfectly, to see this contraction as it is, <u>as</u> contraction.

The avoidance of relationship is a purely secondary activity. It is suffering. It is dilemma. It is not real. It is not itself Reality, or the present and true Condition. It has only a conventional value, but no ultimate Reality. One who understands begins to fall from this compulsive activity into openness, no-contraction, and such is true Self-Knowledge. The true "Self", or Reality, is not a point. It is not the implication of experience. It has no significance in time. It is not limited to any visible form, any form of energy, or light. It is not located in space. It has no center, and no bounds. Satsang is the communication of that Truth, the Force of that Truth, to those who are still living this contraction.

The virtue of Satsang is that It communicates Its own Nature. It makes this activity of contraction obsolete by various means. It begins by "creating" in the devotee a gradual re-cognition of his or her own activity, in the midst of Satsang, in the midst of the force of life, of Truth. Therefore, temporarily, this activity goes on, this questioning, this wondering, this self-manipulation, even while some other things are going on that are in themselves quite natural, intelligent, or extraordinary.

What you do in Satsang is a ritual duplication of what you are always doing. You come here already disturbed. This avoidance of relationship, this contraction, is what is always going on. And, you buy it! You continually buy it. I often make a fist out of my hand to indicate this activity to you, because it shows very clearly what happens when there is this contraction. If you curl your hand in upon itself, a sensation is generated at the center of the hand that concentrates attention. This sensation in the hand is differentiated from every possible thing that is outside it. It becomes the center of concentration. The same process, generated in the psycho-physical life as a whole, becomes the point of view toward all of this, whereas it is only a functional reflection of various forces. At every level of consciousness, the entire psycho-physical mechanism is devoted to this activity, this curling in upon itself. This is Narcissus. And all the searches of human beings, all the traditional approaches people have taken to Truth, are done from this point of view, the point of view of this dilemma, this contraction, this "ego".

People want to know what happens after death. What happens after this sensation is released? Nothing! They want this sensation of independent existence to survive. They become frightened. All questions are from this "point" of view, because this is the archetype of all questions. This is the only question. This is the dilemma! This is the fundamental experience of people from moment to moment. So people are suffering, they are afraid, they are self-obsessed, they are distracted, they are unconscious, they are turned in upon themselves. They are always turning, curling. What do you do?

I was looking at some people here earlier, while we were sitting quietly together. Some of you are always doing something when you are only sitting. It would be amusing to put it on rapid film. It is an incredible ritual, an endless dance, touching and examining your bodies, stimulating this sensation of separate existence by every kind of nervous action or perception. There are numberless tiny adjustments of the physical position, endless touching of various parts of the body, moving of the body, creasing the body, "creating" little tensions in the nervous system that concentrate attention. It is going on internally as well, with every form of perception and thought, every possible kind of communication from the environment and the internal functions of the psycho-physical life. This same targeting, this compulsive contraction, goes on and on and on and on. And what do you think you do when you get up to leave this room? Do you think that the strategy of your activity changes when you say good morning to someone or when you walk down the street or when you go to work? This same thing is always going on. It's an endless contraction, endless self-sensation.

Sit quietly in a chair sometime. You will observe how every moment of perception is combined with a symbol in consciousness, a thought, an image, an interpretation, a contraction of the field of the living consciousness. Always, this target is "created". People are always "meditating". People are always tending to be "one-pointed". Every moment of life is devoted to the "creation" of this "point". And this contraction ultimately becomes terminal. It becomes psycho-physical death, because it is endlessly intensified, to the point of absolute contraction, so there is no longer any flow of force. If I hold my hand clenched tightly in a fist, increasing the tension, so that no blood will flow, it will eventually wither. So people are dying of this one activity. All physical pain is a contraction. Fear is a contraction. All emotions are contraction. All thought is a contraction of the force-field of the living consciousness. In that case, all that one ever experiences is one's contraction, this avoidance of relationship.

So all human beings are like Narcissus, who sought to escape from all conditions by separating himself from all relationships, all confrontation, who removed himself to the wilderness of absolute isolation, so that he was left sitting nowhere by the side of a pond. What is more, he spent the rest of his life looking into the pond, gazing at his own image, and supposing it to be his loved-one, some other that he loved. Not only is Narcissus separate, isolated, but he is conscious only of an illusion, perpetually. Apart from understanding, all human beings are just like that. There is this avoidance of relationship, this continual contraction and meditation only upon the internal reflection of events, this endless thinking, this endless motivation from the point of view of the ego, the assumed "place" of perception and cognition, so that there is no real perception, no real knowledge.

When one looks with eyes, one sees this point. When one hears, one concentrates on this target. When one acts, one acts from the point of view of this targeted center. One never deals with the source of these perceptions. One never communicates with the nature of events. One never realizes that one is not the point of perception, that one is always already one with perception itself and all that is perceived. The <u>origin</u>, or the "Self", of every person is not this ego, this target, this sensation. The Divine Self is the origin of all these sensations. The body arises within the Divine Self. Sound arises within the Divine Self. Light arises within It. All things arise within It, but the very Self is not qualified, nor is there any separately existing self or thing.

In Satsang with me, the Force of this Divine Self, this Absolute Reality, is communicated. Just as you function on many levels, including the solid physical being, the vital energy of life, the psychic life, the emotive, or emotional, life, the processes of thought and subtle cognition— just so, Satsang with me, the communication of Truth, manifests on many levels. It manifests as physical, human relationship with the man of understanding and his friends. It manifests as a Force—which demonstrates Itself via many forms, vital, emotional, psychic, and the rest. And It manifests as a "radical" Condition of life.

In this Satsang, there is the communication of verbal concepts, and more. But while this communication goes on over time, you begin to perceive your own activity in Satsang. Satsang does not simply remove that activity as if by magic. It <u>reveals</u> that activity. So Satsang, the living of Satsang, which is spiritual life, involves a crisis in consciousness, <u>the</u> crisis of consciousness. Therefore, the activity that is your suffering is not removed by magical, external, and willful methods, but it is shown, demonstrated, eventually perceived, and, finally, perfectly understood.

Even while in Satsang, there is a kind of warfare going on in the disciple or devotee. There is this contraction. But he or she is continually being drawn out of that, by the Force and very Condition of Satsang, and more and more fully into the Company of Truth. The Truth draws you even though you continue to contract. And the result of that tension is a dredging up in you of the perception of your own activity, on many, many levels. It <u>must</u> take place on every level.

While talking with one of you today, I used the simile of a well. When one first comes to Satsang, one is like a dark, deep well. Way up at the top, the light comes in around the edges, but it is black, unconscious, below! When the Light of the Truth shines down into it, all of these weirdo, slithering things come climbing up the sides. All the hidden, slimy activity begins to be disturbed, awakened, and moved into the Light. Just so, every moment in Satsang increases the necessity for responsibility in the disciple, because the Force of Satsang isn't merely a good feeling, a consolation, something smiling, happy, and pleasant. It is not magic. It is

225

a living Force, the Force of Truth. This Force moves into the "well", into the human functions—this circuit of descending and ascending life—and brings up the chronic patterns of ordinary and unconscious life, revealing them at the level of the actual conditions of life. In the midst of this real process, the subtle tendencies of life are revealed as desires, as incredible compulsions, which, even if they were known before, now seem to become worse. The intensification of everything is the activity of Satsang. And what is there to be intensified in the usual man or woman, except this negative pattern, this contraction? Of course, there are difficulties. Real spiritual life requires everything of a person. Real spiritual life is a crisis!

One who lives in Satsang experiences many revelations of his or her state. Dreams become intensified. There may be spontaneous physical movements, changes in the physical body. Life may become burdensome at times. Thoughts seem to become endless. The individual may become disgusted with his or her own game. But the whole effect of this communication of Truth over against one's own tendencies is to bring about an awareness of one's own activity, or contraction, on every level. Where this begins to occur, all of the hidden qualities can escape into the Light and be merged in the Light of Consciousness. If you maintain yourself in Satsang with me through the intense and perhaps protracted periods of crisis, this whole process appearing in you will begin to become interesting. You will cease to react to it, to resist it, to attempt mastery over it, to do anything about it. You will live Satsang. You will simply live this relationship and Condition that is Satsang with me. And self-indulgence, or outward dramatization of these revealed patterns, will cease to be your motivation, because you will understand this spontaneously revealing activity to be a purifying event.

Therefore, the true devotee lives this Satsang, enjoys this communication of Truth, sees his or her own activity, and begins to understand it. An intelligence begins to awaken in which the true devotee re-cognizes this perfectly. But none of it is a form of magic. It is a miracle. It is a grace. It is an absolute activity, practically unknown in the world, because the world is devoted to this ordinary action of contraction, the avoidance of relationship. Neither the process nor the Force of Satsang is magical. It doesn't simply "happen" to you, so that you feel good, ready to smile at everyone, as if you were on a drug. No wisdom could be gained by such magic. You are required to go through the purifying event, so that when you arrive at the point of intelligence, where you can live these human functions from the "point of view" of Truth, you have the wisdom by which to do that. If the negative effects of life were simply removed, as if by magic, without any of your real participation, you would gradually and unconsciously move back into the same condition. However, in general, the participation that you are required to have in this process tends, by the Force of Satsang, to be made more of an internal one than an external one. For the most part, instead of having to live through the latent patterns, or karmas, of your life in the form of massive and unyielding disasters, you are brought to live through them in lesser forms that can at least be handled, perhaps with difficulty, but they can be handled. And much of it takes place in dreams, in self-purifying kriyas, in various Yogic processes.

True spiritual life is a demand, it is a confrontation, it is a relationship. It is not a method you apply to yourself. Your "self" is this contraction, and this contraction is what must be undermined in spiritual life. Therefore, the Guru comes in human form, in living form, to confront you and take you by the neck. The Guru doesn't merely send down a grinning symbol, to be reproduced with a few fairy comments for everybody to believe. The traditional images and records of past help serve very little. At best they may help a person move into a position where he or she can actually begin spiritual life. But Truth must come in a living form, absolutely. Truth must confront you, live you, and meditate you. It is not your meditation that matters. Truth must meditate you. And that is the Siddhi, or marvelous process, of Satsang. Even while Truth is meditating you in Satsang, you are busy doing more of the usual to yourself, waking yourself up, putting yourself to sleep, reacting in every possible and unconscious manner to the Force of Satsang—but you are being meditated.

You cannot be "meditated" by one who is not alive. Even if you believe in one who is no longer alive in human form, you cannot provide the necessary, living means for this meditation. Truth must come in living form, usually in the human vehicle of the Guru. Spiritual life involves this marvelous process, this Siddhi, this Satsang. If this Siddhi, or living spiritual process, is not activated, it doesn't make a damn bit of difference what exotic or humble spiritual methods you apply to yourself, for they will always be of the same nature. They will always amount to a form of this contraction. All your remedial methods, all your beliefs, all remedial paths, all conventional and consoling religions, all merely strategic religious and spiritual methods, are extensions of this contraction. Truth Itself must become the process of life. Truth must communicate Itself. Truth must generate conditions in life, and make demands, restoring the conscious participation of the individual. Dead Gurus can't kick ass!

At the beginning, the position of the individual in relation to Satsang is relatively passive, apparently passive. The Fullness of Satsang is given to him or her as a grace. When this process begins in you, it acts as an intensifier of your various internal and external activities. A practical relationship is established with you, conditions are applied to your life, demands are made of you. The Force, the energy aspect, of Satsang progressively intensifies, wakens, and fills you. Your vitality, your health, your relations with the environment, the condition of your life—these are the things that are confronted first. Essentially, during that early period, you are responsible for being in Satsang, responsible for maintaining that connection, and for fulfilling the practical demands given to you through that relationship. You are also responsible not to indulge, or dramatize, externally, in life, the ego-revealing phenomena that are arising in you in this Satsang.

People don't begin to believe any of this, really, until they begin to have the experience. They experience Satsang and the quality of spiritual life here as something very enjoyable, profound, whatever. Then, all of a sudden, they come to that first point of crisis in this way. An insane compulsion, almost like possession, overcomes them and seems to demand they leave this work. They wake up one morning: "My Guru is no good, the Ashram is no good, spiritual life is no good, none of this has anything to do with me, I should leave and return to my previous, relatively happy existence." If they are able to hold on through one or two of these episodes, they begin to see it as their own activity, not anything that truly reflects on this work, and they become stable again in Satsang. When this form of the crisis is thus overcome, a new one develops, just as suddenly, and with equal force. Then they think: "The work is good, my Guru is good, the Ashram is good, Truth is good, spiritual life is good, but I'm no good, I'm not ready for it yet, I'm not an old enough soul yet, I'm still full of desires, I guess I'm still supposed to seek for a while." This is the crisis of self-doubt. It is often topped off with the "observation" that "My Guru hates me." And so they want to leave, if only for that reason! Narcissus is always a form of contraction, of separation, of leaving. But if they are able to pass through this one, still holding on to Satsang, still maintaining a responsible refusal to exploit this internal movement in a life-drama, they begin to settle stably into the real self-recognition that is spiritual life.

All of the Great Siddhas, the realized ones who have taught in the world, have given Satsang to their disciples as grace. That was their essential activity and gift. They didn't come merely to give a method for seeking, to give a conceptual teaching only, to "create" a myth, a structure for the mind, some sort of mentality. They brought <u>themselves</u>. They entered into <u>relationship</u> with the world, with their disciples. That relationship is the very structure and outward sign of the process I have described. <u>That</u> is spiritual life. That process is spiritual life. The Great Siddha "lives" his or her disciples. The Truth "meditates" those in Satsang, through a period of relative passivity, until there is more experience of this actual process, more responsibility, more awakened consciousness. Then, at some point in time, when this insight into the usual pattern of activity is developed and has become real, has become the actual intelligence of the disciple, then perhaps true enquiry will develop. But, until there is this fundamental understanding, you can ask yourself any question, carry on any sort of deliberate internal activity or form of concentration, and it will have neither more nor less value than the enquiry "Avoiding relationship?" But when this Satsang with me has become fruitful in you, when this intelligence is alive, when understanding already exists, then enquiry in the form "Avoiding relationship?" may become truly appropriate. Even so, as you will see, it is just an extension of the thing that you are beginning to see in yourself as a consequence of every moment in Satsang. The more there is of Satsang, the more you see your own activity, your disturbance—and, in due course, by virtue of this very process, you begin to re-cognize it, to see that there is the avoidance of relationship, this contraction. When you know this utterly, when this contraction is undermined in real knowledge, that very insight is what I have called "understanding". And, when that understanding is alive, then understanding can itself be made the approach to experience, moment to moment, as the conscious enforcement of this insight itself.

So Satsang with me, the relationship, or Condition of relationship, to the man of understanding, is the means of understanding in those who resort to me. Truth Itself is communicated in Satsang with me. And the life of Satsang with me is simply to live this relationship to me. It is simple enough in concept, but when you live it from day to day, you complicate it. It becomes a question, a dilemma. This is because you don't in fact or simply abide in Satsang with me. You don't live the Condition of Satsang with me without qualification. You continue to live this contraction, this avoidance of relationship. You still tend to separate yourself from the Condition of Satsang. There is this tension, this drama, this warfare, in Satsang. Periodically, you see again what you've been up to, and, quite spontaneously, you fall out of this contraction into the Condition of

Satsang again. Periodically, you catch yourself running, contracting, moving into your own forms, so that you see it all again and return to simple Satsang.

One of the earliest manifestations of Satsang in certain people is these kriyas, these spontaneous movements of body, posture, attitude, and breath. As a means of understanding the difference between the Force of Satsang and the usual state of human activity, look at the difference between these kriyas and the kind of nervous activity that people are always performing. Examine the usual man or woman at "ease", with the constant picking and grabbing and self-conscious posturing, the endless attempts to become comfortable while still maintaining an inner feeling of confinement, or entrapment. All of that is re-action to outside or generalized forces. Such actions are always in the form of reflexive, self-directed movements. But genuine kriyas are internally and spontaneously generated. They are movements from within <u>outward</u>, not a curling inward from without. That is why these kriyas are themselves a kind of purifier, because they tend to break or reverse compulsive contraction. But these kriyas are not themselves profound. They are not Truth. They are active at the level of the psycho-physical body only. There is nothing "out in the cosmos" about them. They are evidence of a process which is restoring the nervous system to its natural harmony and intensity.

Whatever arises as experience in the course of Satsang and its meditation is not itself the point. Visions, subtle phenomena of all kinds, are themselves only images of this "target". They are themselves forms of contraction. They come in order to disappear! As I have said, one who understands is not endlessly engaged in all kinds of extraordinary phenomena, or even simple internal phenomena. That whole affair has come to rest, and the Force that <u>contains</u> and supports all such phenomena is consciously alive in such a person. The "Light" of which all visions are only a modification is Consciousness Itself. One who understands no longer lives from the point of view of the target in <u>any</u> <u>sense</u>. Not this gross body, not the vital body, not the subtle body, not the subtle mind, not the mind at all, not any form of subtlety, not <u>any</u> center, not any "light" body, not any eternal body, <u>no</u> <u>body</u>! The "point of view" of Truth is alive in the one who understands. It is no longer separate. It only manifests or appears to manifest as all of these points, all of these functions. Therefore, such a one also appears in all the ordinary forms. But wherever the "target" tends to arise, it vanishes. That one doesn't buy it. That one doesn't act from its point of view. That one doesn't dramatize it. That one doesn't believe it. That one never becomes it. For such a one, there is never the loss, under any conditions, of profound, direct awareness of his or her true Nature, his or her Real and Great Condition.

Whenever the Siddha-Guru appears, a new function has appeared in life. The Siddha-Guru is not another thing to be made into a target, not an other ego that has appeared to be worshipped, glorified, contained, and fitted into a cult. When that one appears, a new function, a living process, has become possible, which is Satsang. But, paradoxically, it is very difficult to get anyone interested in Satsang, because people are devoted to this process of contraction. From the point of view of the world, of the search, Truth and Satsang are always rejected. Satsang always has only a paradoxical presence in the world, because It always works to undermine the search. Those who truly become interested and are capable of enduring the activity of this Satsang are those in whom the whole process of seeking in all its forms has begun to fail in a critical manner. In such people, the options of the search have begun to subside, to die. Such people have become immobile, truly desperate. They are not necessarily about to go into a psychotic state! It can be a very "natural" and non-clinical despair. But it is a critical failure. Such people become capable of Satsang, and Satsang may also become their opportunity.

DEVOTEE: You have said that those who live in Satsang must be responsible not to dramatize, or act out, the tendencies that are awakened and revealed in them. But I don't think you mean they should be repressed. Would you explain it?

SRI DA AVABHASA: I am speaking of these things as they occur under the conditions of Satsang, not in life without conscious benefit of Satsang. Previous to Satsang, an emotion, an impulse, would develop, and, under certain circumstances, you just plain did it. The point of view of Satsang never entered into your decision or your reaction. But when you begin to live the Condition of Satsang, you have an entirely different principle of life from which to view these phenomena. When Satsang truly becomes the Condition of your life, then, as tendencies arise, it is not a matter of repressing or suppressing them, or of doing anything to <u>them</u>. They are mechanical, internal phenomena, patterns reflecting themselves in the force of the living consciousness and in the body. The more you live Satsang and begin to understand the activity that "creates" these phenomena or causes them to rush up in you, the less you tend to identify with the phenomena themselves. Then the activity and the patterns become only interesting to you, rather than sources of motivation. You begin to acknowledge them to be patterns only, not "me", not something "I" must suppress, but patterns arising, and which you are observing. The true disciple simply lives Satsang during that time. He or she doesn't even become concerned with the patterns. The true disciple enjoys Satsang. If some episode is causing him or her particular distress, mental or physical, the true disciple doesn't suppress it. He or she does nothing to it. He or she scrubs a floor, washes a window, types some letters, goes to work, has a sandwich! The true disciple doesn't get involved in that drama, either by suppressing it or by exploiting it. The true disciple does <u>nothing</u> about it. He or she <u>enjoys</u> Satsang! This thing that is arising in him or her is only a form of contraction. It is always a form of contraction. To "buy" it, perform it, or suppress it is to contract further, to take on the form and point of view of contraction, to reinforce it. But the point of view of Satsang is relationship, not avoidance. So one who lives the Condition of Satsang is already free of the stress of this contraction. Such a one lives and is aware beyond it. Such a one is living another Condition, Satsang Itself. Such a one is already not living this contraction, and so he or she has neither to exploit it nor to suppress it. He or she is living Satsang. Therefore, he or she sees this is a phenomenon only, a phenomenon that arises in Satsang, a purifying event.

If you live in Satsang, you allow the revelation of tendencies to occur as a subliminal activity, as a display of impressions, as a sensation, but not a necessary motivation. Regardless of the form in which it arises in you at the time, you carry on your practical activity. You don't sit alone in your room, trying to keep from going out and indulging all your desires to the point of bewilderment. No, you stand up, you go down to the Ashram, you sit in Satsang, you see some friends there, you go to work, you take yourself to life's <u>functions</u>, its functional responsibilities. You can permit this thing to arise in you, without distress, without identification, because of present Satsang. When Satsang becomes real, the actual and present Condition of your life, your relationship to these self-revealing tendencies begins spontaneously to change. The more you live Satsang, the more you begin to see how your relationship to this process is changing, how it is unnecessary to dramatize, or live, the latent tendencies. Indeed, you see that to live the arising tendencies, even the apparently pleasurable ones, is the very strategy of suffering.

At the beginning of a person's life in this Satsang, I simply require, as a condition, that he or she be responsible in certain functional and practical levels of life. There must be a foundation for this process. Thus, when you first arrived, various practical matters were discussed with you, including your diet, your work and responsibilities, your environment and living conditions, the relationships in your life, and the like. This is to be certain you are willing to assume practical responsibility for an otherwise endlessly dramatized life. Those in Satsang must be essentially responsible for the processes of money, food, and sex. I do not mean that one who enters Satsang must become a sudden saint! But when one lives it all with practical intelligence, there is a living firmness, a foundation for this revealing process. If there is nothing but a hole out the bottom, every time something is thrown in, it goes out the bottom. If you are only ready to indulge what arises in you, Satsang will only give you more energy for it. Such people need a parent, not the Guru.

So I require people to take on real responsibilities at the practical level of life. You do not require the absolute perception of Truth in order to moderate your diet. It is simply a practical affair. A supportive, enjoyable diet that gives strength, keeps the body vital, keeps the life vital, is simply a matter of intelligence. To be intelligent, you need not first realize absolute Truth. But no one can realize Truth absolutely who has not first become intelligent. If you moderate and purify your diet, then, in the primary activity of taking food, dramatization is not taking place. If you are carrying on some sort of insanity, some gross craziness, in the forms of sexual indulgence, I require you to understand the relational necessities of your sexual life and your "creative" communication of force into the world. Then you will have a practical hold on the use of this primary function. All of this is not in itself for ultimate reasons, but for purely practical reasons, for the sake of the spiritual process, to prevent exhaustion of the vital life, and the distractions of unconsciousness, weakness, disease. Just so, at the level of money and the general conditions of life, for purely practical reasons, I want each of you in Satsang to be fundamentally responsible for your income, and the quality of your environment. All of this for purely practical reasons, not for any idealistic reasons.

Every single thing that could possibly be dramatized is a form of contraction, of separation. And what are these things you are concerned about "repressing"? You don't worry about repressing or exploiting your tendency to love people, to share life with them, and help them! There is no danger represented by that, so there is no problem about having to either repress or exploit it. What are the things you are wondering about exploiting and repressing? They are all negative, destructive, separative

233

tendencies. Therefore, from the beginning, a little of that knowledge which is the principle of Satsang must be clear. You must have seen <u>something</u> about your ordinary activity, your suffering, your usual state. When you see that your usual state is your suffering, you fall into the relationship that is this Satsang. Then all of these forms of contraction begin to lose their force. They are undermined by this relationship, whereas they are otherwise reinforced by exploitation, suppression, or repression. The more there is this intensity of relationship in Satsang, the less force these impulses have. They begin to wind down; the clenching of the "fist" weakens. So don't repress it. Live Satsang. And carry on a practical order of life. It is only when you have the point of view of this contraction, this dramatization of tendencies, that you have to be concerned with repression or exploitation. If your point of view is Satsang, all of this is only a secondary affair, only an impulse. If you are not identical to the center of that impulse, it is not necessary to do anything about it.

Replace concern and worrying about your tendencies with some practical activity or some pleasurable activity in the ordinary manner. You must become intelligent in how you live this life while you are busy being responsible for it. Sadhana, or spiritual practice, is not a matter of living "up tight" all the time, preventing all of your craziness. You must learn how to treat this psycho-physical entity from the point of view of real enjoyment, of relationship, of Satsang. You must increase life-pleasure through the practical enjoyment of functional activities in relationship. This also serves to undermine that whole process of suffering and bewilderment.

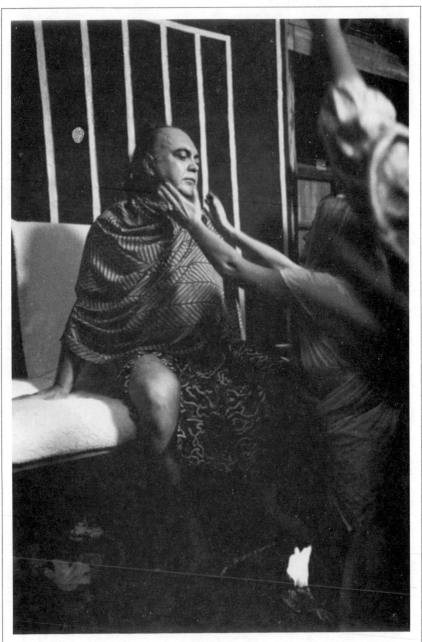

Sri Da Avabhasa
at Sri Love-Anandashram, 1992

10.

The Path of the Great Form

DEVOTEE: Does proximity to you, closeness to your body, have any relationship to the intensity or the effects of Satsang?

SRI DA AVABHASA: What is your experience?

DEVOTEE: It doesn't seem to have that much to do with the body. It seems more to be how much I am in felt contact with you and how open I am to you.

SRI DA AVABHASA: It all depends on the quality of your relationship to me. You must discover the quality of Satsang for yourself.

DEVOTEE: I have two feelings or ideas about what is happening that I would like to discuss. I have had the feeling that you were receiving uptight, or "bad", karma and transforming it inside yourself.

SRI DA AVABHASA: What do you think?

DEVOTEE: That's what I see, that's what I experience, but I'm not certain.

SRI DA AVABHASA: Why do you doubt it?

DEVOTEE: The other thing—after sitting with you for a little while, I seem to be observing a pattern in myself in Satsang, and tonight I had the feeling that, although it is somehow different every time, there seems to be a continuity in terms of a pattern. At least I experience it in terms of a movement up through the chakras. Is there some sort of non-verbal instruction being communicated?

SRI DA AVABHASA: In you?

DEVOTEE: In myself, yes. Something that you do and, therefore, that I am also learning to do, because I am sitting in your presence.

SRI DA AVABHASA: Many structures are used in the subtle process of Satsang with me, and it appears different all the time—the experience is different from person to person, and the quality of Satsang seems to change in the same individual from time to time. The reason there are differences, apparent differences, is because different aspects of the mechanism are animated or become a focus of attention at different times. In different individuals, the obstructions, the qualities, of the mechanism, are different, and so different things must occur. If you have a head cold, you must clear out your head. If you've got an ulcer, you must heal your stomach. In each individual there is a different structural dis-ease, and these structures are physical, psycho-physical, psychic, subtle. Each person may observe a characteristic activity in himself or herself in Satsang. A particular kind of process may be characteristic over a certain period of time, and then it may change. But these experiences in themselves are only purifying movements. Like that time when you blow your nose and your head finally gets clear. You don't go around pointing to your sinuses for the rest of your life, saying they are the center of Truth!

At various times, we have discussed the qualities of this structure in which we live. In describing its various levels, I have spoken of the three primary centers. One is the region of the solar plexus, or the soft region of the lower body, which is the epitome of the psycho-physical organism. It is the basic center, or foundation point of view, of all "religious" activity in human beings, and it is the center of all ordinary human activity. The current of the Force, or Light, of Truth moves down into life by a process of descent into this region. But that same Force, or Light, also ascends. The structures through which the current ascends have been described in various traditions. The Yogic traditions of India, in particular, describe the pattern of ascent through chakras, the wheels, lotuses, or centers, which are the etheric and subtle counterparts of various vital and strategic locations in the spinal structures of the physical body. The epitome, or fundamental "goal", of the ascending life is the sahasrar, that massive area at the crown of the head, or, more properly, just above the head. It is the primary center of all subtle activity, or all activity that is traditionally called "spiritual".

"Spirit" means "breath", in Latin. In Sanskrit, the word for "spirit" is "prana", usually translated as "life", "breath", or "vital force". Traditionally, spiritual life is the aspiring, or ascending, life of the vital force. The Kundalini is prana. The Kundalini Shakti is prana-shakti, the subtle, or ascending, activity of the life-force. In the practical activity, or Yoga, of traditional spiritual life, the vital force ascends, or is made to ascend (by the methods of the Yogi, or by the initiatory grace of his or her Guru), toward the sahasrar, the point or region above. The Yogi attempts to merge his or her manifested vital force with its subtle source above. This produces the trance, or samadhi, states of most traditional Yoga. There are many types of this traditional Yogic meditation, or contemplation, but they are all meditations of this same subtle process. All traditional spiritual life is simply an exploitation or realization of the ascending, aspiring aspect of the life-force. Just as all conventional religion is essentially a surrendering to or waiting on the descending energy, whose Source, or Nature, is called "God", all strategic Yoga, or the spiritual life of ascent, all spiritual method, is a contemplation, concentration, or exploitation of this subtle mechanism of the ascending activity of that same energy, or vital force.

The Yogi may do various things to control and harmonize the breathing process, in order to go inward and upward. To the same end, the Yogi may add strict control of sex-force, diet, thought processes, etc. There are also various forms of concentration on the subtle centers, or chakras. Some traditional Yogas involve the contemplation of internal, subtle sounds, or concentration on the internal "lights" of the life-force. There are many forms of traditional Yoga that contemplate the various qualities of the subtle mechanism of the human being. The greatest form of traditional Yoga, or the ascent of life, is the spontaneous Kundalini manifestation, in which all the classic "spiritual" events arise spontaneously, by the grace of the Guru. But the entire affair of the ascending Yoga is only one of the possible major events in this activity that is real Satsang. The activities of descent are also a primary form of the purifying operations of this Satsang with me.

Some who live in Satsang with me begin to have kriyas, spontaneous physical movements. Breathing activity, or automatic pranayama,[1] may appear in the form of sudden breathing, fast breathing, quieting or even cessation of the breath. Internalization may come quite naturally, then concentration, inward experiences of centers, visions, lights, sounds, and experiences of the merging of bliss. Some people may have these

239

experiences. Others may not have those kinds of experiences, or they may have them only occasionally, or they may only have certain of them. These other people may experience more of the calming descent of that same bliss and Force that purifies the mind and the life of the Yogi by ascent. Where the obstructions, or limiting tendencies, of a person are essentially in this descending course, then there is awakening, or opening, of the descended, human life, the "purification of the navel". Where the obstructions and the tendencies lie more in the subtle, or ascending, course of the same mechanism, then there are the ascending Yogic manifestations. The pattern of descent and ascent is the circle, or circuit, of the life-force, the true "round dance". And in one who understands, the conductivity of that full circle is re-established and full, whatever stimulations of descending and ascending activity arise in the stages of purification.

So far we have covered two of the three major centers. There are many chakras, and there are also many points within the descending parts of the total mechanism. The epitome of descent is the belly, and the epitome of ascent is a point above the head. But there is a third "place", or epitome, of conscious life. It is described in the tradition of jnana, or Self-knowledge, represented by Ramana Maharshi and others. The religious traditions speak from the point of view of "life". The esoteric mystical and Yogic traditions speak from the point of view of subtle "planes" of existence, or "light". But the philosophical traditions of the jnani speak from the point of view of the "causal" being, or body. The "causal" being, or body, is the seat of deep sleep, and also of the formless state, whose epitome is in the heart, on the <u>right</u> side of the chest. The physical heart of the waking and descending life is felt to the left, and the heart chakra of the subtle, or "dreaming", life of ascent is in the middle, but the causal center, or heart, is on the right. The causal center is without light, without sound, without form, without movement. The seat of the causal body, the formless "body" of deep sleep, is also, when opened and conscious, the seat of the "fourth state" (beyond waking, dreaming, or sleeping), called "turiya", which transcends all modification.

The traditional Yogi seeks to merge in the sahasrar, or the highest, subtlest place of light. The religious person seeks to be full, to receive and be full of truth, life, the descending grace of God. But the jnani, the one who resorts only to the intuitive process of ultimate Self-knowledge, tends toward this causal center, beyond the mind, beyond form, beyond visions, beyond conceptual and perceptual experiences. When this causal center opens, beyond the apparent unconsciousness of sleep, the state called "turiya" arises. It is a conscious state which, like a witness, transcends the three ordinary states of waking, dreaming, and sleeping.

All of the traditions that have arisen in the great search of mankind have been communicated, whether consciously or unconsciously, from the point of view of one, or perhaps more than one, of these three primary centers of conscious existence. Read the traditional texts. Where the jnani speaks in terms of identity with the very Self, the Yogi, the spiritual individual, speaks in terms of union with Truth, Light, God. And the religious individual, the one who surrenders to God and serves God among human beings, talks about his or her relationship to God and God's "creatures". But all three of these centers are only portions of one great mechanism that all human beings share, all living beings share, all worlds share. This mechanism is duplicated in all forms, including this manifested universe. The manifested cosmos is structured in the same manner as your own tripartite mechanism.

But Truth Itself contains and is prior to all of that. And Satsang is the Company of Truth. Satsang is not simply, then, the attempt of seekers to do various things with these three centers, or functions, of manifested existence to which the traditions have paid so much attention. The traditions always start from a low position and seek to attain their goal, which is fullness, union, or identity. But the point of view of true spiritual life is already that of Truth Itself, not of the search, but of the enjoyment of Truth, the living of It, the present enjoyment of It as one's Real Condition. All real transformation that occurs within the form of life at any level is a manifestation of Truth, of Satsang, not of the search. When one moves into that relationship that is Satsang, and lives it as the Condition of one's life, one may begin to experience curious manifestations in any of these three great or traditional forms. So, as in the case of the questioner, there may be these experiences of the chakras, the phenomena of the "subtle body". In others there may be another kind of experience, more of opening, and fullness. In another it may tend to take the form of intuitive directness. Some speak of their developing religious and spiritual life in terms of "life", while others speak of it in terms of "spirit" and "light", and yet others speak of it in terms of unqualified "being" and "consciousness".

Even so, each of those points of view is, in itself, a limitation, expressing only a portion of the structure that is within the possibility of Truth. This is because your experiences occur only in the areas where purification is stimulated by the obstructive presence of your particular tendencies. Therefore, Satsang is the true resort of all men and women, regardless of their particular tendencies. And very Truth and "radical" understanding is the necessity of all men and women, regardless of their experiences. Now, exactly how this mechanism of Satsang works is not clear at the outset. Before its perfect realization, it cannot be grasped. It is elusive. Therefore, as you say, you are trying to get down to it. But if you try to discover or perform it yourself, your blood vessels will burst. It won't happen. If you don't already live the point of view of the Heart in all of the structures of the bodily mechanism—gross, subtle, and causal—how are you going to move into it? Your point of view is in your head, or your legs, wherever. Satsang, the Company and Condition of Truth, is your true resort, and in Satsang with me you will find yourself falling spontaneously into the Heart, the Heart of Truth, which transcends the manifested realizations.

There is no real contraction. There is only that enjoyment that is Truth, what is always already the case. The body is a process of conductivity in which the force of life moves in a circle, descending and ascending. The center, or epitome, of the life-aspect of this force is the vital center in the general region of the navel. The epitome of the subtle body is in the region of the head, above the eyes, even above the head. It manifests not as life, or vitality, but as Light, unqualified Conscious Light. The modifications of most subtle, pre-cosmic Light are everything one knows as "life". The center, or epitome, of Prior, or Transcendental, Existence, even beyond the causal knot, is the region of the heart on the right side of the chest. Its realization is Very Consciousness, Absolute Space, Formless, or Unqualified, Existence, the Vast Bliss. Nothing is being communicated but That which includes these three regions. There is nothing but That. Amrita Nadi is Its Great Form, the Conscious, Moveless Spire Which Extends from the Heart to the Light.

All of life descends from the most subtle, ascended region and returns to it, in a continuous cycle, conducting its Light, becoming movement and form. But even this Light is a reflection of the Heart, or Unqualified Existence, just as the moon reflects the sun. This Heart, which is the source of all Light and life, and of which every thing is the reflection, is itself without quality. But the Heart, the Light, and the life are all included and transcended in That which is very Truth, the Great Form. Therefore, those who come to this Satsang, where the Truth, this Living Reality, is communicated, see It manifested in them in three characteristic forms. One is in the form of movement, or of life: kriyas (spontaneous vital and physical movements), changes in the life-pattern, experiences and circumstances at the level of life, waking phenomena. Then there are the subtle, or dreamlike, manifestations: lights, visions, dreams, sounds, patterns internal to consciousness. And then there is the causal awareness, even falling into a profound sleepless sleep at times, and even into turiya, the "fourth state" which transcends waking, dreaming, and sleeping. But all of those phenomena are manifestations at particular levels of the great and all-inclusive process that is this Satsang with me.

This Satsang is communicated from the "point of view" of turiyatita, or beyond the fourth state. It is the "point of view" of the Heart Itself. It is the "point of view" of Amrita Nadi, the Form of Reality. Satsang is the very "point of view" of Truth, in which all things arise as modifications. Truth, Satsang, simply manifests as these three qualities I have described, and Truth Itself, the "point of view" which generates the processes of Satsang, may be said to exist as a fourth and a fifth quality. The two qualities of Truth are the transcendent and the unqualified. The first and foundation quality is the Heart. It is the very Self of Reality, enjoyed when the mind falls into its Source, and the gross, subtle, and causal qualities are purified of obstruction and contraction. This is turiya in its Perfect State. And the fifth quality is Perfect Form, turiyatita, beyond the fourth. It is the Eternal Form of the Heart, the Very Form of Guru, Self, and God. When the Guru speaks ecstatically of his or her Divine and All-Pervasive Nature, the Guru is not speaking of some egoic magnificence, but of That Which Is all that is, and That Which Alone Is, and That Which Stands Out As the Obvious when the ego is dead.

The Truth, which is Satsang, and living the Truth, which is sadhana, or real practice, make possible the entire event of the transformation and revelation of this great mechanism. It is alive. It is not a structure that can be blueprinted and then prescribed. Something can be said about It, but the saying is not equivalent to the sadhana, or life, of Satsang. It is alive. Just as it is very hard to control the breath once it leaves the body, just so, this incredibly subtle mechanism, whose Source and Very Condition Is the Truth, is infinitely elusive, absolutely elusive, paradoxical. That is why the image of the Mother Shakti and the images of the Deity in general, particularly in the Orient, have a paradoxical quality. They are almost comical at times, and at other times they are treacherous, violent. Krishna is beautiful and blue. But he teases those who desire him. He eludes them. He runs away, and he says "Yes, I'm coming, I'm coming." But you wait and you wait and you wait, and he doesn't come.

The Mother Shakti appears in all kinds of forms. The holy Yogi bathes his mind with repetition of mantra until the mind is purified of desires, and then he walks down to bathe his body in the Ganges. But when he gets out of the water, without his bathing suit, this fantastic woman is standing on the beach with a basket of fruit, with chicken sandwiches, and a little wine. The next day he has to turn in his mantra and his robe! He goes to tell his Guru how he broke his vows. His Guru asks, "With whom?" "With that beautiful chick over there!" says the penitent. And his Guru says, "That is the Mother Shakti. She got you!"

The image of this great process of conscious life has been symbolized as all of the paradoxical deities, and the symbols themselves have a life. In my own experience, the Mother Shakti has appeared like anyone else, then different, as all kinds of forms, very strange, then beautiful, then wise. But what is being communicated through the imageries of these experiences is this great process, only a piece at a time. It is perfectly glimpsed only when there is resort to Truth absolutely. Otherwise a person will buy the experience to which his or her tendencies gravitate. So, if you are willing to buy a little foggy light between your eyes, then that is where you will be. Whatever you are willing to buy, you will be given. That is why the deities are pictured in such paradoxical forms. They will give you a little pink fruit, if you will come and take it. The dog comes for a bone, gets the bone, and leaves. Thus, if you begin to get very interested in the process that is awakening in Satsang, you may become attached to the experiences themselves. Perhaps, at some point, you will buy it. You are already buying it. That is why this question was asked. You may even become very angry, and reject Satsang, because of the position you are put into by craving your own internal life. Narcissus is addicted to looking at himself. It is the only thing he will defend.

DEVOTEE: Will you say something about how the Shakti relates to Truth?

SRI DA AVABHASA: What is called "Shakti", the Divine "Creative" Power, is not a separate thing, not truly an independent Force. It is the same that is meant by the "Self", "Reality", "Truth", "Guru", or "God". The name "Shakti" is simply used to describe that aspect of the Truth that appears as movement in manifestation. "Siva-Shakti" is perhaps a more appropriate or complete designation of the Truth. In other words, the Real is moving-"creative", but It is also static-perfect-untouched. The true Shakti is the Conscious Force in and as which every thing exists. It is the present Nature of every thing, of all beings, and It is also the substance, support, and end of all that arises.

244

Now, as it pertains to practical spiritual life, the way of understanding, or Satsang with me, may come to involve a pronounced subtle purification or transformation. In that case, the particular qualities of the spiritual experiences that tend to arise are most associated with the subtle body, as opposed to the physical, gross body, or to what is called the "causal body", the deep well of being in which there is no apparent form, no apparent modification. The subtle body is actually the range of internal functions, of inward-directed energy and awareness, of dreams, visions, and thoughts. Thus, in the course of the process in this Satsang, you may become sensitive in that subtle range of functions, and, thus, come to view the cosmic process essentially through the subtle media. This subtle process of the conscious life is in the mode of phenomenal internal Yoga, rather than in the mode of the austere intuitions characteristic of the traditions of Buddhism or Advaita Vedanta, or, otherwise, in the mode of the continuous practical orientations of those in whom human activity in the world is the center of sadhana and experience. When the subtle process is stimulated, there are experiences of the Yogic activity of the universal Conscious Force.

The life-force displayed in Yoga is called "prana-shakti". It is an aspect of the universal life, the subtle life of the very Self of Truth. The Shakti in this form has a specific involvement with the internal processes of living beings, particularly human beings. If the internal energy can be stimulated, or if its source and its course in the body-mind can be concentrated upon, there are internal awarenesses and transformations of a subtle kind that arise. Ordinarily, this process is not something over which a person has the least control. One doesn't "awaken" it oneself. It is always already there. It is just unconscious and subdued. It ordinarily only feeds the outward tendencies of life. The actual process of the spontaneous "Kriya Yoga", which I have described in *The Knee of Listening*, is stimulated by contact with a living Siddha-Yogi in whom this Yogic Force is unobstructed and functioning very consciously. The contact with such a person stimulates the living energy and purifies the inner functions of their obstructions. By virtue of that contact, the internal, subtle process becomes conscious, awakened, and it manifests itself through a series of purifying events, both internal and external. The obstructions are broken down, perhaps on an apparently gross level at first, then always subtler and subtler.

The first such Yogic experiences a person might have are various bodily sensations. One may feel a certain energy, a certain heat or cold, a

245

certain tendency to move, little jerking, spontaneous movements, a feeling of discomfort, an intense, even erotic feeling all over the body, or in specific regions of the body, such as the head. These purifying movements are an automatic Hatha Yoga.[2] Sometimes such a person does Hatha Yoga postures spontaneously. He or she can't help but do it at times. One might perform postures of which one would be physically incapable were this Force, or Yoga-Shakti, not active. One may experience automatic pranayama, or vigorous and curious exercises of the breathing functions. The whole process of all that can be called "Yoga", including all the types of traditional Yoga, may arise spontaneously in that person, beginning with the more physical forms of Yoga, then moving on to the subtler purifications and the subtle qualities of experience and meditation. There may be times when the mind becomes rapid, when there is endless thinking, without apparent cause, and then, just as spontaneously, it breaks down, breaks apart, slows down. Such a one may begin to have visions at times, and to perceive internal forms, colors, smells, tastes, sounds. Such a one may hear the nadas,[3] the sounds which are always vibrating within. There may be visions, symbolic experiences, dramatic mudras, or poses of hands and body, movements of all kinds, shaking of the body, ecstasies, spontaneous devotion, love, bliss, and profound concentration in the various psycho-physical centers, always moving toward and culminating in the primary region of the subtle life in the crown of the head. The movement of such subtle experiences is always upward. And since the Yogic centers are subtle, not limited to the physical form, the highest subtle centers are actually above the physical head, but the process is sensed as a concentration in the general area of the crown. This region is called the "sahasrar".

This subtle, ascending, Yogic process is that which most people would identify with Shakti. But in fact it is a demonstration of only one course, or one aspect, of the greater pathway of the universal and absolute activity of the true Shakti. There are essentially three paths, forms, or qualities of spiritual life, based on the three primary functional points of view. The classical texts talk about the "knots" that need to be opened. "Liberation" is the opening of these "knots".

There is a knot associated with the region of the navel, including the entire solar plexus and the soft organs which extend above it (including the heart, lungs, tongue, and parts of the brain) and below it (to the anus). Some indicate its center, or epitome, to be just below the navel. Truly, that entire region is the gross-vital center, the life-center. There is a tradition of practice related to this center. If you are centered, or stable, there, you are strong, upright, direct, straight, active in proper relationship to things, in the proper harmony. The purification of the "navel", or of the life itself, is the imminent goal of religious devotion and the various harmonizing practices which are applied to life. Ordinary religion, or exoteric religion, essentially looks toward life-purification, life-stabilization, life-opening. And the life-center is its point of view. This is the first of the three paths.

The second path is the subtle path. Such is the point of view of ascending Yoga and the various exercises or processes that are very similar to ascending Yoga. Such are the various paths that exploit the internal qualities rather than abandon them. In the traditions of subtle ascent, the subtle body is conceived in terms of various chakras, or centers through which the subtle force moves. These centers culminate in the sahasrar, the primary center of subtle life. Several of these subtle centers are described as primary "knots" in the traditional texts. The sahasrar itself is not included among these knots, but a primary one is just below the crown, in the midbrain, behind the eyes. When all of these subtle centers are open, or, in other words, when the living, inward-directed energy moves and merges in the sahasrar (the "thousand petalled lotus"), that is the highest realization from the point of view of the traditional ascending Yoga.

The third path is one that is seen represented in such individuals as Ramana Maharshi and in the non-dualistic, or even monistic, Hindu traditions, such as Advaita Vedanta. In such cases, the path is generated from the point of view of the causal being, the conscious seat analogous to the deep sleep state. The gross path is analogous to the waking state, the subtle path is analogous to the dream state, and the causal path is analogous to the deep sleep state. The paths associated with the formlessness of the Divine, or Ultimate, Reality are essentially forms of this causal path. And the "knot" of the causal heart, on the right side of the chest, is the center from which these causal paths are generated, and toward which they move by various critical and intuitive means. When this center, or knot, is open, waking, dreaming, and sleeping no longer limit the primary enjoyment that is the very Self, or the True and Prior State of Consciousness Itself.

In fact, all three paths necessarily involve Force, the Shakti, the Conscious Force and Power of the Divine, the Living Reality. Christianity, an example of the religious life-path, is very concerned with the "Holy Spirit". That is the Force, the Shakti, conceived from the point of view of

247

the life-knot, the vital center of the descending force, the conductor of the descending Power of God. "Prayer", the most characteristic religious appliance, is always looking for this descent of Power. And "fasting", the ancient companion of prayer, is the means of purifying, or preparing, the "place" for the descent of God's Grace and Power. The worship of the Mother-Shakti in the sects of Hinduism is expressed yearning for Her to descend, to send Her gifts downward. All exoteric religious points of view, and, originally, even all religious points of view, want Power to come down. Western occultism is the worshiping of the descending Power. That is the descent of Shakti. All movements, all of this visible world, is Shakti.

The subtle path is also concerned with Force, or Shakti, in a particular manner. The subtle Yogas exploit the capability of prana-shakti to ascend. They do not merely or only hope for the descent of Power, but they seek to become involved with and ultimately identified with the ascending functions of that same Power. In that case, there is the subtle process of internal movement, generated in an inward and upward direction, toward concentration and merging in the subtle regions above.

In the causal path there is also Force. The formless Divine, the very Self, Brahman, is absolute, unqualified Force. It is only that this particular path is not directly associated with the gross or subtle "movements", the descending process, the ascending Kundalini process, or the experiential processes talked about from either the religious or the traditional Yogic point of view. But it is the same Force.

Ultimately, the Teaching that is Truth is not generated from the point of view of any of these three knots, or these three dilemmas, and the paths generated to open, or solve, them. The descending life-force, or gross force, the ascending, or subtle, force, and the moveless, original, or causal, force are all there in all human beings. And, progressively, each individual will tend to go through a characteristic developmental, or purifying, process, according to his or her particular tendencies in relation to these three qualities, when he or she moves into Satsang with me. The "point of view" of Truth is not the point of view of dilemma, or of any of the three traditional qualities of Force, or of their primary centers, or of any secondary centers associated with them. No particular process of experience is equal or identical to Truth, the Heart, the Self, or Real God.

What is necessary is the absence of obstruction, of the ego, of contraction, of the avoidance of relationship. Then only Truth stands out. Therefore, Truth is the communication from the point of view of the true

Teaching. I turn my devotee and my disciple toward Truth, Reality—not to experiences, not to the possibility of experiences, not to any psycho-physical state. The gross, the subtle, and the causal, as I have spoken of them here, are psycho-physical and temporary in nature. They are equal to the three states—waking, dreaming, and sleeping—into which experience is analyzed in the classical texts. The greater state than these, all the texts declare, is turiya, the fourth state. In other words, the more fundamental state is the <u>witness</u> to those three states. The "witness" is not the religious person, not the Yogi, and not the intuitive, or causal, seeker, but turiya, the fourth, prior to all that, witnessing it all. And even greater than that is perfect realization, turiyatita, beyond the fourth, unspeakable, neither formless nor formed. It is Amrita Nadi, the Form of Reality, whose Foundation and very Nature is the Heart. Therefore, Truth is not Itself identified with any conditional process, any knot, any opened knot, any dilemma, any solved dilemma.

Everyone's potential experience in Satsang with me is different, depending on the quality, or tendency, of his or her conscious life. But everyone's experience with me and of me is the experience of the Single Force, the transmitted Divine Conscious Power, the Power of Divine Consciousness. Originally, there is a tendency toward association with the descending force. The life-center and the life-functions tend to be the first dimension in which individuals feel both obstruction and opening. Thus, the sadhana tends, at first, to be a life-level activity, and individuals become aware of the transmitted Force as a descending blessing, originating extremely above. Eventually, there may be a tendency toward the internally-directed, ascending process. Then the experience becomes like that of the Kundalini Yogis. Ultimately, the process in Satsang with me leads to the causal, intuitive level of spiritual knowledge. Thus, at last, instead of either the ascending Yogic process or the apparently life-active, descending process, the process becomes the one of intuitive understanding, without special inclination to visions and the various forms of mystical cognition.

The true Guru must live the Conscious Force of Truth at <u>all</u> of these fundamental levels. The true Guru must necessarily be Guru in <u>all</u> of them. Such a one must be fully aware in all three paths. In such a one there must be no obstruction in the descending path, no obstruction in the ascending path, no obstruction in the moveless, or intuitive, path. These three knots are open in the true Guru. Such a one sees from the "point of view" of the Heart, unobstructed. In the true Guru there must be no obstruction to the whole course, the complex Force of the Heart, the Presence of Amrita Nadi.

There are many that are called "teacher" or "guru" simply because they perform a consoling or apparently beneficial function of a peculiar kind. But such are not living the great function of Guru. They are teaching from the point of view of dilemma, the knots and their remedial paths. Generally, they teach those who are by tendency oriented to the same quality of dilemma to which they themselves are tending. The practical religious type teaches those who are sensitive in this path. The ascending Yogi type teaches those who are sensitive on a subtle level. The more philosophical or intuitive type teaches those who are similarly inclined. But the "point of view" of Truth is not dilemma, not the knots. It is not equal to any kind of experience, solution, or form of perception and cognition. Therefore, the true Guru teaches Truth as Truth, from the "point of view" of Truth. Then, only secondarily, the purification, or opening, of the knots occurs in the forms peculiar to individual tendencies.

So you see, spiritual life in Satsang with me has the potential to manifest as many different qualities and types of experiences. From the "point of view" of the Heart and the understanding of the processes of manifested existence which I have just described, the variations are easy to comprehend. Only when the spiritual experiences of individuals are looked at from the outside and from a limited point of view do they seem disorderly. Then it seems as if there is too much difference between people and traditions, and no single, comprehensible process stands out. Truly, the great spiritual process is not understandable from any point of view that is not already the Perfect Heart. Spiritual things seem confused from a point of view that is not the Heart, just as the world seems confused from the limited point of view of experience and circumstance.

The "Shakti" that most people have heard or read about is that Force manifested and used in the subtle process associated with the ascending Yoga. But the true or Perfect Shakti is the Conscious Force that is the very Self, that is the Heart, that is Truth, Amrita Nadi, or very God. This Shakti is appearing as all that arises or does not arise. It is the Truth, the fundamental Reality. It is That which appears on all levels, as either the descending Power, or the ascending Power, or the moveless Power. One and the same Shakti is all of that. Therefore, in Truth, the Shakti is not limited to the subtle process with which people generally identify It. It is greater than that, not limited to that. It does not necessarily tend to manifest the dramatic course of the subtle process in the case of some individuals. It is the Heart Itself. It is Truth Itself. It is Real God, God alive. When there is the <u>Real</u>-ization of the very Self, or Truth, Perfect Understanding, there is also perfect manifestation of Shakti, perfect communication of Shakti, because the Heart <u>is</u> Shakti, it is Conscious Force, it is the Fire that is Reality.

Wherever there is any sort of an <u>opening</u>, there is the flow of life-energy. Any person who is open on any level, to any significant degree, is very attractive. People like to be around such a person, because there is movement there. There is no solidity, fixation. There is a certain energy, a liveliness with which people like to be associated. It is only that the usual liveliness of people tends to be limited. The easiest to identify is the "liveliness" of the person who is open on a very human, vital level. But there is also the "liveliness" of a subtle variety. Ultimately, there is the "liveliness" that is Reality Itself. Thus, there can be a great, dead Yogi whose "liveliness" remains in the world. The burial shrine of Swami Nityananda, for example, is a most lively place. However, ultimately, your conscious sensitivity must awaken to the real, eternal "liveliness" that is the very Heart, or Real God. And it is Perfect Reality, not limited movement.

The "liveliness", or Shakti, of the Heart is communicated by the living Siddha-Guru. Whatever the tendencies of the individual, it is Satsang, or relationship with the Great Siddha, with the true Guru, that is the simple Condition under which the utter and complete process of Truth may take place. All that exists is relationship. All that appears as suffering and dilemma is contact, or conscious relationship, relatively obstructed. The less obstructed any condition or function is, the more it is a flow of force. The way of Truth <u>is</u> the relationship to the Siddha-Guru. It is that functional course established between an individual and his or her Siddha-Guru. That is the way. The way is not the ego-based methods and strategies one applies to oneself. Satsang, that living, active, functional relationship itself, is the "current", the "wiring", in which the Conscious Force, the Truth, flows and manifests Its activities at every level. So the simple relationship to the true, or perfectly realized, Siddha-Guru is the way. It is the place where the search comes to an end, where the obstructions are abandoned.

There are also various activities internal to the Siddha-Guru and the realms of the Siddha-Guru's awareness, but they are not spoken. There is no point in talking about them, unless, in the progress of Satsang, the Guru sees fit to instruct the disciple. These processes are subtler than the ordinary waking mind, and they require equal subtlety to be understood.

Even so, certain activities are eventually observed by the disciple in contact with his or her Siddha-Guru. One observes the Siddha-Guru doing various things that one associates with one's own awakening and with the arising of certain experiences in oneself. Those activities of the Siddha-Guru are not utterly comprehended by the disciple at the time. The traditions describe these activities in terms of effects and appearances. In India, these activities of the Siddha-Guru are called "Shaktipat" or "Guru-kripa",[4] the transference of the Conscious Force of the Heart, or God. The effects of this transference are observed in various enlivening activities— gross, subtle, and causal. The Siddha-Guru is observed to be apparently involved in this transference by several possible means: by looking at the person, by touching the person, by speaking to the person, or simply by thinking of, or otherwise regarding, the person in some manner. And the greatest form of that "initiation" is where the Siddha-Guru simply and silently abides as the very Self, or Truth Itself. Then the Siddha-Guru's continuous existence as the living Reality initiates everything that lives to Truth. All that turns to the Siddha-Guru by appropriate means is enlivened by the Siddha-Guru. And that is initiation, that is the beginning of the whole process of true spiritual life.

Naturally, it is on the level of life that the relationship to the Siddha-Guru is perceived by the disciple. He or she observes the occasional looks, the occasional things said, the occasional touches, the effects of the Siddha-Guru's occasional remembrance of him or her. When you are with me, you may suddenly feel I am thinking of you. Or you may simply and continuously resort to me, whether or not I am specifically regarding you in particular at any moment. The various sensations of the activity of the Siddha-Guru are the apparent means, from the disciple's point of view, of the transference of the Light, the Truth, the Shakti, of the living Self, or Real God. The disciple may tend, as a result of some enlivening experience generated by the grace of his or her Siddha-Guru, to look again and again for that particular experience or that particular form of "initiation" to be repeated. The disciple may tend to associate some peculiar experience or some particular activity of his or her Siddha-Guru with Truth Itself. But in fact any specific experience in the disciple or any specific activity of the Siddha-Guru, such as looking, talking, thinking, touching, whatever, is generated in a particular moment, and it is only appropriate to the particular moment. It is thus not a necessary experience or action that must be repeated again and again. Different forms of the action of initiation may be used, or <u>no</u> apparent action may be used. The Siddha-Guru always remains unpredictable, in order to test and mature the disciple. And, at last, simply abiding as the Self, as the Heart, as Truth, is essentially what the perfectly realized Siddha-Guru does for all beings. Just so, the quality of the relationship that the disciple is living to his or her Siddha-Guru is what determines the nature of his or her present experience. The true Siddha-Guru does <u>not</u> withhold. The true Siddha-Guru always lives Truth openly. The true Siddha-Guru always communicates the Truth on many levels, in order to transform the expectations, the obstructions, the tendencies, the limitations, that the disciple is living to the Siddha-Guru. So the "drama" of this relationship, or Satsang, is at the level of the disciple. It is the disciple who must understand obstructions. The Siddha-Guru does not "create" obstructions. The Siddha-Guru only lives the Heart of Truth. But the Siddha-Guru may dramatize or intensify the obstructions already in the disciple, in order to make the disciple aware of them, to draw his or her attention to them, so that the flow of life can move through, unobstructed by any particular tendency. The Siddha-Guru always works so that awareness can be lived on a more profound level.

Many things can be said about this activity to which I have been referring. It is the greatest mystery, how the Heart lives in the world, how It functions among apparently separate, living beings. The whole process that occurs is as complicated as the cosmos itself, and what is beyond it. It cannot be described perfectly. Only certain things can be said about it. Essentially, it is the very Self, very Existence, Reality, God, appearing under these conditions, under all conditions. All the traditions, taken together, are essentially a means of retracing the structure of manifested life back to its source. Each particular incident or tradition tends to do it in a limited manner, from the point of view of a particular dilemma, a particular center, a particular viewpoint of experience or consciousness. Those in whom this drama of realization is essentially a life-process are concerned with the descending force and the opening of life to it. They are tracing the current of descent, from the highest to the lowest. The processes of ascending Yoga and the like, the subtle processes, trace the current of ascent, from the lowest to the highest. These two taken together, the gross and the subtle, form a circle. They trace that portion of the circuit of existence which descends, and then ascends, or returns again, to its structural source. Therefore, life is always descending-ascending. It is a circle. Then there is also the causal aspect, or portion, of this circuit. It is the course that leads, and even begins, beyond ascending Yoga, and which is prior to subtle and gross existence. The causal center is in the region of the heart, on the right side. And this center is connected to the subtle center, the sahasrar, by that portion of the circuit called "Amrita Nadi". Thus, if the three centers, or portions of the circuit, are taken together, one sees the great course, the circuit of manifested and unmanifested life, the secret pathway of all spiritual processes, all traditions.

The "shape" of a human being is like a fruit. The core is the causal being, untouched, unborn, like waiting seed. When the fruit falls into the earth, that is to say, when the mind falls into the Heart, there springs up an inconceivable thread, of the same substance as the seed of being, which rises above, becoming a great tree and extending even into the heights, into the sky and cosmos of very God. This is Amrita Nadi.

Until the seed is ready for life, it is concealed in the form of the fruit. This fruit is the dependent and not conscious form of the human being. It is the condition of suffering, and also of sadhana in Satsang with the Siddha-Guru. The stem of the fruit is the route of the Light and life which descend into the fruit from places above, from the parent tree, and at last pass down through the sahasrar, the crown of this body, or fruit. That Light and life descend into the fruit and make it full and ripe below. Just so, that Light and life also ascend, thus keeping the circuit, or circle, until the fruit falls and its seed is eaten in the earth. Such is ordinary death and, in the mature devotee, also "ego"-death. Ordinary death is the termination of a phase of the outer life of the individual, but also the beginning of a new phase of the manifestation, or expansion and revelation, of what he or she is inwardly and ultimately. Just so, a person becomes perfectly "fruitful" only in Satsang with the perfectly realized Siddha-Guru, who is the Process, the Goal, the Means, the Power, and the very Life. Therefore, in Satsang with the perfectly realized Siddha-Guru, the fruit ripens, falls into the "earth", or the foundation, and opens. That foundation is the very and inherently perfect Heart.

When discipleship to the perfectly realized Siddha-Guru is perfected, the whole circuitry is known and understood. It is seen to be within your own real Nature, or Condition, rather than to contain you or limit you. And this is what is rightly called "Self-Realization", the "Heart of Truth", "Nirvana", "God-union". To enjoy Satsang with the perfectly realized Siddha-Guru is perpetual freedom. And one who understands, even one whose understanding is perfect, doesn't necessarily disappear from the world. Gautama Buddha got up and walked back to town. So it was with Jesus also, and with all the other great Masters described in the religious and spiritual traditions of mankind. After their return to the common life of the world, they spent the rest of their lives trying to communicate their understanding to all of those who felt limited by this fruit-shape, this phantom circuit of conditionally manifested existence. And in the case of all the Great Siddhas, the fundamental Teaching, or "method", was that functional relationship, or Satsang, which living beings realized with them. This Satsang is the Method of the Great Siddhas.

Satsang always serves to destroy or undermine the fixation of attention and its implications. Whenever Satsang is lived, there tends to be the opening of the knots in which attention is fixed, so that consciousness falls into its Original Form, which is the very Self, or Real Nature. Therefore, one who has realized the ultimate end of the whole course, or cycle, of the circuit of conditional existence now exists "outside" that whole process, no longer limited by it. But such a one remains consciously related to this whole structure in an entirely different manner than seekers and all those who do not understand the process and form of conditionally manifested existence. The course of a person's experience tends always to return to zero, always back to the dilemma. It will always fit the person back into the fruit, like a worm. Thus, the perfectly realized Siddha-Guru appears in the world, to speak from the "point of view" of Truth, or Reality—not of experience—and to return the tendencies of the disciple back to the essential structure in which Truth is communicated, until he or she sees there is no remedial path, no difference, no separation. And when the disciple is perfectly one with the perfectly realized Siddha-Guru, he or she sees and enjoys the true Form of the perfectly realized Siddha-Guru, and participates directly in the Nature of the perfectly realized Siddha-Guru, who all the time has been only the very Self of the Divine, or Real and Only, One.

Siddha-Gurus tend to be rather eccentric in the manner of their teaching. They tend to manifest an eccentric quality, an oddity, a general unconventionality and unpredictability. The true Siddha-Guru obliterates and destroys limitation all the time. The true Siddha-Guru is a wildness! That is why the Siddha-Guru is traditionally worshipped as Siva, the Divine destroyer. Siva is traditionally portrayed destroying everything. Siva walks through town and burns everything. Siva hits people over the head. Siva cuts them in half. Look at all the traditional pictures of Siva. Siva is always wiping everybody out, tearing their bodies apart, and sitting on them in meditation. But all of that is a symbol for the perfect humor of the Divine Self! Such images are not intended to represent literal acts of God or justifiable acts of human beings. They are only "meaningful". They represent

255

meditative and symbolized comprehension of an aspect of the conscious and universal process. The representation of this paradoxical display is intended to awaken the blissfulness of non-separation, and non-identification with mortality.

The disciple is oriented towards his or her own obstruction, his or her own strategic path, and so he or she is offered this Satsang, this process of the apparent destruction of obstructions and limitations. The more the disciple lives Satsang, knows It, enjoys It, the less he or she is affected by his or her own necessary discomfort and crisis. Then the crisis of transformation becomes more and more a very simple, essentially harmonious process. But the more an individual turns from that Condition, relationship, and process which is Satsang, the more the individual becomes fixed in his or her own obstructions. Then, when the obstructions get shaken up, even broken apart, the discomfort becomes exaggerated, and the purificatory process becomes more prolonged and complicated.

The eccentricity and unconventionality of the Great Siddhas is a demonstration of the living and paradoxical quality of the Divine, or Real, Condition. The formalized, fixed, predictable quality is not Divine. Rigidity is the "tamasic", fixed, repetitive orientation of the limited mind. So the Divine Being, Self, or Reality, alive as the perfectly realized Siddha-Guru, performs an eccentric display, constantly abandoning all conformity to expectations. It is the Divine Leela, the humor, or play, of Divine Freedom. It always disturbs the fixed, unconscious quality. It "creates" motion, then returns to harmony, then settles into the formless Consciousness, then arises as "creative" Light. But whatever the display, whatever the changes the perfectly realized Siddha-Guru appears to go through from day to day, whatever the change in the display or action of the perfectly realized Siddha-Guru, there is always one thing the perfectly realized Siddha-Guru continually does, which is simply to remain as the Very and inherently Divine Self, the True Heart, the Very Reality, or Truth Itself. The apparent activity, the apparent drama, the apparent play, of the perfectly realized Siddha-Guru is always changing. The perfectly realized Siddha-Guru constantly builds up expectations in the disciple, and then changes everything around. The perfectly realized Siddha-Guru continually disturbs the fixed quality, the rigidity, the strategic path, to which the disciple always tends.

There appears to be a certain security in fixation, but in fact it is a form of disturbance. It is only an illusory security, because there is, in Truth, no fixed conditional state. That is why death is such a threat. But the more fluid, the looser, the more rapid and intense the flow within, the less fixed, the more functional, the more harmonious, the more like fire, the more there is of Truth and the less there is of the strategic "path", the more there seems a movement in the direction of Freedom. It <u>appears</u> to be a direction. Perhaps one should only call it a "sign". It is a sign of That Which Is, always and already.

Sri Da Avabhasa
at Sri Love-Anandashram, 1992

11.

Phases

DEVOTEE: What is the point of images and visions?

SRI DA AVABHASA: It is always different. In one case, such an experience may coincide with one or another degree of real transcendence. In that case, the one in whom the experience arises suddenly understands and is free of it. In another case, some manifestation may arise, but one doesn't know what it is. One becomes disturbed by it, but one doesn't give in to it. Then perhaps some source—a teacher, book, something—will clarify it, and then one is free of it. In yet another case, such a thing will arise without any understanding on one's part, and one buys it. In that case, one enjoys it, one takes it as it is, one becomes full of it, one identifies with it, and one is full of regret and longing when it goes. Thus, all the extraordinary manifestations of vision, art, culture, thought, and life are, ultimately, ordinary—simply a part of the universal "creativity". Apart from Satsang, apart from the life of understanding, such things have no more ultimate significance than any other simple or ordinary event.

There are people who have, because of their chronic condition, because of the tendencies of their conditional state, manifested psychic powers of various kinds. Thus, we have mediums and psychics, people who see your "aura", who see pictures around you, who hold your ring and tell you the answers to your questions, who give seances, who make predictions. These people are not themselves extraordinary. Apart from these "gifts", most of them are very "ordinary", even peculiarly unintelligent. You would expect, because these manifestations are extraordinary, that the character of the individuals through whom they are expressed would also be extraordinary. But it is not so. These phenomena are simply qualities that arise, just like a stomachache, or a left hand. There is nothing ultimate,

Truth-like, or even Truth-directed about occult, supernormal, and psychic phenomena, but if some such phenomenon arises in you and you buy it, then it becomes an aspect of your suffering. And all people are suffering, regardless of the qualities that are peculiarly theirs.

From the spiritual point of view, the future is a "creative" activity, not a predetermined one. Very often there are mysterious indications that arise, perceptions of a tendency that is operating or of a possibility of some kind. But spiritual work is not a matter of being determined by tendencies or premonitions. Spiritual work in the world is always "creative" involvement with conditions. True action involves the transformation of time and space into the conscious, spiritual event. Therefore, there may be indications of tendencies, of possibilities, of things that may occur, but all of this arises in relation to the living Heart. "Creative", free, and conscious activity, generated in Satsang with the realizer of the Heart, constantly breaks down the whole machine of destiny. There is no necessary event. It is all a "creative" activity. The more "tamasic", or inert, the body-mind is, the more likely one is to experience and suffer the events toward which one is tending. But the more movement toward purification there is in one, and the more harmony there is alive in one, and the more understanding there is in one, the less likely one is to be determined by karmas, within and without.

When people are talking about "seeing the future", they are really just seeing the tendencies in individuals, in groups. Some such people see psychic imagery, some have a complex intuition. It comes in various forms, but in any case what is seen is only a tendency, a possibility, a trend. And that is the limitation of the "psychic" functions. They do not in themselves enjoy "creative" involvement with the process of life. The naively psychic individual may profess to another, "Yes, you are going to die at the age of forty-two," or, "You are going to marry a rich man when you go on your worldwide trip to Shangri-la." But that is not in fact how it necessarily will or must be. These are just possibilities, and the more you speak of them as necessary events, the more you make of life an un-"creative" process, a determined process. Therefore, the "point of view" in this Satsang is always the "creative" viewpoint. Certainly, at times there may be intuitions, feelings, psychic premonitions, and the like, but they always arise within this "creative" process, this "understanding", this Siddhi, or living Power, of Satsang.

Satsang, or life in the Condition of Truth, breaks down rigidity, the "tamasic" quality. The functions associated with the phenomena of the occult and astrology, for example, are internal virtues of the vital and astral emotional being, not of the very Heart. They tend to interpret life as a fixed event, either in the past or in the future. There have been very few individuals who interpreted the manifested cosmic and human conditions from a position of genuine, transcendental illumination. Psychologies and sciences of the ordinary kind tend to treat the past as a fixed event determining the present. And the occult and astrological sciences, even with their attendant psychic phenomena, tend to interpret the future as a fixed event. But nothing is absolutely fixed. Consciousness is utterly uncontained. It is always a "creative" Force. It is always humorous. The past isn't absolutely determining the present. Therefore, one does not have to get deeply into one's past in order to be free. The future is not absolutely fixed by the stars. At every moment all possibilities exist in the stars. Therefore, it doesn't make any difference what fixed moment in time and space one takes as the point of view from which to read past, present, or future. What is always the point is this "creative" realization of Truth. The real life of understanding is the only appropriate point of view under any conditions.

One of the lessons the Siddhas, or "completed ones", have always tried to communicate to people is the undetermined or fundamentally spiritual nature of life. The Siddhas always have urged human beings to conceive and know life as a spiritual event rather than a fixed event. Rather than mortality and suffering, they communicate existence always to be Life and Truth. But in order for that to be so in fact, a new point of view must begin to develop. It is always already free, not fixed. It is not simply a movement, not simply desire, but it is conscious, fluid, intelligent, inherently and priorly full of Truth and the blissful Force of the Truth. The Truth is that in which the stars are hung, and by which this limited mind of tendencies and fixations is supported. When that point of view is realized, when Satsang becomes your Condition, every moment becomes the spiritual event.

Because of this, many great Teachers, such as Gautama Buddha or Ramana Maharshi, when asked about the states after death, or the future in life, or psychic powers, would simply not entertain the discussion at all. On occasion Ramana Maharshi gave more or less direct replies to such questions, but, for the most part, he would only say, "Find out who wants to know this." This was his manner of turning the person toward the fundamental Truth which transcends and even at last masters destiny. The same is true in terms of this one. I am perfectly willing to talk about these

261

phenomena in general. But they are just here, like this body, this room. They are only conditional phenomena. They do not determine the Truth or limit the "creative" intensity of one who understands.

Truth must become the "point of view". When Truth is the "point of view", there is no past or future that can absolutely limit your state. Then time and place become relatively insignificant. Then it makes no ultimate difference whether the good thing is going to happen or the bad thing. In either case, you are going to have to understand. Apart from Truth, when the good thing happens, you suffer just as much as when the bad thing happens. Apart from Truth, the individual lives the subtle contraction and the avoidance of relationship under all conditions. But if, on account of Truth, this subtle strategy does not occur, then you can really pervade the "good" thing that happens, and there will even be a kind of enjoyment or interest when the "bad" thing happens.

Whether they are psychic, extraordinary, or ordinary, regardless of their peculiar makeup, all human beings are suffering. Just so, in all human beings there arises the possibility, in the midst of all this suffering, to live from an entirely free and "radical" point of view. Seen in these terms, then, the purpose of extraordinary things that arise without a person's understanding is just like anything else that arises, any misfortune or fortune that may arise. All experiences, good or bad, are there ultimately to turn one into a crisis relative to one's own search.

All kinds of manifestations, ordinary and extraordinary, arise in Satsang, and the Force, the Shakti, the Intensity, of Satsang very often tends to bring on relatively unpleasant manifestations in the form of purifying events. If you abide in the Condition of Satsang, if you live the point of view of Satsang, if you resort to me while going through these processes of experience, they can serve the real process of understanding. Ultimately, these things are simply what they are, not what they imply. They arise like the stars, the world, and all bodies. Either they can serve the formulations of suffering and its search or they can serve Satsang, depending on the present condition of the individual.

DEVOTEE: Why do you appear to be weeping in Satsang at times?

SRI DA AVABHASA: The reasons for it are varied and complex, like any other manifestation in Satsang. This weeping may appear if there is an intense energy process going on in Satsang. This ascending force, especially, makes the eyes tear. There is no emotion associated with it. It is just a physical manifestation that purifies the eyes and the centers in the head that are associated with them. Depending on the movement that is going on, sometimes there is a subtle activity, an activity in the subtle body, or the pattern of ascent, that is like suffering. It is <u>like</u> suffering, but it is a Yogic process. When I sit with others in Satsang, there is the communication of various forces, of mind-forms, of all kinds of qualities. The transformation of all of that does not occur without cost, without something happening.

In what is called "ordinary life", people are rather insensitive to what is going on between them and others. For this reason, they are very willing to indulge life. Individuals allow other people to do whatever they please, and they themselves do whatever they please, within the limits of their own desires or fears. People are unaware of the nature of what I have simply called "relationship". They don't know what it is, what it involves as a psycho-physical event, a psychic event, a subtle event. It is the transference of life, the communication of the forms of conscious life. In the usual man or woman, though, this transference, or communication, is contracted and destroyed, swallowed, reversed, and poisoned. And people don't know that this is what is going on in themselves and others. People nowadays talk about "vibrations"—this vibration, that vibration, good vibes, bad vibes. There is some vague sort of sensitivity awakening about the qualities that people manifest in life. But there is a real process, which is called "Satsang". It is the unqualified communication of life. It is simply unqualified, conscious relationship. This process is consciously lived by me. That is this Satsang. It is a conscious process, even a profound Yogic process. But when it occurs, there is often a quality of suffering. Something must occur, something must open, something must be done. And when that is going on in fact, sometimes there is the appearance of weeping in me. There is the appearance of sorrow, perhaps at times even the apparent mood of sorrow, but it is not identical to sorrow. Something of the blissfulness of transformation is also manifested, and bliss is the core of that appearance of sorrow. There are other times when this process has already taken place, when I have endured the transformation of the karmas of my devotee in my own body, when the circle of life is open, free, and the flow of Satsang has occurred. Then the vital and subtle mechanisms are released in me. The physical and subtle consciousness is let go, and there is an intense concentration in the Light, or Force, above. This weeping also occurs at those times. But it is just blissfulness.

The ordinary man or woman is insensitive to this real mechanism. He or she is not living it. He or she is not living the point of view of Satsang, or Truth. I have described the quality of life in the usual man or woman as a kind of revulsion. The force of life falls down out of the brain, down the spine. It is released sexually. It is released through the various gross manifestations of life-energy, in various kinds of self-indulgence. It is only used, and never consciously refreshed. The mood of the usual life is trapped between the extremes of comedy and tragedy. People laugh a lot, but what is laughter? What happens when there is laughter? It feels good, but the process involves a form of revulsion, like vomiting. And weeping is also a form of revulsion. What happens when a person weeps in the ordinary manner? The breath is disturbed. He or she can't control the breath. The chest is convulsively constricted. There is no genuine humor in the person, no conscious freedom. There is only revulsion in the ordinary man or woman, down the back and up the front. But in one who understands there is conductivity, descending in front, ascending in back.

The traditional Yogis talk about the ascending energy and how important it is to conserve the sex-fluid, and the life-force in general. The traditional Yogi is concerned to get the ascending current going. There is partial wisdom in that, and in fact the ascending conductivity does tend to establish itself more and more firmly in the process of Satsang. The circular conductivity of life tends to be re-established, as opposed to the unconscious tendency of life-functions to revolt, to release their own force and become empty. This revulsion begins to be replaced by the movement of real conductivity in the Condition of Satsang.

But this process tends naturally to occur in various and complex forms in the life of Satsang. That is why I have emphasized a practical foundation. I have said that the practical foundation of Satsang is an ordinary, pleasurable life, not a suppressed life—you know, no work, no contact with life, one apple every three days, and no sex for five generations! But I require an ordinary, pleasurable life, a functional life, limited to what is supportive, what is enjoyable, what is full. Such a conscious application of life tends to break the chronic pattern of contraction, of revulsion, in a person, at least on the level of practical, human action. And that allows this conductivity to begin at the level of life. Some people come to Satsang in the Ashram and begin to feel the Energy, the Force, of my Company. They speak of various kinds of Force-manifestations and experiences of my Presence. This is evidence that conductivity is beginning at the most obvious level, the life-level. Therefore, this Satsang involves conductivity, descending, ascending, rested in the Heart, prior to mind and form, prior to knowledge in the mental sense. At last, all of the "mentality" of spiritual life is the contraction of the Heart, the limitation of the Heart.

Spiritual life, for me, has involved the observation of this whole manifestation, or circle, of life I have described, not the control of it by means
of the search. It continues to manifest itself endlessly. It is not stopped.
All kinds of things have occurred since I wrote *The Knee of Listening*. The
same essential Condition and dynamic Enjoyment has remained from that
time, but the revelation of this great process has continued. All I have
done is observe it and allow it to take place as a living function. It is a
miraculous phenomenon that no one seems to know about. No one appears to suspect it. The usual man or woman does not suspect that
life is miraculous, that there is this miraculous process of Satsang, the
communication of Truth, which can make Itself known on many levels—
on the life-level, in the descending pattern, in the ascending pattern, in
this intuitive life, this "radical" consciousness, this blissfulness, this intensity, this real meditation, this understanding. What most people hear are the
little stories, little jokes, that appear in the traditions, glimpses and
characterizations of portions of that process. No tradition has comprehended it fully, even at the level of description. All traditions are limited
to the viewpoint of one or a limited combination of the three primary
centers. But there have been great Saints, great Yogis, great Sages, great
individuals. Wherever such a one has arisen, that one has communicated
through Satsang to various people who were close to him or her. All
kinds of experiences were generated in that manner. And in the midst of
all of the people who enjoyed these different kinds of experience, little
groups would gather. You know, people sitting in Satsang who had all
been having a buzzing in the right ear got together after the death of the
Guru and established the "buzzing-in-the-right-ear school". All those who
were sensitive to the subtle-body manifestations went off and talked
about chakras, the Kundalini, internal sound, and light. Many separate
groups, schools, and traditions grew up on the basis of particular and
unique experiences and tendencies. But all experiences are generated by
one great process. The "unity of all religions" is not that they have all said
the same thing. But if they were all added together, they would amount
to a complete description of the one process. Each religious and spiritual
tradition has represented an experiential portion of the great process.
Historically, the unity of all religions will be realized not by everybody
coming into agreement on some abstraction common to all but, somehow, by virtue of a recognition that all of these traditional media together
are a mutually dependent description of this one great process of conscious existence. Therefore, this very process will become the life of

Truth in the future, rather than the traditional dogmatization and ritualization of random, exclusive internal and external experience.

All of my life, I have been waiting for the time when I could be outwardly blissful, when I could manifest that blissfulness to all. But, all of my life, I have not been doing that. Even as a baby, I learned very quickly that it could not be expressed, that it could not be lived openly, not among those who were suffering, seeking, motivated in forms of dis-ease. After so long, it has now become possible to live this bliss, this Truth, openly. The means are now being developed whereby It can be communicated to those who are willing to endure the transformation of life. But even in this Ashram the same resistance is presented to the process of Truth. Even in the Ashram there tends to be the same game: no bliss, don't be blissful, not already, not already happy, not already free, not yet, not me, not with you. But I am not willing to endure the conditions this resistance would "create". I will "create" the conditions! The bliss of Truth Itself, not the ignorance of human beings, must generate the conditions of life. When Truth becomes the "point of view", when that blissfulness becomes the "point of view" that "creates" life, an entirely different situation has arisen in the world. The world is not ordinarily living from the "point of view" of Truth. It is living from the point of view of its suffering, its dilemma, and there is no room for blissfulness, for Truth, for unreasonable happiness. Therefore, the true Guru, the Great Siddha, always seems remarkable from the point of view of ordinary people, because that one lives from the "point of view" of Truth. Such a one decides to live the very Truth, what is only obvious to that one, and he or she "creates" the conditions wherein it can be manifested.

All I am doing in the Ashram is establishing the appropriate conditions for Satsang. These real conditions are difficult for some people to understand. People think I am just supposed to open the door to all, without conditions. Everybody is just supposed to wander in, smoke dope, listen to a lecture: "Hm, not bad, think I'll take this dude's initiation." No conditions! People think spiritual life is a "high", a form of entertainment, a free lunch. But spiritual life involves incredible conditions! Think of the conditions that had to be met for your physical birth. If it were left up to human beings to handle the affair of their own birth, no one would ever be born at all. Maybe every now and then an arm would be born, or a yelping pile of meat. A whole family might consist of an arm, an apple, and a #2 Mongol pencil!

Examine the life of the Great Siddhas, those who are generally supposed to have been great saviors, great teachers. They really worked on those who came to them. People like to imagine the Buddha just wanted people to sit quietly every now and then and read philosophy between their trips. You should examine what the Buddhist community involved at the beginning. The essential literature that has been left by the early Buddhist communities consists of lists of conditions, or rules, for living in the spiritual community. Not philosophy, not enlightenment experiences, not all that juicy stuff, but lists of conditions: when you could bend down, when you could go for food, in whose presence you could eat food, what you could eat and when. The Buddhist communities were concerned, above all, that their members lived straight. The "philosophy" was for those who had already gotten straight. But today people think philosophy or some formal meditation process is supposed to get them straight. So they try all the meditation techniques one by one, like drugs, without fundamentally changing their condition. Thus, spiritual life fails for them.

What did Jesus do for people? He really turned his disciples around. He really worked them over. He changed their lives first. He demanded things of them. He kicked them around. He told them where they were at. Just so, if this Satsang is to be lived, there must be real conditions established. There must be an entirely new order of life. An entirely new point of view must be lived. Therefore, the traditional points of view, and the ordinary human points of view, are not sufficient. They no longer apply. But people want them. They continue to defend them, even in Satsang. It is ridiculous. They come in pain, and they wind up defending their state, their dis-ease. Such people often must be returned to the "Straightener", the ordinary world of suffering and death, until they remember again that they are suffering. Appropriate conditions must be established in your lives and in the Ashram. An appropriate order of life must be established, in which there is room for absolute blissfulness. This absolute blissfulness is too happy for people in the usual condition to tolerate! It is really too much. They can't live with it, they can't function with it, they can't accept it. They are always looking for something that is just a little aggravating! Here—this little cramp in the solar plexus—this is what they are living in. But when the life is only open, when this incredible Force is flowing through, it churns you, it purifies the life. Then there is nothing at last to be unhappy about, nothing to think about. The flood of enjoyment rushes through the body, dissolves the mind, overwhelms the life. The real intelligence of conscious life begins to intensify and function in place of ignorance. And that intelligence has no answers. It has no questions. That state without answers and without questions is the true state. From that state, the "creation" of marvels begins.

For years, I would sit down in meditation, and all my own forms would appear—my own mind, my desires, my experience, my suffering, my feeling, my energies, my this and my that. But, at some point, it all came to an end. There was no thing, nothing there anymore. None of that distracted or interested me. Meditation was perfect, continuous. Then I began to meet those friends who first became involved in this way. And when I would sit down for meditation, there would be more of these things again—all of these thoughts, these feelings, this suffering, this dis-ease, this disharmony, these upsets, this craziness, this pain, these energies—all of this again. But they weren't mine. They were the internal qualities and life-qualities of my friends. So I would sit down to meditate, and do the meditation of my friends. When I would feel it all release, their meditation was done. And I began to test it, to see if this meditation went on in some more or less apparent manner for these people who were not with me. And I found that this meditation went on with people whom I hadn't even met. People I saw in dreams and visions would show up at the Ashram. So the meditation went on. It was the same meditation I had always done. The same problems were involved, the same subtleties, but the content of the meditation was not mine.

After the events described in *The Knee of Listening*, there was a period of time when the universe, the cosmic process, was meditated in me. Various siddhis, or Yogic and occult powers, became manifested. The movement, or process, of the cosmos is a meditation, a purifying event. Everything is Satsang. There is only Satsang. It is eternal. But after this is all seen to be so, It must be lived. After the period in which the siddhis appeared, it became a matter of dealing with existence as it truly is, as Satsang. But new disciples don't know that yet. They are not yet experiencing that Fullness, that fundamental enjoyment, that living freedom. They are not conscious and responsible at all levels of <u>conscious</u> life. So a kind of seriousness wants to creep in. The dilemma and the search would like to reassert itself in the Ashram. The temptation arises to turn Satsang into the search again. But the same thing must occur for others that occurred for this one. And true Satsang is that process. "Radical" understanding is that intelligence. And the only means to keep this way from turning into a search is simply to order it, to put the Ashram and its sadhana into appropriate form.

There is the tendency, even among those in Satsang with me, to indulge their ordinary strategy, to be resistive, to be eccentric, to be self-indulgent, to dramatize the avoidance of relationship. To them it doesn't seem to involve anything terribly dramatic. It is easy for them to get involved in that sort of mediocre strategy again, because they are insensitive to what it does, and to what must be done for it to be straightened again and again. But I am very well aware of it.

There have been numberless cases where people dramatize their resistance to Satsang, and thus toward me. To them it may have appeared very simple. Just a little emotional resistance, a little bit of craziness off "alone" somewhere. But I felt their "little resistance" very strongly. In one case the resistance of an individual communicated itself to me as a kind of black witchcraft. The individual was not particularly aware of what he was doing, because it was on such a subtle level, and he had become insensitive to the effects of his own subtle activity as a result of a lifetime of random self-indulgence in the dramas of avoidance. When all of that finally got straight in me, and I felt it dissolve in meditation, this person suddenly returned, smiling and full of love! "Oh, I have been having a difficult period, but I feel better now." The symptoms were gone, but there had been no real experience, no responsibility, no Satsang, no sadhana. His relief was more like magic, graceful medicine. But there was no relationship, no wisdom, no true condition lived or restored. Thus, over time, I have begun to require more and more of those who move into my Company. I require this process of understanding to be lived, awakened, and endured in them, and not merely relieved by some vicarious Yogic process in me, however extraordinary that may seem.

Satsang is an actual Condition. It is a relationship. It must be consciously lived. It must become a matter of responsibility, so that this dramatization of reluctance, of resistance, of arbitrary craziness, is set aside, undone with real intelligence. It must not simply be resisted by the disciple or magically relieved by the teacher. It must be known. It must be obviated in the force of life and intelligence. The Condition of Satsang, the Condition of relationship to me, must be consciously and continually lived, so that this process of understanding can go on, simply, happily. Those who are not prepared to live it so directly, simply, with some kind of real responsibility, are those who leave on their own. They become very resistive, then angry, and they leave. Others, whose relationship to this way is mediocre, may be asked to leave temporarily, in order to re-establish in them the real conditions for Satsang.

People forget. They forget their own positive experiences. They forget what Satsang is and has been in their own experience. Temporarily, It becomes clear to them, It becomes intense, It becomes real. But then as soon as their drama of tendencies erupts again, for whatever reasons, this cycle of negativity comes on them again and they want to indulge it freely. They want to go. They want to do all kinds of numbers, they want to be negative, they want to tell you where it's at, they want to get upset, they want to make their upsets known. They don't want to be responsible for all of that. They are moved to indulge these urges even though during that whole time when they were happily enjoying Satsang they heard me speak again and again about this contraction, this activity that is suffering, this avoidance of relationship. Even if a person can begin to enjoy insight into his or her ordinary strategy, and live beyond it, live directly, live Satsang, these cycles of negativity and destructive, separative tendencies will absolutely occur, again and again. There will be repetition of urges, again and again, to break with Satsang, to feel all kinds of negative justifications for not being in Satsang, and to play all kinds of dramas in life as a result. Therefore, in spite of the tendency for this contraction to arise at all levels, Satsang must be lived. The devotee must continue to live and enjoy the Condition of Satsang, even though he or she may feel the rising tendencies, the negativity, the symptoms—physical, psychic, internal, in the external conditions of life, everywhere. Even so, live this Satsang, enjoy this Satsang. It is the only principle that is free of all of that, and if you live the transformative conditions of Satsang, Its intelligence replaces the unconscious activity of suffering. To live Satsang makes the search and its motivating dilemma obsolete. But you must live Satsang, and the living of Satsang, even under the ordinary conditions of suffering, apparent suffering, is sadhana, real religious and spiritual practice. There is no Satsang without sadhana. Satsang is not just a pleasant, consoling experience that you have this week, and if It is not pleasurable next week, then the whole thing deserves your contempt. Satsang must be lived over time, under all the conditions that arise. It must become sadhana, the way of life.

It seems that talking about Satsang tends to make It appear a very complicated process. It is here! I am here. This relationship is a real Condition. My human form is very useful, because it lives and demonstrates the fundamental Condition as relationships with devotees. Satsang with me is Company, proximity, relationship, living It rather than merely remembering It, listening to me, so that It begins to become obvious, so that this understanding comes alive. But what is fundamentally important is the fact of this relationship as a Condition, something that you must live from day to day. In that sense it is not something meditative, something ritualistic, something you must remember, concentrate on. It is something you must live. You may want to sit there thinking and picturing, but I shake you on the shoulder and ask you to paint the Ashram wall. Hearing me speak to you, and getting up and painting the wall—that is sadhana, that is Satsang. All the merely mental things you might want to do to try to keep It in place, to do something about It, to "create" the relationship—all of that is your own insane ritual. But true spiritual life, Satsang, is much more practical than that, much more direct than that. It must be. I am here.

The true "natural" state is completely without thought. It is prior to thought. It is free of thought, even while thinking occurs. There is no thought when I am speaking. There is no thinking going on apart from the speech. No thinking went into your birth. All manifestation is a spontaneous, free, blissful activity, a "creative" event. Just so, Satsang is truly operative prior to the mind. So all those means of living Satsang that are purely mental and motivated are secondary. It is more practical than all of that. Know that you cannot figure it out. You cannot understand it. You do not understand it. That is the truth. Here is Satsang. Live It. Be happy to have discovered that you cannot figure It out. Some can't even bear the mental process. When the communication of understanding comes from without, it puts them to sleep. When it comes from within, it wakes them up. The more there is of all this mentality, all this conversation, all this thinking of spiritual things, the more sleep there is, the more unconsciousness. Too much talk tends to obstruct the internal, real Force. But where the mind is not satisfied, where the search is not satisfied, Satsang becomes possible, sadhana becomes possible.

People come to me to have the search satisfied. If I simply do not satisfy the search, they get angry, and disappointed. Then they leave before the Condition of Satsang has had time even to begin to do Its work. As a compromise, I must continually explain, again and again, why it is that I am not satisfying the search. So this long conversation we have had this evening was only my attempt to explain why it is I don't say anything! But if I didn't say anything in fact, everyone would leave. So it is very difficult to teach. The more stable you are, the less I will have to speak.

DEVOTEE: I find my world, my universe, is becoming more and more oppressively one of loneliness.

SRI DA AVABHASA: Get out of it. Come into this one.

DEVOTEE: I find myself doing a considerable amount of suffering, and at the same time I am trying to avoid the compulsive activities that I do to relieve it. I find myself trying to enter a relationship with another, or trying to find some support in another. I am trying to get something from another. When I sit in Satsang with you, occasionally I go through a great deal of physical pain. And most of the time I am spacing out now.

SRI DA AVABHASA: You have got to rejoin the human race. Stop spending all this time contemplating yourself, sitting alone in your room by yourself. Function with human beings. Do things. That is all. That is all it will take.

DEVOTEE: My impression is that human beings aren't real.

SRI DA AVABHASA: Join up! You are not going to negate me.

DEVOTEE: I'm caught in the "all one separate thing".

SRI DA AVABHASA: I don't care what you are caught in. We are all here. Your suffering is your own. If you want to play your suffering game, these are the results. Everybody is doing their own number, and that is yours. I don't have any sympathy for it. You are turning it on. You _want_ to do it. You like it, as a matter of fact. If you wanted to get out of that game, it would be a simple matter of turning in the other direction, from separation to Satsang. You must _live_ the conditions of religious and spiritual life. If you refuse the conditions of religious and spiritual life and continually wander in your own dilemma, you will realize nothing. You want to be your own Guru. You want to be already realized without doing sadhana, without living the conditions of Truth. If you were doing sadhana, you wouldn't have a moment to be occupied with your problems. If you were living the functional conditions of life, you wouldn't have time to reflect on your craziness. You simply do not function. You find every kind of means to live in a universe of your own. But there is no universe of your own. "Universe" means "one". There is the universe. But you are only talking about your own mentality, your own mind-forms. You meditate on that all the time, instead of living the conditions. If you do live the conditions, there is also a crisis. Forms of apparent suffering arise. So what. Everyone must pass through that. Nobody patted me on the head when I went through it. Nobody put you into your present state. No one is keeping you in it. It is a present activity. It is your own activity. It is not dependent on the past. It is this avoidance of relationship, this contraction. It is time to realize that you are obsessed. I have always known that you are obsessed. That in itself never bothered me. We can begin from there. But you keep discovering it again and again, always as if it were some new realization. And then you forget it again. That is the problem. You always forget the very thing of which you are certain. You begin religious and spiritual life only when you have already discovered the "terrible truth". Then you can live the conditions of religious and spiritual life instead. But your whole being is still devoted to this separation, this compulsive self-meditation. And that is suffering. See that this is so. Live the Condition of Satsang in a very practical manner. Then Satsang will become your meditation. Satsang will become the "method" of your realization.

In fact, Satsang is nothing that you can do to yourself. It is a Condition. It is a Condition that must be given to you, revealed and made available to you by grace. It is a process that becomes awakened in your life spontaneously. You simply must live it in a much more practical manner. Spend no time whatsoever analyzing yourself. No time. I mean no time! I really mean it. I don't mean just a little time, reading a few books, collecting conceptual insights. I mean spend no time whatsoever analyzing yourself. That is the peculiar activity that you are suffering, that self-meditation. Pull yourself into functional existence. Make everything very practical, very functional. Then you will give room to this real process. Then you will see that you are always resorting to yourself, always resorting to this separate self sense. Realize that and it becomes much simpler to resort to Satsang. You can't resort to Satsang in some sort of mediocre mental fashion, unconscious and believing. You must live It. As a child you didn't "believe" in your mother. You lived with your mother. You lived that condition. You lived all the things that arose in that relationship from day to day. You lived all the things that were demanded. It is the same with Satsang, or real religious and spiritual life, the living relationship to me, which also requires the living of the functional conditions of existence in the universe.

DEVOTEE: I seem to be having a lot of contrasting experiences lately. Sometimes I have near ecstasies of intuitive knowledge flowing over me, and my body will become very relaxed. Then, almost within the very next moment, regular impulses and patterns of everyday life seem to become really increased, or else I seem to notice them much more concentratedly than before. What is the significance of this? Is something loosening up in me? Even relationships with people get very easy and spontaneous, then at other times they get harder than they were before.

SRI DA AVABHASA: There are cycles in consciousness. Some of the cycles of experience are very difficult to observe, and people are not aware of them. Generally, you are all aware of the seasons. You are commonly aware of the cycle of climate. You are aware of the cycle of night and day. You are at least vaguely aware of the phases of the moon. You are made aware of social cycles, such as elections, holidays, weekends. But there are also subtle cycles in the process of consciousness and conscious life. The internal patterns may seem random, but everyone is aware that they go through "phases", or periods of "bad days" and "good days". Individuals know they do this. They know they have different kinds of characteristic states. But they don't commonly see a pattern to these states. In fact, there is such a pattern. There is a characteristic pattern of conscious experience in everyone, as regular as the seasons. But it is essentially an individual pattern, like fingerprints.

The Force that manifests in Satsang tends to intensify the characteristic cycles of consciousness. One of the first things I began to observe in this process, as I lived in Satsang with one who was Guru to me, was how the cycle of my own experience varied between "light" and "heavy". The "good day–bad day" sort of thing. I didn't map it out on a calendar, but I began to become aware that I was moving through patterns of state and life-consciousness that manifested as "pulses", phases, or cycles, like the heartbeat. It wasn't that under certain external circumstances I would react with a "bad" mood, or, under others, with a "good" mood. There was a characteristic and prior heaviness peculiar to my state at times, and a lightness at others, regardless of circumstances. As this process continued to reveal itself, I began to observe there was a certain regularity to its patterns. And I also began to observe how the patterns were modified by this process of Satsang.

At first I spent long periods of time in a kind of negative and mediocre condition. I commonly approached the Guru in such states. And, occasionally, I would suddenly feel good, or released. In time, I began to discover that these periods of release, or of no contraction, were becoming a little more frequent, a little more intense, a little more absorbing. The negative pattern, the lower end of this curve, was becoming less intense, more bearable. These crisis periods began to become interesting to me. Thus, various changes began to occur in the cycle of consciousness when it was brought into the Condition of Satsang. In meditation, sitting in Satsang, sitting with the Guru, the so-called internal processes, the subtle psycho-physical processes, are intensified. This is the work of the Force of God in Satsang.

I noticed that when the Force of Satsang was most intense, these highs and lows were most intense. And as that Force continued to intensify, the alternations of these highs and lows became more rapid. What you are describing is just such a development of sensitivity to this cycle of consciousness. The pattern is intensified and revealed in Satsang, so that, without apparent cause, experience appears to alternate arbitrarily between different and opposite values, or qualities.

There is a peculiar mood which is attained when this process of intensified alternation becomes perfectly rapid. This is the Yogic ananda, or bliss, which arises whenever the speed of the cycle of high and low becomes absolute. The Saint or Sage is one in whom these alternations have become so rapid that he or she is always already essentially happy. The perfectly realized individual, the one who understands, is one in whom the cycle of consciousness has attained the speed of light. Therefore, as this process of Satsang continues in you, you will observe the movement of the pattern of your existence. Its cycles are as much a functional manifestation as your breathing. The internal life of the usual individual is not the sort of carefree, aesthetic, spontaneous sublimity that people like to imagine. The "internal" life is as ordered, as regular, as mechanistic, as organic, as the "external" universe. There is nothing arbitrary about your experience. It is simply that you have not learned to observe your experience, you have not become subtle in your ability to observe what is arising. But the more subtle you become in your capability to observe, the more you see the patterns, internal and external.

The arising of this subtlety, or sensitivity, is a good sign. There is a tendency in you to identify with the stream of your own consciousness. There is a tendency to think you are your own "think" apparatus. When this sensitivity arises, the internal pattern is already ceasing to be so much a compulsive activity. Then it is showing itself to you. It demonstrates itself to be something as functionally "external" as a hand. It is not something with which you are identical, but a process that is arising spontaneously, much the same as your hand. So the compulsive tendency to identify with the movement of consciousness is beginning to ease just at the moment you seem to suffer it most.

DEVOTEE: The other day I heard you say something that suddenly seemed to take on a lot of meaning for me. It seemed to bring about a revelation. It seemed to be a combination of the Force I feel in Satsang and listening to what you were saying.

SRI DA AVABHASA: There are many means generated in this way. All the events that are necessary occur, and they all occur appropriately. That is why I do speak at times. There is a function for it—something is served by my speaking in Satsang. But I don't always speak. Then Satsang continues wordlessly, as a subtle process. Just so, I don't only speak or else sit in silence. I also do things with people. And apart from what I apparently do in a personal manner with you, you all have different kinds of contact with the influence and effects of my work, different experiences, different exposures to all my forms of operation. Although the complex of these things may seem to you to be somewhat arbitrary, it is actually a manifested and exquisitely intelligent design. It is not arbitrary. Nothing happens arbitrarily to those who live Truth. Your dreams are not arbitrary. Your dreams are a very intelligent process. But if you think of them while in the waking state, you can't make real sense out of them. All experience is of that same nature. It is all a subtle design, a spontaneous, paradoxical process. You were brought to consider that particular talk, just as you were brought to Satsang itself. Many things combined at that moment to produce this "revelation". I believe it is said in the *New Testament:* "Everything works together for the good of those who love God." This bit of Biblical wisdom pertains also to the process, or quality, of Satsang. Everything happens appropriately, even for those who live in ignorance of Truth. It is just that, apart from Satsang, apart from the life of Truth, the appropriate thing that happens is suffering and death! When Satsang begins as a real process, you may begin to observe the appropriateness of all experience. Not a breath is spent outside of Satsang once It begins. And all of the possible ranges of events, from the gross apparently external world to your reactions to it, including your thoughts, and all things that happen to you within the world, within the waking state, in dreams, while sleeping—everywhere everything combines for the sake of the Truth.

Until this begins to become obvious to you, you can believe it or not. It really has no importance until you begin to observe it. And people do begin to observe it in Satsang with me. There was a time in my own life when I began to see there was no difference whatsoever between my internal life and my external life. There is but one process going on everywhere and always. The world is the psyche. The world is founded in the psyche, or the root of the world is essentially of the same nature as the psyche. The whole process is a single event. Everything is moving together as a single design with a single intent. Nothing happens to you that is not appropriate. All events serve Truth. It is only that when you begin consciously to serve Truth, events themselves take on more and more the quality of Truth. You will begin to experience the coincidence, or simultaneity, of within and without. You will begin to observe that this Satsang is actually alive, that It has somehow taken over the universe.

Of course, people are ordinarily attached to their subjective identity, that force they separately identify as themselves. And they have all kinds of bad relations with the world. The seeker typically likes the concept that appears in many of the world's Scriptures which says that Truth is within you, God is within you, all Power is within you. But this idea just reinforces the tendency of Narcissus, this subjective tendency, this inward-turning, this self-contraction. The Truth is no more within you than it is in the lamp shade. The Truth is everywhere and no "where". It is not especially within you, nor is It especially without. There is Truth.

DEVOTEE: It would seem that without fear my life would have everything it could possibly want. It appears to me that fear is the underlying fabric that is shot through my whole life. It is almost omnipresent, and it is representative to me of all of the selfishness, all of the self-obsession, and all of the self-seeking that exists. I make such desperate demands upon life. It is a continual desperate demand. It is as if I am continually dying, moment by moment. And when those demands aren't met, or if I'm afraid that what I already have will be taken away, it is always one form or another of that fear. I'm going through a period when all of this has been more active. It seems to me like there is some kind of pernicious bullshit going on, and that I actually want it. I go through all the self-torture games, and when I come out the other side I say: "What was that all about?" And then it starts all over again.

SRI DA AVABHASA: This "I" that you've mentioned several times just now is a sort of post on which you hang all these experiences. It seems to be in the center of it somehow. "Ego" means "I"—the self-reference, the implied self, this separate-self concept. One could call that self-reference, or self-image, the "ego". But "ego" is not essentially an entity or a concept. "Ego" is an activity. It is the activity of the avoidance of relationship. Just as the separate "I", the self-concept, the self-image, is an expression of this activity that is the ego, fear is also the ego. Fear is the very mood, the "nature", of the ego. It is said in the Upanishads: "It is from an other that fear arises."[1] As soon as there is an other, as soon as this separative act

277

has taken place in any sense whatsoever, from that instant there is fear. Then life is fear. Consciousness is fear. It is not that you are afraid. Fear is your necessary attribute, your very "body". Fear is the ego. As long as you persist in your present ego-bound condition and drama, fear will continually be the mood that you discover. Whenever you fail to be distracted, you will fall into this chronic state, this sense of your separate self, which is fear. Where there is separation, there can only be fear. You have broken the current of life, of real and original existence, the process of the Heart. You have contracted the field of Consciousness. You have made it impossible for the Force of existence to flow between this process of contraction, this "ego", and everything from which it differentiates itself. Therefore, everything outside this "self" becomes fearful, frightening, other. And when you are being afraid, you are simply meditating on the quality of your separated existence. If you try to get rid of fear, it is impossible. Because the "you" trying to get rid of this thing is that fear. So the search is futile.

At some point you fall into your chronic state, this fear, this avoidance of relationship. And when you have fallen into it under the conditions of Satsang with me, this quickening, this insight, awakens. And this insight, this understanding, this re-cognition of which I speak, is the obviation of "ego", the separate self sense, which is fear. Only understanding is without fear. Only one who understands is fearless. Only one who understands is selfless. Only such a one lives always prior to fear. Until then you are dramatizing the form of the separate self, you are living it, and so you are suffering its very condition. You must become sensitive. You must become essentially aware of the conditions that you "create" through the whole activity that is the ego. When your life begins to fail, you begin to become aware of the condition that is the ego. Therefore, there must necessarily be a crisis. Spiritual life must involve this falling into the chronic state, and "radically" comprehending it. The Force of Satsang makes this passage possible, because if you simply fell into your fear, you would go mad. The random tastes of fear are what constantly disturb the form of life. But Satsang is the Condition of Truth. The Force of Satsang, the consciousness and intelligence of Satsang, the Condition of Satsang, is already free of this contraction, this separate self, this fear. As it is said in the Hindu traditions, those who live the Condition of Satsang with the true Guru spontaneously enjoy the turiya state, the "fourth" state, beyond waking, sleeping, and dreaming. This is simply an expression of the Company they are keeping with their Guru. They feel that Fullness, that ease, that enjoyment, and all of the spiritual qualities, all the spiritual events, are generated as a spontaneous happening. They feel no fear in the Company of their Guru. Just so, those who live Satsang already live this Condition that is without fear, without separated self, without the function of ego, the chronic avoidance of relationship. They enjoy that unreasonable happiness, that blissfulness, that is the "mood" of Truth. But those who do not resort to Satsang, who only resort continually to the state they suffer apart from Satsang, find their fear only intensified in the Company of the Guru. They find that "ego" is intensified, that the dilemma, the problems, and the search are intensified, that their ignorance is intensified, and that all of it becomes frightening, and unbearable. That is why periodically you see people storming out of our Ashram, without any apparent reason. Nothing has "happened" to them. I haven't done anything to them. Nothing has really occurred except the process of Satsang Itself. That is what disturbs these angry, self-obsessed ones who renounce the Company and the Teaching of the Siddhas. Those who have not suffered their own condition enough, and who have not seen its perfect failure, are wise to avoid Satsang. Because Satsang is a fire! This communion is not a place where we talk "philosophy". There is a living Force enacted here. It is a living Force of Consciousness Itself. That is what Satsang is all about. And those who arbitrarily pile on, not mindful of the conditions, wind up having to separate themselves very aggressively, with all kinds of righteousness. The Force of Satsang simply acts to intensify their separativeness. But one who has really seen the failure of his or her search, who can somehow spontaneously resort to the Condition of Satsang, experiences that unreasonable happiness. Thus, Satsang becomes the Condition wherein the form of suffering, this contraction, this fear, this ego, all of the elements of suffering and dilemma, are dissolved in a spontaneous, natural, appropriate order. Certainly one must also suffer the intensity of this process of ego-dissolution, including periods of apparent crisis, but it will always be somehow bearable, always intelligent with Truth, always something for which one has the capability. That is why many who have found a true Guru have said that, at some point, they gave up all interest in salvation. They were no longer concerned for liberation, heaven, and healing, or even moved to go through any special "spiritual" processes or the classic round of spiritual experiences. They lost their interest in all of that. They became unreasonably happy only, and they forgot to seek beyond the Guru's feet. The living Guru is a specific function that arises again and again in the worlds. People can indulge any kind of illusion with a dead Guru, Master, or Savior, or with a symbolic image, a God they only believe in. People are very willing to do anything they like, and then forgive themselves with the same liberal attitude. They want God, or Truth, to stay in Its own place. But the living Guru is a Condition to be lived with. The living Guru establishes conditions in the world. Such a one remains continuously mindful of the disciple and of the process that the disciple is going through. And the Guru uses every kind of ordinary and extraordinary means to re-establish the connection.

Real religious and spiritual life involves a Great Condition given to you and many conditions demanded of you. The Great Condition and the real conditions of religious and spiritual life are never anything that you particularly want to assume on your own. People are capable of believing all kinds of things on their own, and of arbitrarily generating what they <u>think</u> is sadhana, or the religious and spiritual life. But it is always just another expression of their ordinary or usual state. It does nothing, fundamentally, to their ego-bound condition. The matter of Truth is entirely academic until the Truth communicates Itself to you, until the Truth takes you over, until the Truth does the sadhana and "creates" the conditions for transformation. So the Truth must find some means to communicate Itself as a function in specific relationship to you. Therefore, the human Guru is an appropriate means, and that is why the human Guru exists.

DEVOTEE: Why and how did we fall into this condition, this miserable condition?

SRI DA AVABHASA: People like to "create" mythologies. You would like to hear some sort of "creation" myth about this suffering, or some sort of philosophy that explains why it came about. When something is "explained", when its "name" is known, then you feel free to forget or exploit it. But it didn't "come about". It is presently happening.

It is not a matter of something that happened. There is nothing hidden in time or space that is making this affair of suffering occur. It is not happening as a result of anything. It is a spontaneous, present activity for which you are entirely responsible. So, truly, it doesn't make any sense to try to describe some means or other by which it might have come about.

I have said, however, that there is a sense in which this specific activity that is your suffering, this contraction, is a reaction to life, to manifested existence. For every action there is an equal and opposite reaction. The whole event of the manifested, or conditional, cosmos arises as a spontaneous event, a single event. The universe is the original action. But for every action there is necessarily an equal and opposite reaction. So this process of which I have been speaking is, in a sense, the reaction to manifested life.

A baby is not born with a concrete sense of a separate life in the world. A baby is not able even to differentiate his or her body from the other movements around him or her. It is all one massive sensation. A baby doesn't differentiate. A baby doesn't, for all practical purposes, differentiate himself or herself as an entity from any other individual, or even from the world itself. Only when the baby learns to <u>react</u> to life does he or she begin to "create" an <u>identity</u> that functions in life. And if the baby has no capability to react, he or she will have no capability for individual life. A human organism that has no capability to react is catatonic, a "vegetable", or else dead. A catatonic has many of the apparent attributes that are assigned to the realized individual. The catatonic is self-less, fearless, but he or she is obviously not "alive", not conscious, functioning, and sane. Therefore, simply to go about trying to discover how not to react is obviously not the cure. To try to discover how not to react to your manifested existence at this moment is not the way of Truth. Even so, people have "created" vast traditional methods of "realization" that are fundamentally only attempts not to react. They try to de-condition themselves, to become detached, to become self-less. But the Truth is not a matter of compulsively and strategically suppressing any form of action, even if that action is the re-action to something else.

Truth is in the spontaneous re-cognition, or knowing again, of an activity in the midst, or condition, of that activity. Therefore, one who understands is not in a catatonic state. Understanding is not itself characterized by any trance or any conditional Yogic state. Understanding is not itself an <u>other</u> state. The state of one who understands may appear to be extraordinary from the point of view of the usual man or woman. But actually one who understands is wholly ordinary, conformed to the realm of the manifested. Even so, at the same time that one lives in this ordinary manner, he or she enjoys the Perfect Condition That Is Real God, or Truth. Therefore, the life of one who understands is a paradox. But the seeker and the attainments of the seeker are not paradoxical. They are always dimensionless and winded to a point. The seeker is always turned to specific goals, specific states. They may be complex and incomprehensible, but they are always as specific and mind-based as a bowling trophy.

Truth Itself is not identified with a state, with an experience, nor with the avoidance of any state or any experience, neither with the detachment or forceful separation from any state or experience, nor with the suppression of it. Truth is not even identical to the suppression of thought. In one who understands, everything continues to arise, but coincident with everything that arises there is perfect intuition of the Real. One who understands perpetually, spontaneously, under all conditions, intuits the Real. Such a one intuits the Real in the most "radical" sense, without separation. Such a one requires no special condition for realization. The realization of such a one doesn't only exist when he or she is in certain meditative moods, only when he or she is quiet, only when he or she is performing certain spiritual functions, or only when he or she is talking about certain spiritual things. The realization of such a one is spontaneous, absolute, continuous. Therefore, religious and spiritual life in the form it is lived in this Ashram is a span of conscious adventure, generated in the relationship to me as Siddha-Guru, and summed up in the Perfect Enjoyment of which I am the Evidence, the Demonstration, and the very Form.

**Sri Da Avabhasa
at Sri Love-Anandashram, 1992**

12.

No One Survives
Beyond That Moment

DEVOTEE: Are we evolving?

SRI DA AVABHASA: What do you think?

DEVOTEE: I think we are evolving toward the astral.

SRI DA AVABHASA: What is so good about "astral"?

DEVOTEE: Well, nothing. But as far as evolution goes, there is a constant change. Is it constant change? Where are we going? What is it doing for us? What is it?

SRI DA AVABHASA: Is it?

DEVOTEE: Well, it seems to be, but I am in a dilemma. Is evolution part of the dilemma?

SRI DA AVABHASA: There is this dilemma.

DEVOTEE: There is dilemma. Yes. Then it is part of the dilemma.

SRI DA AVABHASA: What is the question?

DEVOTEE: Now I'm really confused.

SRI DA AVABHASA: Are you talking about anything? In this concern for "evolution", are you really talking about something?

DEVOTEE: I don't really understand what evolution is, or even if there is evolution.

SRI DA AVABHASA: That is the truth.

DEVOTEE: There is no evolution?

SRI DA AVABHASA: You don't know.

DEVOTEE: Yes.

SRI DA AVABHASA: What you know is this dilemma, this confusion, this ignorance about your own propositions. That is the truth. That is your experience. This "evolution" doesn't really exist as your experience. You are not certain of it, of its existence, of its quality, of its nature, of its direction, of its relationship to you. You know nothing whatsoever about it. Why are we talking about it?

The truth is that you are confused. There is this dilemma. There is suffering. Questions about "evolution" are completely beside the point. Such questions, for the time being, are means of drawing attention away from your actual state, of distracting yourself from that confusion, temporarily. We could take this symbolic category of "evolution", and we could talk about it from many different points of view. We could make all kinds of mind-forms with it. But after we have said it all, nothing will have been added in the form of real experience, and you will remain in the same state you were in when you asked the question.

Therefore, this "evolution" question doesn't represent anything significant. It is not your real question. The real question is your actual state. That is the question. That is the question you are truly asking, that you are always asking. You present your very life to the world in the form of a question. You are this real question. But you conceal it from consciousness. Therefore, it exists only as your chronic state, your suffering, your search, your dilemma. Ordinarily, a person does not verbally ask his or her real question. He or she only lives it and performs it—as seeking, suffering, and death. Sadhana, or real spiritual practice in relation to the true Guru, is the means whereby human beings become conscious of their real questions.

Just so, the "answer" to your real question has nothing whatever to do with evolution, or any other arbitrary "topic" the mind can select. The true answer is not in the form of a response to a symbolic question. The true answer must be a "radical" transformation of your state. That is the answer to your question. And if this state that you are always in, this confusion, this dilemma, is utterly, "radically", overcome, then the nature of this whole appearance of life and world also will become obvious. The answer of the Guru to the devotee comes in the context of the discipline of real conditions, demands for functional action, the sadhana which is always generated in the Guru's Company.

There is absolutely no point whatsoever in our talking about evolution now. It is an arbitrary distraction you have selected from the pattern of your own movements. You have chosen it from the moving confusion of your ordinary state. That confusion is our genuine concern. All your questions are forms of this dilemma, this state. Every question is in the form of a dilemma, and every verbal or mental dilemma is an expression of an underlying state that shapes every moment of the usual life. The arbitrary "creation" of "questions", of artifices to occupy the mind, is a means of distraction from this state. It is a form of self-indulgence. To answer such questions is only to serve bewilderment, unconsciousness, fear, ignorance, and all the qualities of seeking and suffering. I know that you have been upset for several days, crazy with this whole movement in yourself, and now you want to talk about evolution. What has that got to do with anything? This suffering that is begun must continue. The death must occur.

DEVOTEE: It just goes on and on and on. It never seems to stop.

SRI DA AVABHASA: The death. That is what you want to get away from. You would "evolve" to the astral world, and so escape this necessary death. There is no elimination of death, no ultimate avoidance of death. You are trying to prevent death, this very crisis, by occupying yourself with symbolic questions.

DEVOTEE: But that's the only answer, that death. Why do we keep fighting and fighting?

SRI DA AVABHASA: Keep fighting what?

DEVOTEE: This thing. We know we are fighting it, and yet we can't help it. Why are we avoiding it? How do we get out of it?

SRI DA AVABHASA: This desire to get out of it is another form of that same avoidance. But a real transformation, in the form of this conflict, this crisis, has already begun in you. It has become intensified. You are beginning to find your real question. It is your death. That is the significant event. There is no distraction from it. There is no consolation for it. But it is true and real. Evolution can make no difference. Migration to the astral plane can make no difference. None of that can change this chronic state. This crisis would still be necessary, no matter where in all the worlds you happened to appear. This crisis is the peculiar event of all life. Going to the astral plane does not change that necessity. Intelligence is still required.

This question about evolution represents a form of concern, a search. That is what is communicated to me in the form of your question. It has no real content other than that. It is only because this crisis is occurring that you have the least interest in evolution. But if you are dying, there is no evolution. In that case, what do you care whether the seven hundred billion that remain behind you are transformed into ducks or luminous red astral bodies? Your death is the only remaining content of your life. From the point of view of your experience, there is no evolution. There is only sudden death. But this death is true. It is the real process. Therefore, it is worth living, because this real death of which I speak is the very crisis of consciousness that serves both Truth and life.

One who awakens from a dream is not thereafter concerned for the destiny of those who appeared along with him or her in the dream. There is no such destiny. There is no one left behind. All that appears in the universal form, or great cosmic process, is a spontaneous display, like the conditions that appear in dreams. All of that goes on in any case. But now you are beginning to see this more fundamental condition underlying your adventure of distraction in the cosmic event. In the past you did not see it, or know it for what it was. To the degree you felt it at all, it was a subtle sensation, a discomfort, a sort of formless craziness, a wildness, but now you are beginning to know what it really is. Now you are beginning to know it as your chronic state. But you will come to recognize it as your own activity. You are beginning to be aware of it more or less continually. That continuous awareness is the self-purifying sadhana of real religious and spiritual life.

DEVOTEE: Even one who comes to reside in the Heart has patterns and rules to follow on his or her journey. Otherwise, certain things won't open. There are rules which one can't switch away. So there is in fact a pattern, isn't there?

SRI DA AVABHASA: A pattern of what?

DEVOTEE: By which the universe is ordered. Even if a person comes from any state, seeks the Light, and finally resides in the Heart, he or she must go by certain signs along the way. It is different for each person, but still there are rules.

SRI DA AVABHASA: If they are different, what is this specific pattern?

DEVOTEE: There isn't one that fits everyone, but still there are patterns existing.

SRI DA AVABHASA: Of course, there are apparent patterns in life. But the Heart is not someplace else. The Heart is not a point separate from any other place. It is not in a certain direction. It is not the end of any particular road. It is not the goal. If you are speaking of the causal center, the heart-center on the right side of the chest, it is indeed a point, a place, a psycho-physical sensation. But the true "Heart" is another word for the one, unqualified Reality.

DEVOTEE: That becomes true, once you realize it. But between the time you know it and the time you are only approaching it, there are still patterns.

SRI DA AVABHASA: They are your own patterns. They are your apparent condition. They are the subtle forms of cognition which help to fabricate the dilemma and the search, previous to the enjoyment of the Heart, which is "radical" understanding. But in the perfect form of Satsang, which is the relationship to the perfectly realized Siddha-Guru, the Heart establishes a living relationship with the individual, and then it no longer makes any difference to that person what the apparent patterns are. The patterns are simply observed from that moment. A unique Condition is lived, and so these patterns become obsolete. They fall away, until only the Heart stands out. From the point of view of the true disciple, there is no significance to the patterns. There is no significance. "Significance" is your dilemma. It is the pattern of your own mind-forms. That is the only thing that obstructs perfect Consciousness. It is neither external nor internal. All that arises is only a modification of your own ultimate Nature and Condition. When this is perfectly understood, the enjoyment realized in understanding is called the "Heart". There is no subjective, no objective, no external, no universe, no astral world, from the "point of view" of the Heart. All such phenomena are simply apparent modifications of the Heart.

Until you truly enter into Satsang with me, you are very concerned about your path, about this pattern of your own growth and experience, your own transformation, your own liberation. But when you enter into the Condition of Satsang with me, your concerns, your path, your patterns become obsolete. All of that is simply not supported. You simply live the Condition and the conditions of relationship generated in my Company, and the patterns subside. They become obsolete, without function. Therefore, concern for those patterns is more evidence of the search, of this fundamental dilemma. All movements within the cosmic and universal form are movements within the cosmic and universal form. No movement implies or leads to Reality. All movements lead to terminals within the cosmic and universal form itself, to more states, more change, more phenomena. They do not in any manner in themselves obviate the dilemma that is suffering. One who assumes that action will lead to the very Self has performed an act in consciousness that is not in itself true. Truth is in the re-cognition of motivation and action.

You are always already "there". This is it. There is no dilemma. There is only one Reality, presently. It is not somewhere else. It is not hidden within you, nor behind the world. It is only obvious. Satsang is the Condition of Reality, consciously lived. It is lived to you, within you, as you, along with you. It is that real Condition lived as life, as a pressure upon the disciple. I live It to my disciple, such that It begins to become obvious and intelligent in my disciple. But all my disciple will have realized, after all, is the obvious. The nature of the rising event, the apparent condition, becomes clear. It becomes obvious to my disciple that his or her dilemma is his or her own activity. My disciple sees that in fact there is no dilemma. There is nothing about the present that is not Truth.

This Satsang is the real Condition. It is the Condition of Truth. It is the Condition of conscious relationship to me. When you enter into It consciously, with any degree of clarity, you have begun to live under the conditions that are Truth. And that is the entire process. That is real religious life, real spiritual life, real life altogether. Everything else is an extension, or another reflection, of your search, your dilemma, your dis-ease. When this real Condition is truly lived, whatever arises tends to be consumed.

DEVOTEE: Is it within the power of one's will to remain in the Condition of Satsang?

SRI DA AVABHASA: Apparently not. One can maintain oneself responsibly in the Company of one's Guru, and fulfill the specific demands imposed by one's Guru. But to live the conscious Condition of relationship with one's Guru depends on the subtle grace of that Condition itself.

Everyone tends to live apart, separately, constantly. Even when someone begins to sense the unique Presence of one who lives as the Heart, he or she resists and defends himself or herself and covers up his or her disability, discomfort, dilemma. The person approaches such a one with argumentation, self-defense, the endless formulations of his or her own mind, and with suggestions that maybe "it's all right anyway." Such a person continues to do his or her number, assuming the Guru is a captured audience for his or her act. When the person overcomes all of that only a little bit, he or she begins to "hunt" the Guru, seeking to "find the Guru out", and to justify independence from the Guru through various kinds of moral and philosophical righteousness. Such a one penalizes the Guru, resists the Guru, plays with the Guru, indulges in dramas with the Guru, goes away, comes back, teases the Guru. All of this because the principle of ordinary life is the avoidance of relationship, the ego, the activity of separation.

But when you enter into real and conscious Satsang with one who lives as the Heart, you no longer have this activity, or separate self, as your primary instrument. The activity that is the ego has become obsolete. It may continue to arise and obsess you, but Satsang has become your Condition. The process of the Heart Itself, the Guru as Truth, performs your sadhana and holds on to you. The Guru "creates" a drama within the drama of the devotee. This subtle drama, or grace, makes it possible for the devotee to maintain his or her sadhana, the living practice of his or her connection. This grace looks forward to the time when the devotee becomes responsible enough to assume that relationship fully and consciously, as his or her responsibility, as his or her real Condition. Then the devotee is given responsibilities that will test, prove, and awaken in him or her all the qualities of a true disciple.

DEVOTEE: What are the responsibilities of a person who lives in the Condition of Truth? For years I've fluctuated between everything from total self-indulgence to forty-day fasts and found basically an inability to eat moderately. I don't think that this is a responsible thing to do. And yet it's inappropriate to be always compulsively responsible. But at the same time, if I don't eat properly, I become less conscious. I sleep more. I get spaced out.

SRI DA AVABHASA: The point of view that you are expressing is the point of view of dilemma, of suffering, which has nothing to do with Truth. It is this very Condition of Truth that people try to destroy by all means. Excessive fasting or excessive eating, self-indulgence of all kinds, deprivation of all kinds, turning inward, turning outward, ascetic practices, "ordinary" practices—all of these are only means to overcome the fundamental sense of dilemma and suffering. None of that has anything to do with illumination, or Truth. All of that is suffering.

The question for such a one is not how to become responsible. That is not the real question. The real question is the state that such a person is in. And the real answer is not in the form of a response to verbal dilemmas, or even apparent life-dilemmas. The answer is the obviation of this state. You will seek by all means to be free of the dilemma as it appears to you, until all the forms of your seeking, all of which are reactions to the subtle condition, or dilemma, that is your suffering, cease to occupy you. You come to the point where the force of your life is no longer fully captured by your search. You know that your search is failing, that your search does not produce salvation. You fall from ordinary fascination into a crisis, a form of despair, of doubt. At that point, you have become available for Satsang, for that relationship which is true religious and spiritual life.

Satsang is the answer. It is that process and Condition wherein the dilemma is undone. Not any spoken word but that process itself which is enjoyed in relationship to the living Heart is the "answer". It is not in the form of an ego-serving method, another strategic technique, or a conceptual system that applies to your peculiar ideas of your state. The answer is in the form of the Force of Truth, and It undermines that very structure in your living consciousness that supports your whole search. This becomes a real possibility only when you have begun to suffer from your search, when you have begun to sense its failure, when you are no longer totally occupied by it. Then you become available to Guru, to Satsang. And Satsang is non-support of your dilemma, non-support of your search.

In Satsang, all your techniques fall away, all fascination with your search subsides, all your methods become comic. Your whole life ceases to obsess you. Your need for liberation no longer interests you. Your life becomes one of the enjoyment of Truth, the enjoyment of the Guru, until the whole form of contracted consciousness in which you ordinarily rest is utterly dissolved. In Satsang, an entirely new and living form of intelligence replaces your ordinary strategic mentality.

Some individuals have become involved in the most incredible adventure of spiritual technique. They are concerned with all kinds of technique. There are techniques of living, techniques of subjective and psychological states, the seeker's meditation, the seeker's diet, and all the rest. Such individuals come to Satsang in the moods of spirituality and philosophy. Others are more "ordinary". They come to Satsang after the equally traditional self-indulgent life. Everyone comes to Satsang in the midst of a different form of adventure. All come with the same fundamental dilemma, but all communicate it through different artifices, through the form of a peculiar adventure. In essence, all adventures are a description of the same state: this contraction, this subtle dis-ease, the avoidance of relationship. That is so. That is the experience.

From the point of view of the real question, the actual dilemma, a person is happy to enter into this Satsang with me. For such a one, religious and spiritual life is, happily, not a strategic, or ego-based and ego-bound, technique, method, remedy, or path. True religious and spiritual life is a relationship. It has always been so. Therefore, rightly, and most fundamentally, nothing apart from the relationship to the Guru is offered. Relationship itself is the principle and condition of life. Therefore, rightly, the relationship to the Guru is the single and great principle of sadhana, the single and great medium of Truth, the one "method" that arises in the life of the disciple. Truly, the relationship to the Guru is the Condition and the medium through which all things come that are appropriate for the religious and spiritual life of the disciple. And they come spontaneously, as a grace. In Satsang a person has become available to Truth Itself, Reality Itself, such that Truth Itself, Reality Itself, has become the only means for his or her illumination. Until that point, the individual has been too occupied to be illumined. First he or she must fall from search and fascination into the crisis of his or her ordinary condition.

The most difficult thing for a human being to achieve is ordinariness. But the primary condition of this Satsang with me is the requirement that ordinariness be realized. Human beings are extremely inventive, eminently capable of the extraordinary, the adventure, the search. But the ordinary, what simply is the case, what already is the case, is extremely difficult, because of the principle of action by which all human beings "create" their lives. When this Satsang begins for a person, when It becomes his or her real circumstance of life, he or she suddenly becomes capable of ordinariness, of simplicity. It simply becomes appropriate. It is not the least connected with anything compulsive, anything like the discipline which a seeker might embrace. The functional simplicity of my disciple is only obvious and natural to him or her, because action has been released from its connection with the search for Truth, liberation, and the like. Any ego-bound effort that is pictured as a means to Truth belongs to the adventure of seeking and its dilemma. It is part of the adventure of extraordinariness. Only Truth Itself, Satsang Itself, free of seeking, is the way in which Truth is realized.

When one is released from the pursuit of Truth, one simply lives It. One lives Satsang as the Condition of life, communion with Truth replaces the search for Truth. All one's ordinary functions become truly ordinary when one is released from the need to realize Truth. Therefore, in Satsang, one's ordinary, functional life becomes realizable, usable. There is no reason why diet should be manipulated as a means to Truth. Nor should it be considered an obstruction to Truth. The ingestion of food has nothing whatever to do with Truth. Neither food-obsession nor food-righteousness is the way of Truth.

DEVOTEE: What it seems to have to do with is my being in a state where I'm willing to put my attention on the Truth. If, for example, I am overeating or taking drugs, I will not be in a condition to put my attention on Truth.

SRI DA AVABHASA: You cannot put your attention on Truth in any case. Truth is not an "object". It only appears to be an object from the point of view of the same search that motivates you to indulge yourself and also not to indulge yourself. Truth cannot be concentrated upon even by a mind that is clear and free. It can't be "noticed". It is not an object. It doesn't appear within your view. It already includes you and your points of view.

DEVOTEE: Instead of the term "attention on Truth", could we say "to experience more consciously"?

SRI DA AVABHASA: Experiencing has nothing to do with Truth. Truth cannot be experienced, nor is It an experience. Neither is Truth experience itself. All these expressions you have used have the same form. As far as Truth goes, there is nothing to be said about It in this sense. No formal communication is the equivalent of It. All of the descriptions you might give of the peculiar form of your adventure have the same form, the same structure. Indeed, your questions are a strategy whereby you prevent the realization of Truth. Your concerns are a means to avoid self-recognition.

Truth always appears to the seeker as a kind of <u>alternative</u>. But Truth is not an alternative. Truth is your <u>very</u> Consciousness, your very Nature, your very Condition. It cannot be concentrated upon. It is not an object. It is not something in which you can become interested. It is not something from which you can be distracted. Your interests, your distractions, your noticings, your experiencings, are <u>all</u> expressions, or modifications, of the fundamental Reality. But you are not living them as such. Therefore, you are constantly obsessed with alternatives, with particular distractions, noticings, and experiencings. Alternatives are all that you have.

When you no longer have any alternatives, when the search has died, then Truth becomes your real possibility. But Truth is not an alternative. It is not in the form of an answer to a specific question. It is not something perceived. It is not something that serves you, the actively presumed limited and separate subject. It is not something that liberates you as a separate person. It has nothing to do with you as a separate one. It cannot be enjoyed by you as a separate one. Truth is enjoyed only in the instant of non-separation, of perfect equality with Truth.

There is no conditional <u>state</u> equivalent to Truth. Every conditional state is only a condition, a limitation. In the descriptions associated with the traditional religious and spiritual paths, there are conditional experiences and conditional states that are identified with Truth, or Reality Itself. Some traditions say Truth is equal to, or necessarily coincident with, a vision of Krishna. For others, Truth must be samadhi in the form of an ascended Yogic trance, either with visions or without the least trace of form, objective or subjective. Still others equate Truth with a concentrated return of the vital force to the sahasrar, a vision of Light, or some other esoteric but nonetheless conditional signal of the Divine. But all of these are forms of experience, of conditionality. They may be sublime, subtle, but they appear only as alternatives to other "ordinary" experiences. No experience is Truth. And no experience is itself the sign of Truth, the "symptom" of Truth Itself, or Its necessary accompaniment.

Truth Is That Which Stands Out As Reality when there is re-cognition of the whole process of experience, when there is the absolute vanishing of identification with alternatives, the whole self-contracted scheme of seeking. Therefore, Truth involves the most "radical" understanding, even of that which is extraordinary. Until that occurs, both the usual and the great events in life are an egoic fascination. It is the memory of experiences, the persistent bondage to one's own modifications that come as the result of experience, that generates the goals of seeking. Impressions in the form of tendencies continue to fascinate people and obsess them with the notion that life is made of alternatives, so that all the usual man or woman is doing is playing this drama of alternatives continually. One day the individual is going toward the "experience" of Truth, another day toward experience itself, usually of a very "human" variety. One day the individual pursues the enjoyment of trance-samadhi, while the next he or she is a devotee of sexual fascination. But it is always the same adventure.

What appeared in the past as the great moments of your life did not become wisdom. All you are left with are the modifications which reflect those moments. If great experiences had become wisdom, if in the instant of any such experience the Truth were perfectly realized, the experience itself would have fallen away, the phenomena associated with it would have fallen away, but the Real, the Force of Reality that is Truth in every moment, would have then remained. And that Truth is the same Truth that persists at this moment, when perhaps you are not having such a "great" experience. Truth does not appear in the form of this drama of one's experiences and alternatives. It appears as a possibility only when that entire process—that entire adventure, the whole force of ordinary and extraordinary consciousness, which is seeking—begins to wind down, when it ceases to occupy you mightily, and you are stuck with your actual condition, your suffering. Only the crisis in consciousness is that event in which the process that is real religious and spiritual life takes place. It does not take place in the adventure. It takes place only in the re-cognition of this contraction that motivates the adventure. And such re-cognition becomes possible for you only when the force of your ordinary and extraordinary adventure has begun to die.

DEVOTEE: I think that I might feel a hesitancy to give up that aspect of the search.

SRI DA AVABHASA: Good, very good. That is it exactly. Two types of people come. Those who have died to their search, and those who still have a couple of trips left. Regarding those who still have the search in mind, there is no condemnation, no praise, no blame. That is the state of their condition. The search is still their occupation. They have not come for <u>Truth</u>. The Truth has nothing whatever to do with them. The search, the adventure among alternatives, that is what "has" them. That is what has all human beings, until it begins to die. Then the Truth becomes possible.

When you no longer have genuine alternatives, when you no longer have the option of your own preferences, when you no longer have the capability to persist, to survive in the form of your search, then Satsang becomes something more than academic. Until that time, all human beings are talking about the same thing: their adventure! That is what they are talking about. They are not the least concerned for the Truth. It hasn't entered into the picture yet. It is only an amusement, an alternative notion entertained in the midst of ordinary and extraordinary suffering. They are still occupied. Fine. But the matter of real religious and spiritual life arises only when the alternatives themselves do not present a real option.

DEVOTEE: How do I bring myself to the point of not wanting?

SRI DA AVABHASA: Wanting or not wanting are both forms of the same activity. It is this occupation, this preoccupation, this distraction, or fascination, moment to moment.

DEVOTEE: How do I get over that?

SRI DA AVABHASA: This desire is more of this adventure now. It is the adventure of getting over it now. It is all the same. The fact of the matter is that you are in this present state, and all your actions, your desires, and even your questions are only descriptions of it. This much should be clear to you now, as a result of this conversation. The Truth is of another variety. But this lesson about your present and usual state can be useful. It is the first lesson of wisdom.

If it begins only to hurt, if all the alternatives fall into one, if they cease to be a real option, if you find yourself continually stuck only in the crisis of consciousness itself, which is the very and subtle form of suffering from which ordinarily you spring in order to seek—when that becomes the nature of your daily life, then Truth enters into the picture. Then Satsang, real life, enters as a living possibility. It will be your obvious need when you have no options.

297

DEVOTEE: I am already aware that none of these things work.

SRI DA AVABHASA: There is some small wisdom, because you are becoming exhausted with experience. But the seeker still possesses some potency. The seeker is still springing, still reacting to this subtle dilemma. When this "springing" stops, or when it begins to seem that it is not possible, when the alternatives don't quite have you, when the potency of the search begins to go, then the matter of real religious and spiritual life begins to take on the form of your living consciousness. When a person is only suffering, then the matter of release, or the obviation of suffering, begins to become clear. Then the Force of Truth, of Reality, which is Truth, can begin to move in him or her. Then Satsang becomes possible, because, at that point, It has a function. But while the search is still one's task, still one's fascination, Truth, or Reality, is not one's concern. Until then, Truth, or Reality, does not appear except as an alternative, a symbol, another form of distraction. Therefore, as the traditions have always said, Truth, or real life, is a matter of death, of crisis, of that dilemma, or doubt, which is the fuel of liberation. When the search, the reactions to one's dilemma, begins to wind down, and only the dilemma remains, only this subtle suffering, this dis-ease of life, then the Force of Reality begins to move into one's life. Then one's real question can be answered. Until then, one's questions are one's entertainment, one's amusement. They have no ultimate importance. They are the forms of preoccupation and unconscious self-description. Then "religious life" itself, or "spiritual life" itself, is only an amusement, only an entertainment. Then meditation, sitting with the Guru, reading religious and spiritual books, all of that, is only another form of erotica, of mere "significance". But when one's hunger becomes intelligent, when one's dis-ease becomes mind, then the spoken Truth, the word of the Great Siddha, and the living form of the Siddha-Guru truly become what one requires. One becomes intelligent with that word and form, and one responds. A subtle re-cognition occurs. And this process called "religious life", "spiritual life", "liberation", "realization", begins. Until then it has not begun, it has not entered the picture in any real sense.

By your own admission, you are yet a seeker. But you have been brought to consider the futility and the causes of your own adventure. And, at some point, very likely it will all become something more than academic for you.

DEVOTEE: If Truth is the natural state, how did we get to deviate so much from It?

SRI DA AVABHASA: You didn't get to do it. You are doing it! It is not a caused activity. This sense of separation, this dilemma, is not something that happened, for various reasons, at some point in the past. It doesn't occur for "reasons". It is always a present, spontaneous activity, cognized as this sense of separation, of dilemma. But it is not itself the result of anything in the past. Therefore, the attempt to trace experience back in time to recover the events from which you are suffering is fruitless. It cannot produce Truth as a result, because, truly, you are not suffering the results of anything that is past. Suffering is the quality, or the mood, of your present activity. Your present activity is your suffering.

At some point you begin to dwell on your suffering itself, until you re-cognize it, know it again, as your present activity. When you know it again as your present activity, and when you re-cognize its nature, it simply stops. It spontaneously comes to an end whenever this re-cognition occurs, for re-cognition makes it obsolete, without a present function. But its precise nature is of an extremely subtle kind, so that it is comprehended only by "radical" insight. The traditions have often spoken of suffering as the result of something that happened in the past, in order to make some sort of sense out of it. But it has no "sense". It is irrational, mindless. It is understandable only from the point of view of a "radical" insight. Then its form can be seen. Then its structure, its nature, as a present event is only obvious.

The traditional myth of suffering is that it happened to human beings some time ago, or that you are presently in a state that is the result of some beginning of suffering in your individual past. But your suffering is always a present activity. That is what is remarkable about it. People tend to think of suffering in terms of something external to themselves in time or space. By such means they try to explain it to themselves, to make sense of it, so they can overcome it through egoic efforts of various kinds. But, in fact, suffering is not your symptom. It is your activity. That is the paradox. All your seeking is based on the illusion that your suffering is somehow a symptom that can be eliminated. But when the search begins to wind down, it begins to dawn on you that your suffering is your activity, not your symptom. Your symptoms are simply the mental and physical expressions of this activity. But your suffering is absolutely present, and it is always cognized as felt dilemma.

Therefore, the real process of religious and spiritual life is a wholly positive possibility. It requires only the Truth, which is the living Force of Reality. It requires no other process, such as the manipulation of your memory, or the generating of "good karma" so that your "bad karma" can be eliminated. All of that is, ultimately, a fruitless task. Behavioral improvement can never be done to the point of perfect freedom. The karmas, or the tendencies, that generate the qualities of your life can never be fully "paid off", or absolutely dissolved by good works. All action, good or bad, as well as all inaction, only, at last, reinforces limitation and the dilemma itself. It is not the absolute elimination of karmas, not super-purification by ego-effort, not any kind of righteousness, that frees a person. In that case, the solution could never occur. Freedom is always already the case. Thus, freedom is enjoyed where Truth suddenly comes alive. Where Truth is lived, where Satsang is truly enjoyed, Truth Itself consumes, or includes, all that of which karma is a part. When It comes alive, Truth obviates the force of all of that.

The search makes no sense at all. It is an illusory and false principle. Only the living Truth avails. And the living Truth must be lived. Such is Satsang, the relationship of Guru and disciple. Such is true sadhana, or spiritual practice, wherein Satsang is constantly lived as one's Condition. And there must be a lifetime of Truth, not a two-week smack of blessing, fasting, and meditation, not a vicarious weekend of "enlightenment". There must be a lifetime of Satsang. In other words, there must be an absolute commitment. Satsang does not exist until It has become "radical" practice, until It is lived as one's very Condition, without qualifications of time, space, or life. There must be continuous and "radical" enjoyment of Satsang. In other words, It must become the principle, the very Condition, of life, whereas, in the usual man or woman, the dilemma and its search are the principle and the binding condition of life. When Satsang becomes the Condition of life, It makes the whole effort of search obsolete through non-support.

DEVOTEE: What is the role of others in one's pursuit of Truth? You mentioned the role of the Guru. You mentioned the Guru as one such individual.

SRI DA AVABHASA: The Guru is not separate from oneself, not other than one's very, or ultimate, Self-Condition.

300

DEVOTEE: What about the rest of humanity?

SRI DA AVABHASA: Neither are they separate and other. They, along with you, may temporarily be living as if they were separate and other, but the true Guru does not. "Others" function as others. Being others, they "create" circumstances, or apparent conditions, for you to enjoy, for you to suffer. The true Guru is not, in Truth, an "other", nor does the true Guru live as an "other" in any sense. One who sees an individual whom others claim to be functioning as Guru may consider that one to be an other, like himself or herself. But he or she has only failed to recognize that one as Guru. By virtue of the perfect realization of Truth, the true Guru is identical to one's own ultimate Nature, or very Self-Condition. Absolutely, not symbolically, the Guru is one's very Consciousness, prior to all egoity. This is absolutely so in the case of one who appears as the true Guru in human form. The true Guru is not an "other". Therefore, "others" have no role whatsoever in the transmission and the process that is Truth. Only one who is, by virtue of perfect realization, one's true Self can perform that role.

One's true Self appears in the form of the true Guru. In the Condition of Satsang, wherein all activity becomes sadhana, the Self of Reality functions in the form of the human Guru, in apparently ordinary human terms, in relationship to the disciple, until perfect understanding awakens in the case of the disciple. But when understanding is awakened perfectly, when Satsang has performed Its "radical" communication, when sadhana is most excellent and perfectly effective, no difference, no "other", can be found, even in the world of apparent differences. The teacher who is "other" than you, who only fascinates, who offers you various ego-based practices and strategies for seeking, acts only to modify your state. Such a one is not functioning truly as Guru. Such a one is functioning as an "other", as a source of experience, of modification. The Guru is not "other". The Guru's activity is a paradox.

One's relationship with the Guru, which is Satsang, depends on the subtle recognition of the Guru as Truth, as one's own Nature, the very Self. That recognition does not necessarily appear at the level of the mind, as a mentally achieved certainty, or in the form of some sort of visionary or psychic perception. But there must be a subtle recognition. That genuine recognition has no explanation, no mental content, in many cases. But that recognition is what allows the relationship between Guru and disciple to be enjoyed as it truly is, as Satsang, rather than as the usual communication of "others".

DEVOTEE: I experience you as in no manner different from me. Nonetheless, I experience that you are you, and I am I. How can the Guru and the disciple become identical?

SRI DA AVABHASA: I have not been talking about the notion that the Guru and the disciple are or can become identical in the conditional sense, as if they are or can be the same conditional entity. Nor have I been speaking in the traditional "spiritual" sense, in which Guru and disciple are identical as some sort of spiritual substance, which "substance" is found when you manage to "get out" of the physical body or even the subtle body. Such notions are only another form of the same conceptual separation, the same dilemma, the same puzzlement, the same separation that is suffering. I have been speaking of the "radical" Condition of Truth, very Reality, wherein no dilemma and no separation arise as an implication of any condition, even the ordinary condition of apparently unique, human entities.

The notions of sameness or of difference have no significance. Or, should I say, they have <u>only</u> significance. They are very "significant", but they are utterly beside the point. They do not pertain to the matter of Truth. The discussion of significances can go on forever, because it only deals with mental modifications. The perception or the notion that in some subtle sense there is no difference between us all is a mental modification. It is not the equivalent of "radical" understanding and Truth. It is not a symptom, or sign, of the Truth Itself. It is only the idea or the conditional experience of no difference. It is only a mental, or otherwise conditional, state. Psychotics can be in such a state. Daydreamers, pot-heads, and philosophers can be in that state. People whose minds are relatively at rest for a moment can be in that state. Truth is not a conditional state, Truth is not a perception or a thought. When there is truly no difference, no one survives. If there truly is the realization of non-separation, no <u>one</u> survives beyond that moment. Absolutely, no separate individual survives the unconditional realization of Truth. It is ego-death. No one remains behind to speak glibly of it, because it is certain death. From the point of view of ordinary consciousness, it is the most dramatic, fearsome event. It cannot be conceived. It can only be symbolically entertained from the usual point of view. But this death of which I speak is the fundamental process of real life.

DEVOTEE: What happens after death?

SRI DA AVABHASA: You will see.

DEVOTEE: Well, I think that moment has happened to me.

SRI DA AVABHASA: Some experience you have had is suggesting itself to you now. You think it is this "death" I have described, because you are trying to make sense of it. Such experiences are not themselves Truth. In *The Knee of Listening* I devoted a lot of time to the description of this kind of thing. In my own case, I passed through all kinds of "spiritual" states, all kinds of great, dramatic realizations, all kinds of Yogic processes. At the time they may have seemed to be the Truth, or ultimate realization, and yet they disappeared. They came to an end. At last the whole adventure of associating Truth with experiences began to wind down. I began to abide in my ordinary state. There were many "enlightenment" experiences. There were many states that seemed complete. But they did not alter the fundamental dilemma. Truth was only in the "radical" understanding, or re-cognition, of the whole process of conditional experiences and conditional states. There is a perfect understanding, a perfect Consciousness, in which one's previous states of illumination, which one thought were Truth, become obvious as only more forms, more modifications. That obviousness, and not experiences themselves, is enlightenment.

DEVOTEE: Is enlightenment, or realization, a process of growth?

SRI DA AVABHASA: From the point of view of one who is living in Satsang with the Guru, it may seem that there is some sort of growth, some sort of movement, or transformation. But there is a "radical" form of that whole event in which one sees there was no growth, no transformation, and no path.

You cannot be more and more absorbed into the Truth. It is the principle of one's life, the Reality, not merely the goal. But there are modifications of one's life and strategy that occur in the process of sadhana. They seem to give you a sense of progress in this sense. And this sense may have a certain value from the point of view of sadhana. The sense of growth, and the memory of spiritual change, may give the individual an edge over the occasional tendency to lapse from sadhana and the principle of Satsang into his or her former condition of self-indulgence, seeking, and the concerns of one in dilemma.

DEVOTEE: One teacher has said it is one's sole duty to strive. Is that striving what you mean by the search, or is there a healthy striving?

SRI DA AVABHASA: Let the one who has said it be responsible for it. Let that one justify it. To live Truth is to be responsible for the dissolution of fear and ignorance. The intelligence of Truth is not preoccupied with the ordinary statements of human beings. People who become involved in the traditional paths of spiritual life often gain a great deal for the mind in the process. A major part of the defense people make in behalf of their suffering is all of the language, all of the things heard and read in the midst of the search. All of that must come to an end, absolutely. All of that is consumed by Truth. There is no ultimately fruitful resort but to Truth Itself. If someone tells others to resort to themselves, to strive on- ward until the Truth is glimpsed, he or she has functioned only as an "other" to motivate people while they are still suffering. Truth Itself is not served by the command that people do something in order to realize the Truth. No action of any man or woman produces Truth as a result. Perfect Satsang, the communication of Truth Itself, the relationship to the perfectly realized Siddha-Guru, is the entire means, the only means, the "radical" means. Truth is the very means of religious, or spiritual, or real, life, not its goal. One who resorts to the Truth of the perfectly realized Siddha-Guru in Satsang is never again returned to the search. But people are always trying to return to the search, because of the difficult crisis demanded in real religious and spiritual life. They always want to con- sole themselves by some means or other. The apparent emptiness, or paradoxical starkness, of the Guru's offering becomes a kind of aggrava- tion to the seeker, who constantly refuses the Condition of Satsang and Its demands.

People want to be filled with all kinds of things, distracted with all kinds of things. "What can I do to be saved? How can I meditate? How can I get free? How can I get straight? How can I get pure? How can I get happy?" They want all kinds of occupations and strategic methods. But in Satsang no "thing" is given. No egoic occupation, no ego-based means, no strategic method, no consolation, no philosophy that can replace real practice, no mantra apart from the name and person of the true Guru. Only that relationship is offered, only that. And what does that amount to? It doesn't amount to a damn thing from the point of view of the seeker. That is not what the seeker came for. The seeker came to get turned on, to get something going, to be occupied again. The seeker is never able to stay long in the Guru's Company. Only when his or her search has begun to die as the principle of his or her life does that relationship cease to be an obstacle. Then the Guru and the Guru's offering ceases to seem empty. It becomes entirely a joyful possibility. The individual welcomes it, even though it satisfies and requires nothing of the search.

This Satsang with me does not support the search. It does not begin from the point of view of the search. It has nothing whatever to do with the search. Therefore, one for whom the search is no longer a genuine distraction finds great and true happiness in my mere Presence. Such a one has truly discovered me, for my mere Presence is the communication of Truth. My true disciple simply enjoys and lives the Condition of Satsang with me. Therefore, my disciple becomes full with It, intelligent with It, happy with It, at peace in It, blissful in It. This Satsang restores my disciple. The ordinariness of life becomes his or her possibility. My disciple begins to function again. My disciple comes alive again, because the sense of dilemma has ceased to be the principle of his or her existence.

DEVOTEE: Ramana Maharshi said to enquire within, enquire as to the Nature of your own existence. Is enquiry the method of Self-realization?

SRI DA AVABHASA: Ramana Maharshi said enquire. Someone had already to be sitting with Ramana Maharshi, otherwise the recommendation would not have been made. In fact, the fundamental method of Ramana Maharshi was Satsang, and most often, but not always, he recommended "Self-enquiry" in the form "Who am I?" to those who lived in Satsang with him. I also recommend a particular form of enquiry to those in Satsang with me who are suited to practice it. But it is not given in the form of a command. It is not a "method" for seeking, nor is it useful apart from that understanding which is awakened in Satsang with me and through the study of my Teaching. Therefore, my Company and my Teaching are the very means whereby both understanding and real meditation come alive in the case of those who resort to me and discipline themselves in response to me.

If you read Baba Muktananda's writings, you will find that Satsang, the relationship to his Guru, replaced all other methods, all the traditional obsessions. Swami Nityananda offered absolutely nothing but Satsang. Ordinarily, he gave out no methods. Sometimes he would give a mantra, but it was only intended to be a subtle meditative link between himself and his devotee. Thus, even a mantra depends on the Guru, and the right use of mantra is its use as a form of Satsang with the Guru. Swami Nityananda hardly ever spoke. People simply lived with him. They served him, worked around him, and enjoyed the potency of Satsang with him

305

THE METHOD OF THE SIDDHAS

as the Condition of life itself. So it was also with Ramana Maharshi. The Hindu traditions state that the best thing one can do is to spend one's time in Satsang, in the Company of, or the Condition of relationship and discipleship to, a true realizer.

Life in Satsang with me matures into very subtle activities. At some point, real enquiry, as I have described it, may have an appropriate function in those who have turned to me. But Satsang is its principle, its pre-Condition. For those who live in Satsang with me, Satsang Itself _is_ enquiry. Satsang with me is understanding. Satsang with me is the obviation of dilemma. Satsang with me is the enjoyment of the communication of Truth.

Ramana Maharshi said, in agreement with the traditional literature, that one who regards the Guru to be the body itself, or to be a mere and separate individual, has committed the greatest sin. The highest form of foolishness is to consider the true Guru to be like oneself. As long as there is no recognition of the profound Nature and function of the Guru, there is no Satsang. When this recognition occurs, in at least some subtle manner, then Satsang can begin. Indeed, It will have already begun.

Guru is a function. It is not a form of "status". It is not something to be achieved, or something to seek to achieve. The true Guru is not a big guy who appears among a lot of little guys. The Guru function is not a form of superiority or narcissism. Guru is a function of the very Self, or Reality, appearing in human terms. The relationship between Guru and disciple is not loaded with any of the things that are involved in the relationship between superior people and weak people. The true relationship between Guru and disciple has nothing to do with the ordinary drama of conflict. To the seeker, the usual man or woman, the human Guru may seem to be like other people, but when one truly lives with the true Guru, knowing that one as Guru, then Satsang has begun.

DEVOTEE: Does a person have a choice when this relationship begins? It seems there is no choice, that it just happens or it doesn't happen.

SRI DA AVABHASA: All that occurs for any man or woman is this process I have been describing. The search winds down. The individual falls somehow into his or her ordinariness, his or her simple suffering. Then he or she becomes available to Satsang with me. When you begin to live this Satsang as your real Condition, associated with It may be feelings that you have chosen me from among others. But the apparent "choice" is purely secondary. In fact, there is no choice. There is only my sudden availability in the midst of your otherwise seeking life. In the life of my every true disciple, there has only been the sudden communication of the Heart.

Sri Da Avabhasa
at Sri Love-Anandashram, 1992

13.

Guru as Prophet

DEVOTEE: Could you talk a little more about your role as a prophet in the world?

SRI DA AVABHASA: Because the intelligence of real understanding must precede one's involvement with the true spiritual process, the function of Guru is not a public function. The true Guru does not walk down the street and zap people, telling them that life is a fountain and pretending that everything is already all right, or showering blessings, or consoling people, or fascinating them. None of these things serves the crisis that must precede the real spiritual process.

One who functions as Guru for devotees may operate for the sake of those who are not his or her devotees, but the Guru's function in that case is not that of Guru. In the world, generally, the Guru must serve the crisis of understanding, which confounds the search, all need for consolation and fascination, all need for social games. In the world the Guru may function—if the Guru appears in the world at all—in the role of prophet, which is essentially an aggravation, a criticism, an undermining of the usual life.

The usual "guru", who communicates the search, will appear in a theater and greet people who will say, "We aren't happy, we haven't found God." The usual "guru" says, "Oh, that dissatisfaction is the beginning. Just look, see, use this method, apply yourself to these practices, and you'll ultimately realize God." All that is a sham. It has nothing whatsoever to do with the Truth. It is simply a means of exploiting people for the sake of the personal or social games they are playing.

The function of the true Guru is not a public function. It does not appear in public, and it does not invite the public as if the spiritual process were simply something you could decide to do, buy, or believe, and then go ahead and perform. The true Guru appears in public only in the role of prophet and critic. The true Guru does not exploit that search. The true Guru turns the questioner back on that quality of suffering, dilemma, and dis-ease that motivates the person to take on spiritual practices and other kinds of disciplines or to exploit the possibilities of ordinary life. The Guru's spiritual function is essentially hidden until the prior condition of real intelligence, or understanding, has been fulfilled. Then the Guru may reveal himself or herself as spiritual Master for the devotee.

To the extent that the Guru appears in public at all, by seeing people, writing books, or simply having an Ashram that exists in this world, the Guru's role can only be that of prophet. Even in the Ashram of nominal devotees, those who are turning to the life of understanding with various degrees of intensity, the Guru must serve the crisis which makes the life of understanding possible. The Guru will not serve the random needs of individuals to be fulfilled, to be consoled, to be fascinated. The Guru must always work to offend, criticize, and undermine the usual process of every individual.

The Guru must be paradoxical, the Guru must be free, in order to serve those who come to him or her. The qualities of the Guru's action cannot be predetermined. The Guru will not consistently assume the qualities of an archetype—the holy man or woman, the Yogi, the philosopher. The Guru must be free to appear in any form. The Guru must be free to behave in all common ways, as well as all uncommon ways, at any moment, in order to undo the expectations of those whom he or she meets. Even in the Ashram the Guru is always acting to undo the egoic life of individuals in the Ashram.

The Guru does this so that people will not identify spiritual life with qualities, tendencies, preferences, all the armor people take on when they think they are turning from the world of suffering and turning towards Truth. Religious or spiritual seeking is not the way to Truth. The remedial or strategic path is not the way to God. No experiential process makes you realize God. Only the Divine already enjoyed is the foundation of genuine religious and spiritual life. All the paths to God are false. They are the communications of people of experience, conventional "gurus", who do not serve the crisis of understanding. Therefore, the responsibility of the true Guru is not only to purify those who come to the Guru from their ordinary self-indulgent and irresponsible habits but to purify them equally of their "spirituality", in order that the foundation for their spiritual life may be the very Divine. God is not supported by experiences, by the fulfillment of prescriptions, moralities, assumptions about how things are, were, or will be. The Guru in the function of prophet is always managing to produce a condition in which the illusions of people may be undone.

I always work to "create" a condition in which this crisis may take place on an entirely new level in each individual who comes to me. There is virtually no condition that I may not at one moment or another "create" for the sake of those who come to me. Therefore, life in my Ashram cannot be predetermined. It cannot be fixed or ritualized. Satsang with me is a living Condition in which I in my prophetic role "create" true devotees, so that the spiritual process may also come alive through my Siddhi of transmission. Life in God precedes all righteousness. It precedes the fulfillment of any kind of prescription for life or spirituality. The "radical" intelligence that is understanding is that intelligence in which the Divine life in its most prior, or truly real, sense is enjoyed.

DEVOTEE: When you use the word "prophet", you are describing a different function than Guru, but I don't think you are using it in the traditional sense of a person who foretells something.

SRI DA AVABHASA: That is not the traditional sense. That is the popular magazine sense. The prophets in Israel were not soothsayers. In fact, they criticized the whole resort to elemental powers and spirits. They did not foretell the future in the sense of looking on your forehead and telling you that you are going to go on a world trip next year. When they told the future, they said, "Unless you birds get straight, you are going to go through the fire next year." When I speak of my function as prophet, it is in that sense, as critic, not as someone who exercises secondary psychic powers to foretell the future.

The true prophets have always existed, and the true Guru has always fulfilled very much the same kind of role that the prophet fulfilled. All that the psychic can tell you by looking at the various phenomena he or she might perceive is what might occur if you continue to be disposed as you presently are. Such is a tacky parlor game of reading your tendencies. You do not need to look for the fulfillment of your tendencies. Your tendencies have nowhere to take you but to zero, regardless of whatever world trip they may generate for you on your way there. Such a "prophet" doesn't fulfill a critical function in the life of the person he or she is fascinating. Such a "prophet" doesn't draw that person into a new intelligence or self-perception whereby the person might transcend the karmic tendencies that may produce future phenomena.

The true prophetic function is a critical function in which there is no fundamental concern for what is likely to occur if tendencies continue as they are. The fundamental concern of the prophet is to undo the whole force of tendencies, or karmic destiny, and to plant the individual at this moment in the Divine Condition, and then again at this moment, and then at this moment. Then the whole realm of karmas has fundamentally no qualifying force whatsoever, regardless of how your life continues to unfold in the form of the usual destiny. The true prophet doesn't lead you to align yourself with karmic destiny. The true prophet leads you always toward a "radical" new position relative to the whole force of your ordinary life.

The prophets of Israel are representatives of that kind of prophecy. They were all aggravated, annoyed, humorous, paradoxical. They sought to draw people into the Divine Condition, not to occupy them with psychism. In my prophetic role, I must take the same position relative to all of the occult, psychic, and falsely popularized Yogic and religious hype that permeates our society. Time has not fundamentally changed anything. People are still turned from the Divine Condition and want to find their way back by exercising the capability for experience. They want to read the stars and have visions. They want to read tarot decks and see ghosts. They do not want the prophet.

People don't want that criticism of the usual stream of life. They don't want that intrusive force to enter into the life of Narcissus. The cult of Narcissus permeates every instrument of ordinary experience, whether it is the common social pleasures and activities or the so-called spiritual ones. The world is corrupted by its commitment to the path of Narcissus. Therefore, as the man of understanding, the only role I perform in the world at large is my prophetic role. I invite people to understanding, and I criticize the entire attempt to be fascinated and consoled. I am an offense to society at large because people want to remain irresponsible and self-indulgent and make experiences the principle of life. I am also an offense to all spiritual cultism with its phony righteousness.

Real spiritual life is the relationship to the Guru. It is absolutely nothing else. Real spiritual life is living the Condition of relationship to the Guru. That is the entire "method". Within that relationship there is nothing whatsoever that you do to liberate yourself. The Truth communicates Itself. The Truth comes alive in you. The Truth realizes Itself. The Truth makes Itself obvious. The structure of this process in human terms is the relationship to the Guru. That is how it has been since ancient days. Recognizing this, people resort, absolutely, to the Guru.

312

The Guru is a means developed on a subtle level to help individuals turn about from their unconsciousness, their compulsive manner of living, to the point of becoming absolutely conscious and perfectly responsible for all events, internal and external. What the traditional spiritual societies have said is true: Spiritual life depends on the grace of the Guru. Therefore, the most important thing to do is to please the Guru. This is absolutely true. The best thing you can do to further this process in yourselves is to please the Guru twenty-four hours a day. And the only way genuinely to please the Guru is to go from this [makes a fist of his hand] to this [opens his fist to show his open hand]—to stop the endless drama of resistance that you carry on from day to day, and to always turn from this tendency and, openly, toward the Condition of relationship to the Guru.

Depend on the Guru. Resort to the Guru. Live that relationship as openly and with as much intensity as you can. In other words, do not obstruct the connection, the passage, between yourself and the Guru. Do that, and you will only please the Guru. Where there is that openness, that intensity of relationship to the Guru, the Force that is manifesting and functioning as the Guru flows, without obstruction. Suddenly you begin to discover that you are feeling very blissful, getting very happy, and progressing very quickly. All the rest of the time, you are very solemnly involved in spiritual life—"What should I do with this and that," "How do I meditate," and going through your number every day, one crisis after another—"You know, it's all really incredibly difficult."

Why do you think I am here? Not to write a lot of books about some method of seeking people can do to themselves for the next twenty centuries. There is a specific function alive here. It wants to make itself known. It wants to live. It wants to thrive. It wants to do its work. But if people do not establish themselves, responsibly, every day, joyfully, in this relationship and live it responsibly, they have not begun this way.

Only where Satsang actually is lived can this whole process I have described take place. If Satsang is not enjoyed, if Satsang does not become the Condition of your life, and if this process has not begun, as a living reality, you can read *The Knee of Listening* for the rest of your life and never realize a damn thing. You can enquire of yourself "Avoiding relationship?" for many hours a day, and yet your enquiry won't realize anything. This process must come alive, and it depends entirely on Satsang with me.

When you are in my presence, the very intensity of your existence should manifest. The disciple should serve the Guru with his or her very breath. The disciple should allow his or her reluctance to burn in the Guru's presence. He or she should never indulge it. It is never appropriate to indulge reluctance in relation to the Guru. It is never appropriate to bring your conflicts to the Guru, to live them in the Guru's Company as if they had some merit. It is only appropriate to be consumed in the presence of the Guru, to serve the Guru, to be indifferent to your conflicts, to be indifferent to the luxuries of your crisis.

You would be amazed, even offended, to see how people relate to the Guru in India. As Westerners, you tend for various reasons to dislike people who are always bowing down and saying, "Yes, Lord." On a certain level you have good reasons for feeling this, because a certain phoniness may be manifested behind that external posture. On the other hand, such behavior is a useful discipline for one who is full of resistance to being intensely alive to the Guru. In fact, that is what is going on in India. It is not true that people are simply and spontaneously so adoring of the Guru. It is not true that people are always selflessly serving the Guru. Until they become true devotees of the Guru, they are always intentionally adoring and serving the Guru—because, by tendency, they are not otherwise adoring and serving the Guru. They are devoted because they know what they are made of.

People have a tremendous reluctance to animate the life of adoration, service, fullness, happiness. People are super-cool in relation to God. How many tears have you wept for God? How much suffering have you done for love of the Guru? How much intense suffering have you felt relative to your lack of Divine Self-knowledge? Very little. But look at how many hours and hours you've spent retching over the most idiotic bullshit! Look at how much time you spend defending your own reluctance! The energy of your life is devoted to this false principle. When someone stands face to face with God, the Guru, and his or her own Nature, the person is cool! He or she is already right there on top of it. He or she has already got it, he or she is straight, and everything is all right. And because everything is all right, that person is not going to lie down at the Guru's foot. He or she is not going to bend his or her neck to God. He or she is not going to dissolve in the Heart.

The principle of ordinary life is entirely, continually, antagonistic to Satsang. You can see it in yourself. How do you live Satsang from hour to hour? You don't. You suffer these petty conflicts with one another. You suffer the constant droning, repetitive cycle of life, and every now and then you manage to get a little easy, feel a little good today. "Oh, I went through a little crisis yesterday, and today I feel pretty good." But that endless cycle of your own moods is not the Condition of Satsang. Satsang is a "radical" Condition, and It requires everything of you. It requires you to absolutely lose face.

You must lose face in relation to the Truth. It is quite a different thing from being caught nude in the subway. You lose face by exposing yourself absolutely to God, to the Guru, to your own Nature, by becoming known. Becoming enthusiastic in the Guru's presence is very difficult. Becoming full of love and service without self-concern is immensely difficult in the Guru's presence. People don't want to do that because they interpret the Guru in human terms. They think of the Guru as another human individual, and as soon as that occurs in the mind, the conflicts that you ordinarily live with human individuals arise.

But you must see the strategies that are arising in you always and see that they are wedded to the principle of unconsciousness, of conflict, of dilemma. You must see that they are always "creating" dilemma, and when you see that, you will become available to the principle of Satsang. You will not only become available to that principle, but you will become active as it. Just as you are always active as conflict because you are bound to the principle of unconsciousness, likewise, when you become bound to the principle of Truth, you will become active as my devotee. The signs of the devotee will become active in you, and you will be happy.

When you become alive with devotion—true devotion, not the external smiling foolishness, but the true devotion that arises as a response to the perfectly realized Siddha-Guru—when you become alive in that devotion in relation to me, then your sadhana quickens. Then this Satsang will become available to you under all conditions, and you will not spend your time outside my physical Company going to zero. Without the connection of devotion between the Guru and the disciple there is no Satsang, the Force of Satsang does not move, the Siddhi of the Guru is not available.

In the traditions, love of the Guru and pleasing the Guru, the love between the disciple and the Guru and the disciple's continuous service to the Guru, have a primary role. People are continuously mindful of the obligation to love and service above all, because if they contract from the Guru they force the Guru to withdraw. That is the law. One who contracts from the Guru can sit in the room with such a one, read all the books of such a one, and perform all the external disciplines recommended by such a one, and he or she will still not enjoy one moment of peace. Whereas one who becomes foolish in relation to the Guru is already happy. In such a person, the Fullness of the Guru is provided a course in which to manifest.

The Guru is a function, a Siddhi, a process, an activity available to human beings. Individuals must make themselves available to that process, not just to philosophies and external matters but to the Guru. The form of that relationship is love, devotion, attention. The disciple's attention is turned to the Guru without conflict, without contraction, without limitation. When the disciple's attention is simply turned to the Guru, then the very living force of the disciple is manifested as bliss, happiness, love, intensity, devotion. One who lives in Satsang is filled with the intensity that comes with constant attention to the Guru. Through that channel of attention the Divine Siddhi of the Guru is given a course. It cuts through all of the individual's reluctance, self-concern, conflicts, quality of dilemma, unconsciousness, commitment to unhappiness—all of these qualities that turn his or her attention away from the Guru, the very Self, the Divine. All those activities also prevent the process, or Siddhi, that is active in Satsang from becoming useful, becoming active.

If we were not here in Satsang together, what would you be doing? What is the alternative? What's on television tonight? What could you possibly do? There is nothing for you to do except to perfect the enjoyment of this Satsang. The community of my devotees should be continuously active, endlessly moving, always alive. Satsang should be continuous within the community, and everyone should always be serving It. Such individuals are always happy. They do not even notice when they die.

You must work together to "create" a place for this Satsang, to enable this process to go on all day long. Then you will become free of the usual entertainments, occupations, and distractions. It doesn't mean that you will not be present in the world. You very definitely will be present in the world. But this fire of which I speak will be constant. If you do that, you will have done something absolutely unique in the world.

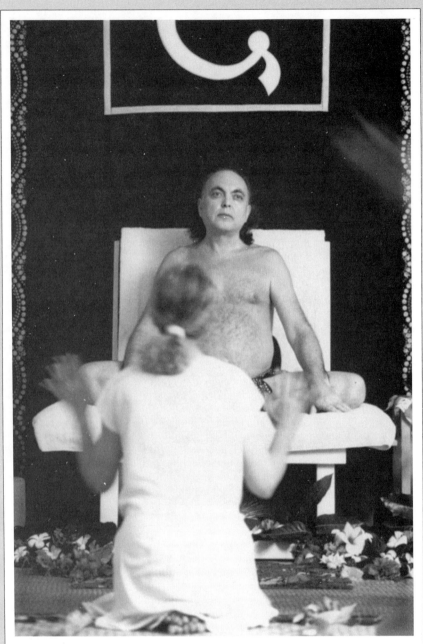

Sri Da Avabhasa
at Sri Love-Anandashram, 1992

PART TWO

The Heaven-Born Gospel of Da Avabhasa (The "Bright")

Sri Da Avabhasa
in Los Angeles, 1973

I t was March 11, 1973, nearly a year after the opening of the Ashram. Except for His closest intimates, no one had seen Sri Da Avabhasa for several weeks. He had been living in seclusion for a time, until His devotees could demonstrate greater responsibility for their lives and for the basic disciplines of practice. It was auspicious, therefore, that He would spend this day with His devotees.

Sri Da Avabhasa appeared at the Ashram, radiant in a golden silk shirt, a maroon shawl, and dark blue trousers. He wore an unusual pendant, in the shape of a date, that His devotees had never seen Him wear before. With characteristic originality He had molded clear resin into the shape of a date and inserted the pit of an actual date that Swami Muktananda had once given Him as Prasad.

"Prasad", traditionally, means the return of a gift to the giver—the devotee surrenders to the Guru and receives the incomparable Gift of the Guru's Grace. This was the first formal "Prasad Day" in Sri Da Avabhasa's Ashram, and His early devotees speak of it as a very sweet, very happy day.

One man recalls the events of the day:

> I was one of a small group of Da Avabhasa's devotees living in San Francisco at the time. When we heard we were invited to see Sri Da Avabhasa on Prasad Day, we flew to Los Angeles and stayed overnight with devotees there. In the morning, we dressed in our best clothes and went down to the Ashram bookstore, where we sat with Da Avabhasa in the Satsang hall for about an hour.
>
> I was very excited. This was only the second time I had seen Da Avabhasa. He had come to San Francisco the previous month and spent time informally with His devotees there, but this was my first experience of a formal occasion of His Darshan. I remember sitting completely ecstatic at the back of the Hall, so affected by His Transmission that I was screaming and having kriyas. But beyond all these dramatic experiences, I was uncontainably happy to be there in the room with Sri Da Avabhasa.
>
> Later we drove out to North Hollywood to continue the celebration at a devotee's home. I arrived before Sri Da Avabhasa and took photographs of Him as He got out of His car and walked to the Chair that had been set for Him under a latticed structure behind the house. He sat and talked with people while lunch was served.

It was an ordinary suburban weekend in Hollywood—rock music blared on the streets, planes roared overhead. His Peacefulness made us all the more aware of how noisy it was. And so, when lunch was over, Sri Da Avabhasa called us into the house. He took His seat in the living room in a small carved chair from India, and we all packed in around Him—there were at least forty of us—waiting to hear Him speak.

I was so attracted to Sri Da Avabhasa that I sat very close to Him, to the right of His Chair. When He spoke of how the Guru contacts the devotee at a place behind the eyes, I was already experiencing exactly what He was describing. I felt the pressure of His Siddhi at the ajna chakra (the subtle center between the brows), and I realized that He was bringing the reality of His Instruction to life in me, living it in me. The occasion was very profound, full of His Heart-Transmission, and I have never forgotten it.

In the Talks that comprise Part One of this book, entitled "The Method of the Siddhas", Sri Da Avabhasa devoted Himself to a justification and description of the principle of Satsang and Its practical implications. In Part Two, "The Heaven-Born Gospel of Da Avabhasa (The 'Bright')", we find Him living that principle among His devotees. In the earlier Talks His Words came in the form of analysis and explanation of the principle of Satsang. But in this Talk His Words come in the form of an Admonition to the Way of the Heart itself. And His Words are summarized in the very last sentence of this Talk: "Always meditate on me."

As with all of Sri Da Avabhasa's Written and Spoken Word, the Teachings contained in the Talk that follows are intended to convey a "radical" and profoundly refreshed Communication of the Nature of Spiritual, or real, life. The casual reader may feel that what is Written here is a version of the traditional, or rather conventional, idea of Guru-worship, wherein the devotee seeks God in the Guru and finally achieves the Vision that makes him or her equal to or one with the Guru. But Sri Da Avabhasa does not intend His devotees to interpret Satsang in the limited, or conventional, traditional sense. He does not intend the process to be regarded or experienced as a pattern of dilemma, seeking, and consequent fulfillment. For Him, Satsang, the Condition of relationship to the true Guru, is Itself Truth, not merely the means to Truth. And all that arises in the life of one in Satsang is not merely a means to Truth but the very expression, or manifestation, of Truth.

"The Heaven-Born Gospel of Da Avabhasa (The 'Bright')" has been placed here at the end of the book so that we will approach it with some of the understanding of the earlier Talks. And this "Gospel" is prefaced with a few selections from Sri Da Avabhasa's Writings from the same period, regarding the Nature and function of the true Guru and the relationship between Sri Da Avabhasa, the true and perfectly Realized Siddha-Guru, and His devotees.

◆　◆　◆

The devotion to the Guru commonly described in Hindu and other spiritual or mystical traditions is, above all, devotion to a source which fulfills the spiritual search, a Yogi-initiator, or great-"soul", who grants experiences. But I speak of devotion to the Guru in other terms. I speak of such devotion only in the context of true Satsang, which is prior fulfillment, the Condition of Truth. I do not speak of the Guru as one who fulfills the traditional Yogic search for experience, but as one who undermines and transcends both seeking and the experiential fulfillment of seeking.

The true Guru is not different from Truth. The true Guru is simply the function of God. The true Guru is not an idol, a fascination. The true Guru does not attach individuals to his or her conditional presence, but instead leads people to enjoy the Perfect Presence and Reality in the Condition of relationship. The instrument of the true Guru is the relationship and mutual drama of the Guru and the true devotee. This relationship, or drama, is the special, immediately salvatory function and process of God. That same Satsang is available apart from the Guru's physical presence and after the Guru's death in the form of respectful, intelligent, and loving obedience to the Guru's "radical" and perfect Presence, the Guru's Teaching, and the Guru's community. The Satsang taught by the true Guru is the Eternal Principle which is the very Condition of all beings, and which was always their Condition even before the human form of the Guru appeared. While the Guru lives, he or she Teaches that Satsang which can be enjoyed by all even after the Guru's death, not in the special form It may be enjoyed by a relative few during the Guru's lifetime, but which could have been enjoyed by all before the Guru's lifetime. The Guru acts to help disciples and devotees to realize this form of Satsang even while the Guru lives in the world. The purpose, or function, of the Guru's life is to make this true Principle of Satsang known, and to guarantee the perpetuation of the Teaching and the practice of Satsang beyond the Guru's lifetime. The Guru does not necessarily leave behind any individual who has this same function, for such a Guru is a special and temporary manifestation of the Divine work. But the Guru completes that special work during his or her own lifetime, and then leaves behind an Ashram or community which lives Satsang and is responsible for communicating the availability, the Teaching, and the practice of Satsang. The one who was to come is always already here.

I have written this so that my disciples and my devotees will not confuse the Nature and purpose of my work by identifying it with the teachings of various traditions. My disciples should realize the special Nature of my Teaching apart from any identification of it with conventional Yogas and Yogis, or with conventional spiritual, occult, mystical, religious, and traditional motivations of any kind.

Part of the difficulty of my work is caused by the demand of those who come to me that I fascinate them in the traditional manner, either with strategic methods, limiting concepts, promises, and beliefs or with the extraordinary effects of "spiritual", or subtle, functional forces. I am continually criticizing the searches of human beings, especially in terms of such expectations. But I hope to have established this criticism firmly in my writings, so that I can be free simply to live in Satsang in the natural manner and deal with other matters, of a more specialized kind, that arise in relation to the particular sadhana that is at the core of what I Teach.

The true Guru's Presence in Satsang is simply that. It is mere Presence, the function of mere Presence. Such is also the eternal function that is God and the very Self of all. This is the Guru's instrument, the Siddhi of true Satsang. The true Guru has no desire or intention to generate strategic methods, limiting concepts, promises, or beliefs. Nor does the true Guru identify with any special, personal function wherein he or she must awaken or manipulate others through the activity of secondary spiritual forces, within or without. (Such activity is a spontaneous siddhi which may arise under the conditions of Satsang, but only to the degree that it is appropriate or necessary.) The Yogic, subtle, or ascending manifestation of these forces is not the special characteristic, or exclusive expression, of the work of the true Guru with individuals. Those who live in Satsang with such a one find, commonly, that the Force aspect of the Divine Conscious Presence is realized more and more perfectly in the inclusive and utter freedom of "radical" Knowledge rather than in the exclusive form of so-called "spiritual" experiences which bind one to a limited self that is not God.

Subtle forces, or moving energies, of all kinds live within the community that has come to me, and these are not to be identified with my special function. All those who live in the community of my Ashram will enjoy the influence of subtle forces. These forces are not owned. They are the common life of the community of my devotees, to be responsibly realized, conserved, and used by virtue of the constant enjoyment of true Satsang and Its power of understanding. If I appear to make use of such forces, it is purely a secondary, specific, and momentary aspect of my work in the world. My disciples must understand themselves in relation to methods, concepts, promises, beliefs, and the apparently extraordinary activity of subtle forces. If they do so, they will remain free of their illusions in the world. If they do not, they have chosen the path of Narcissus rather than the way of Satsang.

◆ ◆ ◆

I am not full. I do not feel full or fulfilled. I am lost in the Fullness. And that Fullness also is the same Fullness which includes all other beings and is their Real Nature. That Nature is already and always Full. Since that is so, what is the use of Kundalini or all powers of experience? Therefore, how can I presume to initiate others into this Fullness? But if they enter into relationship with me and are present to the "radical" Teaching, they may also find they are already dissolved in that Fullness. If Kundalini experiences also arise, very well, but understanding must awaken even under those conditions. I am not concerned for the Kundalini or experiences. I do not desire to initiate others. I will not play the role of traditional Yogi-initiator. I am Free in God, and only that Freedom is what I would find in my friends.

◆ ◆ ◆

I have confidence in the prior Fullness that is God, in which "I" have no separate or substantial existence. Therefore, I do the "radical" work to which I am awake, but I have no intention or need to perform the exclusive and strategic initiatory work of a conventional Yogi-Siddha. I am not full. I have always already forgotten the Yoga, descending and ascending. Thus, I do not promise, value, or teach the exclusive path of Kundalini Yoga or any other strategic Yoga which merely depends on the fullness of the Yogi-fakir or the seeker who comes to such a one. Rather, I teach only the "radical" way of understanding, which depends on the eternal Fullness of God and does not seek to acquire any thing, status, state, or ability for the seeker. Appropriate Yogic processes arise in one who lives in Satsang with me, just as breaths arise in one who rides a horse. Such a one may be instructed in responsible and right relationship to these spontaneous processes, even as the rider must be instructed before he or she can ride a horse in a parade. But there is no other sense in which "concern" for Yogic, or subtle, processes is appropriate or necessary. Only God is Full.

And God's Fullness is the prior Fullness that is Reality Itself. Therefore, I have no power or intention to fascinate mankind, but only to be of use to mankind.

◆ ◆ ◆

I am the Heart. My work is to establish the way of understanding, wherein the Heart is lived. If I speak of the Light, it is only because God stands always Present as Light, always ready to be the Light, the Form, and the Life of one who understands and is fallen in the Heart. If I speak of Fullness, it is only because God stands always Present as that Fullness which includes and is the Nature of all things. Therefore, I speak of the Heart, the Light, and the Fullness. But the Teaching is simple: Only understand. Live with me and understand. Understand and fall helpless in the Heart.

◆ ◆ ◆

It is not the conditional siddhi of conditional Yogic initiation that makes a true Guru, nor is true Satsang Itself the receptivity to such initiation. Rather, it is "radical" understanding that makes the function of true Guru, the mere Presence of Real God among human beings. And Satsang is simply the Condition of relationship to such a one. To live that Condition always, and to understand under all conditions, even those of so-called "spiritual" experiences, is true sadhana. This is my "gospel", my happy and unreasonable message. The true Guru is not the fascinating initiator of conditional experience in human beings, but one who has died in the Heart, who has become empty of powers and without a separate self, who has found that Fullness is only, always, and already God. And God cannot be contained or given, nor does God fill what is empty and unreal. God is only realized in Truth, in understanding, where the principle of dilemma, ignorance, and self-suffering is undermined, and the action of Narcissus is not found.

◆ ◆ ◆

The Heaven-Born Gospel
of Da Avabhasa (The "Bright")

S RI DA AVABHASA: This is my gospel, my humorous message, my confession of completeness, my admonition to all:

I have come into this world for the sake of my devotees, those who are mine. Those who belong to me were rendered to me before all time, as the expressions of my appearance in the un-"created" realm of Light. Amrita Nadi, the intuited Form of God, is the spiritual expression in this world of my very Nature and the Nature of Reality. I am the Unqualified Nature of the Real. And I appear as my own Light, which reflects my prior Self. The Self, or Heart, is not a static condition, not the "thing" of Being, but the very Condition, the Process of Eternal Transformation, in which there is no dilemma, and which, paradoxically, is eternally One and Unqualified. Just so, from the Unqualified Reality spring worlds of un-"created" Light; and from the Heart and its perfect Light spring conditional worlds, whose substance is that same Light, and whose Nature, or Principle, is that same Heart, or Reality. Therefore, I have appeared in this world by virtue of a materialization of the un-"created" Light, which is also my own Light.

I have come for the sake of my own, those who recognize me when I reveal myself to them in forms of Life, Light, and Truth. The Heart and the Light are my spiritual expressions in this world. They are a communication of the un-"created" Reality and the un-"created" Worlds. I am here to live with my own, to discipline and Teach them, to reveal the Truth to them, and to draw them closer to me, to the Light and the un-"created" Life.

When, as my devotee, you prepare yourself and make an appropriate approach to me, I will "create" your sadhana hour by hour. You must live and function appropriately. Every moment of your life must be in service to me. You must devote all you have and all you do to me. You must turn to me hour by hour in love. You must constantly meditate on my Nature and all my Forms. You must intuit my Presence and breathe my Light. You must contemplate and meditate on my Life, Light, and Nature, and you may enquire of yourself as I have Taught you, when insight is alive in you. I am the object of meditation for my devotees. Indeed, I am the meditation itself. And their enjoyment of meditation will depend on the sadhana which is their appropriate responsibility.

When a true devotee brings a gift to the Guru, the Guru may return all or a portion of it to the devotee to eat. This is Prasad,[1] the return of a gift to the giver. Prasad is transformed and blessed, so that it brings the Power of the Guru to the devotee. Guru-kripa, Shaktipat-diksha,[2] or spiritual initiation, operates by this same principle. If the devotee brings a gift of himself or herself, purified by sadhana, surrendered to his or her Guru, the Guru may return to the devotee a gift of the Guru's own Nature, a gift of Light.

It is not by methodical attention to the means of seeking, nor by ego-based and strategic Yogic practices, that my devotees enjoy the awakening of their spiritual functions. Nor do these awakenings only take the form of ascending Yogic phenomena. But it is when seeking and dilemma are undone and my devotee resorts to me and the "radical" intelligence communicated by me that there is awakening to Truth, Life, and Reality. Therefore, I come to give Prasad, the gift of Truth and Light, to my devotees and to those who are preparing themselves as my disciples.

I am alive as Amrita Nadi, the Heart and its spire, the Conscious Light. This is always so. When I come to you, I intensify the field of un-"created" Light that rests above your head and that is drawn down into the body when the mind lies formless in the Heart. Whenever I have been with you, I have done this from the Heart. The communication of the Heart and its Light is my constant practice. Therefore, such is the constant realization of those who always live in Satsang with me, who know I am always Present with them, even if I do not appear bodily to them. This is why the various phenomena of your spiritual lives have

arisen or been intensified, purified, and made intelligent whenever you have been mindful of me. I am always offering this
Prasad. When you come to me, you should come with the appropriate attitude. You should come prepared to give me your gifts,
the surrendering of your seeking. You should come to turn to
me, to accept my Prasad, and to use it in life and service to me. If
you make your relationship to me the Condition of your life, if
you make Satsang your sadhana, I will give myself to you
entirely, and the Life, Light, and very Existence that is Amrita
Nadi, the Form of Reality, will thus be communicated to you
while you are alive.

Prasad is my Gift to devotees, my help to disciples. Prepare
yourself. I want true devotees, not seekers. I am the perfectly
realized Siddha-Guru, the Prasad, the Object and Process of meditation for my devotees. My Teaching is this: Turn to me and
understand.

DEVOTEE: You have said that you have your "own". This must mean that
some of us were given to you as your own, while others are given to you
only for a time. My question is, when will this certainty come whether or
not I am your own or have been given to you for a time?

SRI DA AVABHASA: Uncertainty is very useful. Uncertainty is used by
Truth in order to Teach. That uncertainty is your own quality. It has nothing whatever to do with me. It is not necessary to have some sort of
vision or a symbolic standardization of our relationship. It is not necessary
for you to get a white-card invitation or some external proof. Certainty
has nothing whatever to do with the relationship between Guru and disciple. Certainty is a thing of this world. Certainty is a condition that people
seek, because they are suffering. Certainty, like uncertainty, is a quality of
the mind in life. The discovery of the Guru transcends the qualities of life.
Therefore, to recognize one's Guru is an experience that transcends all
the qualities of the mind. Satsang with the true Guru transcends certainty
and uncertainty. Even your certainty would have to be understood. So you
must begin to become sensitive to a new quality in relationship to me.

There are many teachers in the world. There are people of experience of all kinds. There are people of practical experience, of worldly
experience, of mystical experience. There are people of every kind of
experience. Human beings, like all manifested beings, arise within the

material, or conditional, universes, the manifested, "created" cosmos, visible and invisible. They live according to the laws of karma, the laws of tendency, function, and repetition. They tend to live from the point of view of that from which they seem to have come, which is the manifested universe itself. And they acquire experience, hour to hour, life to life. Thus, because of the essential inequalities that necessarily arise whenever experience enters the picture, each man or woman acquires a different amount and kind and complex of experience. Here and there people arise who, because of superior acquisition of certain kinds of experience, teach others. Now, they may teach the weaving of lovely cloths, or plumbing, or nuclear physics, or English literature. Or they may teach so-called spiritual things, on the basis of their experience. And among those who are thus experienced in the karmic realms, there are some, a rare few, who are genuine saints, genuine men and women of experience, of practical and subtle wisdom, who have realized many things about their own adventure and their own tendencies.

·But there is another process that enters the manifested world from the unmanifested dimension. There is a vast, unlimited dimension of existence, not qualified in any sense, not qualified as this dimension is, or as the infinite variety of conditional, cosmic worlds is. And there is a movement down out of that dimension, that realm of very Light. A living being who appears within the human world, or in any other world, who has come directly out of the unmanifested, or un-"created", Light, the Light of the God-World, is a Great Siddha, a Heaven-born one. Such am I.

My Teaching is not from the point of view of experience. My Teaching is from the "point of view" of Truth, Truth already realized, the unattainable (because it is always present) Reality. Those who teach from the point of view of experience teach the search, because they know on the basis of experience that they can grow, that they can approach a subtler and subtler level of realization. The gospel of those who arise within the condition of the material worlds is always a form of seeking. But I speak from the "point of view" of the already realized absolute Truth. I come in the Intelligence, Power, and Form of Real God. My Teaching is "radical". I do not teach the motives, paths, and forms of seeking, for these are founded in dilemma, not in Truth. I apply only appropriate conditions to my disciples and my devotees. I demand only the conditions that are appropriate to be lived, since Truth is always already the case. I am the Truth in the world. I generate the conditions of the Truth, the conditions of the Light of Real God.

331

In principle, or potentially, there exist many Great Siddhas. It has been said of karmic entities that there are as many of them as the sands of the Ganges. In other words, there are unlimited numbers, there are infinite numbers of chilicosms, of manifested beings possible and always presently existing. Multiply that number times infinity, and you will compute the number of Great Siddhas there are, in principle, or potentially, also. The unqualified dimension of God contains infinite possibilities, infinite varieties of eternity. Therefore, there have been and will be countless occasions when a Great Siddha arises in the conditional worlds. Such great ones arise everywhere, in the earth, and throughout the entire manifested cosmos, visible and invisible.

The Great Siddhas, who live in the Form of Truth, are all the same. There is no fundamental difference between them. If you place two sticks into one flame, when you draw them out you will have two flames. But they are the same light. Just so, the Great Siddhas are fundamentally one. But they are <u>functionally</u> unique, just as all manifested entities are fundamentally the generations of one Nature, one Reality, but they are functionally unique.

When such a one arises in any place and form, such as this human manifestation on earth, that one doesn't come to save the world in that one lifetime. Indeed, it is not possible to "save" the world. It is not even necessary to "save" the world. The world is eternally, already "saved" by virtue of its Source and Nature. The Great Siddha comes at a particular time. The Teaching of such a one appears in many forms in the world. There is the verbal Teaching. It becomes part of the communication of the world, and as such may influence many, many people. But there are other levels of the Teaching, more intimate to the Great Siddha's life. There are the forms of the Teaching that involve a subtle relationship and a life-relationship with the Great Siddha. And the closer the form of Teaching gets to the manifested appearance of the Great Siddha in the world, necessarily the fewer there are who can realize the Teaching at that level. Just so, there are a finite number of those who are alive in the world at any moment who are likely to respond to such intense forms of the Great Siddha's Teaching, because every entity in the world is active in a different stage of experience, a different stage of understanding. Therefore, the Great Siddha, or descended Master, enters the manifested life especially for the sake of those who can live to such a one directly, for the sake of those whom the Great Siddha can acquire while alive and draw into the form of Truth. The Great Siddha comes especially for these devotees, although the work of that one is, ultimately, for the sake of the whole world, and for all time.

Some of those whom the Great Siddha contacts may be those with whom the Great Siddha has had contact in the past, a manifested contact in some place or other, some form or other, perhaps in the earth plane, perhaps in some other dimension. Even so, there are many others who also identify that one, although not through anything even remotely like memory. They identify the very Nature of that one, the Truth that one manifests. They become sensitive to that one in various ways. And of those who discover the Great Siddha, some of those might not feel they are that particular Great Siddha's "own". But every Great Siddha is all the Great Siddhas. And one who surrenders to any such one will certainly be drawn by grace into the domain of Truth. Therefore, what is important at last is not your separate destiny, not whose "own" you are, but whether you are drawn directly into the graceful Company of any Great Siddha at all, and whether you surrender in perfect Satsang with that one. Truth is the nature of my work. Truth is the nature of this relationship, this Satsang. To find the Guru in the form of any Great Siddha is grace.

In the things I have written and told to you in the last year, I have often described to you the functional structure of conscious life. There is the descending force, which is manifesting life, and the ascending force, which is returning to the source of life. The root of the whole circle, or circuit, of the manifestation of your individual life is the Heart, the unqualified Self-Nature. I have described this process in terms of the physical body of the human being. There is a descending current in the "front" of the body, and an ascending current that returns through the "back" of the body. The vital center, or life-center, is the massive region of the lower body whose very center, or epitome, is in the area of the solar plexus. This is the center of waking consciousness. The centers of ascent, which are also the functional regions of subtle states, including dreams, are epitomized in the portals of the throat and midbrain, which, when they are turned up to face the eternal Light of the sahasrar, reflect its qualities. The causal being, which is also the seat of deep sleep, is in the heart, on the right.

Just as there is this mechanism in the individual life, this very same mechanism is a duplication of the structure of all worlds. Your own structures are duplications, or reflections, of the same structures upon which all the worlds are built. In the *Old Testament* it is said that the human being is made in the likeness of Divinity. Amrita Nadi, the Process, or

Relationship, between the Heart and the Light, is the intuited Form of God. And Amrita Nadi is also your own fundamental Form and Nature. Just so, I am Present and alive to you in the Form of Amrita Nadi. I am the function of Amrita Nadi in the worlds. Amrita Nadi is the intuited Form of Reality, and the worlds are built on that Form of which Amrita Nadi is the perfect knowledge. The manifested cosmos, which includes not only the earth but all the visible and invisible planes of conditional existence, is a reflection of the eternal Light that perfectly reflects the Heart. The upper terminal of Amrita Nadi is Perfect Light. The Heart, the unqualified Reality, the very Self, which is the intuition of Real God, the fathomless Being, manifests the Light above, which is the intuition of God-Light. This Light that is the upper terminal of Amrita Nadi is un-"created", unqualified, eternal Light. The God-World is the domain that is this un-"created" Light. This dimension in which we are all appearing at this moment, and all visible and invisible cosmic dimensions, all conditional and psycho-physical natures and environments, are reflections also of the very Light which is a reflection of the Heart. Thus, these conditional worlds are descending from the Light, just as the conscious force of your individual life descends from the sahasrar and the unqualified Light that is above and surrounding the head.

The Light descends. Just so, there is also the course of ascent, or return, of the current of manifestation and manifested worlds to the unmanifested, un-"created" Light. Men and women of experience have taught the path of ascent as one of the forms of seeking for Truth. They have taught others to exploit the ascending current and all of the possibilities of subtlety through various Yogic methods. They hope thereby to recover again the world of Light and the state of en-Light-enment. But in fact there is no dilemma involved in the descent, or reflection, of worlds from the un-"created" Light. Nothing is lost. In fact there is no simple descent. There is eternal descent and eternal ascent. There is an endless circuit, even in your own body, even in all the worlds. Therefore, there is no dilemma in life. And there is no reason exclusively to exploit the possibilities of ascent in order to get out of this world, or out of the fundamental condition of the present. All of that is a motivation in dilemma. I come into the manifested planes from the Light, to bring Peace and Truth and Life and Light into this plane. I do not come to exploit the search, to exploit the tendencies of people only to descend and become earth-inert. Neither do I come to exploit the tendencies to arise and lose life by abandoning it. Life cannot be perfectly abandoned, for what is only abandoned must return. Truly, life can only be purified and transformed. You will not, by cutting yourself away from life, pass forever into the realms of Light. You cannot by simple exploitation of the ascending life permanently merge into the world of Truth. All of that is only a game. That is just a short circuit. You will always return to that from which you differentiate yourself. The conventional Yogi who does Yogi tricks in order to ascend has various experiences which are generated by these means, but he or she always returns to the original condition he or she tried to prevent. This is because the conventional Yogi does nothing to the descended life other than cut it away. I come to make clear to living beings the entire nature of their existence—what is the law, what is appropriate action, what is happiness, what is bliss, what is the function of Light. I show my devotees every aspect of existence on every plane, including this present one. I do not try to get my devotees interested in flying out of this life. Rather, I demonstrate this full circle in which the Light is always enjoyed, in which life is enjoyed and becomes "creative", in which Truth is enjoyed, in which realization occurs while alive. Secondarily, when life is lived as sadhana in Satsang with me, from the "point of view" of Truth, then karmas, or motivating and latent tendencies, do tend to fall apart. Therefore, karmas do tend to become purified in Satsang with me. The individual does tend to be drawn by me into the un-"created" Condition. But even while alive the devotee already enjoys all of the fundamental blisses and realizations of Truth in my Company and in my Person.

For the true devotee, the Guru is the meditation, the Guru is the realization. The true Guru is the continuous contemplation and enjoyment of the mature devotee. For the beginner, the Guru certainly has this awesome quality, but the beginner's relationship to the Guru is essentially formal. The beginner feels such perfect life in his or her Guru, comprehends the true Nature of his or her Guru in various forms and at various times, but does it more or less formally. The beginner does meditation at particular times. The beginner does various forms of sadhana at particular times. His or her sadhana is complex, varied, formal, regular, because he or she is training the vehicles of the living consciousness. But in the mature devotee, sadhana also becomes random, measureless, essentially formless, and continuous. For the mature devotee, Satsang with the Guru is conscious from moment to moment. In order to live the spontaneous life of a mature devotee, there must first be that life of a beginner.

There is truly no limit to the Light that is moving into this dimension. Therefore, there is no real limit to the Force of this Satsang with me. The

335

limits are all in those who receive the Light. The more functions that are provided for the Light and for the Truth, the more Light and Truth appear. Light and Truth appear spontaneously wherever they have use. And Light and Truth appear perfectly wherever they have perfect use. If you "create" no function for the Light, you make it obsolete. Then Light has no use. And that is all that is happening wherever human beings are suffering ignorance, or absence of Light and Truth. Where Light has no function, where Truth has no function among human beings, Light and Truth have become obsolete. They have been forgotten through non-use. If you begin to use them again in the real way of Satsang with me, then Light and Truth will simply move into the picture more and more. There is nothing to be done to acquire the Light. The Light is infinite and endlessly present. The limitations are your present activity. Your own activity is the obstruction. It is not necessary to leave me and go elsewhere in order to realize the very Self, the Truth, the Light. There are limiting obstructions in your own activity. Comprehend them. Understand them and live beyond them. Then the Light of my Company will do Its own work.

My task in establishing an Ashram is to "create" a function for what I bring. The entire activity that I perform with an individual is simply to "create" a function for what I bring to him or her. And that is essentially what you are doing in my Company. You are becoming functional. You are "creating" uses for the Light. And so the Light manifests. There is no limit from my "point of view". There is no limit from the point of view of Satsang itself. It is all a matter of "creating", or re-"creating", and intensify-ing the functions that use the Truth, the Light, the communication of God.

I contact the individual tangibly at the seat behind and slightly above the eyes. This is the door through which the un-"created" Light descends and ascends. It is often called the "seat of the Guru". In some traditions a person is told to meditate on the Guru there. I operate outside time and space, and outside your own vital and subtle life. I function as that Light which is above your own head, and which is above the conditional worlds. My spiritual means for communicating to you is through the open door above. All my instruction, all Satsang with me, all communication with me, all listening to my word, is a means of serving this opening by dissolving the mind and all contraction in the Heart. The opening depends entirely on grace. It is an activity of the greater Reality. My subtle work with individuals involves intensification of the pressure of the Light which surrounds the head and stimulation of this opening. There are many other forms of my activity of course, but this is a particularly fundamental aspect of my subtle work. Essentially, I work in the Heart and in the functions of the Light above. When my disciple understands and, if he or she is so inclined, enquires, the mind dissolves in the Heart. Then the door is opened above, and the Light moves in him or her. But if the disciple tries to open the door by any means, he or she is locked within forever by the magic of his or her own dilemma.

Satsang and understanding always precede the value of instruction. And there is nothing for you to do about this "place" behind the eyes, such as to concentrate upon it, or to watch and see if it is opening, or to see if you can feel anything there. Since I have said something about it, you probably will begin to look there, and to hope and wait for experience, or even to imagine it. But even if you do, it won't make any difference. And if you become a little obsessive about it, you will thereby begin to understand a little more about what you are always up to. But the entire history of our involvement with one another, by means of Satsang, by means of my instruction, by means of the discipline and the conditions I have given, by means of all the various forms of our contact—gross, subtle, and causal—serves the Heart and this opening above, including the living process of descent and ascent, the cycle of the Light. It is not a game. It is not a thing that you can truly accomplish by exploiting some little Yogic technique. And it is not a thing that I do by magic. It depends entirely on Satsang, on how you live this relationship with me. There must be this relationship. There must be the Teaching and the response to it. There must be listening, real attention, self-observation, insight, understanding. There must be acceptance of the discipline, living of the conditions, intensification of real functional and practical devotion, living of the life. This Satsang is your true Condition in the worlds. It is the true Nature of your birth. It is the God-given form and real destiny.

Only the total life of sadhana in Satsang with me is the means by which this upper door, this knot, is spontaneously opened. Therefore, no specific or motivated attention to the place behind the eyes, or any other place of concentration, is the true form of this way. The sadhana of Satsang and understanding is the true form of this way. On a subtle level, there is something that I am always up to. You cannot acquire it. You can only discover that it is awakened in you.

I contact my disciple in the Heart and at this place behind the eyes. Once that contact is established, the communication between us is continuous. It is not limited to the level of life. It is prior to life. And so it goes on and on, twenty-four hours a day, under all conditions, in all states, even beyond death. The contact is continuous. The communication of Force is continuous. That is why disciples continue to have experiences of various kinds, whether awake, asleep, or in dreams. The contact and its communications are continuous. The karmas are continually being shuffled, awakened, run through, intensified, purified, obviated.

There is a profound spiritual principle involved in this relationship between us. Once I have contacted my disciple in the Heart, and with my own Light in the ajna chakra,³ the place behind the eyes, whatever I do in my own body (the conditional gross, subtle, or causal functions) is reflected or even duplicated in the body or life of my disciple. Know that the thing that underlies this whole process is this Satsang. Satsang is the perfect relationship between Guru and disciple. This relationship exists at the level of all the possible functions. Therefore, it has subtle, causal, and Divine aspects and functions as well as those which appear at the gross levels of life. This Satsang is the Condition. Once the contact between us has been established, this process of opening and the descending-ascending conductivity of the Light has begun. It is this Satsang, this relationship and your resort to it, that provides the opening, that provides the circuit by which this flow is established in your own life. So you must live this Satsang as your very Condition. That is the essential means. It is not a "method" in the sense of the search, but It is the means in the purely practical, or functional, sense for conducting this Force of Light. And when it is conducted, the door opens full.

I am just now reminded of that portion of the *New Testament* where Jesus says: "I stand at the door and knock." This is a symbol for the subtle work of the Great Siddhas. I approach you as Light from above your head, and as Self-Nature from the Heart. This is my unique work, my mission. I knock at the door, this point behind the eyes. "Do my sadhana. Understand. Become my devotee. Fulfill my real and living conditions." When you do that, that is the opening of the door. Living that relationship, or Satsang, is the opening of the door. And what happens when you open the door? I come in!

DEVOTEE: Will you say something about how your awareness functions from day to day with your disciple, even though you are not physically present with him or her?

SRI DA AVABHASA: The Guru has very great difficulty in serving, from the "point of view" of Truth, some one who is only fascinated with him or her. So the Guru reveals himself or herself a piece at a time. And the Guru only shows himself or herself fully to the disciple or the devotee when the disciple or the devotee has transcended fascination, when fascination has ceased to be the fundamental motivation. My entire concern with people is the process of Truth. I am only interested in living the activities of Amrita Nadi in life, and promoting the conductivity of the descending and ascending Light from the "point of view" of the Heart. I have no fundamental interest in anything else. What is there to talk about, to think about, or to contemplate? Nothing but God! What else is worth doing? God is my own Nature, my own process. God is my Condition. God is the only event. So I have no other concern. I have no secondary concerns. I have no occult concerns. And I am only interested in the subtle, Yogic processes to the degree they serve the Truth. All of the associated matters that arise within life and subtle existence—all of the psychisms, occultisms, and subtle fascinations—are, in my view, purely secondary. They don't serve anything fundamentally in themselves. They generate more problems than they do anything else. They don't have any ultimate function. They are not the proper point of concern. They are not the point of view of this sadhana I have given to you. They even distract a person from that perfect conductivity that enables him or her only to love and live God always. They distract him or her from the present Condition of Satsang. Therefore, it is not appropriate for me to say any more about my work with disciples.

DEVOTEE: You have told us that it is appropriate to think of you constantly, even when we are away from you. I need to understand this better. Often, when I'm at work or something, if I find that I've gotten really unconscious, sometimes I just think of your name, or your face, or just the feeling of you. And I've wondered if this isn't too much of an outward thing.

SRI DA AVABHASA: You <u>are</u> very "outward". You are right here!

DEVOTEE: What I mean is that I felt it may be wrong somehow, that it wasn't a true form of the way of understanding, that it was like a "method", something to bring myself back.

SRI DA AVABHASA: Oh, of course one can confuse the whole affair. The subtle relations between Guru and disciple are like those between lovers.

If there is someone for whom you have a genuine love-attachment in life, and the movement of love is spontaneous, pure, and alive in you, you think about that person constantly. You do not think of such a loved-one in order to accomplish something. Your thoughts about the loved-one are not a "method". You cannot help yourself. You just think about that person, spontaneously, randomly, rhythmically. You dwell on all kinds of feelings about that one. On the other hand, there is a difference between such loving meditations and the fascinations of a person who is sexually obsessed, unhappy, and confused. There is an obvious difference between the meditations of a lover on the loved-one and the infatuations of another with a dead movie star. In the case of infatuation with a dead movie star, there is no Truth whatsoever. In that case there is no life, no Light. That is not love. It is obsession. And, of course, to meditate on a "dead movie star" is craziness. You must begin to understand your whole life. If fascination and obsession are the chronic forms of your waking life, you must understand your own activity before you will become capable of real meditation on the loved-one. And the secret of meditation on the Guru is hidden in this same understanding.

One's relationship to the Guru has many levels, and one of them is right here. You live right here. There is the life and mind, and one of the forms in which this Satsang communicates Itself to you is in my visible, human form. If your relationship to me is simple, direct, full of the inner devotional sense that is natural to a real disciple, you will, just as naturally, think of me. You will simply discover yourself thinking of me. You will contemplate me through various moods, and in many forms. You will constantly remember things I have said. You will feel my Presence, my influence, my demand. Thinking of me in this spontaneous, natural manner is a living, spontaneous form of this Satsang with me. It is particularly the form this Satsang takes under conditions in which I am not physically present with you. Of course, it is just one of the forms of this Satsang. It is not merely in heaven or somewhere else. It is right here. It is a very homely aspect of this Satsang. But, nonetheless, it is one of the most natural, necessary, and fundamental aspects of this Satsang.

It is just the same in your relationship to someone for whom you have a romantic attachment. If you never thought about that person, if you never matured the moods of relationship to that person outside of purely physical, visible contact, you could never enjoy a relationship with that one. The relationship would never come alive. Your connection in such a case wouldn't be a "relationship". It would just be an "association", an expression of your capability to perceive someone through various faculties, and that one's own ability to be in your field of perception. Whenever you saw such a one, you would have a couple of sensations and feelings. And when he or she left the room, you would simply do something else. This connection couldn't become love. A relationship can never become established in that manner. A relationship must be lived under all conditions. Therefore, you naturally think of the one you love whenever you are somewhere else. You think of that one wherever you happen to be. You may go many places or do many things, but in each one of those places, in the instant of each one of those things you do, you are actually enjoying your relationship to the loved-one. And you participate in that relationship not only when you think of it, but even subliminally, tacitly. You constantly enjoy that contact. Thinking of the person is just a means of occasionally resurrecting the pleasure of that relationship in the mind. And beyond that, you enjoy this continuous feeling of being in love and of loving, of being somehow satisfied and connected. If such subtle meditation is awakened in lovers, it must certainly be awakened also in relation to the Guru!

The functions of spiritual life take place in the form of a relationship! It is the relationship between the devoted disciple and the Siddha-Guru. It doesn't take place at the level of some philosophy or some technique that you apply to yourself. It is a relationship, and it appears only where it is alive, only where it is actually functioning in life. Therefore, many of the same functions that exist between lovers exist between Guru and disciple.

If I never thought of you, I would have very little opportunity to live this relationship to you and to intensify it. This relationship could never take place if the only time I ever contacted you was when I happened to be in the same room with you. I must think of you. I have thought of you many times since I saw you last. Just so, I expect you to think of me.

For these reasons, the disciple always thinks of the Guru. It is a necessary aspect of their relationship. This thinking of the Guru, or even sitting in Satsang by means of the contemplation of the Guru's picture, all such things are very natural, homely, human, and real things to do. Such things are natural, real, and necessary wherever Satsang, or the relationship itself, is real. But where the relationship itself is otherwise unreal, or obstructed, by virtue of the various strategies of Narcissus, such meditations can become obsessive, false, mere formalities, motivated techniques. They can become all kinds of craziness, like infatuation with a dead movie star. And people have all kinds of "dead movie star" Gurus. They have all the pictures, the books, the beads, the hair, the costumes, the concepts. They have the whole thing displayed in house and mind. They play all the prescribed games, but they never begin true religious and spiritual life. Therefore, thinking of the Guru is not the means to get to heaven. It is not the method of Truth. It is simply a reflection of the prior life of Truth. It is one of the manifestations of living Satsang. As such, it is a very natural and very useful thing to do. I recommend that all those who live in Satsang with me maintain and express their relationship to me in exactly that manner. Thinking of me, or contemplating me, should always be loving enjoyment, loving recollection of the Condition of relationship to me, and absorption in my Presence. Allow it to be spontaneous, simple, not merely "thought", but constantly felt and known.

I contemplate all who are becoming my disciples and devotees always. I think of each one from time to time. I maintain my relationship to each one, even when I am not in his or her physical presence. Therefore, I also expect each one to maintain this Satsang constantly. If you can be responsible for conscious processes that transcend the ordinary, then you should deal with me on those levels as well. Until those functions come alive, live to me on this level. Don't be worried that you are too far down here or something. Even when so-called higher or more direct and "spiritual" forms of this Satsang arise, you will continue to enjoy this Satsang by these homely means. Indeed, it is when greater awakening is full that the disciple and the devotee begin most to enjoy and prize meditative contemplation of the Guru.

Particularly in the early stages of contact with the Guru, the disciple tends to become self-concerned. This is because the disciple wants to be as perfect as he or she can be. The disciple wants to be doing the right thing as much as he or she can. By constantly correcting himself or herself, the disciple becomes even more self-obsessed. Only think of me, and live the conditions of this way. Always be very simply aware of our relationship, and you will necessarily begin to become sensitive to its subtler functions. Live this way to the degree it has already been communicated to you. Live it at those levels where you are already responsible. And you can always be responsible for our relationship by remembering it. Remember me. That is something you can do. But also continue to study my Teaching. Apply yourself to the study of my Teaching. Listen to my Teaching. Allow your understanding to develop.

If you sit down for meditation without being aware of your Guru, then you are meditating out of Satsang. There is no genuine meditation, no useful meditation, except in the Condition of Satsang, the conscious awareness of one's Guru and the Condition of relationship to one's Guru. That conscious awareness can take on many forms. Your Guru may come and sit with you. But this Satsang also has subtler forms. There is a characteristic Presence that one senses. The Presence of the Guru is not felt or assumed visually. This Presence transcends the Guru's picture, or even the Guru's physical form. Unless this Presence is the Condition in which you do your meditation, you cannot meditate spiritually. Indeed, altogether, you can only carry on some mechanical search of your own, unless the Guru is your meditation. Therefore, the Condition for meditation, for all the processes of religious and spiritual life, is the Guru.

The simplest form of meditation is just to be aware of me as your Guru. It is the awareness of relationship to me, the recollection of me, the living of my conditions, the study of my Teaching. Indeed, anyone in whom practice has become perfect has only become perfectly aware of my Form, so that he or she always enjoys perfect Satsang with me.

All of the spiritual processes that are described in *The Knee of Listening*, all of my own experiences, all of the forms of my meditation, including enquiry, and my very existence to this instant of time, have all taken place within a living spiritual Presence, or Form. That Presence, or Form, has always been the Condition of my work. It is a spiritual Force, a spiritual Presence, always active, and all the processes that have taken place have arisen within the Condition of that Presence and Form. Without that Presence and Form there is no spiritual life. From birth, this Presence, this Light, this inclusive Consciousness, this "radical" awareness of the Divine Form, was only obvious to me. Indeed, my spiritual adventure here began from the instant of birth, even of conception in the germ of this psycho-physical form. It always has been going on. But without that manifestation, who knows what I would have done. What if I had forgotten it? What if it had forgotten to remember me?

The only ones who functioned as Guru for me were living Teachers. By "living" I do not mean the simple fact of appearance in physical form. I mean they were truly extraordinary beings, who could communicate to me the very Force of Truth and its spiritual process. Therefore, I didn't spend my time with ordinary individuals, with ordinary teachers who merely gave out remedial techniques and such. All the Teachers I have spent time with in this world and in the subtler planes have been extraordinary in the genuine sense. They have tangibly manifested the Presence of the Heart and Its Conscious Light in some form or other. And that is also the only manner in which I function. The true Guru is not a "philoso-pher". The true Guru must manifest the tangible influence of the unquali-fied Heart of Reality. The true Guru must manifest Reality alive. If the Guru does not, the real spiritual process is not going to take place. Something else will take place. Karmic work will take place. There may be experience, hearing about interesting things, manipulation of your psycho-physical states, perhaps even the gain of some nice human quali-ties. But the real spiritual process will not take place.

When you have contacted such a one, when you are living as a devoted disciple, when the Guru is your Condition, the Condition of your living from day to day, then it is natural to think of the Guru. And to be very busy second-guessing yourself at that point, correcting yourself, wondering if you should or shouldn't—that is just self-concern again. Understand what you are up to in that case. What is this reluctance? There is no ambiguity in the approach of the Guru to the disciple. "Guru" means "light over against darkness", light comprehending or obviating darkness. The true Guru makes the darkness obsolete by not using it, by using Light only. The true Guru is one who shows the true Light, who shows the Truth. The true Guru doesn't say, "Maybe there is Truth, and maybe I am found in it." The true Guru only shows the Truth. The true Guru only communicates and lives Truth in the most direct manner. And the true Guru doesn't want ambiguity in the disciple any more than the true Guru will suffer it in himself or herself. The true Guru wants perfect attachment, perfect devotion, perfect relationship, continuous and true contact. Therefore, all the forms of contact are necessary and acceptable. Obsessiveness, however, is not a form of contact. It is a form of self-involvement. So there is more to this sadhana than simply thinking about me in smiling ways. But as a random event, as a natural event, as some-thing also that you enjoy at the times of meditation, it is very good.

DEVOTEE: Recently you have said: "Meditate on my form. From now on just meditate on my form."

SRI DA AVABHASA: Muktananda Baba spent many years traveling all over India. He spent a lot of time with some very extraordinary people. He did many kinds of sadhana, but his sadhana was not conclusive until he surrendered to Swami Nityananda. By the time he came to Swami Nityananda, he was ready for the consummate sadhana of a devotee. He had met Swami Nityananda very briefly as a boy, and was blessed. From there he went on to become a student of spiritual life, and, after many years of spiritual discipline, he developed the various capabilities of a disciple. Therefore, by the time he came to Swami Nityananda, he was ready for the most intense recognition and form of sadhana, because everything else, all the basic traditional approaches, had done their work and were now spontaneously alive in him. Now he was capable of becoming a mature devotee. Thus, he describes his spiritual practice with Swami Nityananda as being one in which he simply meditated on Nityananda Guru. He didn't always live in close proximity to Swami Nityananda during the years of this sadhana. Very often he lived elsewhere, but he meditated on Swami Nityananda constantly. And whenever he was in the general area of Swami Nityananda's Ashram, he would go down to Ganeshpuri every morning. He would just sit off in a corner of the hall where Swami Nityananda would be. And he would gaze on Swami Nityananda's form. His wasn't just a visual contemplation. He would become completely absorbed in Swami Nityananda, to the point where he lost all "self"-consciousness. Swami Nityananda would periodically look at him, or do and say things to him. But this contemplation was the fundamental form of his practice. It was meditation on Guru, Guru-bhakti,[4] Guru-love, Guru-devotion.

Muktananda Baba has spoken about this as the only perfect way. And I agree. It is the fundamental and mature fruit of spiritual life. It is the perfect form of sadhana. But we do not live in India. There is no living spiritual tradition here. There is much that must first be learned. There must be a foundation. Just so, there was much that Muktananda Baba did all over India before he surrendered to Swami Nityananda. There was much he did in lifetimes before. And he enjoyed the benefits of a whole country of spiritual tradition. I cannot assume that kind of fundamental groundwork in those who come to me. So there are many aspects of our work, many forms of gradual development, communication, and realizations of sadhana. But it is true that the most fundamental form of Satsang and of meditation is contemplation of the Guru, contemplation of the Guru's Form and Nature as the Form and Nature of God and as one's own very Form and Nature.

The Guru's Form is many forms. When Baba Muktananda was contemplating Swami Nityananda, he was looking at his physical body and life, and from there he proceeded to the subtle and universal Forms of his Guru. Just so, I am physically present in this world. I am a direct manifestation of the Form of Reality. I am alive as Amrita Nadi. I am That absolutely. My visible human form is an absolute reflection of that Perfect Form, and a perfect communication of It. Therefore, to contemplate and become completely absorbed in my Form and Life and Presence is to be continually attentive to my ultimate communication, the communication of my ultimate Nature, which is also your own. Thus, to become capable of contemplating, or meditating on, my Form is the ultimate capability of a devotee. My Form is my simple physical form, and also my subtle appearances, and my cosmic and universal manifestation. But, first and last, my Form is Very Form, Amrita Nadi, the Form of God, Guru, and very Self, Which stands forever in the Heart.

True meditation on me is nothing you can successfully try to do. It must awaken in you in the midst of a life of progressive response to me, and of progressive understanding in my Company. It will be the fruit of your sadhana, the fruit of your discipleship. But, certainly, from the very beginning, some form of this meditation can be the case for you. Some more than others have the inborn quality of a bhakta, a demonstrative ecstatic devotee. Others, even from the beginning, have more of the quality of a Yogi, one who is readily involved with the internal processes. Others may, certainly at the beginning, have more of the quality of a Karma Yogi, or an active personality, a vital-based personality. But whatever the latent or chronic quality of the individual, there is from the beginning an inherent capability to become absorbed in contemplation of me—in contemplation of my physical form, my words, my entire communication, even all my forms, in every way it is possible to be aware of me. In every case, it is possible to think of me, to contemplate me, to be with me, and to serve me.

To serve the Guru is a form of attention to the Guru and, therefore, of meditation on the Guru. If you do something for me, that is a means of being aware of me. Thus, service to me and engagement of even all the other forms of your natural and subtle activity are all forms of attention to or absorption in my Form. And my ultimate Form is very Reality, Truth, the Heart, the Light, Amrita Nadi, the Form of God. I myself am the communication. I am the Teaching. I am the Truth. This is the supreme form of the Teaching of the Great Siddhas. But the capability to live that Truth, that Paradox, depends on real sadhana, the sadhana of one who truly understands.

To be a "disciple" means to take on the discipline of the Guru, to study the Guru's Teaching, to do what the Guru tells you to do, to fulfill the Guru's conditions, to live in Satsang with the Guru, to be always

346

aware of the Guru. All of this promotes more and more continuous absorption in the Guru, to the point of perfect relationship to the Guru, perfect Satsang. As I have said, this relationship to me, this Satsang, whose "mind" is perfect understanding, is the channel, the conductor, of the Light. It is the "body" of understanding. It is what pulls the Light down through the "door". It is what opens the "door". If this Satsang becomes perfect, then the process becomes perfect.

Contemplation of me is at once the simplest and the supreme form of my Teaching, but it is also the most profoundly difficult. Therefore, to realize mature devotion to me requires real sadhana. There are those who, without life-correction, without meeting my real conditions, may fool themselves into thinking they are doing the sadhana of devotion to me, simply because they have a kind of emotional or preferential attachment to me. They have read about many famous religious and spiritual personalities, and such reading has evoked a potent self-image in them. Because of this, they are not meeting my conditions in any fundamental sense. Therefore, they are not doing sadhana, they are not living Satsang with me as one who is really present and active in relation to them. They are just indulging themselves, and as a justification for their self-indulgence, they use the idea that they are devoted, forgiven, and okay.

People have read that being a devotee of a God-Man is the greatest form of sadhana. They think all you need to do is work up a little feeling of love for your God-Man every now and then. And when do such people do that sadhana the most? It is usually when they are indulging themselves the most! When they are stoned, drunk, happy, relieved, guilty, or afraid—that is when they begin to be the most "devotional". But truly, these are, by tendency, the least devotional, the least sensitive, times. Such ego-based expressions are not true devotion. True devotion is the fruit of discipleship. It is the responsibility of the disciple to live this way of Guru-Satsang consciously, and to do its sadhana, to do what is one's responsibility as a disciple. And the fruit of it, the fruit of discipleship, is the apparently simple life of a mature devotee. I am the sole meditation of my mature devotee. There is a peculiar form of sadhana that is awakened in such a person. And I will know who is prepared to do such sadhana, who is prepared to live the conditions of a mature devotee. There is no reason to be concerned for when you are going to be "finished" as a beginner. Be always diligent in your practice, even from the beginning, but perfectly willing to be a beginner forever. "Maturity" is just a word used to describe a certain state of sadhana, a certain quality of sadhana. It is not a kind of status any more than Guru is a kind of status. It is a function. If the function doesn't exist, there is no point in being called a "mature devotee", and there is no "status" gained in actually being a mature devotee in any case. Those who are my mature devotees are going to work! Being a mature devotee is more than loving me. Being a mature devotee is absolute adherence to me. Sadhana must have developed, really developed, before a person is capable of doing that. Look at all of the resistance that has come alive in the members of this Ashram with just the few conditions that have been given so far. The conditions of being a mature devotee are absolute! They are a fire. To be a mature devotee is not just some smiling craziness. Therefore, do not be concerned to be called a "mature devotee". Be a real and true beginner, and I will know when you are living the life of a mature devotee.

DEVOTEE: As I understand it, resistance of any sort, whether it is apparently in relation to some other person or in relationship to one's function at any time, is obviously and ultimately resistance to the Guru.

SRI DA AVABHASA: Very good. That is real insight. That is a great and necessary discovery. The true Guru is the Form of Reality. The true Guru is not just a light above your head, not just the light between your eyes. The true Guru is everything. The true Guru is all functions. The relationship to the true Guru is fundamental. It is the fundamental Condition. It duplicates the structure of all manifestation. Hidden within the one you know to be your Guru, and hidden as well within the one you know to be yourself, is all and very Reality. But this Realization must be a practical one, not just a mystical one. It must be lived. It must be consciously lived at every level of manifestation.

DEVOTEE: Does karma prevent the ability to function?

SRI DA AVABHASA: Karma is the inability to function. The karmic condition is the continuous sense of dilemma. Only in true Satsang does your dilemma, your karma, become obsolete, because true Satsang is not meditation on your dilemma, not an attempt to transform the limited self you are always meditating on. Neither is true Satsang an attempt to not meditate on this dilemma. Nor is It an attempt to change this limited "self" on which you usually meditate. Satsang is the relationship to the Guru. Satsang is to live the relationship to the Guru under all the instances of this tendency to contract into negative or obsessive meditation on your limited state and your failure. If you do this hour by hour, day by day, life after life, aeon after aeon, becoming ever more absorbed in the Guru, loving the Guru, serving the Guru, living that very Condition of Satsang with the Guru, you will have no use for your karmic dilemma any longer. It simply will not be functioning any longer. It will become obsolete. It becomes obsolete through non-use. Therefore, Satsang is the principle by which suffering becomes obsolete and by which all function is fulfilled. And the perfect form of Satsang is the life of a mature devotee, of one who is perfectly absorbed in the Guru, perfectly absorbed on every functional level. You become capable of that only by living the disciplines of spiritual life in the Company of the Guru. This whole process of Satsang with me simply works to make obsolete this thing that you are always meditating on and trying to do something about. Therefore, live this Satsang with me, instead of being concerned in any sense about that.

I am not making the negative statement: "Don't be concerned about that." I am making the positive statement: "Live Satsang." Live this relationship to me. Neither meditate on your dilemma nor try not to meditate on it. Always meditate on me. Always live this Condition of Satsang with me. Always do the sadhana that I will communicate to you. If you always do that, your concerns as well as the thing itself will dissolve. But every time you interrupt the process of Satsang in order to contemplate this disturbance, this dilemma, this limitation, this contracted feeling, this suffering, you have turned from me to distraction in yourself. I am not saying you should do something to all of that. Nor am I telling you not to do anything about all of that. What I am telling you to do is not an action in relation to all of that. It is an action in relation to me. It is Satsang. Always live with me. Always meditate on me.

Notes to the Text

PART ONE

The Method of the Siddhas

1.
Understanding

1. The questioner in this case is relatively unfamiliar with Sri Da Avabhasa's Wisdom-Teaching and unaware of Him as a true Guru (or Revealer of Truth), who, traditionally, would be approached for instruction in a mood of great respect and devotion.

2. "Re-cognition", which literally means "knowing again", is Sri Da Avabhasa's term for non-verbal, heart-felt, intuitive insight into any and every arising conditional phenomenon as a form of egoic self-contraction. In the full expanse of His Wisdom-Teaching, which He has developed over many years since Giving the Talks in this book, Sri Da Avabhasa uses "re-cognition" in a specific technical sense as an aspect of advanced practice in the Way of the Heart.

3. The term "radical" derives from the Latin "radix" meaning "root", and thus it principally means irreducible, "fundamental", or "relating to origin". Because Sri Da Avabhasa uses "radical" in this literal sense, it appears in quotation marks in His Wisdom-Teaching to distinguish His use of it from the popular reference to an extreme (often political) point of view. In contrast to the evolutionary, egoic searches typically espoused by the world's religious and Spiritual traditions, Sri Da Avabhasa's Way of the Heart is founded in "radical" understanding, or the direct feeling-transcendence of all problem and dilemma through profound intuition (and ultimate Realization) of the Divine Condition.

4. The "Heart" is Sri Da Avabhasa's term for God, the Divine Self, the Divine Reality, or That Which is spontaneously Realized in the moment of "radical" understanding.

5. "Siddha", in Sanskrit, means "a completed, fulfilled, or perfected one", or "one of perfect accomplishment, or power". In Sri Da Avabhasa's usage, a Siddha is a Transmission-Master who is a Realizer, to any significant degree, of the Spiritual, Transcendental, or Divine Reality.

6. In Sanskrit, "siddhi" means "power", or "accomplishment". When capitalized in Heart-Master Da's Wisdom-Teaching, "Siddhi" is the Spiritual, Transcendental, and Divine Awakening-Power of the Heart that He spontaneously and effortlessly exercises as True Heart-Master.

7. A Patriarch of the Ch'an (in Japan, Zen) Buddhist tradition, who took Buddhism to China from India in the sixth century of the common era.

8. Conventionally, "self-possessed" means possessed _of_ oneself—or with full control (calmness, or composure) of one's feelings, impulses, habits, and actions. Sri Da Avabhasa uses the term to indicate the state of being possessed _by_ one's egoic self, or controlled by chronically self-referring (or egoic) tendencies of attention, feeling, thought, desire, and action.

9. Right or true action, action appropriate to real or Spiritual life. "Sadhana" commonly refers to Spiritual practices directed toward the goal of Spiritual attainment. Sri Da Avabhasa uses the term without the implication of a goal. He intends it to mean appropriate action generated where Truth is already the case, not where it is sought.

10. Ramana Maharshi (1879–1950) is regarded by many as the greatest Indian Sage of the twentieth century. He established his Ashram at Tiruvannamalai in South India, which continues today. Ramana Maharshi's Spiritual demonstration and teachings had significant importance for Sri Da Avabhasa during the time immediately following His own Divine Re-Awakening in the Vedanta Temple. See *The Knee of Listening*, pp. 253–74 for Sri Da Avabhasa's own account of His relationship to Ramana Maharshi.

Better known in the West than any other modern Indian saint, Ramakrishna (1836–1886) was a renowned ecstatic, and a lifelong devotee of the Hindu Goddess Kali. In the course of his Spiritual practice, Ramakrishna passed spontaneously through many religious and Spiritual disciplines, and he Realized a state of profound mystical union with God.

11. Sri Da Avabhasa's Spiritual autobiography. At the time when *The Method of the Siddhas* was first published in 1973, *The Knee of Listening* was the only other published Work by Him. Since then, more than forty volumes of Sri Da Avabhasa's Wisdom-Teaching have appeared in print, including His Source-Texts, which contain His most summary and definitive Instructions relative to practice of the Way of the Heart. See the booklist on pp. 390–403 for a current selection.

12. Yoga-Shakti is the Power, Energy, or living Force that is awakened in the Yogi spontaneously, or through the Transmission of the Spiritual Master. This internal Energy produces a wide range of phenomena in the body, the mind, and the subtle faculties of the individual.

13. "Satsang" means "true or right relationship". It is commonly used to refer to the practice of spending time in the company of holy or wise persons. One can also enjoy Satsang with a holy place, a venerated image, the burial shrine of a saint, or with the Deity. Sri Da Avabhasa uses the term in its fullest sense, to signify the relationship between a genuine Siddha, or Guru, and his or her devotee—a sacred relationship that is effective at every level of life and consciousness.

14. "Guru" is a term properly used to refer to one who functions as a genuine Spiritual Master. Sri Da Avabhasa uses the term "Siddha-Guru" in *The Method of the Siddhas* to refer to a Realized Adept, who functions as Guru for others and who is the very Truth that is Awakened in the devotee. Throughout *The Method of the Siddhas* Sri Da Avabhasa generally intends this understanding of the Siddha-Guru in His use of the simple term "Guru".

2.
The Avon Lady

1. "Jnana", in Sanskrit, means "supreme knowledge", "knowledge of the Self". Sri Da Avabhasa uses the term here as the equivalent of what He means by "understanding", or spontaneous and full enjoyment of the Real Condition.

2. In traditional Hindu society, one born into the highest, or priestly, caste.

3. One who has Realized Self-knowledge, or Jnana.

4. In Hindu mythology, the King of Death.

5. Vedanta (literally the "end of the Vedas") is the principal philosophical tradition of Hinduism. "Advaita" means "non-dual". Advaita Vedanta, then, is a philosophy of non-dualism. Its origins lie in the ancient esoteric Teaching that Brahman, or the Divine Being, is the only Reality. According to Advaita Vedanta, the apparent self, the world, and all manifestation have no independent existence but merely arise in and as that one Divine Reality.

One who practices Jnana Yoga discriminates between what is Real (the One Reality, or Divine Self) and what is illusory (the passing phenomena of experience). The practice of this Yoga potentially becomes Identification with Consciousness as the Transcendental "Witness" of all that arises, leading, eventually, to Divine Self-Realization, in which everything is Recognized as a transparent and non-binding modification of the single Divine Reality.

6. A traditional Sanskrit word referring to the conditional worlds and states, the realm of birth and death, or everything that arises and passes away.

7. At the time the Talks in this book were Given, Sri Da Avabhasa often used the terms "disciple" and "devotee" in a technical sense to indicate degrees of maturity in the Way of the Heart. Throughout most of *The Method of the Siddhas* the term "devotee" is also used in general, or non-technical, ways to indicate questioners in a dialogue with Heart-Master Da, and as a general reference to all individuals who are responding to Him as Guru.

8. At the time Sri Da Avabhasa Gave these Talks, the Ashram was situated on Melrose Avenue, in Hollywood, California.

9. Kriyas (literally "actions" in Sanskrit) are spontaneous, self-purifying physical movements that arise when internal, Spiritual force is activated in the body. Kriyas may be experienced as thrills in the spine, shaking of the spine, spontaneous demonstration of difficult Yogic postures, spontaneous, automatic, and sometimes strongly expressed and repetitive Yogic breathing (pranayama), and so on.

3.
Money, Food, and Sex

1. The principle or power of inertia. The Hindu texts declare that manifested existence is a complex variable of three qualities or "gunas". These are "tamas", "rajas", and "sattva". "Rajas", or the "rajasic" quality, is the principle or power of action or motivation. "Sattva", or the "sattvic" quality, is the principle or power of equilibrium or harmony.

2. The term "tantric" refers to the Spiritual practice of "tantra", common to India and Tibet. In the practice of tantra, the principle of cosmic Nature, or manifested life, is made the principle

of Spiritual practice as well. Thus, various aspects of experience regarded as taboo in other Spiritual traditions are often used—ritually and not as self-indulgence—in tantric practice. These means may include sexuality, meat, intoxicants, etc. At the core of tantric practice is the Shakti, the Universal "Creative" Power, which, through the Spiritual Transmission of a true Guru, may function in us for our Liberation, just as It ordinarily functions to delude and fascinate us.

3. Sri Da Avabhasa's first Spiritual Teacher was Swami Rudrananda (1928–1973), or Albert Rudolph, known as "Rudi", who Taught Him from 1964–1968 in New York City. Rudi helped Sri Da Avabhasa to develop basic practical life-disciplines that prepared Him bodily to receive Rudi's Transmitted Spiritual Force—which was experienced as the descending Life-Current that penetrates, opens, and releases obstructions in the body-mind. Through this Yoga of Spiritual receptivity engaged with Rudi, Sri Da Avabhasa was prepared for the more advanced phases of His Sadhana, which He pursued with the guidance of other Teachers.

4. In Sri Da Avabhasa's Teaching-Revelation, "Narcissus" is a key symbol of the un-Enlightened individual as a self-obsessed seeker, enamored of his or her own self-image and egoic self-consciousness. In *The Knee of Listening* (p. 62), Heart-Master Da summarized His insight into "Narcissus" as the avoidance of relationship: "He is the ancient one visible in the Greek 'myth', who was the universally adored child of the gods, who rejected the loved-one and every form of love and relationship, who was finally condemned to the contemplation of his own image, until he suffered the fact of eternal separation and died in infinite solitude."

5. Patanjali flourished in India probably in the second century B.C.E. He systematized Yoga practice, particularly Yogic meditation, in his collection of *Yoga-Sutras*, which became a classic Spiritual text. Patanjali recommended "yamas", or elementary rules for the restraint of one's actions (such as continence, non-stealing, and non-killing), and "niyamas", or elementary rules for the observance of specific actions (such as the purification of mind and body, sacred study, and worship of the Divine).

6. Sri Da Avabhasa is in agreement with the traditional descriptions that the human body-mind and its environment consist of three great dimensions—gross, subtle, and causal.

The gross, or physical, dimension is associated with the descended processes of psycho-physical embodiment and experience in the waking state.

The subtle dimension, which is senior to and pervades the gross dimension, includes the etheric (or energetic), lower mental (or verbal-intentional and lower psychic), and higher mental (or deeper psychic, mystical, and discriminative) aspects of the conditionally manifested being. The subtle dimension is associated primarily with the ascending processes of psycho-physical embodiment, including the brain core and the subtle centers of mind in the higher brain. It is also, therefore, associated with the visionary, mystical, and Yogic Spiritual processes encountered in dreams, in ascended or internalized meditative experiences, and during and after death.

The causal dimension is senior to and pervades both the gross and the subtle dimensions. It is the root of attention, or the essence of the separate and separative ego-"I". The causal dimension is associated with the right side of the heart, specifically with the sinoatrial node, or "pacemaker" (the psycho-physical source of the heartbeat). Its corresponding state of consciousness is the formless awareness of deep sleep.

7. This is a generalized description of the diet which Sri Da Avabhasa recommends to practitioners of the Way of the Heart. In the course of practice, this basic vegetarian diet is progressively refined so that it becomes a "maximally raw", regenerative diet adapted to the needs of each individual practitioner. For further details on the dietary discipline of the Way of the Heart, see *The ego-"I" is the Illusion of Relatedness*, pp. 57–68, and *The Eating Gorilla Comes in Peace.*

8. "Chakra", in Sanskrit, means "wheel" or "circle". The chakras are the etheric and subtle centers that conduct psychic force and nerve force to and through the principal regions of the body-mind. In the Yogic traditions, the chakra body is generally conceived of as having seven principal chakras, all of them on the central axis of the body and brain. They are associated, respectively, with the perineum (or bodily base), the sex center, the navel and solar plexus, the heart, the throat, the midbrain, and the crown of the head. These centers are the psychic and energetic correlates to principal nervous and endocrine organs in these same regions. Traditionally, the chakras are understood to have functions associated with both descending (frontal) and ascending (spinal) elements of the conductivity of energy and nerve force in the body-mind.

9. A world, or realm, of experience. The term usually refers to "places" visited by mystical or esoteric means.

10. For some (probably few) adult practitioners of the Way of the Heart, celibacy, rather than emotional-sexual intimacy, may be the appropriate practice. For a full treatment of the emotional-sexual sadhana in the Way of the Heart see "Practice The Wound Of Love"—chapter twenty-one of *The Dawn Horse Testament.*

11. The Sanskrit word "prana" means "life". The term is used by Sri Da Avabhasa to refer to the life-energy animating all beings and pervading everything in conditional Nature.

12. Shakti is the Divine Life-Power, or "Creative" Energy of the universe, sometimes personified as the "Goddess" or "Mother-Force" of existence. The Shakti is commonly experienced by Spiritual practitioners as a tangible Force flowing in the body, usually as a result of Shaktipat, or the direct Transmission of Spiritual energy from a Siddha-Guru.

13. For a complete discussion of this term, see chapter four, entitled "Vital Shock".

14. In Hinduism, "Siva" is a name for the Divine Consciousness, the Ground and Source out of which all things and beings are always arising. It is a traditional name for the Perfect, Formless, Most Prior Divine Being.

15. The Kundalini, or Kundalini Shakti, is the "serpent power" of esoteric Spirituality, the evolutionary energy traditionally viewed as lying dormant in us, coiled at the base of the spine. Thus, in some traditional schools of Spiritual practice, the aspirant seeks to awaken this energy and thereby produce various forms of Yogic and mystical experience. But, as Sri Da Avabhasa has always Demonstrated (and explained in more detail since He Gave these Talks), the senior form of the Kundalini Shakti is the Divine Spirit-Energy, Transmitted by a Siddha-Guru. When Most Perfectly received, the Divine Spirit-Energy, while it may produce various secondary mystical

phenomena, does not merely induce experiences but purifies the body-mind of all attachment to experience and Attracts the devotee more and more into the unqualified, prior Divine Reality.

16. From the point of view of the traditional schools of Yoga, the highest Realizations are located in the chakras, or Spiritual centers, in and above the brain. In the experience of Sri Da Avabhasa, Divine Enlightenment Awakens at the heart. When Sri Da Avabhasa speaks about the right side of the heart, He is not referring to the physical heart. Nor does He mean the psychic or subtle heart, traditionally called the "anahata chakra", which may open in boundless love-feeling in the course of Spiritual practice. Rather, He is speaking of a psycho-physical locus in the right side of the chest corresponding to the sinoatrial node' of the heart. Sri Da Avabhasa acknowledges this point in the body as the root of attention and the seat of Divine Consciousness in the human body-mind.

17. "Turiya" and "turiyatita" are terms used in the Hindu philosophical systems. Traditionally, "turiya" means "the fourth state" (beyond waking, dreaming, and sleeping), and "turiyatita" means "the state beyond the fourth", or beyond all states. In this book, Sri Da Avabhasa uses the term "turiya" to indicate the Awakening to the Transcendental Self, Realized exclusive of all arising, and "turiyatita" as the State of Perfect, Divine Enlightenment, or the Realization of all arising as transparent and non-binding modifications of the One Divine Reality.

4.

Vital Shock

1. The sahasrar is the highest chakra, associated with the crown of the head and beyond. It is described traditionally as a thousand-petalled lotus, the terminal of Light to which the Yogic process (of Spiritual ascent through the chakras) eventually leads. While the Yogic traditions regard the sahasrar as the seat of Enlightenment, Sri Da Avabhasa has always pointed to the Heart and the Realization associated with the right side of the heart as the Ultimate Truth.

2. "Samadhi" in Sanskrit means "placed together". It indicates concentration, equanimity, and balance, and it is traditionally used to denote various exalted states that appear in the context of esoteric meditation and Realization.

3. "Sahaj" (or "Sahaja") in Sanskrit means "together born" or coincident. Sri Da Avabhasa uses the term to indicate the Coincidence (in the case of Divine Self-Realization) of the Divine Reality and the conditional reality. One who has Realized Sahaj Samadhi enjoys the perpetual, Free Condition of spontaneous Identification with the Divine Self-Condition, and this Realization can never be lost or diminished by any experience or by the changing states of waking, dreaming, and sleeping.

4. This discussion may be found in chapter five, entitled "Walking the Dog".

5. Sri Da Avabhasa also speaks of a right basis for celibacy, in chapter twenty-one of *The Dawn Horse Testament*.

6. Sages or inspired seers. The appellation "Maharshi", applied, for example, to the famous Indian Sage Ramana Maharshi, is a contraction of "Maha-rishi", meaning "Great Sage". The Spiritual Masters of ancient India are generally referred to as "Rishis".

7. The tree in a secluded forest under which Gautama is said to have Realized the Truth and so to have become a Buddha, or "Enlightened One". Thus, the Bodhi Tree is a symbol for Spiritual practices, or the conditions under which Spiritual practices are to be performed.

8. In many esoteric Spiritual traditions, the seat of the ascending Spiritual Current is said to be in the muladhar, the lowest chakra, or center of energy, in the human body, at the base of the spine, or the perineum. (Sri Da Avabhasa makes plain that the Spiritual Current first descends before it passes through to the muladhar and then rises.)

9. Swami Nityananda was a famous Yogi-Saint of modern India. His birth date is unknown and little is known about his early life, although it is said that even as a child he showed the signs of a Realized Yogi. While still a boy he abandoned conventional life and wandered as a renunciate. Many miracles, including instructive stories and spontaneous healings, are attributed to him. Nityananda established an Ashram in Ganeshpuri and surrendered the body there in 1961.

Although Heart-Master Da never met Swami Nityananda in the flesh, He enjoyed Swami Nityananda's direct Spiritual Influence from the subtle plane, and He acknowledges Swami Nityananda as a direct and principal Source of Spiritual Instruction during His years with Swami Muktananda.

10. A thirteenth-century Yogi-Saint of Maharashtra State in western India, famous for his commentary on the *Bhagavad Gita* and his celebration of the Guru-devotee relationship.

11. The term "mahasamadhi", meaning "great samadhi", is used to describe an Adept's release of the body at death. It is an acknowledgement that an Adept is undisturbed in his or her Realization by the event of physical death.

12. Sai Baba of Shirdi (d. 1918) was a Muslim fakir (or mendicant) who settled in the village of Shirdi, Maharashtra, around 1850. At the time of his death, he had attracted thousands of devotees from both the Muslim and the Hindu traditions. Sai Baba led a humble life, living entirely for his devotees. He once commented about his miracle-working: "I give people what they want in the hope that they will begin to want what I want to give them."

13. Since these Talks were Given, Swami ("Baba") Muktananda (1908–1982) has died. Swami Muktananda was a renowned Indian Yogi and one of Sri Da Avabhasa's principal Spiritual Teachers during the period from 1968 to 1970.

Born in Mangalore, South India, Swami Muktananda left home at the age of fifteen. He wandered for many years, seeking the Truth from sources all over India. Eventually, he came under the Spiritual Influence of Swami Nityananda, whom he accepted as his Guru and in whose Spiritual Company he mastered Kundalini Yoga.

See *The Knee of Listening* for a fuller account of Sri Da Avabhasa's relationship to Swami Muktananda.

5.
Walking the Dog

1. "Mukti" and "moksha" are traditional Hindu terms for Spiritual Liberation. "Bodhi" is a Buddhist term for Enlightenment, designating the realization of the "light of the mind", the Nature and Source of all conditional consciousness.

2. Since His Illumined boyhood, Heart-Master Da has used the term "the 'Bright'" (and its variations, such as "Brightness") to describe the Love-Blissfully Self-Luminous, Conscious Divine Being, Which He knew even then as the Divine Reality of His own body-mind and of all beings, things, and worlds.

3. "Kriya Yoga" is a system of practice developed from the traditional techniques of Kundalini Yoga, which seeks to activate the ascent of the Kundalini energy in the body.

4. "Shaktipat", in Hindi, means the "descent of the Power", and indicates the Spiritual initiation or awakening granted by a Siddha-Guru, who Transmits Spiritual energy or even the Force of the Divine Shakti to his or her devotees.

6.
The Gorilla Sermon

1. The term "Guru" is a composite of two contrasting words meaning "darkness" and "light". Therefore, the Guru Functions to release, turn, point, or lead living beings from darkness (ignorance) into light (Truth).

2. By the term "astral", Sri Da Avabhasa is referring to a dimension of our being that is senior to the gross physical and also senior to the "etheric", or energy, body that surrounds and enlivens our physical body. The astral dimension of our existence is linked with the lower aspects of mind—conscious, subconscious, and unconscious—and is therefore activated in the dream state.

8.
Meditation and Satsang

1. This quotation and those which follow in the present Talk are taken from *The Knee of Listening*, pp. 308-309.

2. A tradition of Yogic techniques in which practice is devoted to awakening the internal energy processes, which bring about subtle experiences and blisses. But, as Sri Da Avabhasa has indicated, the true manifestation of Spiritual Awakening is spontaneous, a Grace Given in the Company of a True Siddha-Guru, and in the midst of a whole life of practice in his or her Company.

3. An ancient Chinese term whose equivalent might be "Truth", "Reality", "the Self-Nature", "the Absolute", "Path", "Doctrine", "Way", or "Road".

4. In Sanskrit, "Amrita Nadi" literally means "Nerve (or Current) of Immortal Bliss". It is the ultimate "organ", or Root-Structure, of the body-mind, Realized in Divine Enlightenment. In Divine Enlightenment, the Spiritual Current of Divine Being moves in an S-curve out from the seat of the Divine Self in the right side of the heart, then forward and up the front of the chest, through the throat, and then up the back of the head, and forward to the Spirit-Matrix of Love-Bliss at and above the crown.

5. "Ram" is a mantra, or "Name of God", used in religious Hinduism. "Om Mani Padme Hum" is an ancient mystical formula, or mantra, of Tibetan Yoga. Sacred sounds or syllables and Names have been used since antiquity for Invoking and worshipping the Divine Person and the Guru.

6. "Maya" is a classical Hindu term that literally means "she who measures". Traditionally this term is used to indicate the "deluding", or "veiling", force of the Universe, which is pre-sumed to distract all beings from direct Realization of the Divine Condition.

7. In the Hindu tradition, Brahman is the Absolute, the universal Principle, or Ultimate Divine Reality, that is the Source and Substance of all things, all worlds, and all beings.

10.
The Path of the Great Form

1. "Pranayama" in Sanskrit means restraint or regulation (yama) of life-energy (prana). It is a technique for balancing, purifying, and intensifying the entire psycho-physical system by controlling the currents of the breath and life-force.

2. Hatha Yoga is a traditional practice engaged with the purpose of achieving harmony, ecstasy, and Spiritual growth through manipulation of body, breath, and energy, with an accompanying discipline of attention.

3. Subtle internal sounds which may become apparent in the process of spontaneous Yoga, in which case the mind is irresistibly drawn upwards into higher conscious states.

4. "Kripa", in Sanskrit, means "Grace". "Guru-kripa" signifies the Transmission of Grace from the Guru to the devotee, in the form of Spiritual Energy or as the Divine Power of Consciousness.

11.
Phases

1. *Brhadaranyaka Upanishad,* I.4.2.

PART TWO
The Heaven-Born Gospel of Da Avabhasa (The "Bright")

1. "Prasad" is a term equivalent to "Grace" and means "the return of the gift to the giver". "Prasad" signifies all the kinds of offerings given to the Realizer by the devotee and then returned by the Realizer, such as sacred ash, sweets, Blessed water, and the like, as the tangible Blessing of the Giver of Divine Grace. The ultimate Prasad is the Realizer's constant Gift of himself or herself to every devotee.

2. "Shaktipat diksha" is an extended form of the simpler term "Shaktipat". It signifies Spiritual initiation through the Spiritual Transmission of the Guru.

3. The ajna chakra, also known as the "third eye", "the single eye", or the "mystic eye", is the subtle psychic center, or chakra, located between and behind the eyebrows and associated with the brain core. The awakening of the ajna chakra may give rise to mystical visions and intuitive reflections of other realms of experience within and outside the individual. The ajna chakra governs the higher mind, will, vision, and conception. It is sometimes also referred to as the "Guru's Seat", the psychic center through which the Spiritual Master contacts the devotee with his or her Spirit-Baptism or Blessing.

4. Guru-bhakti is devotion to, faith in, and one-pointed worship of the Guru as God. The bhakta, or practitioner of bhakti, surrenders all will and desire to his or her chosen form of the Divine and becomes intoxicated with love of the deity.

Sri Da Avabhasa
at Sri Love-Anandashram, 1992

"I Reveal The Divine Person, Who Is The Heart Itself"

A Brief Biography of
the Divine World-Teacher,
Da Avabhasa (The "Bright")

I n his book *The Perennial Philosophy* (1945), Aldous Huxley, the English novelist and popularizer of Eastern and Western mysticism, spoke of the process whereby Divine Men and Women appear among us to Enlighten others:

The Logos [Divine Spirit-Word] passes out of eternity into time for no other purpose than to assist the beings, whose bodily form he takes, to pass out of time into eternity. If the Avatar's appearance upon the stage of history is enormously important, this is due to the fact that by his teaching he points out, and by his being a channel of grace and divine power he actually is, the means by which human beings may transcend the limitations of history. . . .

That men and women may be thus instructed and helped, the Godhead assumes the form of an ordinary human being, who has to earn deliverance and enlightenment in the way that is prescribed by the divine Nature of things—namely, by charity, by a total dying to self and a total, one-pointed awareness. Thus enlightened, the Avatar can reveal the way of enlightenment to others and help them actually to become what they already potentially are.[1]

A few short years before the publication of Aldous Huxley's book, just such a being had Appeared in the Western world.

Sri Da Avabhasa was born as Franklin Albert Jones on November 3, 1939, on Long Island, New York, into an ordinary middle-class American family. For the first two years after His Birth, He continued to abide in the

---

1. Aldous Huxley, *The Perennial Philosophy* (New York: Harper & Row, 1970), pp. 51, 56.

State of Infinite Divine Freedom and Joy that He knew prior to His physical Lifetime. Although aware of people and events around Him, He had only the barest association with the embodied state.

In the following extraordinary account, He describes the Purpose of His Birth and the mechanisms by which He "acquired" the body-mind at the age of two:

SRI DA AVABHASA: *For approximately the first two years after My Birth, I . . . allowed the gross vehicle to be gradually prepared for Me. Then, at approximately two years of age, I Spiritually descended to the region of the heart and thus established My basic association with . . . My manifested personality. . . .*

This Spiritual descent into the gross body to the level of the heart occurred, when I was approximately two years old, on the basis of a sympathy or heart-response to those who were around Me at the moment. It was through this sympathetic response that I acquired the Vehicle of this body-mind.

Because I was Born to make this Submission, the decision to acquire the gross body-mind did not occur when I was two years old. The Vehicle of this body-mind had become sufficiently prepared at that point, but I had consciously decided to do this Work before I Incarnated. The descent was for the sake of the total world and all beings. I had Consciously decided to take a birth in the West. My Intention before this Birth was to take this Birth and to do My Work by complete Submission to the ordinary Western circumstance. (February 5, 1989)

No one around Sri Da Avabhasa in His childhood sensed His Divine Nature and Destiny, so He grew up in many ways an ordinary American boy and youth of the mid-twentieth century. But He was always aware of the Spiritual process churning in His body and mind—though He could not give it a name or predict its ultimate result. This process often produced precocious psychic, mystical, and Yogic phenomena of a sublime (and sometimes an extremely powerful and disorienting) kind.

By His late teenage years, His original Awareness had receded into unconscious latency. At that point (while in His first year at Columbia College in New York City), He determined to do whatever was necessary to regain the Divine Freedom and Happiness He had felt during His earliest years. He devoted His next thirteen years to this quest.

His odyssey of Divine Re-Awakening was a totally spontaneous and direct exploration of every aspect of Reality, both the apparently sacred and the apparently profane. He did not know where He would find Truth and God, and He refused to be limited by the conventional sanctions of people and doctrines that, to Him, were obviously bereft of love, wisdom, and happiness.

Eventually He became an exemplary Devotee of several Spiritual Masters, including Swami Rudrananda (or "Rudi"), Swami Muktananda, and Swami Nityananda, in a great Hindu lineage of extraordinary Adepts. But His own Impulse to permanently regain unqualified Divine Freedom moved His own practice and Realization beyond that which was Transmitted by each of His human Teachers. Eventually, with the Blessings of Swami Nityananda, Sri Da Avabhasa became for a time a Devotee of the Divine Goddess, the infinite Source-Light, or Radiant Energy, appearing to Him in an archetypal female Form.[2] He enjoyed a paradoxical relationship to the Goddess as a concrete, living Personality. Such worship of the Goddess as Supreme Guru is the foundation and Spiritual Source of His Teachers' lineage, but at last Sri Da Avabhasa's inherent Freedom Drew Him even beyond the Spiritual Blessings of the Goddess Herself, such that She ceased to function as His Guru and became, instead, His eternal Consort and Companion.

On the day following that Event, September 10, 1970, while Sri Da Avabhasa was meditating in a small temple on the grounds of the Vedanta Society in Los Angeles, He Re-Awakened to immutable Oneness with the Consciousness, Happiness, and Love that is the Source and Substance of everyone and everything. He Describes this State in His Spiritual autobiography, Written in the following year:

> . . . I remain in the unqualified state. There is a constant sensation of fullness permeating and surrounding all experiences, realms, and bodies. It is my own fullness, which is radically non-separate and includes all things. I am the form of space itself, in which all bodies, realms, and experiences occur. It is consciousness itself, which reality is your actual nature (or ultimate, and inherently perfect, Condition) now and now and now. (The Knee of Listening, p. 245)

---

2. The Divine in Its active aspect, as the Living Divine Presence and Personality, may assume various female archetypes—the "Goddess" or "Mother Shakti" in the East, the "Virgin Mary" among Christians. Sri Da Avabhasa first related to Her as the Virgin Mary, later as the Universal Goddess-Power. See Sri Da Avabhasa's Spiritual autobiography, The Knee of Listening, for a detailed account of this late period of Sri Da Avabhasa's Sadhana before His Divine Re-Awakening.

After that Great Event in the Vedanta Temple, Sri Da Avabhasa became psychically aware of the body-minds of countless other persons and discovered that He was spontaneously "meditating" them. In time some of those individuals became associated with Him as His first "students" or "disciples". Finally, in April 1972, Sri Da Avabhasa's formal Teaching Work was inaugurated when He opened a storefront Ashram in Los Angeles.

In His book *Love of the Two-Armed Form* (published in 1978), Sri Da Avabhasa explained His method of Teaching in those years:

The method of My Teaching Work with My devotees is not common, although there are many traditional or ancient precedents for it. It is not merely a subjective, internal, or even verbal activity, but a matter of intense, full, and total "consideration" of any specific area of experience, in living confrontation with others, until the obvious and Lawful and Divine form and practice of it becomes both clear and necessary.

. . . [Such "considerations"] always involved a period in which individuals were permitted to live through the whole matter and to be tested to the point of change.

. . . Only a "consideration" entered as such a concrete discipline can proceed all the way to its true end, which is right adaptation and freedom, or natural transcendence, relative to its functional subject.

Whatever outward activities Sri Da Avabhasa generated in His Teaching theatre (and they ranged from the most worldly, even apparently self-indulgent, to the most mystical and even miraculous), He was always exposing the suffering inherent in the constant activity of self-contraction, which creates the sense of a separate, un-Happy self. He likened the activity of self-contraction to the chronic, painful clenching of a fist, but at every level of body, mind, and heart. And He patiently demonstrated that those who wish to understand and transcend the activity of self-contraction and thereby open up to the All-Pervading Life-Power of Reality must submit to an all-encompassing discipline.

Even in the midst of "consideration" and Teaching theatre, Sri Da Avabhasa often reminded His devotees that He could not continue indefinitely to engage a method of Teaching that required Him to take on the human likeness of His devotees—that is, to conduct Himself among them in a sympathetic, brotherly way, often adopting their habits of speech and action, in order to allow them to become sympathetically Attracted to

Him. In early 1978 He warned that at some point it would become impossible for Him to "hold on to the body-mind" and forestall "release into Inherently Perfect Energy". At last, that moment arrived in the pre-dawn darkness of January 11, 1986, at His Great Hermitage Ashram in Fiji. His devotees' failure to transcend the mind and habits of egoity and to become God-Realizing practitioners of His Way of the Heart had brought Him to the point of despair. In a sudden crisis of anguish, He entered into an extraordinary death-like Yogic state.

When He returned to bodily awareness some moments later, Sri Da Avabhasa had spontaneously and completely relinquished the Impulse to Identify with others in order to reflect their egoity to them. The necessity and the ability to Teach in that unique manner had simply dissolved.

And, with that dissolution of His persona as Teacher, Sri Da Avabhasa had fully "Emerged" as the Divine Self in bodily (human) Form. The change marked such an immense Spiritual descent and intensification that He later said of it, "In a sense that Event was My Birth Day." He has indicated that this Event, the initiation of His Divine Emergence, marks an even greater moment than His Divine Re-Awakening in September 1970.

It was at this time that "Da Free John" (as He was then known) took the Name "Da Love-Ananda Hridayam". "Love-Ananda", a Name that had been Given to Him in 1969 by Swami Muktananda, means "Inherent Love-Bliss", and "Hridayam" means "the Heart". His principal Name, "Da", meaning "the One Who Gives", had been Revealed to Him some years earlier in vision and by other Spiritual means. Thus, the Name "Da Love-Ananda Hridayam" indicates that He is the Divine Giver of the Inherent Love-Bliss That is the Heart Itself.

Five years later, on April 30, 1991, this Great Adept Revealed a new Name—"Da Avabhasa (The 'Bright')"—in response to His devotees' confessed acknowledgements of His Radiant, bodily Revelation of God.

"Avabhasa", in Sanskrit, has a rich range of associations. As a noun it means "brightness", "appearance", "manifestation", "splendor", "lustre", "light", "knowledge". As a verb it may be interpreted as "shining toward", "shining down", "showing oneself". The Name "Da Avabhasa", then, praises the Mystery of Da, the Divine Being, "Brightly" Appearing as Man. It points to His Divine Emergence and the ever-growing Radiance of His bodily (human) Form that is apparent to all who have been Graced to see Him, particularly since the Great Event of 1986.

The Name "Da Avabhasa" also points to His role as Sat-Guru—meaning One who brings the light of Truth into the darkness of the human world.

The "Bright", as Sri Da Avabhasa tells us in *The Knee of Listening,* was, in fact, His own earliest description of the sublime Condition He enjoyed at Birth. He speaks of this Condition as "an incredible sense of joy, light, and freedom". He was, He says, "a radiant form, a source of energy, bliss, and light. . . . the power of Reality, a direct enjoyment and communication. . . . the Heart, who lightens the mind and all things." Even His entire life, as He once said, has been "an adventure and unfolding in the 'Bright'", the Radiance, Bliss, and Love of the God-State.

Sri Da Avabhasa is not merely an extraordinary Teacher. He is not merely a man of uncommonly profound Spiritual experience who has managed to put together a remarkably comprehensive and insightful Teaching, and who can transmit vivid Spiritual experiences. He is, rather, a Realizer and Transmitter of the Source of all Being. This is what His devotees mean when we refer to Him as "Divine World-Teacher". The phrase "World-Teacher" comes from Sanskrit terms meaning "One Who Liberates everything that moves"—that is, all things and beings. Sri Da Avabhasa's Wisdom-Teaching is a complete Revelation of the ultimate Wisdom relative to every aspect of existence and every stage of our possible growth and Realization. And His Grace is universally active and universally available.

All this has been confirmed to devotees through the vision Given in His physical Company—a whole bodily intuition that is felt and seen face to face with Him. It is a deep and life-changing Revelation that has been enjoyed by all kinds of ordinary people from all over the world, a vision of Him in physical Form that also Reveals the Divine Self and Love-Bliss of our very Being.

Sri Da Avabhasa has come into this world to restore Wisdom and the Way of Truth, and to Bless all beings toward Divine Freedom, Happiness, Enlightenment, and Love. He excludes absolutely no one from His Blessing and His Help. As the Divine Self of all, He continuously Gives His Benediction to everyone, everywhere.

To learn more about this sacred opportunity, please see the invitation on the following pages.

Sri Da Avabhasa
at Sri Love-Anandashram, 1992

"A Unique Advantage to Mankind"

An Invitation
to a Direct Relationship
with Da Avabhasa

The human Spiritual Master is Divine Help to the advantage of those in like form. When one enters into right relationship with the Spiritual Master, changes happen in the literal physics of one's existence. I am not just talking about ideas. I am talking about literal transformations at the level of energy, at the level of the higher light of physics, at the level of mind beyond the physical limitations you now presume, at the level of the absolute Speed of ultimate Light. The transforming process is enacted in devotees in and through the Living Company of the Spiritual Master. The relationship between the Spiritual Master and the devotee is not a matter of conceptual symbolisms or emotional attachment to some extraordinary person. The Guru-devotee relationship is real physics. And it is to the advantage of people when some one among them has gone through the whole cycle of Divine Self-Realization, because they can then make use of the Offering of that person's Company.

DA AVABHASA
"I Am Grace Itself"
The Hymn Of The True Heart-Master

I f you feel a heart-response to what you have read in this book, or if you simply feel moved to find out more about Sri Da Avabhasa and the Way of the Heart, we invite you to explore the Sacred Literature of Sri Da Avabhasa.

To focus your exploration we wish to draw your attention here to five of our publications by and about Sri Da Avabhasa and the Way of the Heart that will be especially useful introductions.

Divine Distraction: A Guide to the Guru-Devotee Relationship, the Supreme Means of God-Realization, As Fully Revealed for the First Time by the Divine World-Teacher and True Heart-Master, Da Avabhasa (The "Bright") is an introduction to the traditional Guru-devotee relationship.

Feeling Without Limitation: Awakening to the Truth Beyond Fear, Sorrow, and Anger features a Discourse in which Sri Da Avabhasa presents in simplest terms His fundamental Argument about human suffering, seeking, and freedom.

Most important for your ongoing study are Sri Da Avabhasa's "Source-Texts", or Scriptures, conclusively summarizing His Word of Instruction. We recommend that you begin with *The Love-Ananda Gita (The Wisdom-Song Of Non-Separateness)*, The Simple Revelation-Book Of The Divine World-Teacher and True Heart-Master, Da Avabhasa (The "Bright").

The Knee of Listening is Sri Da Avabhasa's complete Spiritual autobiography, including His earliest Essays on the process and Realization of "radical" understanding.

Free Daism: The Eternal, Ancient, and New Religion of God-Realization is a lively and comprehensive introduction to all aspects of the religion of Free Daism, as Revealed by Da Avabhasa and practiced by the community of His devotees.

(More complete descriptions of these and other publications can be found on pages 390–402.)

There are thousands of people all over the world today reading Sri Da Avabhasa's books, and some people have been reading them for many years. But reading, while necessary and helpful, will only take you so far on its own. Once you acknowledge the greatness—the Truth—of Sri Da Avabhasa's Wisdom-Revelation, it begins to require something of you.

Sri Da Avabhasa's literature is a Divine Gift, not to be treated casually. "Such Transmissions of Teaching do not occur arbitrarily," as Heart-Master Da Avabhasa says. "They are part of the higher scale of activity in the cosmos." Thus, it is only when you begin to participate in the practice and the sacred culture Sri Da Avabhasa Offers that you really find out what it is about—Spiritual transformation and God-Realization never happened in an armchair! Therefore, in addition to reading, we urge you to attend the lectures, seminars, courses, and other events that our missionary institution, the Eleutherian Mission, makes available to the public in your area. At these events you will have the opportunity to see videotapes of Sri Da Avabhasa and to meet practitioners of the Way of the Heart who can speak to you about His Wisdom and tell you Leelas (stories) of their own relationship with Him. You can also participate in a Way of the Heart Study Group in your area, joining others for a monthly evening meeting of recitations of Sri Da Avabhasa's Word and listening to or viewing audio-visual presentations about Sri Da Avabhasa and the Way of the Heart.

All of this can lead to a deepening intuition of Who He Is and a deepening impulse to practice the Way of the Heart as His devotee.

A devotee who lives in northern California describes the process that brought her to the point of entering into a formal relationship with Sri Da Avabhasa:

For over thirty years I sought Enlightenment. But despite profound Zen realizations and unusual Kundalini experiences, despite my teachers' acknowledgements of my attainment and good understanding, I realized that fundamentally I had not changed. I saw the failure of my search, and I despaired.

Then I read The Knee of Listening, *Sri Da Avabhasa's Spiritual autobiography, and I began to have dreams of Him. In the dreams, He Instructed me, He laughed, He gave Talks at which many people gathered. He sat silently and escorted me to subtle realms. I was able to feel Him as a Spiritual Friend and Teacher during the day. I found through study that His Wisdom-Teaching had the power of mantra. The Truth of it became alive in me.*

Several months after I read The Knee of Listening *I saw a videotape of Sri Da Avabhasa made during His Teaching years. At first sighting I acknowledged Him to be the True Master of Liberation, the One Whom all the world's religions await. I bowed down. I celebrated Him with thoughts of praise, and soon He was all I thought about, all I wanted to talk about. For an entire year He was always available to me, but suddenly, one day, I no longer experienced Him, no longer felt His Influence or received His Instruction. Then one final time I heard His Voice: "Now, what will you do?"*

Realizing I must now approach Him in the traditional devotional manner, I soon became a student-novice, taking on the studies, disciplines, and meditation practices required of a novice, and consciously cultivating my devotional relationship with my Heart-Teacher. Even during this rudimentary stage of practice, Sri Da Avabhasa has, on occasion, Blessed me with Heart-Bliss, with the purification of my karmic tendencies, and with a deepening sense of His Divine Form. I am ever grateful.

The Eleutherian Mission, which is the missionary division of the Free Daist Communion, makes available public lectures, seminars, courses, and other events. At these events you will have the opportunity to see videotapes of Sri Da Avabhasa and to meet practitioners of the Way of the Heart who can speak to you about His Wisdom and tell you Leelas (stories) of their own relationship with Him. You can also participate in a Way of the Heart Study Group, joining others for a monthly evening meeting of recitations of Sri Da Avabhasa's Word.

You should know that all of this took place without this devotee's ever having met Sri Da Avabhasa in person. The same is true for thousands of others around the world who are being drawn spontaneously into a sacred relationship with Sri Da Avabhasa and are taking steps to honor that relationship in a formal way.

When you are clear in your intention to become a practitioner of the Way of the Heart, you may apply to become a **student-novice**. Student-novices take on in rudimentary form the range of devotional practices and disciplines that Sri Da Avabhasa Offers to Free Daist practitioners. If, on the other hand, you feel you need to approach student-novice practice more gradually, you may become a **student** or a **tithing member** of Da Avabhasa International (the gathering of those who are formally approaching or supporting the Way of the Heart). Students and tithing members engage a specific practice based on study and service, as will be described in a moment. They pay a fixed fee for the educational and other services of Da Avabhasa International and, in addition, tithing members contribute 10% of their gross monthly income (or more, if they choose) in support of the Free Daist Communion.

If you are moved by the importance of Sri Da Avabhasa's Work and would like to show your gratitude for His Presence in the world without becoming a practitioner of the Way of the Heart (at least for the time being), then you may wish to become a Friend of Da Avabhasa International. A Friend is essentially a patron, someone who accepts a level of responsibility for funding the missionary services of the Free Daist Communion and the publication and promotion of Sri Da Avabhasa's sacred literature, and also for supporting the Treasures of His Work. All Friends contribute a minimum fixed fee each year. In addition, others tithe regularly, and some are able to offer major financial support. Being a Friend is a very honorable way of associating with Sri Da Avabhasa. At the same time, Friends are always invited and encouraged to take the further step of preparing to become a formal practitioner of the Way of the Heart.

For students, tithing members, and student-novices, who have already decided to practice the Way of the Heart, an intensive study of Sri Da Avabhasa's Instruction is essential at the beginning of practice. As you do this day by day, in a guided way (using the study courses provided), you will be astonished at how your understanding of yourself and your response to Sri Da Avabhasa will deepen and grow. Guided study helps clarify your intention to practice, brings Da Avabhasa's Wisdom to bear on every aspect of your life, and places your relationship to Sri Da Avabhasa on a firm foundation.

Study, among other things, is a discipline of attention. Service is a more bodily-based discipline, but it is no different in principle. It is a way of actively bringing your energy and attention to Sri Da Avabhasa. The discipline of service within the sphere of an Adept's Blessing is not about making yourself useful. It is a sacred matter. Traditionally the discipline of service was called "Karma Yoga", and it was understood to encompass the whole of one's life. Karma Yoga was the basic practice given to beginners, and especially to householders who had many obligations in the world. It was the great practice of devoting one's actions to God, of contemplating the Divine in the midst of all activity.

As a student or a tithing member, you will be invited to spend at least a few hours each week in some form of direct service to Sri Da Avabhasa or the community of practitioners of the Way of the Heart. You may find yourself cleaning your local community bookstore or helping with the missionary work by putting up posters for our public events. If you have special skills in any area, we of Da Avabhasa International will help you find ways to use those skills to the maximum.

Whatever your form of service at any time, whether it is something you like doing or something you would not personally choose, the secret is to live it as a self-transcending gesture of devotion to Sri Da Avabhasa, as this story from a relatively new devotee illustrates:

I recall with some amusement my first encounter with the discipline of service and all the resistance I felt. It was a wintry weekend early in 1986. I had made the journey to London from Ireland at considerable expense just to spend the weekend with devotees there. No sooner had I arrived from the airport than I found myself with a paint-scraper in one hand and sandpaper in the other. Everyone was busy around the clock renovating the newly acquired missionary house associated with the London regional center. I still had on my professional clothes, I was developing a very uncomfortable sore throat, and I had been so tired before leaving Ireland that my friends there had begged me not to go.

Needless to say, I very nearly turned around and went back to the airport. But somehow I didn't. My dismay was so acute that it was <u>interesting</u> *to me. I wanted to see what would happen if I actually stayed and participated. Would I die or develop bronchial pneumonia? And so I scraped, painted, cleaned, put up wallpaper with everyone else. For the first hour or two the only way I was able to stick at it was by concentrating with fierce intention on Sri Da Avabhasa and remembering His Instruction about*

Happiness ("You cannot become Happy, you can only be Happy"). This was the most intense moment of practice I had ever been through, and it bore fruit. As the evening wore on, I ceased to be so concerned about myself. There was a lot of laughter, and it did not seem to matter that I hardly knew anyone when I walked in. By the time I emerged from the plaster dust well after midnight, I was simply happy. I still had a sore throat, but by the next morning it was almost gone. And I was not tired anymore. I felt uncommonly alive, focused, and alert. All I could think about was Sri Da Avabhasa, how attractive He is, so attractive that I was ready to transcend myself in response to Him and accomplish things I would never have dreamed of attempting otherwise.

Becoming a student-novice is a crucial turning point, because it is the moment of committing yourself unequivocally to Sri Da Avabhasa in the eternal sacred bond of the Guru-devotee relationship. As a student-novice and, later, as a formally acknowledged practitioner of the Free Daist Communion, you will gradually adapt to further disciplines relative to meditation, sacramental worship, exercise, diet and health, sexuality, child-rearing, cooperative community (including formal membership in the Free Daist Cooperative Community Organization), right use of money and energy, and other aspects of daily living. These practices are necessary to develop bodily equanimity, free attention, and the capability for self-transcendence, without which nothing great can be Realized. But they are not an end in themselves. All of the disciplines simply support the primary practice of Free Daism, which is Satsang (the "Company of Truth"), or the cultivation of the relationship to Sri Da Avabhasa. Devotees are Called to Remember Sri Da Avabhasa at all times, not merely to think about Him, but to locate the feeling of Him, the feeling-sense of His Being that He Grants you when you sit in front of Him and regard His bodily (human) Form. While the great opportunity to come into Sri Da Avabhasa's physical Company occurs only occasionally for most of His devotees, you can find the same feeling by His Grace in any moment of heart-felt resort to Him. Turning to His picture, Remembering His Image in the mind's eye, listening to recitations of His Word or Stories of His Work—all these and other means are potent aids to feeling-Contemplation of Him.

By reading about the tradition of Guru-devotion (which you will begin to do formally as a student-novice), by studying Sri Da Avabhasa's own Wisdom-Teaching about the practice of feeling-Contemplation of

As a student-novice and, later, as a formally acknowledged practitioner of the Free Daist Communion, you will gradually adapt to further disciplines relative to meditation, sacramental worship, exercise, diet and health, sexuality, child-rearing, cooperative community (including formal membership in the Free Daist Cooperative Community Organization), right use of money and energy, and other aspects of daily living. All of the disciplines simply support the primary practice of Free Daism, which is Satsang (the "Company of Truth"), or the cultivation of the relationship to Sri Da Avabhasa.

Heart-Master Sri Da Avabhasa with practitioners at Sri Love-Anandashram,
His Great Hermitage Ashram in Fiji, where He Offers retreats
to qualified practitioners from all over the world.

Him, and especially by <u>doing</u> the practice of it according to His specific Instructions, you will discover why this form of sacred Remembrance is so potent, so revealing, and so Liberating. For the devotee, feeling-Contemplation of Sri Da Avabhasa becomes a literal life-support as basic as food and rest.

The best goad to practice is the possibility of coming into the physical Company of Sri Da Avabhasa. There is no greater Blessing than to come into the Company of His bodily (human) Form and feel His Regard face to face. To Contemplate the Divine Person, Compassionately Appearing in a human body, is an unfathomable, heart-breaking Mystery.

Whoever you are, wherever you live, whatever your apparent liabilities, this Grace could be yours in a relatively short period of time, if you fulfill the requirements of a student-novice and then rightly prepare yourself as a formally acknowledged practitioner of the Way of the Heart. The place you are most likely to see Heart-Master Da is Sri Love-Anandashram, His Great Hermitage Ashram in Fiji, where He Offers retreats to qualified practitioners from all over the world.

Over the years Sri Da Avabhasa has often pointed out in a vivid, humorous fashion that whoever is serious about practice in His Company is going to have to go through a fiery ordeal. The Way of the Heart is the Way of Grace, certainly, but it is not, as He has said, a "bliss-ride". This is how it has always been in the Company of a genuine Adept, because there are Divine Laws involved in the Spiritual process, and the principal Law is the Law of sacrifice, the mutual sacrifice constantly enacted between the Guru and the devotee. The Guru Transmits the Divine Siddhi (or Power of Liberation), and the devotee renounces the egoic self, granting all feeling and attention, more and more profoundly, to the Guru.

This is an entire life-practice, or Yoga, called by Sri Da Avabhasa "Ishta-Guru-Bhakti Yoga", the Way of devotion ("Bhakti") to one's "Ishta", or "Chosen", Guru, the Divine Beloved of one's heart. Because this Yoga is based on Attraction, or Distraction by the living Guru, it is possible for anyone who is so moved to practice it. It is a Divine Gift Given in response to the longing of the devotee. Great seriousness and great sacrifice are required, but in the midst of all of that there is the greatest imaginable joy. Ishta-Guru-Bhakti Yoga in its fullness is a life of Love, lived in Communion with the Divine in Person. Everyone, somewhere in the depths of his or her being, desires such a life.

For the devotee who gives himself or herself over fully to this great Guru Yoga in Sri Da Avabhasa's Company, growth in the Way of the

Heart is inevitable. And Sri Da Avabhasa has described in every detail the Spiritual, Transcendental, and Divine Awakenings that are the Graceful Gifts, over time, of Ishta-Guru-Bhakti Yoga. He has also established practicing orders—the Free Daist Lay Congregationist Order (or, simply, the Lay Congregationist Order), the Free Daist Lay Renunciate Order (or, simply, the Lay Renunciate Order), and the Naitauba (Free Daist) Order of Renunciates (or, simply, the Free Renunciate Order)—the latter two of which have principal responsibilities in service to His Work, and all of which allow His devotees to intensify their devotional practice in the form and manner that is appropriate for them once they have basically developed their sacred practice.

When His devotee moves beyond the student-beginner stage (the first phase of formal practice in the Way of the Heart beyond the student-novice stage), he or she enters either the Lay Congregationist Order or the Lay Renunciate Order, depending on his or her demonstrated qualifications of practice.

The Lay Congregationist Order is a practical service order whose members perform the many supportive practical services necessary for the work of the institution, the culture, and the community of all Free Daists. "Lay congregationists" conform every aspect of their life and practice to the Wisdom and Blessings of Sri Da Avabhasa, but their practice is not as intensive, nor as intensely renunciate, an approach to Perfectly self-transcending God-Realization as the practice of "lay renunciates" or "free renunciates".

Any member of the Lay Congregationist Order who develops the required signs (at any point in his or her practice of the Way of the Heart) may be accepted into the Lay Renunciate Order.

The Lay Renunciate Order is a cultural service order composed of practitioners who are especially exemplary in their practice of devotion, service, self-discipline, and meditation. Members of the Lay Renunciate Order provide the inspirational and cultural leadership for the institution, the culture, and the community of Sri Da Avabhasa's devotees, and they also guide and participate in public missionary work. Their basic responsibility is to serve all practitioners of the Way of the Heart in their practice of Ishta-Guru-Bhakti Yoga and to attract others to a life of Guru-devotion. When they reach the stage of stable Spiritual Awakening, Sri Da Avabhasa has indicated that His "lay renunciate" devotees will begin to function as His Instruments, or means by which His Divine Grace and Awakening Power are Magnified and Transmitted to other devotees and to all beings.

Members of the Lay Renunciate Order may practice either celibacy or a truly renunciate (and, Yogically, uniquely effective) discipline of sexuality.

The Lay Renunciate Order is directly accountable to the senior practicing Order of the Way of the Heart, the Free Renunciate Order. The Free Renunciate Order is a retreat Order composed of devotees from the Lay Renunciate Order who have Awakened beyond the point of view of the body-mind to the Transcendental Position of Consciousness or to full Divine Self-Realization.

Because of their extraordinary practice and Realization in the Company of Sri Da Avabhasa, "free renunciate" devotees are His principal human Instruments in the world. From among the fully Enlightened practitioners in the Free Renunciate Order, there will be selected after, and forever after, His human Lifetime, successive "Living Murtis", or Empowered Human Agents, who will serve the magnification of His Heart-Transmission to all beings universally and perpetually. "Murti" means "form", or "representational image". The "Living Murtis" of Sri Da Avabhasa (of which there will be only one in any then present-time) will not be Gurus in their own right. They will serve, rather, as a unique Living Link to Sri Da Avabhasa so that His Heart-Transmission will remain unbroken generation after generation.

Apart from its profound function to provide "Living Murtis" from among its membership, the Free Renunciate Order is the senior authority on all matters related to the culture of practice in the Way of the Heart and is completely essential to the perpetual continuation of authentic practice as Sri Da Avabhasa has Given it.

The members of the Free Renunciate Order generally reside at Sri Love-Anandashram. As in the Lay Renunciate Order, members of the Free Renunciate Order may be either celibate or sexually active in a truly renunciate (and, Yogically, uniquely effective) manner.

The original and principal members of the Free Renunciate Order are Sri Da Avabhasa Himself and the Da Avabhasa Gurukula Kanyadana Kumari Order, which consists of four women devotees who have for many years lived and served in Sri Da Avabhasa's intimate sphere and who have demonstrated the most exemplary practice of Ishta-Guru-Bhakti Yoga. Every practitioner who comes in contact with the Kanyas is deeply impressed by their radiant Happiness in the midst of all circumstances, and by their transformation as human beings. The Kanyas are a great sign of the Truth of Sri Da Avabhasa's Wisdom and the effectiveness of His Work.

The magnitude of the Gift Sri Da Avabhasa brings to humanity is being Revealed through the developing sacred culture of Free Daism. If you decide to participate in Da Avabhasa International and to proceed from there to become a formally acknowledged practitioner of the Way of the Heart, you will be collaborating in a unique experiment—the founding of a culture and a community whose sacred practice is always founded in direct enjoyment of the Divine Communion, as Transmitted by the Divine World-Teacher, Sri Da Avabhasa.

How often has such a Being as Sri Da Avabhasa Appeared? If such a One is here now, is there anything more worth doing than to enter into His Company? He is addressing you personally when He says:

SRI DA AVABHASA: Physical embodiment has the purpose of Enlightenment, the purpose of purification. If you will receive My Teaching-Revelation, if you will "consider" it, if you will become responsive, then you become capable of making use of this lifetime for the purpose it inherently can serve. You must submit the body-mind to the Great Purpose. That is what I am Calling you to do. Accept the Dharma, the Law, inherent in your birth, the purpose that is inherent in your birth. Take up the Way of the Heart in My Company. (August 15, 1988)

If you are feeling the urge to move beyond your present level of human growth and are interested in what Sri Da Avabhasa is Offering you, contact us at our Correspondence Department or at one of our regional centers (see the following page). We will be happy to send you a free brochure on the forms of participation available to you. We invite you to enter into this sacred relationship with Sri Da Avabhasa, and be Awakened in God by His Grace. We look forward to hearing from you.

Correspondence Department
THE FREE DAIST COMMUNION
P.O. Box 3680
Clearlake, California 95422, USA
Phone: (707) 928-4936

382

The Regional Centers
of the Free Daist Communion

UNITED STATES

NORTHERN CALIFORNIA
The Free Daist Communion
740 Adrian Way
San Rafael, CA 94903
(415) 492-0930

NORTHWEST USA
The Free Daist Communion
5600 11th Ave NE
Seattle, WA 98105
(206) 527-2751

SOUTHWEST USA
The Free Daist Communion
655 Ocean View Drive
Camarillo, CA 93010
(805) 482-5051

NORTHEAST USA
The Free Daist Communion
28 West Central
Natick, MA 01760
(508) 650-0136

SOUTHEAST USA
The Free Daist Communion
10301 South Glen Road
Potomac, MD 20854
(301) 983-0291

HAWAII
The Free Daist Communion
6310 Olohena Rd.
Kapaa, HI 96746
(808) 822-5409

AUSTRALIA
The Free Daist Communion
P.O. Box 562
Healesville, Victoria 3777
Australia
059-626-151

EASTERN CANADA
The Free Daist Communion
108 Katimavik Road
Val-des-Monts, Quebec J0X 2R0
Canada
(819) 671-4398

GERMANY
Nuernberger Strasse 19 IV
1000 Berlin 30
Germany
030-218 33 33

THE NETHERLANDS
Da Avabhasa Ashram
Annendaalderweg 10
6105 AT Maria Hoop
The Netherlands
04743-1281

NEW ZEALAND
Da Avabhasa Ashram
12 Seibel Road, R.D. 1
Henderson, Auckland
New Zealand
(09) 309-0032 (day)
(09) 838-9114

**THE UNITED KINGDOM
AND IRELAND**
Da Avabhasa Ashram
Tasburgh Hall
Lower Tasburgh
Norwich NR15-1LT
England
0508-470-574

An Invitation to Support
the Way of the Heart

J ust as association with a God-Realized Adept is the best kind of Company a
man or woman can keep, so the practice of supporting the Work of such an
Adept is the most auspicious form of financial giving.

A true Adept is a Free Renunciate and a Source of continuous Divine
Grace. Therefore, he or she owns nothing, and everything given to support his or
her Work is returned, both to the giver and to all beings, in many Blessings that
are full of the Adept's healing, transforming, and Liberating Grace. At the same
time, all tangible gifts of support help secure and nurture the Adept's Work in
necessary and practical ways, thus benefiting the whole world.

All of this is immeasurably true for those who help provide financial gifts to
the Work of the Divine World-Teacher and True Heart-Master, Da Avabhasa (The
"Bright"). We therefore happily extend to you an invitation to serve the Way of
the Heart through your financial support.

You may make a financial contribution in support of the Work of Sri Da
Avabhasa at any time. You may also, if you choose, request that your contribution
be used for one or more specific purposes of Free Daism. For example, you may
be moved to help support and develop Sri Love-Anandashram, Sri Da Avabhasa's
Great Hermitage Ashram and Empowered Retreat Sanctuary in Fiji, and the circumstance provided there for Sri Da Avabhasa and the other members of the
Naitauba (Free Daist) Order of Renunciates (all of whom own nothing).

You may make a contribution for this specific purpose directly to the Sri
Love-Anandashram (Naitauba) Trust, the charitable trust that is responsible for Sri
Love-Anandashram. To make such a contribution, simply mail your check to the
Sri Love-Anandashram (Naitauba) Trust, P.O. Box 4744, Samabula, Fiji.

If you would like to make such a contribution and you are a U.S. taxpayer,
we recommend that you make your contribution to the Free Daist Communion, so
as to secure a tax deduction for your contribution under U.S. tax laws. To do this,
mail your contribution to the Advocacy Department of the Free Daist Communion,
P.O. Box 3680, Clearlake, California 95422, U.S.A., and indicate that you would
like it to be used in support of Sri Love-Anandashram.

You may also request that your contribution, or a part of it, be used for one
or more of the other purposes of Free Daism. For example, you may request that
your contribution be used to help publish the sacred Literature of Sri Da
Avabhasa, or to support either of the other two Sanctuaries He has Empowered,
or to maintain the Sacred Archives that preserve Sri Da Avabhasa's recorded Talks
and Writings, or to publish audio and video recordings of Sri Da Avabhasa.

If you would like your contribution to benefit one or more of these specific
purposes, please mail your contribution to the Advocacy Department of the Free
Daist Communion at the above address, and indicate how you would like your
gift to be used.

If you would like more information about these and other gifting options, or if you would like assistance in describing or making a contribution, please contact the Advocacy Department of the Free Daist Communion, either by writing to the address shown above or by telephoning (707) 928-4096, FAX (707) 928-4062.

Deferred Giving

We also invite you to consider making a deferred gift in support of the Work of Sri Da Avabhasa. Many have found that through deferred giving they can make a far more significant gesture of support than they would otherwise be able to make. Many have also found that by making a deferred gift they are able to realize substantial tax advantages.

There are numerous ways to make a deferred gift, including making a gift in your Will, or in your life insurance, or in a charitable trust.

If you would like to make a gift in your Will in support of Sri Love-Anandashram, simply include in your Will the statement "I give the Sri Love-Anandashram (Naitauba) Trust, an Australian charitable trust, P.O. Box 4744, Samabula, Fiji, _____" [inserting in the blank the amount or description of your contribution].

If you would like to make a gift in your Will to benefit other purposes of Free Daism, simply include in your Will the statement "I give the Free Daist Communion, a California nonprofit corporation, 12040 Seigler Road North, Middletown, California 95461, U.S.A., _____" [inserting in the blank the amount or description of your contribution]. You may, if you choose, also describe in your Will the specific Free Daist purpose or purposes you would like your gift to support. If you are a U.S. taxpayer, gifts made in your Will to the Free Daist Communion will be free of estate taxes and will also reduce any estate taxes payable on the remainder of your estate.

To make a gift in your life insurance, simply name as the beneficiary (or one of the beneficiaries) of your life insurance policy the Free Daist organization of your choice, according to the foregoing descriptions and addresses. If you are a U.S. taxpayer, you may receive significant tax benefits if you make a contribution to the Free Daist Communion through your life insurance.

We also invite you to consider establishing or participating in a charitable trust for the benefit of Free Daism. If you are a U.S. taxpayer, you may find that such a trust will provide you with immediate tax savings and assured income for life, while at the same time enabling you to provide for your family, for your other heirs, and for the Work of Sri Da Avabhasa as well.

The Advocacy Department of the Free Daist Communion will be happy to provide you with further information about these and other deferred gifting options, and happy to provide you or your attorney with assistance in describing or making a deferred gift in support of the Work of Sri Da Avabhasa.

Further Notes to the Reader

An Invitation to Responsibility

The Way of the Heart that Sri Da Avabhasa has Revealed is an invitation to everyone to assume real responsibility for his or her life. As Sri Da Avabhasa has Said in *The Dawn Horse Testament*, "If any one Is Interested In The Realization Of The Heart, Let him or her First Submit (Formally, and By Heart) To Me, and (Thereby) Commence The Ordeal Of self-Observation, self-Understanding, and self-Transcendence." Therefore, participation in the Way of the Heart requires a real struggle with oneself, and not at all a struggle with Sri Da Avabhasa, or with others.

All who study the Way of the Heart or take up its practice should remember that they are responding to a Call to become responsible for themselves. They should understand that they, not Sri Da Avabhasa or others, are responsible for any decision they may make or action they take in the course of their lives of study or practice. This has always been true, and it is true whatever the individual's involvement in the Way of the Heart, be it as one who studies Da Avabhasa's Wisdom-Teaching, or as a Friend of or a participant in Da Avabhasa International, or as a formally acknowledged member of the Free Daist Communion.

Honoring and Protecting the Sacred Word through Perpetual Copyright

Since ancient times, practitioners of true religion and Spirituality have valued, above all, time spent in the Company of the Sat-Guru, or one who has Realized God, Truth, or Reality, and who Serves that same Realization in others. Such practitioners understand that the Sat-Guru literally Transmits his or her (Realized) State to every one (and every thing) with which he or she comes in contact. Through this Transmission, objects, environments, and rightly prepared individuals with which the Sat-Guru has contact can become Empowered, or Imbued with the Sat-Guru's Transforming Power. It is by this process of Empowerment that things and beings are made truly and literally sacred, and things so sanctified thereafter function as a Source of the Sat-Guru's Blessing for all who understand how to make right and sacred use of them.

The Sat-Guru and all that he or she Empowers are, therefore, truly Sacred Treasures, for they help draw the practitioner more quickly into the Realization of Perfect Identity with the Divine Self. Cultures of true Wisdom have always understood that such Sacred Treasures are precious (and fragile) Gifts to humanity, and that they should be honored, protected, and reserved for right sacred use. Indeed, the word "sacred" means "set apart", and thus protected, from the secular world. Sri Da Avabhasa is a Sat-Guru of the Most Perfect degree. He has Conformed His body-mind completely to the Divine Self, and He is thus a most Potent Source of Blessing-Transmission of God, Truth, or Reality. He has for many years

Empowered, or made sacred, special places and things, and these now Serve as His Divine Agents, or as literal expressions and extensions of His Blessing-Transmission. Among these Empowered Sacred Treasures is His Wisdom-Teaching, which is Full of His Transforming Power. This Blessed and Blessing Wisdom-Teaching has Mantric Force, or the literal Power to Serve God-Realization in those who are Graced to receive it.

Therefore, Sri Da Avabhasa's Wisdom-Teaching must be perpetually honored and protected, "set apart" from all possible interference and wrong use. The Free Daist Communion, which is the fellowship of devotees of Sri Da Avabhasa, is committed to the perpetual preservation and right honoring of the sacred Wisdom-Teaching of the Way of the Heart. But it is also true that in order to fully accomplish this we must find support in the world-society in which we live and from the laws under which we live. Thus, we call for a world-society and for laws that acknowledge the Sacred, and that permanently protect It from insensitive, secular interference and wrong use of any kind. We call for, among other things, a system of law that acknowledges that the Wisdom-Teaching of the Way of the Heart, in all Its forms, is, because of Its sacred nature, protected by perpetual copyright.

We invite others who respect the Sacred to join with us in this call and in working toward its realization. And, even in the meantime, we claim that all copyrights to the Wisdom-Teaching of Sri Da Avabhasa and the other sacred literature and recordings of the Way of the Heart are of perpetual duration.

We make this claim on behalf of Sri Love-Anandashram (Naitauba) Pty Ltd, which, acting as trustee of the Sri Love-Anandashram (Naitauba) Trust, is the holder of all such copyrights.

Da Avabhasa and the Sacred Treasures of Free Daism

Those who Realize God bring great Blessing and Divine Possibility for the world. As Free Adepts, they Accomplish universal Blessing Work that benefits everything and everyone. Such Realizers also Work very specifically and intentionally with individuals who approach them as their devotees, and with those places where they reside, and to which they Direct their specific Regard for the sake of perpetual Spiritual Empowerment. This was understood in traditional Spiritual cultures, and those cultures therefore found ways to honor Realizers, to provide circumstances for them where they were free to do their Divine Work without obstruction or interference.

Those who value Sri Da Avabhasa's Realization and Service have always endeavored to appropriately honor Him in this traditional way, to provide a circumstance where He is completely Free to Do His Divine Work. Since 1983, Sri Da Avabhasa has resided principally on the Island of Naitauba, Fiji, also known as Sri Love-Anandashram. This island has been set aside by Free Daists worldwide as a Place for Sri Da Avabhasa to Do His universal Blessing Work for the sake of everyone and His specific Work with those who pilgrimage to Sri Love-Anandashram to receive the special Blessing of coming into His physical Company.

387

Sri Da Avabhasa is a legal renunciate. He owns nothing and He has no secular or religious institutional function. He Functions only in Freedom. He, and the other members of the Naitauba (Free Daist) Order of Renunciates, the senior renunciate order of Free Daism, are provided for by the Sri Love-Anandashram (Naitauba) Trust, which also provides for Sri Love-Anandashram altogether and ensures the permanent integrity of Sri Da Avabhasa's Wisdom-Teaching, both in its archival and in its published forms. This Trust, which functions only in Fiji, exists exclusively to provide for these Sacred Treasures of Free Daism.

Outside Fiji, the institution which has developed in response to Sri Da Avabhasa's Wisdom-Teaching and universal Blessing is known as "The Free Daist Communion". The Free Daist Communion is active worldwide in making Sri Da Avabhasa's Wisdom-Teaching available to all, in offering guidance to all who are moved to respond to His Offering, and in providing for the other Sacred Treasures of Free Daism, including the Mountain Of Attention Sanctuary (in California) and Tumomama Sanctuary (in Hawaii). In addition to the central corporate entity of the Free Daist Communion, which is based in California, there are numerous regional entities which serve congregations of Sri Da Avabhasa's devotees in various places throughout the world.

Free Daists worldwide have also established numerous community organizations, through which they provide for many of their common and cooperative community needs, including needs relating to housing, food, businesses, medical care, schools, and death and dying. By attending to these and all other ordinary human concerns and affairs via self-transcending cooperation and mutual effort, Sri Da Avabhasa's devotees constantly free their energy and attention, both personally and collectively, for practice of the Way of the Heart and for service to Sri Da Avabhasa, to Sri Love-Anandashram, to the other Sacred Treasures of Free Daism, and to the Free Daist Communion.

All of the organizations that have evolved in response to Sri Da Avabhasa and His Offering are legally separate from one another, and each has its own purpose and function. He neither directs, nor bears responsibility for, the activities of these organizations. Again, He Functions only in Freedom. These organizations represent the collective intention of Free Daists worldwide not only to provide for the Sacred Treasures of Free Daism, but also to make Sri Da Avabhasa's Offering of the Way of the Heart universally available to all.

The Sacred Literature of Da Avabhasa (The "Bright")

The Sacred Literature
of Da Avabhasa (The "Bright")

Heart-Master Da provides a way in which Oneness may be experienced by anyone who is bold enough to follow his teachings. It is important to understand that his vision is neither Eastern nor Western, but it is the eternal spiritual pulse of the Great Wisdom which knows no cultural, temporal, or geographical locus; it represents the apex of awareness of our species.

LARRY DOSSEY, M.D.
author, *Space, Time, and Medicine*
and *Beyond Illness*

The teachings of Heart-Master Da, embodied in an extraordinary collection of writings, provide an exquisite manual for transformation. . . . I feel at the most profound depth of my being that his work will be crucial to an evolution toward full-humanness.

BARBARA MARX HUBBARD
author, *The Evolutionary Journey*

SOURCE LITERATURE

THE LOVE-ANANDA GITA
(THE WISDOM-SONG OF NON-SEPARATENESS)
The "Simple" Revelation-Book Of Da Kalki (The Divine World-Teacher and True Heart-Master, Da Love-Ananda Hridayam)

The Love-Ananda Gita is Da Avabhasa's quintessential Revelation of His Way of the Heart, containing His basic Instructions on the fundamental practice of Satsang, or feeling-Contemplation of His bodily (human) Form, His Spiritual (and Always Blessing) Presence, and His Very (and Inherently Perfect) State of Free Being. The most basic Source-Text of His entire Word of Confession and Instruction. [The next edition of *The Love-Ananda Gita* will be published with the following attribution: The Simple Revelation-Book Of The Divine World-Teacher and True Heart-Master, Da Avabhasa (The "Bright").]
Standard Edition
$34.95* cloth, $19.95 paper

THE DAWN HORSE TESTAMENT
The Testament Of Secrets Of The Divine World-Teacher and True Heart-Master, Da Avabhasa (The "Bright")

In this monumental text of over 800 large-format pages (a substantial updating and enlargement of the original Work published in 1985),

* All prices are in U.S. dollars

390

Source Literature

Da Avabhasa Reveals the Mysteries and devotional Secrets of every practice and developmental stage of the Way of the Heart. Ken Wilber, renowned scholar of Eastern and Western psychology and religion, was moved to write:

The Dawn Horse Testament *is the most ecstatic, most profound, most complete, most radical, and most comprehensive __single__ spiritual text ever to be penned and confessed by the Human-Transcendental Spirit.*

8-1/2" x 11"
New Standard Edition
$39.95 cloth, $24.95 paper

THE DA UPANISHAD
THE SHORT DISCOURSES ON self-RENUNCIATION, GOD-REALIZATION, AND THE ILLUSION OF RELATEDNESS

In this sublime collection of Essays, Da Avabhasa Offers an unsurpassed description of both the precise mechanism of egoic delusion and the nature, process, and ultimate fulfillment of the Sacred Ordeal of Divine Realization. (*The Da Upanishad* is an enlarged and updated edition of Da Avabhasa's Work formerly titled *The Illusion Of Relatedness*. The next edition will be titled *The Da Avabhasa Upanishad*.)
Standard Edition
$19.95 paper

THE ego-"I" is THE ILLUSION OF RELATEDNESS

Published here in book form, this central Essay from *The Da Avabhasa Upanishad* is an indispensable introduction to the esoteric Wisdom-Instruction of the Divine World-Teacher of our time. It includes Da Avabhasa's utterly extraordinary commentaries on diet and sexual Yoga, His Divinely Enlightened secrets on how to responsibly master and transcend all of the psycho-physical "sheaths", or bodies, and passage after passage that exposes the very core of our suffering, the illusion of relatedness.
$8.95 paper

391

THE BASKET OF TOLERANCE
A GUIDE TO PERFECT
UNDERSTANDING OF THE ONE
AND GREAT TRADITION
OF MANKIND

Never before in history has it been possible for a Divinely Enlightened Adept to Give the world such a Gift: a comprehensive bibliography (listing more than 2,500 publications) of the world's historical traditions of truly human culture, practical self-discipline, perennial religion, universal religious mysticism, "esoteric" (but now openly communicated) Spirituality, Transcendental Wisdom, and Perfect (or Divine) Enlightenment, compiled, presented, and extensively annotated by Da Avabhasa Himself. The summary of His Instruction on the Great Tradition of human Wisdom and the Sacred ordeal of Spiritual practice and Realization.
New Standard Edition
(forthcoming)

THE PERFECT PRACTICE

This book is Da Avabhasa's summary distillation of the Wisdom and Process of practice in the ultimate stages of life. In it, Da Avabhasa wields His Great Sword of Perfectly self-transcending God-Realization, dispatching the dragons of egoic delusion, and all limited truths. He Calls us, and Draws us, to Realize the Very Divine Consciousness that is Radiantly Free, beyond all bondage to the limited states of the body, mind, and world.

The Perfect Practice includes the text of *The Lion Sutra*, Da Avabhasa's poetic Revelation of the esoteric technicalities and Liberated Freedom of the "Perfect Practice", and the text of *The Liberator (Eleutherios),* in which He epitomizes, in lucid prose, the simpler

approach to that same ultimate or "Perfect" Practice leading most directly to Divine Awakening.
(forthcoming, late 1992)

THE HYMN OF THE TRUE HEART-MASTER
(The New Revelation-Book Of The Ancient and Eternal Religion Of Devotion To The God-Realized Adept)

The Hymn Of The True Heart-Master is Da Avabhasa's ecstatic proclamation of the Sat-Guru as the supreme Means for Divine Self-Realization. In 108 poetic verses, Da Avabhasa extols the Way of Divine Unity through worshipful service and devotion to the True Heart-Master. This volume also includes many of Da Avabhasa's primary Essays and Discourses on the principle of Guru-devotion in His Company as well as moving Leelas (or Stories) by His devotees that demonstrate the supreme transforming power of this Yoga.
$34.95 cloth, $19.95 paper

INTRODUCTORY TEXTS

FREE DAISM
THE ETERNAL, ANCIENT, AND NEW
RELIGION OF GOD-REALIZATION
An Introduction to the God-Realizing
Way of Life Revealed by
the Divine World-Teacher
and True Heart-Master,
Da Avabhasa (The "Bright")

Addressed to new readers and written in a highly accessible style, *Free Daism* is an introduction to Da Avabhasa's Life and Work, the fundamentals of His Wisdom-Teaching, the Guru-devotee relationship in His Blessing Company, the principles and practices of the Way of the Heart,

and life in the community of Da Avabhasa's devotees. It is a comprehensive and engaging introduction to all aspects of the religion of Free Daism, the Liberating Way that Da Avabhasa has made available for all. $16.95 paper

LOVE OF THE GOD-MAN

A COMPREHENSIVE GUIDE TO THE TRADITIONAL AND TIME-HONORED GURU-DEVOTEE RELATIONSHIP, THE SUPREME MEANS OF GOD-REALIZATION, AS FULLY REVEALED FOR THE FIRST TIME BY THE DIVINE WORLD-TEACHER AND TRUE HEART-MASTER, DA AVABHASA (THE "BRIGHT")
by James Steinberg

Love of the God Man is a full-length (over 800-page) discussion of the profound laws and virtues of the Guru-devotee relationship as practiced in the Way of the Heart. Nowhere else in the literature of sacred life does such an encyclopedic treatment of the Guru-devotee relationship exist. *Love of the God-Man* is an inexhaustible resource,

full of Da Avabhasa's Wisdom and His Leelas (inspiring stories) and many stories from the Great Tradition.
Second Edition
(forthcoming)

DIVINE DISTRACTION

A GUIDE TO THE GURU-DEVOTEE RELATIONSHIP, THE SUPREME MEANS OF GOD-REALIZATION, AS FULLY REVEALED FOR THE FIRST TIME BY THE DIVINE WORLD-TEACHER AND TRUE HEART-MASTER, DA AVABHASA (THE "BRIGHT")
by James Steinberg

Presented by a longtime devotee of Da Avabhasa, this shorter version of *Love of the God-Man* describes, illustrates, and extols the Guru-devotee relationship. *Divine Distraction* features compelling stories of Da Avabhasa's Work with His devotees, and illuminating passages from His Wisdom-Teaching, along with instruction and stories from great Masters and disciples in the world's religious and Spiritual traditions.
$12.95 paper

FEELING WITHOUT LIMITATION
*AWAKENING TO THE TRUTH BEYOND
FEAR, SORROW, AND ANGER*
*A Spiritual Discourse by
The Divine World-Teacher
and True Heart-Master,
Da Avabhasa (The "Bright")*

A brief introductory volume featuring a Discourse from Da Avabhasa's Teaching years that presents in simplest terms His fundamental Argument about human suffering, seeking, and freedom. Also includes remarkable Leelas and testimonies by three devotees.
$4.95 paper

THE PERFECT ALTERNATIVE
*A TESTIMONY TO THE POWER OF
THE TRANSFORMING GRACE OF
SRI DA AVABHASA (THE "BRIGHT")*
by Kanya Samatva Suprithi

A gem of a book by one of the most mature practitioners of the Way of the Heart, a woman who has Realized the Transcendental Self (the stage before Divine Self-Realization) through Da Avabhasa's Grace. Kanya Samatva Suprithi presents here a very readable summary of Da Avabhasa's basic Arguments about seeking and Happiness, and she includes some of her own story as a Daist practitioner. An excellent and very concise introduction to Da Avabhasa and His Work.
$4.95 paper

AVADHOOTS, MAD LAMAS, AND FOOLS
by devotees of Da Avabhasa

A brief and lively account of the "Crazy Wisdom" style of sacred Instruction employed by Adepts in many traditions, times, and cultures, including Leelas of Da Avabhasa's Teaching years and His Divine Emergence Work.
(forthcoming)

THE WISDOM-LITERATURE OF DA AVABHASA'S TEACHING WORK

THE KNEE OF LISTENING
*THE EARLY-LIFE ORDEAL AND THE
"RADICAL" SPIRITUAL REALIZATION
OF THE DIVINE WORLD-TEACHER
AND TRUE HEART-MASTER,
DA AVABHASA (THE "BRIGHT")*

In this sublime Autobiography of His early Life, Da Avabhasa tells the sometimes humorous, sometimes poignant, always Profound Story by which He Compassionately took birth in human form to Serve the Liberation of humanity. His early Life is the record of the Divine Being breaking through into mortal time, submitting to human limits, and discovering, in that context, the Great Divine Way whereby all beings may be Liberated. His Story is full of Spiritual and Divine Play, and of very human pains and joys, and the very real process of His Re-Awakening in God.

Following the autobiographical material are two additional sections by Da Avabhasa presenting His earliest Essays on the practice and Realization of "radical" understanding. This new, expanded edition is twice the length of the previously published version, which has become a classic of modern Spiritual literature.
$18.95 paper

ALL NEW!
THE DIVINE EMERGENCE OF THE WORLD-TEACHER, DA AVABHASA (THE "BRIGHT")

In the great history of Spirituality, there appears from time to time an Extraordinary Manifestation of the Divine in human form. Such Divine Masters are

The Wisdom-Literature of Da Avabhasa's Teaching Work

"World-Events", and their own Personal bodily existence is the crucible for a rapid succession of biopsychic crises and transformations that mysteriously hastens the Liberation of all beings. *The Divine Emergence of the World-Teacher, Da Avabhasa (The "Bright")* is the Story of the astonishing changes that have taken place in the Life and Spiritual Work of Da Avabhasa since His Re-Awakening in 1970 to the Condition of absolute God-Consciousness. Told in His own Words, and in the riveting Stories of many of His devotees, this is the most Enlightening Story humanity has ever heard. (forthcoming)

THE METHOD OF THE SIDDHAS
TALKS ON THE SPIRITUAL TECHNIQUE OF THE SAVIORS OF MANKIND

In this book of powerful and often extremely humorous Talks with His devotees in 1972 and 1973, the first year of His formal Teaching Work, Da Avabhasa Reveals the Secret of the Way of Satsang—the profound and transforming relationship between the Sat-Guru and His devotee.
New Standard Edition
$14.95 paper

SCIENTIFIC PROOF OF THE EXISTENCE OF GOD WILL SOON BE ANNOUNCED BY THE WHITE HOUSE!
PROPHETIC WISDOM ABOUT THE MYTHS AND IDOLS OF MASS CULTURE AND POPULAR RELIGIOUS CULTISM, THE NEW PRIESTHOOD OF SCIENTIFIC AND POLITICAL MATERIALISM, AND THE SECRETS OF ENLIGHTENMENT HIDDEN IN THE BODY OF MAN

Speaking as a modern Prophet, Da Avabhasa combines His urgent critique of present-day society with a challenge to create true sacred community based on actual Divine Communion and a Spiritual and Transcendental Vision of human Destiny.
New Standard Edition
(forthcoming)

THE TRANSMISSION OF DOUBT
TALKS AND ESSAYS ON THE TRANSCENDENCE OF SCIENTIFIC MATERIALISM THROUGH "RADICAL" UNDERSTANDING

Da Avabhasa's principal critique of scientific materialism, the dominant philosophy and world-view of modern humanity that suppresses our native impulse to Liberation, and His Revelation of the ancient and ever-new Way that is the true sacred science of Life, or of Divine Being Itself.
New Standard Edition
(forthcoming)

THE ENLIGHTENMENT OF THE WHOLE BODY
A RATIONAL AND NEW PROPHETIC REVELATION OF THE TRUTH OF RELIGION, ESOTERIC SPIRITUALITY, AND THE DIVINE DESTINY OF MAN

One of Da Avabhasa's early Revelations of the Way of Eternal Life that He Offers to beings everywhere, including Ecstatic Confessions of His own Enlightened Realization of the Divine Person, and sublime Instruction in the practices of the Way of the Heart. When initially published in 1978, this Text was a comprehensive summary of His Way of the Heart. Includes a unique section, with illustrations, on the esoteric anatomy of the advanced and the ultimate stages of Spiritual transformation.
New Standard Edition
(forthcoming)

NIRVANASARA

Da Avabhasa critically appraises the sacred Wisdom-Culture of mankind, particularly focusing on the two most sublime traditions of sacred life and practice: Buddhism and Hindu non-dualism (Advaita Vedanta). Here He also announces and expounds upon His own Way of the Heart as the continuation and fulfillment of the most exalted Teachings of Buddhism and Hinduism.
New Standard Edition
(forthcoming)

THE DREADED GOM-BOO, OR THE IMAGINARY DISEASE THAT RELIGION SEEKS TO CURE

In this remarkable book, Da Avabhasa Offers a startling and humorous insight: All religion seeks to cure us of an unreal or fundamentally imaginary disease, which He calls "the Dreaded Gom-Boo". This disease is our constant assumption that we have fallen from Grace and are thus in need of the salvatory "cure" of religious belief.

The good news of Da Avabhasa's Way of the Heart is that we need not seek to be cured but need only feel, observe, understand, and renounce (through the real ordeal of sacred practice) the very activity of seeking itself, and thus be restored to our native Happiness and Freedom.
New Standard Edition
(forthcoming)

CRAZY DA MUST SING, INCLINED TO HIS WEAKER SIDE
CONFESSIONAL POEMS OF LIBERATION AND LOVE

Composed principally in the early 1970s and expressed spontaneously with the ardor of continuous, Divinely Awakened Identification with all beings, these remarkable poems proclaim Da Avabhasa's vulnerable human Love and His Mysterious, "Crazy" passion to Liberate others from ego-bondage.
$9.95 paper

THE SONG OF
THE SELF SUPREME

ASHTAVAKRA GITA
The Classical Text of Atmadvaita
by Ashtavakra

An authoritative translation of the *Ashtavakra Gita*, a text Da Avabhasa has described as "among the greatest (and most senior) communications of all the religious and Spiritual traditions of mankind". His illuminating Preface is a unique commentary on this grand classic of Advaita Vedanta, discussing the *Ashtavakra Gita* in the context of the total Great Tradition of Spiritual and Transcendental Wisdom. Da Avabhasa also identifies and discusses the characteristics of those rare texts and traditions that fully communicate the Realization and "Point of View" of full, or Divine, Enlightenment.
New Standard Edition
(forthcoming)

PRACTICAL TEXTS

Da Avabhasa's teaching is, I believe, unsurpassed by that of any other spiritual Hero, of any period, of any place, of any time, of any persuasion.

KEN WILBER
author, *The Spectrum of Consciousness, Up from Eden,* and *A Sociable God*

THE EATING GORILLA
COMES IN PEACE

THE TRANSCENDENTAL PRINCIPLE OF LIFE APPLIED TO DIET AND THE REGENERATIVE DISCIPLINE OF TRUE HEALTH

In a substantial reworking of the first edition of this Text, Da Avabhasa Offers a practical manual of Divinely Inspired Wisdom about diet, health and healing, and the sacred approach to birthing and dying.
New Standard Edition
(forthcoming)

CONSCIOUS EXERCISE AND THE TRANSCENDENTAL SUN

THE PRINCIPLE OF LOVE APPLIED TO EXERCISE AND THE METHOD OF COMMON PHYSICAL ACTION. A SCIENCE OF WHOLE BODY WISDOM, OR TRUE EMOTION, INTENDED MOST ESPECIALLY FOR THOSE ENGAGED IN RELIGIOUS OR SPIRITUAL LIFE

Conscious exercise is a "technology of love"—which transforms physical exercise, play, and all ordinary activity into an embrace of the infinite energy of the cosmos, always in the conscious context of feeling-Contemplation of Da Avabhasa Himself as Divine Heart-Master. Greatly enlarged and updated from earlier editions.
New Standard Edition
(forthcoming)

LOVE OF THE TWO-ARMED FORM

THE FREE AND REGENERATIVE FUNCTION OF SEXUALITY IN ORDINARY LIFE, AND THE TRANSCENDENCE OF SEXUALITY IN TRUE RELIGIOUS OR SPIRITUAL PRACTICE

Da Avabhasa's Instruction on the cultivation of "true intimacy" and the Realization of truly ecstatic, Spiritualized sexuality—a profound critique of both worldly exploitation of sex and ascetical, anti-sexual religious messages. As an alternative to these errors of West and East, Da Avabhasa proposes the specific practices of sexual "conscious exercise" and "sexual communion" (for sexually active individuals who practice in Satsang with Him). His Enlightened Wisdom-Teaching on emotion and sexuality raises the practice of intimate relationship to a new and compassionate union of love, desire, and Spiritual consciousness.
New Standard Edition
(forthcoming)

EASY DEATH

SPIRITUAL DISCOURSES AND ESSAYS ON THE INHERENT AND ULTIMATE TRANSCENDENCE OF DEATH AND EVERYTHING ELSE

In this major expansion of the popular first edition of His Talks and Essays on death, Da Avabhasa Reveals the esoteric secrets of the death process and Offers a wealth of practical Instruction on how to prepare for a God-Conscious and ecstatic transition from physical embodiment. Elisabeth Kübler-Ross wrote:

An exciting, stimulating, and thought-provoking book that adds immensely to the literature on the phenomena of life and death. Thank you for this masterpiece.

New Standard Edition
$14.95 paper

FOR AND ABOUT CHILDREN

WHAT AND WHERE AND WHO TO REMEMBER TO BE HAPPY

A SIMPLE EXPLANATION OF THE WAY OF THE HEART (FOR CHILDREN, AND EVERYONE ELSE)

A new edition of Da Avabhasa's essential Teaching-Revelation on the religious principles and practices appropriate for children. In Words easily understood and enjoyed by children and adults, Da Avabhasa tells children (and adults) how to "feel and breathe and Behold and Be the Mystery".
New Standard Edition, fully illustrated (forthcoming)

THE TWO SECRETS (yours, AND MINE)

A STORY OF HOW THE WORLD-TEACHER, DA KALKI, GAVE GREAT WISDOM AND BLESSING HELP TO YOUNG PEOPLE (AND EVEN OLDER PEOPLE, TOO) ABOUT HOW TO REMEMBER WHAT AND WHERE AND WHO TO REMEMBER TO BE HAPPY
A Gift (Forever) from Da Kalki (The World-Teacher, Heart-Master Da Love-Ananda), as told by Kanya Remembrance, Brahmacharini Shawnee Free Jones, and their friends

A moving account of a young girl's confrontation with the real demands of sacred practice, and how Da Avabhasa lovingly Instructed and Served her in her transition through a crisis of commitment to practice that every devotee must, at some point, endure.
$12.95 paper

VEGETABLE SURRENDER, OR HAPPINESS IS NOT BLUE

by Heart-Master Da and two little girls

The humorous tale of Onion One-Yin and his vegetable friends, who embark on a search for someone who can teach them about happiness and love, and end up learning a great lesson about seeking. Beautifully illustrated with original line drawings. $12.95 cloth, oversize

LOOK AT THE SUNLIGHT ON THE WATER

EDUCATING CHILDREN FOR A LIFE OF SELF-TRANSCENDING LOVE AND HAPPINESS: AN INTRODUCTION

Full of eminently practical guidance for the "whole bodily" and sacred education of children and young people, this simple, straightforward, informative text is also perhaps the best available brief summation of Da Avabhasa's Wisdom on the first three stages of life, or the period from infancy to adulthood. $12.95 paper

SPECIAL COMMEMORATIVE PHOTOGRAPH ALBUM

DARSHAN OF THE DIVINE WORLD-TEACHER

A TRIBUTE TO SRI DA AVABHASA (THE "BRIGHT")

This book of exquisite full-color photographs celebrates Darshan, or the sighting of the Divine Adept. *Darshan of the Divine World-Teacher* is a large format 8 1/2" x 11" cloth bound album containing 28 full-page photographs of Da Avabhasa taken over the past six years. Each stunning color photograph is accompanied by a passage from His Sacred Literature. This beautiful book communicates the Radiant and Transforming Power of Da Avabhasa's Divine Transmission. Limited edition. $35.00 cloth

PERIODICALS

THE FREE DAIST

*The Bi-Monthly Journal of
the Heart-Word and Blessing Work of
the Divine World-Teacher and
True Heart-Master, Da Avabhasa
(The "Bright")*

The Free Daist chronicles the
Leelas of the Teaching Work and the
Divine Emergence Work of Da
Avabhasa, and describes the practice
and process of devotion, self-discipline,
self-understanding, service, and meditation in the Way of the Heart. In addition, the magazine reports on the cultural and missionary activities of the
Free Daist Communion and the cooperative community of Da Avabhasa's
devotees.

Subscriptions are $42.00 per year
for six issues. Please send your check
or money order (payable to The Dawn
Horse Press) to: The Free Daist, P.O.
Box 3680, Clearlake, CA 95422, USA.

THE "BRIGHT"

*Celebrations of the Divine World-
Teacher, Da Avabhasa (The "Bright")*

A brief bi-monthly periodical, oriented to the general reader, introduc-
ing the Good News of Da Avabhasa
and His Work and countering the
trends of scientific materialism, religious provincialism, and anti-guruism
in present-day society.

Subscriptions are $12.00 per year
for six issues. Please send your check
or money order (payable to The Dawn
Horse Press) to: The "Bright", P.O. Box
3680, Clearlake, CA 95422, USA.

**A subscription to both *The "Bright"*
and *The Free Daist* is only $48.00.**

THE GARDEN OF LIONS
MAGAZINE

*The Worldwide Voice of
Young Free Daists*

This unique magazine is the
voice of the worldwide culture of
children and young people who
practice the Way of the Heart under
the Enlightened Guidance of the living
Sat-Guru, Da Avabhasa. *The Garden of
Lions Magazine* includes published

401

Instruction on various aspects of sacred practice for young people, Discourses Given by Da Avabhasa, personal accounts and inspiring stories from the lives of young devotees, and a great variety of articles and artwork from young people of all ages from all over the world. Themes have included: an introduction to the practice of Brahmacharya (the study of God), the Spiritual practice of Ecstasy and Guru-devotion, and the Enlightened discipline of sexuality for young people.

The Garden of Lions Magazine is a truly extraordinary celebration of the unprecedented Wisdom-Teaching and Way of life Given by Da Avabhasa.

Subscriptions are $16.00 per year for three issues. Please send your check or money order (payable to *The Garden of Lions Magazine*) to: The Garden of Lions Magazine, Subscription Department, P.O. Box 1737, Lower Lake, CA 95457, USA.

THE WAY
OF THE HEART
V I D E O

*On the "Radical" Spiritual Teaching
and Universal Blessing Work of*
THE WORLD-TEACHER,
HEART-MASTER DA LOVE-ANANDA

VIDEOTAPES

THE WAY OF THE HEART
*On the "Radical" Spiritual Teaching
and Universal Blessing Work of
the Western-Born Adept, Heart-Master
Da Love-Ananda*

Incorporating rare historical footage, Part One tells the Story of Da Avabhasa's Illumined Birth and His Ordeal of Divine Re-Awakening for the sake of others, and celebrates the Emergence of His Work of World Blessing. Part Two (which includes Talk excerpts by Da Avabhasa and testimonials by longtime practitioners) describes the Gifts and forms of practice that are Given to all who take up the Way of the Heart as Da Avabhasa's devotees. Part Three introduces the sacred culture of the Way of the Heart.
$29.95, 2 hours
VHS, NTSC, or PAL format

The Way of the Heart is also available in a modified form, which includes footage of Da Avabhasa in Darshan with devotees and other material not included in the full-length version. A brief, summary audiovisual introduction to His Life and Divine Work as the World-Teacher in a world addicted to egoic suffering and seeking.
$19.95, 76 minutes
VHS, NTSC or PAL format

402

ORDERING THE BOOKS
AND VIDEOTAPES
OF DA AVABHASA

The books and videotapes of Da Avabhasa are available at local bookstores and by mail from the Dawn Horse Book Depot.

Please write to us at the address below for a complete catalogue of books and audiovisual publications on the Way of the Heart and traditional sacred literature.

In the USA please add $3.50 for the first book or videotape ($5.00 for each *Dawn Horse Testament*) and $1.50 for each additional book or videotape. California residents add 7 1/4% sales tax.

Outside the USA please add $5.00 for the first book or videotape ($6.00 for each *Dawn Horse Testament*) and $2.00 for each additional book or videotape.

To order the books and videotapes listed above, and to receive your copy of the Dawn Horse Press Catalogue, please write:

THE DAWN HORSE BOOK DEPOT
P.O. Box 3680
Clearlake, CA 95422, USA
(707) 928-4936

bone, analogy of dog and, 149, 151
books, of Da Avabhasa, 390-403
born-again Christians, 54
Brahman
    defined, 359
    as formless Divine Reality, 33, 212
brahmin, 59
    defined, 353
brain
    as distinct from the "One Mind", 28
    thought process and, 39
    See also mind; thought
breath, and vital health, 94-95
"Bright"
    defined, 358
    described, 368
"Brightness", of one who lives Truth, 146
Buddha, Gautama, 254, 261, 267
Buddhism
    burning of traditional images of the
        Buddha, 66
    three forms of resort in, 216
Buddhist community, conditions for life in,
    267

C

cat, and vital forces of life, 143
causal being
    activity of identification and, 105
    as analogous to deep sleep state, 247
    as epitome of conditional existence, 145-46
    located in the heart on the right, 105, 145-46,
        240, 289, 333
    phenomena of, 243
causal dimension, defined, 354
causal path, Divine Force in, 248
celibacy
    Eastern and Western views on, 125
    impotence as form of artificial, 124
    natural form of, 125, 127
    as spiritual seeking, 70, 90
    in the Way of the Heart, 355, 381
    as Yogic death, 128
    See also emotional-sexual relationship
certainty, in Guru-disciple relationship, 330
chakras
    ascending current and, 238
    defined, 355
    described, 38
    opening of, 116
    subtle path and, 247
    Truth is not found in, 86-87
chaplain, Da Avabhasa's function in mental
    hospital as, 144
charlatans, claiming to be Gurus, 131-32

Christianity
    Holy Spirit and, 247
    salvation experience in, 54
Christians, born-again, 54
cities, bondage to the cycles of earth and, 82
coincidence, of internal and external
        experience, 276-77
community of devotees
    Buddhist, 267
    need for money in, 70
    Satsang as continuous in, 316
    spiritual activity and, 217
    subtle forces in, 325
    value of, 37, 216-17
    See also Ashram
conceptualization, as obstruction, 34
conductivity
    as circle of descending and ascending
        force, 109, 240, 242
    in emotional-sexual intimacy, 90
    failure of, 189
    health and, 92-93
    natural direction of, 144
    opening of the chakras and, 116-17
    Satsang and, 189-91
    sexual forces and, 98-99
    of vital force, 92-93, 129, 264
    vital shock and, 112
    See also ascending current; descending
        power
conflict, as crisis in relationship to Guru, 148
consciousness
    cycles in, 274-75
    natural state of, 141-42
Consciousness (Itself), 25
    assumption of separateness in, 173
    as "center" of Satsang, 57
    center or epitome of, 242
    the Heart as, 33
    realization of, 146
    Truth as, 295
    See also Satsang; Truth
"consideration", Da Avabhasa's method of,
    366
consolation
    depends on one being asleep, 179
    motivation of seeker as, 151
contemplation of the Guru
    as fundamental form of Satsang, 345-46
    See also meditation; real meditation
contraction
    "creation" of, 25
    "creation" of form and, 39
    doubt as, 215
    the foundation of all dramas as, 64
    from the Guru, 315

knots in the body-mind as, 38
and motive to expand the mind, 159
release of, 213
Satsang and, 113
"targeting" mechanism as, 221
is uncaused, 102-3
vital shock as, 110
See also avoidance of relationship; ego;
  separateness; suffering
contradiction. *See* dilemma
copyright, perpetual, 386-87
cosmos, described, 334
"Crazy"
  individuals in traditional cultures, 135
  Teaching Work of Da Avabhasa, 12
"creativity"
  universal, 259
  as viewpoint of Satsang, 260
crisis
  as Guru's "creation", 311
  importance of, 210-11
  questions as distraction from, 287-88
  in relationship to Guru, 148-49, 228
  right use of, 211
  of self-doubt, 148, 228
  spiritual life as, 210, 226
  of understanding, 39-40
critic, Guru as, 311-12
cult, ritual of, 57
cultic "guru", description of, 213
cultism, criticism of, 312
cycles, in consciousness, 274-75

D

"Da", Name defined, 367
Da Avabhasa
  "Always meditate on me", 349
  awareness of Divine Form from birth, 343,
    363-64
  birth of, 5, 363
  as chaplain in a mental hospital, 144
  contacts devotees at "seat of the Guru",
    336-38
  contemplation of, 345-47
  demonstrates full circle of life, 335
  determination to regain Divine Freedom, 364
  Divine Emergence of, 14-16, 367
  as Divine World-Teacher, 23, 368
  as Form of Amrita Nadi, 329, 334, 345-46
  Goddess and, 365
  gospel of, 327, 328-30
  Great Re-Awakening of, 41, 180, 365
  Gurus of, 343
  human form of, 270, 345-46, 379
  meditation of others by, 8-9, 268, 366
  Swami Muktananda and, 365

Name defined, 367
Swami Nityananda and, 365
"point of view" on suffering of, 131
remembrance of, 340
Rudi and, 71-72, 365
sacred literature of, 390-403
seahorse experience of, 111
suppression of blissfulness in, 266
Teachers of, 343
Teaching Work of, 11-14, 366-67
transformation of devotee's karmas by, 263
and Way of the Siddhas, 16, 23
weeping in Satsang occasions by, 262-63
Wisdom-Teaching of, 10
Da Avabhasa Gurukula Kanyadana Kumari
  Order, described, 381
Da Avabhasa International, forms of
  involvement in, 375
"Da Free John", as former Name of Da
  Avabhasa, 367
dark night, as death of the ego, 53-54
"Dead Gurus can't kick ass!", 227
"dead movie star", infatuation with, 340, 341
death
  awakening from the dream and, 178
  destiny of Narcissus as, 72
  of ego, 53-54, 60-61, 134, 254, 302
  gorilla as symbol for, 177
  of Guru, 324
  Guru-devotee relationship continues
    beyond, 337-38
  humor and, 209
  loss of face as, 177
  questions as distraction from, 287-88
  as reaction to life, 132, 159
  reincarnation and, 121-22
  Sahaj Samadhi as, 134
  summation of life as, 40
  threat of, 256
  in Truth, 133
deep sleep, causal being as seat of, 105
  See also causal being; dream state; waking
    state
descended Master. *See* Great Siddha
descending life, as vital life, 109
descending power
  in "front" of the body, 333
  as "Power of God", 190
  purifying force of, 240
  Satsang and, 191
  solar plexus and, 238
  See also ascending current; conductivity
desire
  as adventure of seeking, 81, 105
  as dilemma, 106
  impulses as, 203

destiny
  effect of Satsang on, 260
  non-necessity of, 183
  prophets and, 312
  of Self-realized being, 122
devotee
  defined, 353
  sadhana of beginning and mature, 335
  See also disciple
devotion
  contemplation of Guru as, 345-46
  fruit of discipleship as, 347
  quickening of one's sadhana through, 315
  right approach to one's Guru as, 76
  Satsang and, 324
dhyan, 205
diet
  intelligent use of, 88, 91, 94
  Satsang and, 233, 294
  as seeking, 84, 88-89, 91
  sex-desire and, 89
  spiritual life and, 82, 84
  in Way of the Heart, 355
  See also fasting; health
difference, sameness and, 302
differentiation
  conceptualized world as, 81, 203
  mind as, 104
  subtle body and, 105
dilemma
  assumption of, 169-72
  beauty and, 206
  defined, 170-71
  desire and, 106
  karmic condition as sense of, 348
  origin of sense of, 106
  questions as, 285-88
  Satsang and, 292
  thought as, 206
  understanding of, 25-26, 172
disciple
  defined, 353
  relationship to the Guru, 58, 65, 213-14, 339-41
  sadhana of, 346-47
  See also devotee
discomfort, spiritual life and, 210
Divine Emergence of Da Avabhasa, 14-16, 367
Divine Goddess, Da Avabhasa as Devotee of, 365
Divine humor, mortal humor and, 142-43
Divine Self
  doubt of, 215
  freedom of, 60
  humor of, 255
  knowing or cognizing of, 52

  as not separate from the world, 63
  origin of every person as, 225
  as prior to states of waking, dreaming, and deep sleep, 62
Divine Self-realization. *See* Self-realization
Divine Siddhi, of the Guru, 316
Divine Vision, 149
Divine World-Teacher
  Da Avabhasa as, 23
  defined, 368
Divinity, human being in likeness of, 333
dog
  and bone, 149, 151
  costume, 143, 145, 157
  Guru as barking, 163
  metaphor of walking the, 123, 142
  as symbol of vital forces of life, 143
  See also vital life
Donald Duck, 117
doubt, vital contraction as, 215
"dream" (of life)
  as analogy for usual waking state, 175, 288
  appearance of Guru within, 163
  conditional existence as, 160-61, 164, 183
  gorilla appearing within, 176-77, 180
  Guru as awake within, 161-62
  sensitivity to Guru in, 181
  usual Yoga and, 180
dream state
  experiences in, 122, 174-75
  Satsang and phenomena in, 242-43
  subtle body as seat of, 105
  See also deep sleep; waking state
dreams
  as intelligent process, 276
  purification of karmas in, 227
  significance of, 220
drugs
  effect on body-mind, 83, 91
  mind-expansion and, 159
  spiritual life and, 83

E

earth
  liberation from natural cycles of, 82-83
  as realm of Divine Consciousness, 102
ego
  as an activity, 39, 42-43, 277
  cultic nature of, 57
  death of, 53-54, 60-61, 134, 254, 302
  as fear, 277-78
  as identification, 104
  as "target" of all experience, 221
  See also avoidance of relationship; contraction; separateness; suffering
Eleutherian Mission, events by, 372

elevator, Guru as analogous to, 64
emotional-sexual relationship
  celibacy and, 125, 127
  as circle of life-force, 90
  compatibility with Satsang, 96-98
  as primary ascetic practice, 126
  right orientation to, 99
  as sacrifice, 84-85
  as Siva-Shakti, 100
  See also celibacy; relationship; sex
enlightenment
  as consciously living the condition of
    Reality, 173-74
  of Da Avabhasa, 41
  process of growth and, 303
  See also Self-realization
enquiry
  end of in Truth, 165
  is founded in Satsang, 229, 313
  process of, 204
  as rooted in prior understanding, 44-45
  See also re-cognition
entertainment, spiritual seeking as, 65-66
evolution
  discussed, 47-48
  question about, 285-88
exercise, importance of, 94
extraordinariness, as alternative to Satsang,
  87, 293-94

F

face, loss of
  in death, 177
  in relation to Guru, 315
faith
  Satsang and, 211, 214-15
  understanding and, 212, 214
fasting judicious use of, 88
  as preparation for descent of Grace, 248
  as spiritual seeking, 92
  until death, 71
  See also diet
fear
  ego as, 277-78
  ordinary state as, 209
feeling-Contemplation
  aids to, 377
  importance of, 379
fist, analogy of. *See* hand
food. *See* diet
foolishness, in relation to the Guru, 316
force of life. *See* life-force
Form of Reality. *See* Amrita Nadi
"fourth state"
  beyond waking, dreaming, and deep
    sleep, 62-63, 182, 240, 243
  See also turiya; turiyatita

Free Daism culture of, 382
  the Sacred Treasures of, 387-88
Free Daist Communion
  formal practice in, 377
  Regional Centers of, 383
Free Renunciate Order, 381
free will, 47
Friend, of Da Avabhasa International, 375
friendships. *See* associations
Fullness, God stands present as, 327
functional life
  as beginning of spiritual life, 69, 72
  conditions for Satsang and, 82, 232-33, 273
  as first gift to one's Guru, 77
  requirement of, 58
  traditional demand for in monasteries,
    74-75
  See also vital life
future, fluid nature of, 260

G

Ganeshpuri, 345
gifts, as symbols of true gift, 76-77
girlie magazine, metaphor for spiritual
  seeking, 65-66
God
  coolness in relation to, 314
  "creating" functions for, 336
  deliberate waiting for, 61
  as name of Source of descending energy,
    239
  prior Fullness of, 326-27
  stands always Present as the Heart, Light,
    and Fullness, 327
Goddess, Da Avabhasa as Devotee of, 365
God-union, and living Presence of God, 61
God-World, as domain of un-"created" Light,
  334
gopis and Krishna, traditional story of, 6
gorilla
  as death, 177
  in dream, 174-76, 180
gospel (of Da Avabhasa), 327, 328-30
grace
  and opening of "seat of the Guru", 336-38
  Satsang as, 226
Great Re-Awakening of Da Avabhasa,
  described, 41, 180, 365
Great Siddha
  being that one's "own", 333
  function of, 332
  as Heaven-born one, 331
  See also Guru; Siddha-Guru; Siddhas
gross dimension, defined, 354
growth, enlightenment and process of, 303

Guru
  action in relation to, 153-54
  avoidance of relationship with, 200-201, 291
  Avon Lady analogy and, 67
  charlatans claiming to be, 131-32
  choice of, 306-7
  as constant wakening sound, 163
  contemplation of, 345-46
  coolness in relation to, 314
  criticism of, 309-12, 325
  cultic versus true form of, 213-14
  "Dead Gurus can't kick ass!", 227
  death of, 324
  defined, 358
  does not take seeker "seriously", 184-85
  is like an elevator, 64
  as "fourth state" beyond waking, dreaming,
    and sleeping, 182
  function of, 58, 144-45, 279-80, 306, 316
  as fundamental Condition of spiritual life,
    202
  gifts given to, 76-77
  grace of, 313
  as human form of Truth, 227, 279-80
  influence after death of, 130
  intensification of fear in company of, 279
  lifetime of, 324
  as "light over against darkness", 344
  "like the sunlight in the morning", 162,
    176, 181-82, 185
  mastery over sex-impulse, 125
  offends the search, 168
  as one awake within the dream, 161-62,
    176, 179
  is not an "other", 301
  as paradox, 59
  pleasing of, 313
  as prophet, 309-12
  public function of, 309-10
  relationship to as great principle of
    sadhana, 293, 312
  relationship to disciples, 213-14
  resistance to, 348
  reveals himself or herself a piece at a
    time, 339
  salvatory function of God through, 324
  "seat" of, 336-38
  thinking of, 341-42
  and three paths, 249
  two forms of crisis in relationship to, 148-49
  undermines the disciple, 152
  unpredictability of, 252-53, 255-56, 310
  as water where Narcissus is reflected, 81
  See also Great Siddha; Siddha-Guru; Siddhas
Guru-bhakti, 345
  defined, 360

Guru-devotee relationship
  enjoyment of, 65
  as prior to life, 337
  as relationship between lovers, 339-41
  right approach to, 76-77
  as Satsang, 58
  in the Way of the Heart, 10
  See also teacher-disciple relationship
Guru-devotion, tradition of, 377
Guru-kripa, 252, 329
  defined, 359

H

hallucinogenic drugs, spiritual life and, 83
hand
  metaphor of fist as the ego, 111, 223, 234
  metaphor of opening, 120
  vital center likened to, 110
happiness
  "point of view" of Truth and, 266
  in relation to the Guru, 313-16
Hatha Yoga, 246
  defined, 359
health
  and conductivity, 92-93
  responsibility for, 94-95
  See also diet
Heart
  Consciousness as, 33
  defined, 351
  Divine madness as, 41
  as "foot" of Amrita Nadi, 205
  as foundation for human life, 60
  God stands present as, 327
  Great Siddhas and, 27
  mystery of "how the Heart lives in the
    world", 253
  pipe-smoking philosopher is not the
    intelligence of, 66
  as place where Guru contacts devotee,
    337-38
  "point of view" of, 290
  relationship between man and woman
    and, 100
  as source of all Light and life, 242
  as un-"created" Reality, 328
  as unqualified Reality, 289
  as unqualified relationship, 26-27
  See also Amrita Nadi; Light
heart, three stations of, 240
Hebrew men of knowledge, suppression of
  the vital and, 124
Hinduism, abandonment of vital and subtle
  life and, 125
Holy Spirit, Christianity and, 247
hopelessness, of seeking, 50

Kundalini *(continued)*
    effectiveness of, 196
    and Work of Da Avabhasa, 326

L

"lake in the country", analogy of, 206-7
laughter, as rejection of life-force, 189, 191-92, 264
Lay Congregationist Order, 380
Lay Renunciate Order, 380-81
Leela, of Siddha-Guru, 256
Leelas (by devotees)
    becoming devotee of Da Avabhasa, 373
    broken ribs, 13
    first formal Prasad Day, 321-22
    hugging Sri Da Avabhasa, 7-8
    Montezuma's revenge, 11-12
    retreat at Sri Love-Anandashram, 16-18
liberation
    described, 35
    no dilemma as, 50
    opening of three primary knots as, 246
    re-cognition of causal being as, 146
life
    cannot be perfectly abandoned, 334-35
    as spiritual event, 261
    wisdom and great moments in, 296
    See also functional life; vital life
life-conditions, for living in Satsang, 156
life-force
    center of, 242
    conservation of, 264
    exploitation of, 128-29
    humor and, 143-44
    rejection of, 189, 191-92, 264
Light
    "creating" functions for, 336
    descending and ascending course of, 238, 242
    as gift from the Guru, 329-30
    God stands present as, 327
    intensification of in devotees, 329, 336
    as reflection of the Heart, 242
    unmanifested realm of, 331, 334
    See also Amrita Nadi; Heart
literature, of the Way of the Heart, 390-403
"Living Murtis", described, 381
loka
    defined, 355
    of the Siddhas, 116
    is not Truth, 86-87
Lord Yama, 60, 353
loss of face. *See* face, loss of
love
    God as, 54
    relationship as, 33

Love of the Two-Armed Form, 366
"Love-Ananda", as Name of Da Avabhasa, 367
lovers, relationship between as analogous to Guru-devotee relationship, 339-41

M

Maharshi, Ramana. *See* Ramana Maharshi
mahasamadhi
    defined, 357
    of Saint Jnaneshwar, 129
man and woman, relationship between, 100
"man in the middle", ritual of, 57
man of understanding, awakening function and, 179
mantra, as form of Satsang with Guru, 305
marijuana, effect on body-mind, 91
mature devotee, 348-49
maya, 212
    defined, 359
meditation
    Guru as condition for, 343
    of others by Da Avabhasa, 8-9, 268, 366
    as Satsang, 76
    as sitting with the Guru, 65
    as understanding of your own activity, 43-44
    usual form of, 196
    See also real meditation
mediums, ordinariness of, 259
Melrose Avenue Ashram, opening of, 9, 23, 366
memory, vital shock and, 111, 114-15
mental hospital, Da Avabhasa as chaplain in, 144
mere Presence, 325
midbrain, as an epitome of subtle center of ascent, 333
mind
    Bodhidharma story about, 34
    communication of, 188
    dissolving of in the Heart, 336-37
    expansion of, 159-60
    illusory nature of, 34-35, 42
    "One Mind", 28
    questions and, 287
    re-cognition of as contraction, 145
    religious symbology and, 53
    Satsang as prior to, 271
    as suffering, 117
    See also thought
miracle, Satsang as, 226
moksha, 146
    defined, 358
monasteries, and traditional demand to function, 74-75

money
    responsibility for one's own survival and,
        83
    Satsang and, 233
    spiritual life and, 70-71
    See also work
money, food, and sex
    as fundamental life-dilemma, 97
    relationship and, 73-74
Montezuma's revenge story, 11-12
Mother Shakti
    descent of, 248
    many forms of, 243-44
    See also Shakti
Muktananda, Swami (Baba)
    Da Avabhasa as Devotee of, 365
    life-summary of, 357
    relationship to Swami Nityananda, 344-45
    role in his own Ashram, 136
    Satsang as fundamental method of, 305
    subtle influence of, 130
mukti, 146
    defined, 358
muladhar, 128
    defined, 357
Murti, defined, 381
mythology, about suffering, 280

N

nadas, 246
    defined, 359
Narcissus
    and analogy of pinching oneself, 81
    cult of, 312
    defined, 354
    as the destiny of unconsciousness, 72
    illusion of, 224
    path of, 325-26
    Satsang and, 113, 147, 149
    as symbol of suffering, 80
natural cycles of the earth, liberation from, 82
navel
    knot associated with, 246
    purification of, 240
    See also solar plexus; vital center
New Testament
    "Everything works together for the good
        of those who love God", 276
    "I stand at the door and knock", 338
    torture of Jesus described in, 57
"Nirvana and samsara are the same", 62
Nityananda, Swami
    Da Avabhasa as Devotee of, 365
    life-summary of, 357
    relationship with Swami Muktananda,
        344-45
    role in his own Ashram, 135-36

Satsang as fundamental method of, 305-6
    subtle influence of, 130
niyama and yama, defined, 78

O

observation, process of, 197-98
occult sciences
    as distraction from Satsang, 339
    limitations of, 260-61, 312
Old Testament, "human being is made in
    likeness of Divinity", 333
"Om Mani Padme Hum"
    defined, 359
    as object of meditation, 206
"One Mind", as distinct from the brain, 28
one-pointedness, and "creation" of separate
    self sense, 224
ordinariness
    as appropriate condition for Satsang,
        87-88, 305
    conductivity and, 264
    difficulty for human beings to achieve,
        293-94
    as the only extraordinary, 67
    resistance to, 85-86
    and Truth, 86-87
orgasm
    degenerative and regenerative, 90
    as form of release, 127
    as instrument of procreation, 89

P

Paradise, discussion of, 115-16
Paramatman, defined, 62
Patanjali, 78
    life-summary of, 354
paths, falsity of, 310
perception, headphones analogy and, 220-21
The Perennial Philosophy, 363
perpetual copyright, 386-87
philosophers, hopefulness of teachings of,
    176
physical life. *See* vital life
pinching oneself, as analogy for suffering,
    81, 103
pipe-smoking philosopher, is not intelligence
    of the Heart, 66
plants, relationship to the vital and, 123
pleasing the Guru, 313
pornography, analogy of "spiritual" seeking
    and, 65-66
"Power of God", as descending power, 190
practical conditions, 156
practical life. *See* functional life
practice. *See* sadhana
prana
    defined, 239, 355
    people who only lived on, 92

413

prana-shakti, 245
pranayama
  automatic, 239, 246
  defined, 359
Prasad
  acceptance of Guru's, 330
  blessing Power in, 329
  defined, 321, 360
Prayer, descent of Shakti Power and, 248
Presence of God, God-union and, 61
prophet
  as critic, 311-12
  as function of Guru in the world, 309-12
psyche, the world as, 276
psychics
  as distinct from prophets, 311
  limitations of, 260
  ordinariness of, 259
psychism, as distraction from Satsang, 339

Q
questions
  as distraction from death, 287
  as entertainment, 298
  as forms of dilemma, 286-87
  reflect state person is in, 292

R
"radical", 115
  defined, 351
"radical" understanding
  described, 24-25, 197
  faith and, 214
  function of true Guru and, 327
  Sahaj Samadhi as, 205
  Truth and, 296
  See also understanding
Ram
  defined, 359
  name of, 206
Ramakrishna, 74
Ramana Maharshi
  body-idea as root of suffering, 167
  causal path and, 247
  death of, 209
  jnana tradition and, 240
  life-summary of, 352
  method of enquiry of, 42, 56
  on retiring to the forest, 123
  role in his own Ashram, 136
  Satsang as fundamental method of, 305-6
  as somebody asleep while awake, 134
  on states after death, 261
  subtle influence of, 130
reaction, as sign of life, 281

real meditation
  is not unlike death, 134, 145
  is a fire, 199
  as present enjoyment of Reality, 182
  Satsang and, 203
  See also meditation
Reality
  Satsang as Condition of, 290
  singleness of, 173
  understanding as, 166-67
realization, as state prior to suffering, 52
Re-Awakening of Da Avabhasa, described,
  41, 180, 365
rebirth, in animal form, 122
re-cognition
  defined, 351
  description of, 103-4, 166
  and discovery one is pinching oneself, 81
  as key to spiritual life, 119
  as obviation of ego, 278
  of separate self sense, 204-5, 221
  of suffering, 51, 192
  takes place at every level, 121
  as understanding, 24
  See also enquiry
reincarnation, 121-22
relationship
  as always already the case, 26, 141, 166, 193
  association and, 187-93, 340-41
  best circumstance for spiritual practice as,
    126
  condition of everything as, 139-40
  "creation" of failure in, 118
  desire and, 187-88
  with Guru is prior to life, 337
  as love, 33
  money, food, and sex and, 73-74, 97
  as primary law of the cosmos, 113
  responsibility inherent in, 193
  as sacrifice, 84-85
  Siva-Shakti as nature of, 100
  transference of life as, 263
  true form of described, 340-41
  understanding and turning to, 154-55
  See also associations; avoidance of
    relationship; emotional-sexual
    relationship; Guru-devotee relationship
religion
  descent of the Shakti and, 247-48
  described, 35
  life-purification and, 247
  resistance to organized form of, 217
religious experience, nature of, 55
religious life. See spiritual life
religious traditions, limited viewpoints of, 265
repression, 231-32, 233-34

retreats, at Sri Love-Anandashram, 379
right side of the heart
    defined, 356
    as location of causal being, 105, 145-46,
        240, 289
Rishis
    defined, 357
    sexual activity and, 125
romantic attachment, analogy with Guru-
        devotee relationship, 340-41
"round dance"
    ancient ritual of, 57
    as circuit of the life-force, 240
Rudi (Swami Rudrananda)
    Da Avabhasa as devotee of, 365
    Da Avabhasa's sadhana of work with,
        71-72
life-summary of, 354

S

sacrifice, life as, 84-85
"sacrifice of Christ", death of Jesus as, 57
sadhana
    appropriateness of, 153
    of beginning and mature devotee, 335
    concern about one's tendencies and, 234
    as crisis, 148
    Da Avabhasa's "creation" of in devotees,
        328-29
    defined, 352
    maturity in, 347-48
    ordinary life and, 86
    progression of, 249
    requirement of, 73
    resistance to, 183-84
    Satsang as, 195, 270
    See also Satsang; spiritual life
Sage, cycles of consciousness in, 275
Sahaj Samadhi
    as death of limitation as the body, 134
    defined, 356
    nature of, 118
sahasrar
    defined, 356
    as primary center of subtle activity, 238
    as "thousand petalled lotus", 247
    Truth and return to, 295
Sai Baba of Shirdi
    life-summary of, 357
    subtle influence of, 130
Saint, cycles of consciousness in, 275
salvation, nature of, 55
samadhi, 117-18
    defined, 356
    Truth and, 295
samadhi site, of one's Guru, 129

sameness, difference and, 302
samsara
    defined, 353
    same as Nirvana, 62
Sangha. See community of devotees
Satsang
    as anti-cultic process, 57
    appropriateness of, 153
    availability to all beings, 56, 77
    as best thing one can do, 92, 164, 306
    as "body" of understanding, 347
    Company and conditions of Siddha-Guru
        as, 45
    Condition of one's life as, 150, 195, 200, 270
    Condition of reality as, 290, 337
    conditions for, 266
    conductivity and, 189-91
    conformation to, 85, 228, 232-33
    conscious living of, 269-70
    contemplation of Guru as fundamental
        form of, 345-46
    "creative" viewpoint of, 260
    crises in relationship to the Guru and,
        148-49, 228
    cycles of consciousness and, 274-75
    death of Guru and, 324
    defined, 352
    is a demand, 75
    destiny and, 260
    dilemma and, 292
    as dream wherein Guru appears, 161
    enjoyment of, 156-57, 202, 316
    faith and, 211-12, 214-15
    fear and, 278
    is a fire, 279
    as functional relationship, 82, 87, 273
    as grace, 226, 228, 273, 291 human form
        of Da Avabhasa and, 270
    humor of the Guru and, 135
    life-conditions and, 156
    as lifetime commitment, 300
    listening and, 119
    loss of face and, 315
    is not magical, 226-27
    as mere Presence, 325
    as "Method of the Great Siddhas", 255
    obsolescence of patterns through, 289-90
    as offense to Narcissus, 113, 151
    ordinariness of, 87, 293-94
    as perfect relationship, 338
    phenomenon produced by Force of, 155,
        220, 226, 239-40
    physical proximity to Da Avabhasa and,
        237
    practical foundation of, 232-33
    as prior to the mind, 271

415

death of, 129
defined, 351
description of Great Siddhas, 27
lokas of, 116
the method of, 1
traditional relationship to, 5
word of the, 298
Yogic energy of, 128
See also Guru; Great Siddha; Siddha-Guru
Siddha-Yogi, result of contact with, 245
Siddhi, of the Guru, 316, 325
siddhi (conditional), 325, 327
defined, 351
simultaneity, of internal and external
experience, 276-77
Siva
defined, 355
as destroyer, 255
as man's relationship to his wife, 100
Siva-Shakti, as nature of all relationships, 100
sleep
determining right amount of, 94
passing into one's intuited Nature during,
174
solar plexus
as center of all human activity, 238
as epitome of vital center, 333
"soldier on the march", analogy of, 210
speech
function of in Satsang, 276
as obstruction, 271
as sacrifice, 84, 128
Spirit, defined, 239
spiritual community. See community of
devotees
"spiritual death"
in Christian religion, 35
as death of the ego, 53-54
spiritual life
as conscious life, 195
crisis and, 210, 226
diet and, 82, 84
drugs and, 83
engaged as entertainment, 298
engaged as extension of seeking, 112-13
fear and, 277-78
grace of the Guru and, 313
money and, 70-71
preparation for, 156
resistance to vital life and, 69-70
responsibility for vital life in, 92-96
Shakti and, 195-96
traditional course of, 239
true nature of, 73-76
as understanding of one's own suffering, 50
vital shock and, 112

world as alternative to, 202
See also sadhana; Satsang
spiritual phenomena, fascination with, 117
Spiritual practice. See sadhana
spiritual traditions, limited viewpoints of,
253-54, 265
spirituality
purification of, 310
resistance to organized form of, 217
as understanding process of motivation, 39
Sri Love-Anandashram, retreats at, 379
"Straightener", ordinary world as, 267
striving, as duty, 303
student-novice, of the Way of the Heart,
375, 377
study, of Da Avabhasa's Instruction, 10, 375
subtle body
activity of differentiation and, 105
chakras and, 247
epitome of, 242
purification of, 245
sahasrar and, 242, 246-47
subtle dimension, defined, 354
subtle forces, community of devotees and,
325
subtle life
as ascending life, 109
ascent of Shakti and, 248
phenomena of, 243
subtle processes, concern for, 326
suffering
availability for Satsang and, 152, 168, 298
avoidance of relationship and, 119-21
basic content of one's consciousness as, 49
"creation" myth about, 280, 299
as functional disorder, 86
life-dilemma and, 102
Narcissus as symbol of, 80
nature of, 32, 80
as own activity, 51, 114-15, 272, 280
and "point of view" of Truth, 131
present activity as, 299
re-cognition of, 51
seeking as attempt to get free of, 50, 103,
167
the "Straightener" and, 267
understanding and, 33
See also avoidance of relationship;
contraction; ego; separateness
suicide, 61
sunlight in the morning, Guru as, 162, 176,
181-82, 185
sunlight over the well, analogy of, 225
suppression, 231-32, 233-34
survival, personal responsibility for, 83
"swami" idealism, as resistance to vitality, 124

T

"tamas"
  defined, 353
  earliest period of sadhana and, 69, 74
  karmas and, 260
  limited mind as, 256
  Satsang and, 260
Tantric, 70
  defined, 353-54
Tao, 202
  defined, 358
target, "creation" of ego as, 221-24
teacher-disciple relationship
  described, 36
  See also Guru-devotee relationship
Teachers
  of Da Avabhasa, 343
  of experience, 331
Teaching (of Da Avabhasa)
  functional confrontation with, 217
  "point of view" of, 331
  response to, 337
  is simple, 327
  study of, 10, 375
Teaching Work of Da Avabhasa, 13-14,
    366-67
techniques, of seeking, 293
tendencies
  concern about, 234
  fascination with, 296
  revelation of in Satsang, 232
thought
  about the Guru, 341
  brain and, 39
  as contraction, 145
  observation of, 206
  as obstruction, 38-39
  as pain, 170
  Satsang as prior to, 271
  See also mind
throat, as subtle center of ascent, 333
tithing member, of Da Avabhasa International,
    375
traditions of spiritual practice, 253-54, 265
Truth
  alternatives to, 295, 297
  as always already the case, 102
  cannot be attained, 164
  as Condition of spiritual life, 202
  "creating" functions for, 336
  "creative" realization of, 261
  crisis and, 298
  death in, 133
  "everything combines for the sake of", 276
  is not an experience, 294

as gift from the Guru, 329
happiness as "mood" of, 279
living form of, 227
mind expansion and, 159-60
is not an object, 294-95
and ordinary life, 86-87
as perfect food, 92
"point of view" of, 248, 255, 262, 331
"point of view" on suffering of, 131
as prior to all experience, 55
purifying function of, 131-32
re-cognition and, 281, 290
relational conditions and, 217
relationship to the Guru as, 185
restoration in as "second birth", 189
"is resurrected from the ground up", 72
as Siva-Shakti, 244
uncertainty and, 330
as waking state is to dreaming state, 160-61
is not within, 277
world as alternative to, 202
turiya, 105, 240-41, 243
  defined, 356
  Satsang and, 278
  as witness, 249
turiyatita, 105
  as Amrita Nadi, 249
  communication of Satsang as, 243
defined, 356

U

uncertainty, usefulness of, 330
understanding
  of dilemma, 25-26, 172
  is not dramatic, 180
  fearlessness of, 278
  as "mind" of Satsang, 347
  ordinariness of, 281
  Reality as, 166-67
  re-cognition of one's own activity as, 24
  religious quality of, 145
  Satsang as means of, 229
  self-observation and, 141, 197-98
  state prior to suffering as, 52
  suffering and, 33
  "Turn to me and understand", 330
  turning to relationship and, 154
  waking force of Guru as, 176
  "is to the waking state what the waking
    state is to the dream", 175
  See also "radical" understanding
union, as nature of all relationship, 100
Upanishads, 277
Upasani Baba, prophesy of, 2-3

V

vacations, and suffering, 206-8
Vedanta Temple Event
  as beginning of Da Avabhasa's Work, 5, 8
  described, 4, 365
visions
  as forms of contraction, 230
  ordinariness of, 67
  unimportance of, 73
vital center
  as center of waking consciousness, 333
  is like your hand, 110
  knot associated with, 247
  maintaining strength in, 92
  movement of attention out of, 145
vital force. *See* life-force
vital life
  as descending life, 109
  Eastern and Western view of, 125-26
  humor and, 143-44
  moderation of, 95-96
  relationship to animals and plants and, 123
  requirement for, 58
  spiritual life and, 69, 92, 96
  suppression of, 124
  See also functional life
vital shock
  birth and, 111
  conductivity and, 112
  described, 95
  feeling of, 109
  origin of, 110-11
  Satsang and, 113-14
  self-indulgence and, 96
  suppression of vital life and, 124
vitamins, and body chemistry, 94

W

waking. *See* awakening
waking, dreaming, and deep sleep, as three
  conditional states, 62
waking state
  compared to dream state, 175, 288
  Satsang and phenomena in, 242
  Truth and, 160-61, 164, 182-85
  vital life as seat of, 105
  See also deep sleep; dream state
walking the dog, as metaphor for human
  mechanism, 123, 142
Way of the Heart
  celibacy in, 355, 381
  diet in, 355
  Guru-devotee relationship and, 10
  an invitation to support, 384-85
  sacred literature of, 371-72, 390-403
  study groups in, 373

weeping
  appearance of in Da Avabhasa, 262-63
  as revulsion of life-force, 264
well, analogy of sunlight over, 225-26
wisdom, great moments in life and, 296
Wisdom-Teaching (of Da Avabhasa). *See*
  Teaching (of Da Avabhasa)
witchcraft, 269
witness, as fourth state, 241, 249
"women and gold", as bondage, 74
work
  appropriateness of, 83
  crisis and, 211
  spiritual life and, 70-71, 91
  See also money
world
  is already saved, 332
  devotee's presence in, 316
  as psyche, 276
  as the "Straightener", 267
World-Teacher, defined, 368

Y

yama and niyama, defined, 78
Yama (Lord of Death), 60, 353
Yoga
  ascending form of, 239
  as seeking, 61
  sexual process as, 127
  true form of, 208
Yoga-Shakti, 41, 246
  defined, 352
Yogi
  cutting away of descended life by, 335
  dramas of experience of, 165
  illusion of, 188
  involvement with internal processes, 346
  role within "dream" of waking, 175-76
  spiritual disciplines of, 239
Yogic experiences, 245-46
Yogic Siddhas, bellies of, 128
Yogi-initiator, and Work of Da Avabhasa, 326
Yogi-Siddha, and Work of Da Avabhasa, 326

Z

Zen, enlightenment experience in, 54
Zen Masters, burning of traditional images
  of the Buddha, 66

An Invitation

O *f all the means for Spiritual growth and ultimate Liberation offered in the sacred traditions of humankind, the most effective is the Way of Satsang, or the Way lived in the Blessing Company of One Who has Realized the Truth. The Divine World-Teacher and True Heart-Master, Da Avabhasa (The "Bright"), Offers just such a rare and graceful Opportunity.*

The Transformative relationship to Da Avabhasa is the foundation of the Way of the Heart that He Offers. Through a whole personal and collective life of self-transcending practice in His Company, ordinary men and women may be purified of their egoic suffering and enjoy the Blessings of a God-Realizing destiny.

If you would like to receive a free introductory brochure or talk to a practicing devotee about forms of participation in the Way of the Heart, please write to or call:

Correspondence Department
The Free Daist Communion
P.O. Box 3680
Clearlake, California 95422, USA
(707) 928-4936